Vamping the Stage

MUSIC AND PERFORMING ARTS OF ASIA AND THE PACIFIC

Series Editor: Fred Lau

Vamping the Stage

FEMALE VOICES OF ASIAN MODERNITIES

Edited by
ANDREW N. WEINTRAUB
and BART BARENDREGT

University of Hawai'i Press
Honolulu

Paperback edition 2019

Printed in the United States of America

24 23 22 21 20 19 6 5 4 3 2 1

Library of Congress Cataloging-in-Publication Data

Names: Weintraub, Andrew N., editor. | Barendregt, Bart A., editor.
Title: Vamping the stage : female voices of Asian modernities / edited by Andrew N. Weintraub and Bart Barendregt.
Description: Honolulu : University of Hawaiʻi Press, [2017] | Selected papers from two conferences, convened as part of the Voices of Asian Modernities Project (VAMP), held September 4–6, 2013, in Leiden, the Netherlands, and April 4–6, 2014, at the University of Pittsburgh. | Includes bibliographical references and index.
Identifiers: LCCN 2016058133 | ISBN 9780824869861 (cloth ; alk. paper)
Subjects: LCSH: Popular music—Asia—Congresses. | Women singers—Asia—Congresses. | Women entertainers—Asia—Congresses. | LCGFT: Conference papers and proceedings.
Classification: LCC ML3500 .V36 2017 | DDC 781.63082/095—dc23
LC record available at https://lccn.loc.gov/2016058133

ISBN 978-0-8248-8148-1 (pbk.)

University of Hawaiʻi Press books are printed on acid-free paper and meet the guidelines for permanence and durability of the Council on Library Resources.

CONTENTS

CHAPTER 1

Re-Vamping Asia

WOMEN, MUSIC, AND MODERNITY IN COMPARATIVE PERSPECTIVE

Andrew N. Weintraub and Bart Barendregt

> Where else have gender and sexual identities been so explicitly and exhaustingly performed as on the pop stage and dance floors of the twentieth, now twenty-first century?
> —Barbara Bradby and Dave Laing, "Introduction to 'Gender and Sexuality' Special Issue"

Two busloads of tourists from mainland China arrived at the Teresa Teng Museum in southern Taiwan to pay homage to the legendary Taiwanese pop diva who died in 1995 (Hsu 2015). Banned by the Chinese government in the 1970s, her songs about individual desire and romantic love were considered harmful to the project of nation building, and her body was judged too sexy and glamorous for mainland taste. After Deng Xiaoping opened the door to foreign trade, investment, and cultural products in 1978, Teng (born Deng Lijun) was one of the first to introduce Chinese popular songs (*gangtai yinyue,* lit. "Hong Kong–Taiwan music") about romantic love—"not love for the homeland, the party, or Chairman Mao, but rather romantic love between a man and a woman" (Baranovitch 2003, 11).[1] A popular saying of the late 1970s was that "old Deng [Xiaoping] rules by day, little Teng [Lijun] rules by night" (Gold 1993, 909n8). For the visitors to the museum, beckoned by Teng's vocal prowess, "here was Teng's majestic music bringing the estranged people of China and Taiwan together—and, importantly, it was on the latter's terms" (Hsu 2015). How did a woman's voice and her sweet melancholic love songs mediate this political rapprochement?

According to one prominent music critic, the time was ripe for Teng and her soft and slow-tempo songs to achieve success in mainland China because "the musical style on the mainland during the revolutionary period [w]as 'lacking in *yin* and abundant in *yang*' (1988), meaning overly masculine and lacking in femininity" (Baranovitch 2003, 12, quoting Jin Zhaojun). Teng's lyrics provided a space "for the expression of individuality or the self *(ziwo, zijue)* and a sense of women's consciousness *(nuxing yishi)*" (Moskowitz 2010, 21). Under these conditions of gendered modernity, Teng's success was rapid and far-reaching: "China was like a dry field in which a match had been thrown" (Baranovitch 2003, 12).

Teng was a model of inter-Asian modernity whose voice crossed linguistic, national, and generational borders. "From Singapore to Japan, Miss Teng was a superstar and brilliant linguist. She sang in Mandarin Chinese, Cantonese Chinese, Japanese and English, and in recent years she had lived in Japan and become popular among both the young and the old" (WuDunn 1995). As a symbol of economic exchange, "Teresa Teng" signified a "reified commodity to mediate, indeed to create, interpersonal bonds" through consumption (Chow 2007, 113). Fans attributed Teng's popularity to her syrupy sentimental ballads and "the quality of her voice—economical, confident, tinged with a bit of plaintive longing. She wasn't the brashest singer, nor did she possess dazzling range—critics and fans referred to her style as 'elegant whispering'" (Hsu 2015).[2] Even after her untimely death in 1995, Teng continued to perform with other artists in 2009 and 2013—as a hologram—dressed in her trademark white gown ("Superstar Teresa Teng" 2015). To mark the twentieth anniversary of her death, Taiwan's postal service issued stamps with her portrait. She was a persistent figure of the Asian diva, in life and in death. Beloved by the masses but perceived as a threat (moral or otherwise) to the reigning political regime, Teresa Teng's voice and body, in concert with so many Asian songstresses throughout the twentieth and twenty-first centuries, symbolize the triumph and tragedy of gendered modernity.

Vamping the Stage is a collection of fifteen chapters about the ascendancy of female singers and entertainers in Asian popular music cultures from the early twentieth century to the present. This interdisciplinary volume aims to properly historicize the artistic sounds, lyrical texts, visual images, and social lives of female performers in Asian popular music. Women surfaced as popular icons in different guises and in different Asian countries through different routes of circulation. Within the exploitative and divisive conditions of colonialism, female performers developed unique ways to combine novel and foreign musical elements with the vernacular and familiar. The ascendency of women as performers paralleled, and in some cases generated, developments in wider society such as suffrage, social and sexual liberation, and women as business entrepreneurs and independent income earners and as models for new lifestyles. Further, these female performers often emerged from the underclasses of society and had been engaged in activities with low social prestige and little remuneration. They moved from the margins to the mainstream, and in their wake, Asian pop cultures followed.

These female performers were not merely symbols of times that were rapidly changing. Nor were they simply the personification of global historical changes. Female entertainers, positioned at the margins of different intersecting fields of activities, created something hitherto unknown: they were artistic pioneers of new music, new cinema, new forms of dance and theater, and new behavior, lifestyles, and morals. They were active agents in the creation of local performance cultures, of the newly emerging mass culture, and the rise of a region-wide and globally oriented entertainment industry. Through the present day, female performers, willingly or not, have often taken on a role of the modern woman challenging conservatism, morality, and religion. Calling for changes in attitudes and lifestyle, they have evoked attraction and admiration, as well as derision and conflict.

Vamping the Stage addresses the following themes:

(1) The historical, cultural, and social conditions through which women achieved prominence in popular music in Asia
(2) The relationship between female entertainers and modern media in different parts of Asia from the twentieth century to the present
(3) The aesthetic forms and practices through which women's voices were produced, circulated, and consumed in Asian popular music
(4) The meanings about women and gendered relations that audiences derived from popular music in Asia

In this introductory chapter, we define our terms and map out the rationale, methodology, and intellectual framework for the book. We aim to connect various theoretical ideas of the book with multiple fields; references are meant to point to exemplary models of scholarship rather than comprehensiveness. "Re-Vamping Asia" places the book in conversation with work in Asian studies that emphasizes cultural critique, multidisciplinary approaches, and inter-Asian connections. In the section titled "Asian Traditions of Modernity," we trace some of the ways that authors have used this vexing concept by emphasizing localized genealogies of the modern and claims to modernity, rather than a rigid overarching definition of the term. Modernity is important for our study as it marks the emergence of stardom and celebrity, new kinds of technologies, new forms of circulation, new kinds of aesthetics, new opportunities for women, and new forms of gender relations in Asia. Although women have often been neglected in studies of modernity, the section "Women, Music, and Modernity" links our book to studies that privilege women as prominent social actors in music and raise questions about the politics of gender in the performing arts. Each of the authors in this book claims that popular music, however that is defined in specific places and times, is a site of encounter in which the voices of women play a transformative role. "Popular Music of Asia" puts gender in dialogue with popular music studies. "Technologies of the Modern" refers to entertainment technologies as a modern condition that made it possible for women's voices to become audible through music recordings, radio, and onstage performance. It is the "voices" of Asian modernities that we leave for the final section of this introduction. We briefly summarize multiple valences of "voice," the central feature of this book, as they pertain to each chapter. In this way, we hope that the book will contribute to the increasingly growing field of voice studies in comparative and cross-cultural perspective.

Re-Vamping Asia

Vamping the Stage is the first book-length historical and comparative examination of women and popular music in Asia. The coverage of this volume is intentionally broad across space and time. The book addresses colonial, postcolonial, and late-modern conditions of culture as they relate to women's musical practices and their changing social and cultural identities throughout Asia. We do not claim that Asia is a homogeneous cultural sphere that can be regionally circumscribed or that the activities of female singers can be enumerated as a list of common elements or practices in all times and places. Rather, the book places the topic of female singers and popular music in broad debates about gendered relations and the ways popular musical expression has been used to articulate modernities in various Asian contexts and time frames.

The authors of this book consider "Asia" in terms of geography (albeit variously imagined and always unstable) and as a method for developing new approaches to the study of Asian subjectivities that are grounded in specific social and historical conditions rather than categories that privilege the West as the primary point of reference. Much has been said and written about the (arbitrary) invention of "Asia" as an area of study and the supposed crisis in Asia studies of the late 1990s, as well as its subsequent "afterlives" in the 2000s (Miyoshi and Harootunian 2002). Many Asian studies scholars tend to agree on the need to rethink their field of study, although generally such efforts have focused on often hazy premises and definitions rather than the urgency for new analytical procedures, for example, how to better do comparative research on and with Asia(ns) (for a Southeast Asian studies example, see Huotari 2015).

Comparison is at the heart of our project. We appreciate area studies' deliberate interdisciplinary effort and their urge to move beyond sheer "methodological nationalism" (Wimmer and Schiller 2002). We likewise welcome the kind of research in which nation and state are never simply natural givens or the sole arenas in which culture and society are to be defined. It is area studies' comparative edge that seems able to capture the lure of popular cultural expression across time and borders, addressing populations not necessarily bounded by a single language or sole citizenship. Yet we do take seriously the often voiced criticisms toward what some scholars have come to define as a more "traditional" area studies approach: the "politically motivated myths" that some areas, regions, or even whole continents in time have come to stand for (Lewis and Wigen 1997); the theoretical preoccupations and predispositions of certain disciplines over others in some area study paradigms (see, for example, the contributions in Szanton 2004); and the always lingering risk of essentializing cultures and people who inhabit those areas.

In a passionate plea for area studies, the anthropologist Jane Guyer (2004) noticed how area studies had become more of an arena than an agenda, with some areas changing far more vibrantly than the scholars and programs now studying them. The initial response among social scientists was to get rid of area studies altogether, favoring new paradigms such as international or globalization studies—and loathing area studies' supposed lack of generalizable knowledge and methodological rigor. However, others have continued to treasure what they see as potentially more in-depth and context-sensitive knowledge. They have argued for an approach that can potentially shed light on the experience of people in a particular part of the world and the ways globalization leads them to define "new myths of identity and place" (Burgess 2004, 127).

The call for a new kind of area studies approach has paradoxically resulted in, on the one hand, a return to (mostly social scientific) disciplines and, on the other, a move away from rigidly defined disciplinary approaches. In the latter case, for example, scholars have injected area studies with cross-disciplinary research on media and the arts to illustrate how popular practices such as cabaret, film, and music easily manage to cross borders and, in the process, take on new meanings. Similar efforts to reinvigorate Asian studies have argued for the study of much smaller, more consistent subregions or a move *beyond* the region at large that emphasizes the global connectedness of Asia(ns). Instead of geographical boundedness, scholars have preferred to look at oceans, flows, routes, and diaspora or at the comparison of hitherto marginal communities living in the borderlands of many Asian societies (Baud and Van Schendel 1997; Scott 2009). Blaming area studies for their alleged lack of historicity, still others have preferred to go back in time and look at both colonial and postcolonial epochs, claiming that Asia has never truly been "in place" anyway but that hybridized identities, artistic genres, and performers have made Asia as much part of the West as the West has been part of the everyday lives of Asians for a very long time (for examples, see Cohen 2010). Such a focus on contemporary hybrid identities and practices has especially taken hold in the field of Asian American studies and, to a lesser extent, in the transcultural studies promoted by some

European universities and research centers in their aim to understand "the multi-layered interactions between and within Asia and Europe" (see, for example, "Asia and Europe in a Global Context," Heidelberg University). Following Purnima Mankekar and Louisa Schein, our project seeks to "invoke an Asia in medias res, always in production. We conceive of Asia as an assemblage of ideas, histories, and images, the very construction of which is haunted by heterogeneous legacies and memories of empire, and vastly different histories of racialization" (2012, 15).

The idea of Asia may historically be European (Wang 2007) and is obviously reinforced by subsequent notions of "Asia as empire" or "Asia as Cold War legacy." But well into what many scholars see as the "Asian century" and confronted with various "Asian challenges," the much-needed revitalization of area studies is no longer restricted to or expected to happen from the traditional centers of scholarly knowledge production about Asia.[3] In asking, "what is left of Asia?" Yan and Vukovich (2007) not only refer to some of the aforementioned critiques on area studies but also add yet another important trend of destabilizing the category of Asia: the increasing interest for Asian studies within Asia itself. These interests are largely fed by a post–Cold War "reregionalization process" that comes with the rise of new and powerful economically driven networks within the region, a flourishing of imaginaries found in the realm of popular culture, and a growing awareness among politicians, intellectuals, and academics.

To many Asian scholars, the alleged crisis in Asian studies is more of a crisis in Western social sciences and humanities itself, as, from their point of view, preoccupations with global and fluid categories are but a product of time and therefore constantly need to be problematized. They argue for new analytical procedures, "which can at once explicate alternative epistemological imperatives relevant to regional academic practices and recognise their coeval standing in the enterprise to decentre and pluralise knowledge" about the region (Goh 2010).

Whereas many of these new area studies initiatives tend to be self-Orientalizing, inspired by national interests and/or outright chauvinistic in scope, others have used a cultural studies approach to scrutinize Western ways of producing knowledge on all things Asian. Ethically inspired journals such as *Critical Asian Studies*, *positions: asia critique*, and especially *Inter-Asia Cultural Studies* are often mentioned in this respect. An argument widely brought forward by the proponents of such critical regionalism is that "Asia" has too often been imagined from the perspective of the West. Whereas the need for comparison is rarely questioned, imagining and translating one culture in terms of an "other" should not be the prerogative of Western scholars, nor is Western knowledge any longer the measure of all things. In understanding Asian societies and their people, we need other frames of reference that do not exclusively focus on the West. In the book *Asia as Method,* Kuan-Hsing Chen proposes that by "using the idea of Asia as an imaginary anchoring point, societies in Asia can become each other's points of reference, so that the understanding of the self may be transformed, and subjectivity rebuilt. On this basis, the diverse historical experiences and rich social practices of Asia may be mobilized to provide alternative horizons and perspectives" (2010, 212). Koichi Iwabuchi (2014) explains how, with the rise and fame of K-pop or J-pop, inter-Asian referencing is not simply academic theorization but an increasingly common practice in which Asian neighbors are looking to each other as reference points for defining alternative modernities and subjectivities. In another inter-Asian example, Iwabuchi shows how the concept of *mugukjeok* captures the local Korean experience of mobility better than the English-language term "transnational" and how the Korean experience of *mugukjeok* has much more in common with its Japanese equivalent, *mukokuseki.* Comparisons between the Japanese *geisha* and Korean *gisaeng* (chap. 5), both referring to a courtesan-like singer, or the Iranian *mutrib* (chap. 11) and Asian equivalents such as the Indian *devadasi* (chap. 8) or Pakistani *mujrawali* may similarly provide new insights. Such a comparative perspective is useful for tracing routes of circulation across national boundaries, which bypasses the binary East/West model of modernity.

As Iwabuchi states, social scientific theory's urge for generalizations may aim to be universal in character, yet theory is constructed in particular locations and in specific historical situations (2014, 47). Even general theories require translation. Inter-Asian referencing may help construct innovative theories derived from non-Western contexts and may help us understand modern trajectories of Asian countries in a new critical light. This does not mean that we simply get rid of the "West as method" (Chen and Chua 2007, 1) or that we deny the role of borrowings from the West in the formation of Asian subjectivities. Inter-Asian referencing may provide us with the means to analyze how certain concepts may have emerged in various Asian societies and how they can be seen as transformations or "iterations" of each other rather than simply borrowings and translations from the West. An inter-Asian approach opens up the frame of multiple borrowings, such as Bart Barendregt shows in chapter 10, on the Islamist pop of the Malaysian diva Siti Nurhaliza, for whom the East/West dichotomy is less of an issue and other frames of reference are incorporated instead, both Asian and Muslim.

In line with such an approach, we will not privilege the relationship between Asia and the West, although it does receive ample attention here due to the powerful historical presence and influence of Western popular music in Asia. Inter-Asian roots and routes receive as much, if not more, attention. But some caution is needed here in order to counter the tendency of inter-Asian referencing (like its area studies predecessors) to result in a single and unproblematic Asia. Rather, as Chen writes, Asia must remain at all times a historically fluid category in constant need of interrogation (2010, 215). It is important to problematize the object of analysis, as much inter-Asian referencing still seems to be based on the category of the nation-state. In "Conceptualizing East Asian Popular Culture," Chua therefore traces the circulation of popular cultural products not within one single country but rather across 1980s East Asia. This move allows for the "discursive construction of an 'East Asian Popular Culture' as an object of analysis" (Chua 2004, 202). The analysis is contingent on understanding the relative dominance of production, export capacity, local specificities of audience consumption, and the meanings generated by these products. But in focusing on East Asian instances of regionalization, such work should not obscure the fact that not all Asian societies equally welcome this newfound East Asian sensitivity but rather choose to see it as soft power, Oriental Orientalism, or "marginal imperialism" (Yue 2006, 22). Much of the work so far also tends to be very contemporary in scope, describing what is a relatively recent form of inter-Asian traffic. More historical studies, such as the ones compiled here, are needed, and other "possible Asias" (Yan and Vukovich 2007, 12) need to be taken into account, such as Thai pop culture, Indian pop culture, and the Malay Muslim communities of insular Southeast Asia, to produce a truly inter-Asian framework (Chua 2012, 8). Lastly, moving away from the West-and-the-rest opposition, such novel analytical efforts need not be reserved for Asian scholars only (see also Chow and de Kloet 2013) but may well go beyond the long-lingering insider/outsider dispute, as hopefully this volume also attests.

Inter-Asian referencing, as promising as it may be, does not equally inform all of the contributions in this volume. However, its contours are easily recognizable, as demonstrated in several chapters in this book. In sum, the authors in this book are interested in Asia as a part of the world with some potentially rich historical connections within, between, and beyond the scope of the nation-states constituting today's Asia.

Although the coverage of geocultural areas in the book is quite expansive, we did not conceptualize this volume as a survey. It was not our intention to include every country in Asia (by some accounts, comprising some fifty countries in all). Rather, we selected these chapters for their thematic focus, methodological interest, and analytical acuity. Including Farzaneh Hemmasi's chapter on Iran, for example, provides an excellent chance to further problematize the notion of "Asia" as it is commonly understood in scholarship about Asia. On the one hand, Iran is often deemed to be culturally distinct from other Asian societies, yet this depends on one's vantage point and/or historical perspective.[4] Iran and the Middle East more generally are considered "The Orient" as historically understood from the perspective of Western scholars; from the outside looking in, Iran is part of "Asia" (Tavakoli-Targhi 2001). Many Iranians also see themselves historically and today as part of the (civilized) "Eastern" world, using the term *sharghi* or "Eastern" to describe their culture, as opposed to *gharbi,* "Western." Hemmasi's chapter on the Iranian singer Googoosh adds to rather than detracts from the topic of female voices and Asian modernities. Hemmasi's treatment of both Islam and the Iranian diaspora in the United States further problematizes "Asia" as a concept. As a "border study," Iran lends itself to exploring the challenges and limits of the inter-Asian referencing approach we have chosen to emphasize in the book. For example, chapters by Hemmasi and Barendregt demonstrate how Islam is not well represented by geographical terms like "Asia."

Asian Traditions of Modernity

Modernity comes with (a) history and has "only an ambiguous and impermanent relationship to the reality we seek to describe" (Mee and Kahn 2012, 4). The study of modernity in political, social, and critical thought bears the uncomfortable burden of that history, due to the concept's (again) almost exclusive roots in a particular Western historical time frame, the correlation between European modernity and colonialism, and its relationship to modernization theorists' Eurocentric orientation and zealous insistence that things get better the more modern we become.[5]

Modernity was one thing in the age of empire, when the projects of colonialism, science, and capitalism were intimately intertwined (see Barlow 1997; Prakash 1999), leaving an indisputable and continuing impact on much of the Asian region. But it morphed into something quite different during the dawn of Asia's postcolonial era, in which modernity became a project and a vehicle of newborn nation-states—a project that gave Asian governments such as Japan "bragging rights to cosmopolitan achievements, placing [the country] on a par with other industrial countries" and defining the country as "not a mere 'modernizer' following a Western model but on its own terms through achievements that went beyond other nations" (Christine R. Yano, chap. 6 in this volume). How do we account for these different kinds of modernity?

Scholars in the late 1990s introduced alternative takes on modernity, with a 1999 article in *Public Culture* (Gaonkar 1999) about how modernity continues to "arrive and emerge" but no longer from the West alone. These studies coincided with comparable calls to study other modernities away from that very same West and in their own right (e.g., Rofel 1999).[6] Were these expressions of a singular modernity (Jameson 2002) or possible alternatives to such a modernity? And if they were alternatives, alternatives to what? As useful as the concept of alternative modernities was to the debate, it seems highly unlikely that modernity had its origins in the West and then became indigenized or contaminated once it traveled eastward. Rather, countermodernities have always been part and parcel of the modern, or as Wendy Mee and Joel Kahn argue, modernity was plural all along (2012, 6). Along similar lines, Shmuel Eisenstadt, in a much-cited essay, has argued that "the best way to understand the contemporary world—indeed to explain the history of modernity—is to see it as a story of continual constitution and reconstitution of a multiplicity of cultural programs" (2000, 2).

Multiple-modernities scholars typically have been interested in variation and continuity, critiquing the acultural idea of convergence propagated by many modernization theorists.[7] In spite of the fashionability of the multiple-modernities paradigm, critics have questioned its shallow conceptualization and seeming inability to methodically compare modernities. The reluctance to address more normative questions about how to measure progress in each of the modernities has similarly come under scrutiny. In short, whereas modernization theories have tended to be quite normative, multiple-modernity studies have a tendency to be relativist (Wagner 2012; Dirlik 2013). Modernization and multiple-modernity paradigms coexist and are (too) often interchangeably used, while lacking proper definition. Volker Schmidt (2010) rightly points out that both paradigms in fact focus on different (although related) phenomena, with adherents of the multiple-modernities paradigm being overall better equipped to study the cultural variation we also aim to do in this volume, rather than looking at varieties within the political and economic spheres.

Modernity therefore is not something that is easily, if ever, to be defined. Nevertheless, it is important to trace and analyze the way people at various times and in different places have used the concept (Rabinow 1989; Vickers 1996; Cooper 2005). In a similar vein, Arif Dirlik suggests that the globalization of modernity "needs to be comprehended not just in the trivial sense of an originary modernity reaching out and touching all, even those who are left out of its benefits, . . . but more importantly as a proliferation of claims on modernity" (2010, 29). He adds that so-called traditions are no longer used to contrast with modernity, as they once were in modernization discourse, but that "they are invoked increasingly to establish claims to alternative modernities (but only rarely, to alternatives to modernity)" (ibid.). The claim of modernity may thus have a singular source in Western history—and there are certain commonalities from one place to another—but such claims to the modern are manifold. In contrast to Dirlik, the multiple-modernities approach seems the most fitting for the historical and comparative purposes of this book. Following our conclusions in the section "Re-Vamping Asia," "when 'Asian' is not as homogenous as the term implies, there should be different modernities across Asia" (Chu and Man 2010, 14).

Modernity is not static but rather struggles to become, as it refers to processes of profound social transformations and accompanying forms of politics (nation-state), economics (capitalism), technology (mass media), and culture. Modernity is a slow process, not something that happens all of a sudden. We are not talking about an eschatological modernity, a kind of modernity that has a linear trajectory (as framed in modernization theory or as synonymous with things coming from the West and spreading out). We are also keen on studying modernity as a project that is necessarily unfinished and in constant need of transformation. In line with scholars such as Peter Wagner (2012), we aim here to study modernity's successive changes as people and societies have felt the need to make their present situation better.

Many scholars have likewise commented on how Asian modernities are not only always necessarily unfinished but also unevenly distributed. Articulations of the modern are haunted by other exclusionary modernities, be they religious, traditionalist, or gendered in scope (Harding 2008; Kahn 2001). In spite of the term's normative ring, we are fully aware of "modernity's darker sides" (Mignolo 2007), the very coexistence of modernity's emancipatory ideals with institutions such as colonialism, patriarchy, or genocide, as demonstrated in Soojin Kim's contribution in this volume dealing with the US military government as a driving force in shaping Korean modernity (chap. 9). Joshua D. Pilzer thus attests to how many early twentieth-century East Asian films and songs starring Asian divas centered on narratives of women's hardship (chap. 5 in this volume). While some of these stories relate to women suffering the traces of the "premodern," many of these narratives are about women suffering due to processes we normally associate with modernity. Pilzer writes, "the preponderance of women in cinema and song in early East Asian popular culture was not exclusively because women were convenient metaphors, exemplars, or metonyms of modernity, or anything else, but because colonial popular culture was in this way engaged in the regulation of the sexes. If these figures were voices of East Asian colonial modernity (its mouthpieces), then these voices were granted only under certain conditions—the conditions of female suffering."

In sum, rather than an essentialized Euro-American model of modernity, from which alternative or multiple modernities derived, we prefer here to track distinct genealogies of modernity starting from the perspective of the local (Mee and Kahn 2012). Modernity should be studied relationally and situationally, within localized and time-bound debates (Geschiere, Meyer, and Pels 2008). We do so by following certain social actors—in our specific case, female popular entertainers in Asian societies—and document how they have differently experienced and commented on the political, economic, and cultural transformations they were part of. We aim to track how such commentaries materialized in new forms of expression like film, literature, and especially popular music. As "social texts" about modernity, music, film, and literature marked a transition between something old and something new. Those social texts are subject to all sorts of interpretations and readings and therefore are continuously on the move and giving rise to new subjectivities, new ways of seeing oneself in the world, and new ways of relating to others. How do/did people experience those social (in)stabilities? What specifically does the conjuncture of women's voices and modernities look like in different eras and locations? In order to track such genealogies of modernity, the contributions in this volume juxtapose the dynamics of place, human agency, and technological innovation and focus on the production of new musical styles and emergent new audiences and new lifestyles as inspired by Asian female performers.

We thus choose to study modernity as both a discursive construct and an experimental project within Asia that often involved power-laden encounters between Asia and the West. Studies of Asia's entertainment industry at the turn of the twentieth century provide examples of this interplay between traditional and modern and East and West but also show some of its complicating histories and unexpected trajectories. Studies by Andrew Jones and Taylor Atkins are exemplary in this regard. In *Yellow Music,* Jones (2001) describes the contours of China's Jazz Age. Originally coined after Scott Fitzgerald's tales of the 1920s rise of mass entertainment in Hollywood, the term "Jazz Age" is instrumental in showing how China's is not a belated or incomplete modernity, how modern jazz music is shaped in a wider transnational context, and how invention in the West does not necessarily imply the dissemination of Western civilization. Jazz in Shanghai's musical mecca, for example, was coproduced by people of at least twenty different nationalities for whom the new sounds and technologies issued a call and a challenge to experiment with what was novel. Similarly, E. Taylor Atkins (2001) writes about another Asian jazz haven, Japan, and the efforts by Japanese musicians to liberate the music from its foreign models. Atkins points out how jazz offered a sophisticated life form of not only music but also dance, fashion, and other modalities for expressing modernity. Those modalities not only transformed Japan into a mass consumer culture but also were used to achieve cultural parity with the West as well as with other modern Asian locales closer to home, including Shanghai. These works prove how jazz's histories away from what are usually considered the entertainment centers of the world may provide us with wholly new insights on modern ideas and practices. Placing jazz music outside an exclusively Western mode of linear progress may help us think about its incongruities, not only the much reiterated dichotomy of black versus white musicians (problematized by Asian musicians appropriating the genre) but also the much disregarded role of collective communities (versus the individual genius of the artist) in defining what is modern. Such an approach may help us focus on modernity's other temporalities, spaces, and subjects that are silenced in such dominant accounts, most crucially the much neglected role of female performers (Lipsitz 2007). Lila Abu-Lughod reminds us to be "skeptical of modernity's progressive claims of emancipation and critical of its social and cultural operations and yet appreciate the forms of energy, possibility, even power that aspects of it might have enabled, especially for women" (1998, 12).

Inspired by the aforementioned works, we aim to redirect the study of modernity away from both the nation-state and its elites, without neglecting their crucial contributions. We take up the invitation by the anthropologist Joel Kahn (2001, 2003), who urges us to move beyond "exemplary modernity" as dictated by authorities and intelligentsia, choosing to pay due attention to the cultural orientations of modernity as they surface in the realm of the popular and the everyday. Struggles over the meanings of modernity, objectifying stories that self-designated moderns tell about themselves (Mee and Kahn 2012, 7), are nowhere more explicit than in the entertainment industry. How do people in everyday life reflect on modernity, what "language" do they use, and how do they express how the modern is made, unmade, and remade in music?

A shift from the exemplary to the popular modern should not ignore the fact that the protagonists of the popular work as easily with hegemonic narratives as they do with alternatives to what may seem like a monolithic "national-modern." We intend to study the ways that modern ideas, practices, and technologies have been appropriated from elsewhere, including the West, and (in line with "Re-Vamping Asia") how they have been transformed from one Asian context to another. In addition to Kahn's more inclusive popular view of the modern, we emphasize a comparative perspective to show how cultural orientations of modernity become reembedded in particular social constellations and help shape their expression and transformation (Mee and Kahn 2012, 8). Following the important work done in inter-Asia studies, we actively seek, through music, to explicate "how common experiences of modernization, urbanization, westernization and globalization are experienced similarly and differently in other Asian contexts" (Iwabuchi 2014, 52).

In sum, whereas typical histories of the arrival and emergence of things modern have mostly focused on Western male actors and have privileged politics and economy over culture, our contributors here try to unsettle and interrogate such accounts by focusing on female actors away from the West, or in dialogue with the West, to historically situate how popular music has provided them with the means to articulate the modern.

Women, Music, and Modernity

Scholars have noted that women are often ignored or left out of accounts of modernity (Felski 1995; Pykett 1995; Ardis and Lewis 2002). In contrast, this book foregrounds the individuals, the gendered ideologies, and the popular music industries and music through which women's voices came to enjoy a prominent and oftentimes powerful place in Asian modernities. It highlights the marginalized histories of female singers in Asia.

Modernity and morality are often discursively produced as absolute and universal categories. In contrast, comparison is a central analytical component of this project. An analysis of women, gender, and sexuality in comparative perspective enables us to illuminate the often abstract notions of modernity and morality in specific historical and material circumstances. For example, women entertainers in multiple locations have often been castigated for allegedly threatening the moral fabric of societies in Asia by singing or dancing in public. The case studies in this volume illustrate the variable nature and meanings of morality across Asia as they relate to culture (Ricardo D. Trimillos, chap. 12), religion (Tan Sooi Beng, chap. 4; Bart Barendregt, chap. 10), and nation (Yifen Beus, chap. 3; Farzaneh Hemmasi, chap. 11).

By examining the local historical and cultural specificities of women in Asian popular music, we aim to understand the conjuncture that enabled women's voices to emerge simultaneously with modernities in Asia. This comparative approach to Asian modernities, although focused on Asia, provides useful data for studies of modernity in world and global history (or what Arif Dirlik [2007] has called "global modernity").

Our approach differs from previous projects on female subjectivities and global modernity in its scope and orientation. For example, the Modern Girl Around the World Research Group focused on the emergence of a new kind of young woman around the first half of the twentieth century (1920s and 1930s) who challenged social conventions and stereotypes (for example, the dutiful daughter, mother, or wife) (Weinbaum et al. 2008). The Modern Girl project, however, emphasized visual iconography in art, advertising, journalism, and cinema, whereas *Vamping the Stage* focuses on music, sound, the voice, and performance. It is our contention that music, sound, the voice, and performance mark women's agency in different and important ways. Numerous examples point to voices relating to bodies in particular ways. For example, the voices of playback singers in Indian film were disembodied—they were heard but not seen—lending them a different valence than the flashy and fashionable image of the modern girl. Film promoted the idea of fragmentation by splitting the body and the voice. Further, the Modern Girl project identified the nearly simultaneous emergence of modern forms of femininity around the globe. In this project, we wish to identify ruptures and discontinuities that complicate the notion of an emergent type of the Modern Girl, in particular in and between Asian societies. We focus on the variety and richness of sound and music made by modern women. The modernities in this book do not belong to a particular historical period because modernity happened unevenly and in different scales and modes in Asia. In many cases, sound and music in performance introduced a disruptive element and a way of challenging normative modes of gender and sexuality.

Studies of pioneering women in popular performing arts of Asia have shown how ideas of performance were instrumental in the construction of new identities, through questioning and rejecting conventional forms of presentation. For example, Asian performers play with ideas of "glamour" (defined as dressing up, allure, and enchantment), "camp" (artifice and exaggeration), and "kitsch" (sentimentality and melodrama) for strategic ends. These ideas, and others, allow us to map the ways in which performers have articulated their own (counter) hegemonic positions in specific contexts. This volume reveals how women in popular music have contributed to new processes of social differentiation, of culture formation, and of history making.

Conscious subversion of gendered behavior, parody, and strategic use of cultural stereotypes not only have been instrumental in the making of new fashions but also have found their way to a larger audience and society as a whole. Asian entertainment industries have as such not only seen the rise of the Asian diva but also offered a productive platform for performers, both male and female, to experiment with the effeminate and other alternative forms of masculinity, cross-dressing, and sheer travesty. The book considers these forms, among others, as effects of female voices of modernity.

This volume joins a body of work, including several important multiauthored anthologies, that traces the relationship between women, gender, music, and culture in comparative perspective. Women's musical activities were largely devalued in scholarship about music until the 1970s (Bernstein 2004). In the 1980s, several studies addressed this lacuna by documenting the prominent role of women in music (for an excellent historical study of the Western art music canon, see Bowers and Tick 1986). Feminist approaches of the late 1980s raised questions about gender, power, and the social construction of difference in music. *Women and Music in Cross-Cultural Perspective* (1987), edited by Ellen Koskoff is a pioneering ethnomusicological study about culture-specific gender ideologies (the "proper" or "ideal" roles of women and men in a society) that inform musical ideas and practices, and the uses and functions of music that inform social relations of gender. The 1990s marked the development of feminist music criticism and the publication of a number of field-shaping studies on music and the social formation of gender identities (McClary 1991; Solie 1993; Cook and Tsou 1994); the launching of *Women & Music: A Journal of Gender and Culture* in 1997; scholarly legitimation of popular music; and the emergence of queer musicology, inspired by feminist approaches to music, that challenged heteronormative representations of gender and sexuality (Brett, Wood, and Thomas 1994). The scholarship is too vast to summarize here, but a few multiauthored books provide a springboard for the present volume. *Embodied Voices: New Perspectives on Music History and Criticism* (1994), edited by Leslie Dunn and Nancy Jones, focuses on the female voice and vocal music in Western culture and emphasizes cultural meanings about subjectivity, the body, and sexual difference generated in performance. *Sexing the Groove: Popular Music and Gender* (1997), edited by Sheila Whiteley, foregrounds the poetics and politics of constructing "masculine" and "feminine" identities in popular music (mainly rock). The essays in *Music and Gender* (2000), edited by Pirkko Moisala and Beverley Diamond, present richly contextualized studies of music and the dynamics of gender in diverse musical cultures; the authors are sensitive to the way that research is shaped by the subject position of the author. *Women's Voices across Musical Worlds* (2004), edited by Jane Bernstein, is a cross-cultural and cross-historical approach to the study of women and music that includes an excellent bibliography. *Women Singers in Global Contexts* (2013), edited by Ruth Hellier, emphasizes biography, lived experience, and personal subjectivities of individual women musicians through ethnographic case studies. The unique contribution of *Vamping the Stage* is our emphasis on historical particularities of female singing stars as central actors in the popular music of Asia. As a way of drawing these case studies together, we discuss commonalities and divergences among the performers discussed herein.

As professional singers, women were wage earners and laborers in the realm of popular music. Some of them, including Zhou Xuan, Anna May Wong, Lee Mi-ja, Patti Kim, Misora Hibari, Titiek Puspa, Siti Nurhaliza, and Googoosh, enjoyed substantial economic rewards. Those who achieved successful careers became powerful economic actors who often supported husbands and children and family members. Stars had counterparts in the real-life experiences of women in the sex and entertainment industries of comfort women (Pilzer, chap. 5 in this volume).[8]

Women's images and voices were mediated through sound recordings, film, TV, posters, and other media. As commodities, their voices, images, and stories about them were marketed and sold. This raises the following questions: Were female singers allowed to make decisions on their own, or (and to what extent) were they dependent on larger male-dominated entertainment industries already in place? Did they have any agency in determining how they wanted to be seen and heard? Was their "prominence" in music and film really just another example of women's voices, bodies, and images being exploited for profit by a male-dominated industry?

A study of star singers may help to answer these questions. In film, stars were "intimate strangers" to audiences who connected the screen character or recorded singer with the real person. This was especially true for women. For example, in China of the 1930s, separating the screen character and the real star was an option only for men, not women. Gossip about women's voices, bodies, and sexual lives had important implications for the construction of female subjectivities, as fans idolized stars and authorized them to "speak for" them. In popular discourse, women were the subject of gossip about their private lives, especially their sexual relationships. The Indonesian singer Waldjinah carefully managed her public image as a counternarrative to the gossip about her personal life in newspaper reports (Russell P. Skelchy, chap. 13 in this volume). She manipulated her image in order to create counternarratives to those images of her as sexually promiscuous.

This book documents the many ways that women performers challenged the representations of existing gendered norms in entertainment media. Although the "real" lived experience of women may have been highly constrained and limiting due to restrictive ideological systems dominated by men, popular female singers maneuvered within those systems. For example, Zhou Xuan reshaped the screen archetype of an oppressed yet persevering female entertainer of the 1930s into China's "New Woman." In many cases, these female artists used technology to express modern ideas. Tan Sooi Beng (chap. 4 in this volume) shows how women's alternative lifestyles and modern music in Malaysia of the 1950s signaled a critique of the hegemonic West and Malay Muslim patriarchal society. The Japanese diva Misora Hibari's "ambivalent" sexuality presented an alternative to either masculine or feminine stereotypes (Yano, chap. 6 in this volume). A variety of Korean dance divas who emerged with the modernization of the 1980s presented a new bold image of female sexuality (Hee-sun Kim, chap. 14 in this volume). These dance divas stand in contrast to the two dominant *trot* singers of the 1960s and 1970s: the dutiful and virtuous Lee Mi-Ja and the progressive and urbane Patti Kim (Soojin Kim, chap. 9 in this volume). The dance divas paved the way for the eroticized K-pop performers in the 2000s.

Women performed gender onstage, and these gendered performances became central reference points for discourses about female subjectivities. The identities they performed onstage were not meant to reflect their "real" lives or some static notion of identity. Taking a cue from Judith Butler (1990), their performative selves were pivotal elements for shaping their own identities as well as broader representations about women's subjectivities. For example, in chapter 12, Ricardo D. Trimillos shows how two singers performed different but complementary types of femininity in Filipino popular music. Both singers mastered the culture of the colonial Other and enacted a colonial gaze onstage, one the "good girl" associated with the *ilustrado* nineteenth-century Spanish and the other the "bad girl" of the American colonizer. Performance gave them a way to negotiate with these colonial gazes in order to displace their power. These alternative forms of representation challenged types of the "good girl" and the "bad girl" and helped to create "alternative modernities" (Gaonkar 1999;

Chakrabarty 2000). The "good girl / bad girl" dynamic is highlighted in chapters by Bart Barendregt, Yifen Beus, Soojin Kim, and Amanda Weidman, and this pairing has implications for historical constructions of female identities in Malaysia, China, Korea, and India, respectively.

Women served as symbols of the nation in postcolonial national projects (Yuval-Davis 1997). Some even enjoyed prestige as the "voice of the nation" (Danielson 1998, 1).[9] Titiek Puspa's career is forever linked to Indonesia's first two presidents, Sukarno and Suharto. She served as the mother, wife, and sister in the national family. And yet her life did not abide by those roles, and she did not always perform according to the desires of her symbolic father/husband/brother. These competing desires are read as the disruptive tensions and conflicts of modernity (Andrew N. Weintraub, chap. 7 in this volume). The Iranian singer Googoosh's representation of herself as a national symbol in exile provides an alternative form of national belonging that challenges the authority of male patriarchy (Hemmasi, chap. 11 in this volume).

On the other hand, due to the power of women's voices, they were sometimes considered "dangerous," leading to discourses about control, regulation, and censorship. Due to the metaphorization of women's voices as seductive, singers in Muslim societies were prohibited from singing in public, except under restricted conditions (see contributions by Tan, Barendregt, and Hemmasi in this volume). The fact that women's voices came from women's bodies was part of why they were considered dangerous. In a fascinating account from Syria, Marwan Kraidy shows how the celebrity singer Assala's voice and body, through the spectacular media of television and the Internet, rebelled against the autocratic Assad regime during the uprisings of 2011, by "fracturing the cult that sutures the nation to the body of the dictator" (2015, 176).

In these modernizing societies, there was a tremendous amount of anxiety over the female voice and female singers' conduct in public. What was so dangerous about women's bodies? How did local codes of conduct restrict or challenge the singers we study? How were female voices subject to policing, gossip, or coverage by the popular press, and what are the stereotypes or moral anxieties being employed? How and for what were these stereotypes legitimated?

The terms "femme fatale" and "vamp"—a woman who uses sexual attraction to exploit men—capture this discursive element of these women's identity, in which they were the object of both desire and fear. We connect this element with the musical term "vamp." In jazz and popular music, a vamp is a short, simple introductory passage, usually repeated several times. In classical music, it is an ostinato; in hip-hop, it is a loop; and in rock, it is called a riff. Musicians lay down a vamp, a fixed and unchanging chord sequence, so that others can improvise. It is the stable ground on which a shifting and unpredictable improvisation is performed. In this sense, a vamp is the stage for improvisation, creativity, and change. It is a dangerous and risky space but also one that is full of transformative possibilities.[10]

Popular Music of Asia

Popular music—mass-mediated, commercialized, and consumed by large groups of people—developed in Asia during the first half of the twentieth century in conjunction with emergent forms of nationalism, new electronic technologies, urbanization, and modern lifestyles. One of the most striking characteristics of its early years was the proliferation of female performers, often drawn from existing local theater or entertainment traditions that were changing into new fields such as cinema and advertising. Female singers played a central role as stars whose musical careers and public lives attracted great interest from entertainment entrepreneurs and political actors, as well as ordinary people. Women's voices, mediated through new technologies of film and the phonograph, changed the soundscape of global popular music and resonate today in all spheres of modern life.

The case studies in this book illuminate the histories of popular music in China, Japan, India, Indonesia, Iran, Korea, Malaysia, and the Philippines. However, this is not strictly a book about the genres, industries, media, audiences, and musicians that constitute popular music in those places. Rather, these case studies highlight the dynamic lives of women whose musical activities helped to shape modern societies, lifestyles, and identities. The emphasis of this book is on popular music, but we do not divorce music from other artistic forms, including dance and film.

We use the term "popular music" even though we know that any precise definition of that problematic term will vanish into thin air as soon as we write it into existence.[11] However, it is important to explain why we are using it and why it lacks precision. In this section, we circumscribe the topic of popular music as both an object and a field of study.

As an object of study, popular music evades precise definition. The varieties of popular music discussed in this book are so diverse that it would be futile to define "popular music" in terms of a singular musical style or a list of musical elements. But what does the music sound like? Despite its stylistic diversity, there are some important general comments to be made in relation to popular music and style in Asia. Scholars have noted that styles of popular music in Asia are stylistically derivative of Euro-American popular music (Mamula 2008, 33; Lockard 1998, 53). In this view, Westernization and cultural imperialism overwhelmed local cultures and generated a number of imitations: Yellow Music, Cantopop, *enka*, pop Indonesia, and the list goes on. Whether those forms of music sound anything like their Western genre counterparts is a matter for debate—derivative according to whom and what categories of listening?—but even if they did (or do), their social contexts and localized meanings set them apart. This claim opens up interesting historical questions: does a genre like Indonesian pop indeed *sound* like American pop, and if so, when did that happen, and why is that the case?[12] Analysis of musical style yields important insights, and there is ample room for comparison, as shown in several of the chapters in this volume (Tan, chap. 4; Yano, chap. 6; Weintraub, chap. 7; Trimillos, chap. 12).

However, focusing solely on the sonic elements moves us away from important questions about musical production, context, reception, and meaning. The cultural imperialism thesis ignores the agency of musicians, producers, engineers, manufacturers, and distributors, not to mention consumers, who are all active makers of musical meaning in specific socioeconomic and political contexts. Finally, the strong inter-Asian influence of Japan, India, and Korea, as well as the impact of Middle Eastern ideas and sounds on popular music of Asia, is largely unacknowledged in these narratives about Western hegemony.

We retain the term "popular music" because it points to the changing musical practices of production, circulation, and consumption as those practices come into contact with mass media, commercialization, urbanization, nation-building, modern social class structures, and the spirit of modernity.[13] This is a tale of music and its relationship with profit, industries, markets, and ownership. Where were the opportunities for women on recordings, film, radio, and live performances? How were women's voices turned into commodities? Under these conditions of modernity, popular music cultures took hold and continue to manifest themselves in diverse ways. The music, heard in streets, cabarets, nightclubs, brothels, and bars and through new technologies like radio and television, was exciting and new, reflecting and shaping the realities of people living in rapidly modernizing societies. In today's listening spaces of public transportation, shopping malls, and iPods, popular music signals changing artistic practices, novel forms of circulation, and new modes of consumption.

Many forms of commodified, mass-mediated, urban music that embodied the spirit of modernity are not covered in this book. And while many prominent women were trendsetters in individual genres of music, they are not included in our purview. We do not intend to present an argument about what is popular and what is not; we are not attempting to police the boundaries of "the popular." In fact, we are more interested in popular music as a crossroads or border crossing that brings competing desires into dialogue with each other. Our focus is on the histories of female singers in mass-mediated commercial music who made a significant impact on the way people understood and practiced gendered ideologies in various societies in Asia.

This book makes an important contribution to popular music studies, which grew out of media and cultural studies of the 1970s. Moving away from popular music as an object toward an ideological process has been a productive move that owes a profound debt to Stuart Hall (1981). In Hall's classic formulation, "popular culture is neither, in a 'pure' sense, the popular traditions of resistance to [these] processes; nor is [popular culture] the forms which are superimposed on or over them. It is the ground on which the transformations are worked." These symbolic and material dialectics resonate in all of the essays in this book. On the one hand, popular culture is populist: it represents the culture, values, behavior, and interests "of the people" (Hall 1981, 234). On the other hand, popular culture simultaneously articulates with commercialization, state formation, and manipulative cultural industries that often work against the interests of "the people." There are numerous examples of elite audiences in popular music, as demonstrated in several chapters of this book. But in order to reach and speak for "the [interests of] people," popular music must somehow provide counternarratives to those structures of dominance. In this way, audiences and producers (among others) are linked together in the process of production (Negus 1996). We aim to show how popular music is part of complex social relations that bring different ideological interests into dialogue.

Popular music is a space for branching out in all sorts of ways (religion, sexuality, politics, music). In this way, popular culture is not a distraction or an escape or a fantasy: it is a contact zone for defining one's self in relation to others (Lipsitz 1994). In this in-between space, popular culture is an evolving hybrid language, the kind that often works against the rules rather than follows "correct" and standardized norms. For example, the Chinese singer Anna May Wong evoking nineteenth-century German lieder, the Korean singer Lee Mi-ja doing fox trots, and the Indonesian singer Titiek Puspa channeling Ella Fitzgerald all work against fixed racial and national stereotypes.

What is special or unique about the relationship between popular music and changing gendered ideologies? There is not one answer to this question because the uses and functions of popular music cannot be reduced to simple homologies, such as the "music of resistance" or "the music of manipulation." Popular music can reinforce the dominant social structure, and it can lay the groundwork for social change. One of the most fascinating elements of music is that its cultural and political meanings, and its effects on people's lives, are unpredictable; for example, despite the efforts of market studies, producers cannot predict the success of songs or artists (Middleton 1990). Each author in this volume constructs an interpretation of the ways in which popular music was embedded in people's social lives and helped to shape conceptions of modern ways of life. As people identified with sounds, songs, artists, and scenes, they formed taste cultures and communities around the new ideals of modern lifestyles.

We seek to understand how people make meaning out of sounds, images, bodies, and performance within particular social conditions. Popular music, because of its desire to appeal to large and diverse audiences, is always open to multiple interpretations. Female singers have been responsible for creating countermeanings about gender ideologies. The Japanese star Misora Hibari, who embodied the voice of postwar Japan, transgressed gendered norms onstage through cross-dressing, dance movements, and bodily gestures (Yano, chap. 6 in this volume). The Filipino singer Katy de la Cruz used her raspy voice and eye movements to transform a song about a duck egg into a sexual commentary on men who have trouble getting an erection (Trimillos, chap. 12 in this volume). These counternarratives about male hegemony may be useful to compare with meanings that emerge (in other media) out of language or other kinds of artistic practices.

The notion of the "popular" implies that the music appeals to vast numbers of people. While this facile definition is often invoked, there are numerous examples of popular music that were not "popular." Several chapters in this book point to music as a space of danger, trouble, and conflict. Popular music can be a site of ideological clashes: high and low culture, class conflict, generational divisions, state–civil society relations, and religious differences. For example, in Iran after the revolution of 1979, women were prohibited from singing solo in public before audiences including adult males to whom they were not closely related, due to the perception that their voices exerted a seductive force over males.

In focusing on the popular, we also hope to contribute to the field of Asian popular culture studies. The burgeoning field of Asian popular culture studies is deeply implicated in the academic study of the popular and quotidian but is equally (and notoriously) implicated for its lack of a well-defined methodology and singular obsession with the present. The often shallow theorizing of historical dimensions in Asian popular culture studies is in particular need of historiographical remediation. Further reflection on the introduction of new media technologies and the historical role they have played in carving out what is considered to be popular is one potentially rich area of exploration.

Technologies of the Modern

Novel technology is often equated with modern times. Not coincidentally, media technologies have been formative of Asian postcolonial nations (for an Indonesian example, see Mrázek 2002; and Barker 2005). One of the most noteworthy trends in this respect has been the development of national media: national recording companies, radio, television, and film in which new technologies are central to imagining new forms of collectivity and identification. Throughout the twentieth century, new media technologies have enabled newfangled ways of making music, linking hitherto distinct musical genres, blending them into new styles, and triggering debates about what is regarded as authentic and traditional. Moreover, new trends in musical technology often signal or at least sonically coincide with wider socioeconomic changes, as Jacques Attali (1985) and more recently Michael Denning (2015) have demonstrated.

Mass-media technologies changed the way that people hear music: the forms they hear, the places where it can be heard, and the times for listening. These technologies turned music into something popular or well liked by masses of people. But perhaps more importantly than the broad appeal of new technologies is the fact that they engendered new forms of identification. For example, in colonial Malaya of the 1950s, the microphone brought listeners "closer" to Malay Muslim singers and engendered a more intimate personal relationship between singers and listeners. In the same period, the gramophone record distanced singers' bodies from public performance, releasing them from the social condemnation of women singing in public. Singers created personal styles in order to distinguish themselves from one another in the marketplace (Tan, chap. 4 in this volume). In India, playback singing in film was not simply a technology of matching a star's body and voice through filmic projection and simultaneous sound recording; it was a cultural and historical phenomenon. Playback singing produced new forms of stardom and increased opportunities for women to enter the public sphere (Weidman, chap. 8 in this volume). In Korea, cinema songs marked the emergence of colonial female pop stars, the colonial and wartime sex industries, and the identification of women's bodies as national bodies (Pilzer, chap. 5 in this volume).

New kinds of identities and audiences became audible through new cultural technologies. The voices of singers in popular music and film were heavily mediated and remediated via technologies of microphones, sound recording, radio, and digital software, among others. For example, in Chinese cinema of the early twentieth century, "voices and vocal performances were filtered, reconstructed, rearticulated, rendered audioable, even burdened by the technologies of sound recording and audiovisual syncing" (Yiman Wang, chap. 2 in this volume). Yiman Wang's chapter shows that different star singers performed different agendas on-screen within the particular ideological conditions of early twentieth-century China offscreen. In a study of colonial radio in the Dutch East Indies, Philip Yampolsky (2014) argues that it was the incorporation of elements from European and American ("Western") popular music of the 1920s and 1930s that defined music as modern. Tan (chap. 4 in this volume) similarly describes how female artists-entrepreneurs in colonial Malaya were constantly adapting to foreign popular music trends and new sound technology of the times. Women singers learned and adapted singing styles and instruments, inserting piano, drums, and other Anglo-American elements in the recorded folk songs of the 1930s and early 1940s. Incorporating technologies from elsewhere, such as amplification, thus led to new hybrid forms, and in the aftermath, the first supraethnic and truly national entertainment genres blossomed, including genres such as *bangsawan* in Malaya, *hiburan* in Indonesia, *enka* in Japan, and *sinminyo* in Korea (see the contributions by Tan, Weintraub, Yano, and Hee-sun Kim in this volume).

Media technology has also been instrumental in shaping how certain roles in the Asian entertainment industry are typically coded as male—for example, the role of producers or sound engineers—whereas other tasks are deemed more appropriate for females. Francesca Bray states succinctly that "one fundamental way in which gender is expressed in any society is through technology," and in "the contemporary world, technology is firmly coded male" (2007, 38). Modern tales of technonationalist miracles and innovations are male-centric in character, overlooking both the ways technology is firmly embedded in social relations and also how new and old technologies alike have been appropriated in innovative ways by female users, two features we hope to redress in this volume.

Cheris Kramarae comments on how social relationships are best studied as organized and structured by technological systems that allow or encourage certain kinds of interactions and prevent or discourage others: "The histories of these specific innovations can lead to a general discussion of how all technological practices—including innovation, creation, production, maintenance and use—affect the ways, places, times and content of talk, writing and publishing," or in our case, popular music (1988, 2). Newly introduced technologies historically tend to upset existing social relations in unpredictable ways. New technologies also have fed the mostly middle-class fantasy of what such new technologies may or may not be able to do. This has included moral panics, for example, over the fear of female phone operators and their female voices intruding into the domestic household. Struggles over the meaning of new technology thus have defined insiders and outsiders, with jokes about minorities, the rural population, and especially women marking such a technological divide (Marvin 1988).

Commercial recordings of Asian music were made as early as 1902 to accompany the expanding phonograph industry (Gronow 1981). New technology posed a challenge that was quickly taken up by, among others, a surprising number of female artists and entrepreneurs who were quick to recognize the potential of technology for raising the female voice in public. Gerry Farrell notes how "the twin mediums of photography and recorded sound turned Indian music and musicians into saleable commodities" and how female performers were among those pioneering the new technologies (1997, 58). At the turn of the twentieth century, the Indian bourgeoisie viewed musical performance as suspicious due to its overt association with alcohol, salons, and female courtesans who, devoid of earlier aristocratic patronage, were now left to their own fate (for an Iranian parallel, see Hemmasi, chap. 11 in this volume). Mediated (and much condensed) formats brought the performances of these courtesans out of the underbelly of society safely back into the homes of the Indian bourgeoisie, where they added to the "modern stigma" of listeners who could afford to pay for imported phonograph technology. Catalogues and record sleeves contributed an air of decency to the courtesan and turned her into an icon of modernity. Amanda Weidman (2003) comments on how the introduction of novel media technology did not so much replace tradition as lead to contemplation about what was considered tradition and what passed as modern. Moreover, with the belief that modern equipment could register the real and enable ways to distinguish and hear such real sounds, processes of standardization were well under way. Condensing performances that lasted hours (or days) into short three-minute recordings left little room for improvisation or extrapolation.

The amplification of the female voice in public spaces has proven to be both emancipatory and regulatory in character. In West Java, the use of amplification in traditional puppet theater performances enabled female singers to be heard over the male puppeteer and contributed to their dominance in performance (Weintraub 2004). Technology boosted the fate of certain divas well beyond national borders, including Umm Kulthum, whose performances were broadcast in large parts of Asia (Danielson 1997). But in other instances, novel technology restricted the performance of female artists and marginalized others. Yiman Wang describes in her contribution to this volume how the performance of cultural hybridity and cosmopolitanism by Hollywood's most famous Chinese star, Anna May Wong, was undermined by the inception of sound. Commentators reviewing Wong's first talkie, *Flame of Love,* lamented that "one great 'treasure' of the silent film, as embodied by Wong's 'incredibly subtle and expressive art, enhanced by her exotic appeal,' was unfortunately destroyed by the 'introduction of dialogue.'" In a similar vein, Neepa Majumdar (2009) shows how, in the transition from silent movies to talkies in India, some artists who used their own voices in talkies soon lost public appeal. For others, it meant a pathway to stardom, as they became skillful at lip-syncing to the songs of the playback singers Lata Mangeshkar and her sister Asha Bhosle in mainstream Indian cinema.

The introduction of new technologies is frequently accompanied by changes in auditory perception, sonic recontextualization, and contrastive listening practices (Ochoa Gautier 2014), and such shifts often lead those who are involved to reflect on the very notion of what passes as a "genuine voice." Moreover, media technology may have done a great deal to determine what male and female voices were expected to sound like. In the context of the British entertainment industry, Kay Dickinson (2001) has commented on the pop singer Cher's 1998 hit single "Believe" and especially its use of the timbral modifier known as a vocoder.

Invented in Germany in 1939, this technology has long been the mainstay of male musicians performing futuristic electronica music, such as Kraftwerk, and representing an inorganic cyborg-like quality. With an increased use by female performers, the contemporary vocoder now successfully lends itself to a novel construction of female musical corporeality and "prompts us to think through some newer possibilities for women's profitable social mobility through music and beyond" (Dickinson 2001, 9). At the same time, Barbara Bradby and Dave Laing differ with Dickinson on the potential challenge of such manipulated voices/bodies and coding as "female," questioning the attribution of agency in the construction of Cher as an ageless diva: "Cher's use of the vocoder sonically highlights her use of plastic surgery, used by (or using?) women globally in pursuit of the 'normality' of white middle-class femininity" (2001, 296). More research is needed to determine the extent to which samplers, vocoders, and Auto-Tune software are shaping what the ideal Asian female voice is supposed to sound like.[14] Jennifer Milioto Matsue's contribution to this volume (chap. 15) offers one fine illustration of such research, showing how the virtual idol Hatsune Miku's disembodied voice enjoys a flexibility that exceeds that of the human singer, with a vocal identity that can be easily manipulated and controlled. Miku as an animated character is most typically rendered with a young female voice to match her young female body, but prosumers have also programmed the vocal synthesizer software to stress Miku's gendered ambiguity. Matsue's contribution comments on a number of genres of Japanese music in which we find a similar play with gender, but Miku's case provides an arguably more radical example of playing with and possibly escaping strict gender roles in Japanese society.

Matsue's contribution has us attuned to the ways technology coproduces notions of gender and modernity. Technology's role and its impact is nowhere simply deterministic, but it affords a variety of potentialities that, depending on cultural context, may or may not be accessible. Almost every culture has its own sound ideologies and prevailing social hierarchies, hierarchies that are easily shaken up by the emergence of novel technology. Gendered hierarchies offer a case in point and thus may help explain the moral panic and uproar that has often accompanied the rise of the Asian vamps, divas, and modern muses described in this volume.

The Poetics and Politics of "Voice"

This book reflects multiple valences of "voice" as a key concept in the social construction of gendered identities in Asia.[15] A voice is a sound-producing instrument of the human body and a sign that points toward intentionality, expression, and meaning (Dolar 2006, 14–15). Voices call attention to agency and subjectivity and the historical and material contexts through which they are embodied, mediated, circulated, and consumed. Placing women's voices in social and historical contexts, the contributors critically analyze salient discourses, representations, meanings, and politics of "voice" in Asian popular music of the twentieth century to the present day.[16]

We are particularly interested in women's singing voices but do not exclude speaking and other kinds of voices in popular music.[17] In our focus on individual performers, voices come to stand for singers and their bodies, musical practices, public images, and social lives. In this section, we do not attempt to sketch out all the various meanings of voice and to measure them against the ideas in this book.[18] Rather, we aim to highlight the meanings of "voice" in practice that have emerged out of the case studies.

Amanda Weidman writes that in South India, "it is precisely *within* modernity that the voice comes to occupy such a privileged position" (2006, 6). Within the institutional structures of power that characterized colonial modernity (Mitchell 2000; Erlmann 1999), ideas about the voice as a metaphor for bourgeois subjectivity and the self merged with the material and sonic practices of spoken and sung performance. "Voice" became a sign for the coemergence of these two meanings, which points to what Weidman refers to as the "politics of voice": the discursive and ideological production of "voice" that enabled it to achieve significance within the conditions of modernity.

What does it mean that there were so many *women's* voices in these emergent modernities of Asia? Did women have a greater voice in modern times compared to premodern times? Was this an effect of the "modern girl around the world"? What role did female stars of popular music and film play in the sonic ascendency of women? In order to answer these questions, we examine specific cases in which voices were made audible. We also examine which singers did *not* become prominent and which voices were silenced or disempowered in Asian modernities.

One of the main arguments of this book is that voices are not unmediated essences (metaphorical of individual identities) that are simply waiting to be expressed. The problem with this position, in general, is that a voice does not simply map onto a person's inner emotions, as if there were an authentic or essentialized voice that flows naturally out of the body. This view also ignores the important role of mediation and new technologies that are central to popular music and the creation of listening publics (for more about this point, see the previous section in this introduction, on media technologies).

In *The Voice of Egypt*, Virginia Danielson writes about the Egyptian star singer Umm Kulthum, who became the "cultural symbol of a nation" (1997, 1). In Lebanon, Fairuz was a metaphor for the nation (Stone 2010, 144). In this volume, chapters by Hemmasi, Weintraub, and Yano describe similar cases of women as voices of nations in Iran, Indonesia, and Japan, respectively. These studies raise historical questions: *when* and under what conditions did female singers become marked as the voice of a place, a time, and a social collectivity?

As women achieved prominence in popular music of Asia during the early twentieth century, they began to "have a voice" and started using their voices to challenge dominant ideals. In colonial Malaya, new forms of commercial urban entertainment engendered a new kind of female performer. Women became professional singers and film stars with money, independence, and power. Female singers began singing about social progress, women's rights, and virtuous behavior (Tan, chap. 4 in this volume). The singing voice was the medium for women to become agents of change.

In prerevolutionary Iran, Googoosh, Iran's most famous and beloved pop vocalist of the twentieth century, was a symbol of other people's projections; although she appeared in films and sang on recordings, she did not possess her own "voice." The lack of agency, or the lack of her own voice, was what made her an instrument of the state and the voice of a nation (Hemmasi, chap. 11 in this volume).

On the flip side of these stories about empowerment is the image of the suffering woman as a symbol of the modern. The musical voices of Korean "comfort women," a euphemism for the Japanese military's wartime system of sexual slavery during the Asia-Pacific War (1931–1945), expressed the real-life experiences of suffering girls and women. Pilzer's chapter in this volume shows how the voices of East Asian pop stars and the voices of comfort woman were entangled, as dystopian twins (chap. 5).

In a broader sense, the voice activates an affective and emotional bodily identification with events, characters, and places through which people can recognize themselves. What effects did these voices have on listening publics? What feelings or emotions did these voices arouse in people? How do voices *do* their affective work? How did women's voices represent collectivities and help give voice to others?

The way that a woman's voice helped people to construct their own subjectivities is the subject of Yano's chapter in this volume (chap. 6). Misora Hibari's multilayered voice embodied the contradictions of modernity in postwar Japan of the 1960s and 1970s. Best known for *enka*—sentimental balladry reputed to express "the heart/soul of Japanese"—she shed tears onstage to symbolize the hardship and suffering of Japan's past. But her voice also produced songs in diverse repertoires of American rockabilly, African American jazz, and Latin dance tunes, among others, that symbolized the ideals of reconstruction, renewal, and the mobility of the Jet Age. The mix of indigenized Japanese music and a cosmopolitan repertoire appealed to diverse audiences and resonated with the push-and-pull experience of modernity. Hibari's voice expressed the tensions and contradictions of modernity and enabled her to become the "people's singer" of Japan.

Within popular music and film, voices map onto character types that people use to create models for behavior. Weidman describes how female playback voices in Indian film since the 1950s resonate with a complex classification system and associations with female character types "that represented 'good' women (mothers, wives, chaste girlfriends) and those who represented 'bad' women (the overly educated, rich, Westernized, and hypersexualized female characters who were either foils to the heroine or were themselves eventually reformed and brought into the fold)" (chap. 8 in this volume). L. R. Eswari's voice and performance style helped to define a woman's place within an Indian and specifically Tamil modernity in the 1950s and 1960s against both the West and North Indian hegemony.

Categories of femininity were performed in vocal music of the Philippines during the twentieth century. Trimillos contrasts the vocal style of two Filipina vocalists, the jazz singer Katy de la Cruz and the chanteuse Pilita Corrales, to frame a discussion of stereotypical character types and their embodiment in theatrical performance (chap. 12 in this volume). Vocal skills, techniques, sounds, and aesthetics solidified these categories. Cruz, with her frontal delivery, bright sound, and signature raspy quality, stood for the *contrabida,* a more proactive and assertive female figure. On the other hand, Corrales, whose vocal production was medial and whose vocal sound was rounded and clear, embodied a more passive figure who was subject to external control (the *bida*). Their singing voices helped to perpetuate these shared cultural values in practice.

The Indonesian singer Waldjinah's "voice" refers to her musical voice as well as to her public persona in popular print media. Russell P. Skelchy describes the tensions that Waldjinah felt about the representation of her image in popular print media (chap. 13 in this volume). This issue is especially salient in Indonesia, where gossip about sexual exploits can easily tarnish a female singer's reputation (and, paradoxically, where it can *help* a male singer). In interviews, for example, women often "give up" their voice to have a male figure speak for them, rather than suffer the consequences that come with being alone and considered sexually available. However, Waldjinah chose her battles wisely. Waldjinah struggled to "have" her voice in the way she was portrayed, much like Umm Kulthum in Egypt (Lohman 2010; Danielson 1997).

Similarly, Yifen Beus explains in her chapter on the Chinese actress-singer Zhou Xuan how personal hardship and suffering clearly added to the power and perceived authenticity of the star's voice. Zhou's on-screen role as the "wandering songstress" mirrored her personal search for true love and happiness. It also became her professional nickname, which was frequently used in advertising and public relations materials. It was this "mythical" nature of her personal story that allowed Zhou to play her tragic cinematic roles with piercing persuasion, blending "reality and fiction, gossip and truth, in the construction of her public image" (chap. 3 in this volume).

And yet we must be careful not to confuse a highly audible female voice with an individual singer's individual agency (Weidman 2014). There is not necessarily a direct correspondence between the singer and the singer's authorship or between the singer and the meaning of the sung text (Brackett 1995). There are so many layers of mediation that go into production, not to mention the multivocality of other actors: producers, songwriters, musicians, arrangers, among others. This raises the question, whose voice (is being voiced)?

Echoing the views of the early twentieth-century philosopher Theodor Adorno (1941), "voice" may refer to the dominant and manipulative culture industry.[19] Despite the reductive nature of Adorno's framework in terms of dominance *or* resistance, in the case of popular music, it is important to specify other "voices" that inform the production of popular music.

Voices may serve state propaganda or orthodox religious and fundamentalist ideas. In modernizing South Korea of the 1960s, the state expressed its "voice" by regulating lyrics, foreign elements, and vocal style of popular music (Soojin Kim, chap. 9 in this volume). The government restricted Japanese-inspired *trot,* while it promoted American-inspired pop. Music performances were heavily monitored by the military and regarded as pure entertainment. While male singers tended to depict modernization in a singular way, female singers expressed contrasting attitudes to gender identities, morality, and modernization. The voices of Lee Mi-ja *(trot)* and Patti Kim (standard pop) helped to construct the collective consciousness of Korea during the 1960s.

These issues are especially salient for female singers whose voices were mediated by male figures. Googoosh, for example, did not compose her own songs but was supported by a production "team." As such, it was easy for others to objectify her. Similarly, in Lebanon, Fairuz was manipulated by her family and lacked autonomy or "a voice" (Stone 2008, 157). Titiek Puspa composed her own lyrics and melodies but not the harmonic progressions or instrumental parts. Umm Kulthum did not compose her songs but exerted artistic control over which songs she would sing and where she performed (Danielson 1997, 129). The facts do not take anything away from the creativity and musicality of these women, who were expert interpreters, or the impact they had on listeners.

VAMP (Voices of Asian Modernities Project)

This book is the result of scholarly papers presented at two conferences as part of the Voices of Asian Modernities Project (VAMP), a consortium between the

University of Pittsburgh, Leiden University, and the Royal Netherlands Institute of Southeast Asia and Caribbean Studies (KITLV). The conferences allowed us to have extended conversations about these issues, to share our work with others, and to develop our ideas collaboratively.

An initial two-day conference took place September 4–6, 2013, in Leiden, the Netherlands. The conference was funded by the Leiden University priority cluster Asian Modernities and Traditions and directed by Bart Barendregt. We received thirty-five abstracts, and fourteen participants (including seven from the United States, four from Asia, and three from Europe) were invited to present papers at the first conference. The second conference, directed by Andrew Weintraub and hosted by the Asian Studies Center at the University of Pittsburgh, took place April 4–6, 2014. For this conference, we received twenty-seven abstracts, and fifteen participants (including seven from the United States, four from Asia, two from Canada, and two from Europe) were invited to present papers. The total number of sixty-two abstracts attests to the strength of this area of inquiry.

We could not include all of the papers in this book; many of them were excellent but not directly related to the themes of the resultant publication. The chapters focus on female singers in popular music of Asia, but the contributors do not share a methodology. Rather, our goal was to create cross-talk among multiple fields: music, literature, history, anthropology, communication, film studies, cultural studies, women's studies, performance studies, and Asian studies. The authors are all experts in their fields, with knowledge of the language, history, and societies of the people they study. All of the chapters are deeply grounded in places and contexts, and data are rigorously analyzed and interpreted. We wanted an interdisciplinary approach that would cast the net widely in order to attract a wide audience.

Acknowledgments

The Leiden priority cluster Asian Modernities and Traditions (AMT) sponsored the first conference, with additional support from the Institute for Cultural Anthropology and Development Sociology, as well as from the Royal Netherlands Institute of Southeast Asian and Caribbean Studies (KITLV). The Pittsburgh conference was sponsored by the Office of the Provost; the University Center for International Studies (UCIS); the Global Studies Center (GSC); the Asian Studies Center (ASC); the Kenneth P. Dietrich School of Arts and Sciences; the Humanities Center; the Gender, Sexuality and Women's Studies Program; the Japan Iron and Steel Federation Endowment (JISF); and the Department of Music at the University of Pittsburgh.

Notes

Epigraph. Bradby and Laing 2001, 295.

1. Media technologies had made Teng's voice audible in the People's Republic of China through unofficial channels even before Deng Xiaoping's Open Door Policy in 1978 (Brace 1992, 139–40).

2. The book cover of Moskowitz 2010 asks, "Why, if the music is as bad as some assert, is it so central to the lives of the largest population in the world? To answer, [Moskowitz] highlights Mandopop's important contribution as a poetic lament that simultaneously embraces and protests modern life." Teng and the *gangtai* musical style in social and political context are discussed in Brace 1992; Baranovitch 2003; and Moskowitz 2010.

3. These concepts merit critical interrogation, but this is not the place for it.

4. When Iran is considered part of Asia, is it Southwest, West, or Central Asia? Or, as historians have suggested, is it Asia Minor?

5. For recent examples of modernization theory, see Kumar 2005 (in sociology) and Inglehart and Welzel 2005, 2010 (in political science).

6. For recent summaries of the debates about singular versus plural or commonly experienced versus alternative modernities, see Chu and Man 2010; Mee and Kahn 2012; and Protschky 2015.

7. For a more thorough critique of such convergence theories and more specifically the scrutiny of the idea that industrialization, Westernization, and capitalist absorption may result in a cultural convergence of Asia (especially its newly affluent classes) and the West, see the essays in Pinches 1999, especially the introduction.

8. The dual nature of women performers in Asia has interesting parallels with nineteenth-century opera divas, who were defined by a male gaze to be pretty, eroticized, fantasy objects that entertained for the pleasure of others. Disempowered, the figure of the prima donna or diva stands outside social norms and cannot be defined as wife or mother. But these singers were also a metaphor for female empowerment because they "had a voice" (Pope 1994).

9. The valorization of Umm Kulthum is exceptional, given that professional singers in Egypt were often held in low esteem and considered disreputable (Nieuwkerk 1995).

10. This claim contrasts with Doane's idea that femmes fatales lack empowerment and agency (1991).

11. Numerous authors have noted the difficulty in defining the term, including Middleton 1990, 3–7; and Shuker 2013, 5–6.

12. For the emergent middle classes in mid-1970s Indonesia, Western music signified progress, development, and "high" status, whereas local Malay music signified tradition and backwardness (Remy Sylado, quoted in Surawijaya 1991, 53).

13. These are the categories mentioned in Peter Manuel's excellent overview of world popular music in *Oxford Music Online* (2001).

14. In a similar vein, Bart Barendregt and Els Bogaerts describe how Europeans and Eurasians acting as indigenous Javanese and echoing traditions of vaudeville, jazz, and minstrelsy aroused widespread anxieties (2014, 11). "Sounding black" (Stras 2007) or "sounding Asian" in this case clearly profited from profound technological changes, as "the visual indeterminacy of the aural media precipitated a crisis for the American audience, for it highlighted the potential for black music and voices to 'pass' as white, and vice versa" (2007, 209). Yiman Wang's contribution in this volume (chap. 2) similarly provides an illustration of how Asian female artists have managed to pass as European and the other way around.

15. Quotation marks around the term "voice" signal its multiple meanings, as well as the political, economic, and ideological conditions that enable certain voices to speak and on behalf of whom, while others are silenced (Spivak 1988). In musical terms, what enabled certain singers to sing, and on behalf of whom? If musical style can be compared to language, what musical "languages" did/could women use?

16. Dunn and Jones note that "voice" is often understood only as the speaking voice and only in terms of language (1994b, 2). They suggest using the term "vocality" instead of "voice" to signal an important shift from the metaphorization of voice to a broader conception that is nonverbal, performative, and embedded in cultural context (ibid.). We prioritize sound, performance, and culture, but we retain the term "voice" to emphasize individual "voices" of women singers.

17. For example, Amanda Weidman notes that "effects" of laughter, crying, sighing, or heightened speech are often inserted into film songs of India (chap. 8 in this volume), and Christine Yano discusses the spoken recitative delivered by the *enka* singer Misora Hibari (chap. 6 in this volume).

18. For an excellent overview of the scholarship on anthropology and voice since the 1990s, see Weidman 2014.

19. The problem with Adorno's view of popular music is that (a) meaning is produced at the point of production and analyzed in terms of the "music itself," and (b) manipulation and control form the ground on which meaning is made. In this view, control or resistance to control are the only two possible meanings yielded by popular music. We maintain that meaning is constructed in historical and social contexts and that popular music can produce a multiplicity of meanings in concert with those historical and social contexts.

References

Abu-Lughod, Lila. 1998. *Remaking Women: Feminism and Modernity in the Middle East.* Princeton, NJ: Princeton University Press.

Adorno, Theodor. 1941. "On Popular Music." *Studies in Philosophy and Social Science* 9:17–48.

Ardis, Ann L., and Leslie W. Lewis, eds. 2003. *Women's Experience of Modernity, 1875–1945.* Baltimore: Johns Hopkins University Press.

Atkins, E. Taylor. 2001. *Blue Nippon: Authenticating Jazz in Japan.* Durham, NC: Duke University Press.

Attali, Jacques. 1985. *Noise: The Political Economy of Music.* Minneapolis: University of Minnesota Press.

Baranovitch, Nimrod. 2003. *China's New Voices.* Berkeley: University of California Press.

Barendregt, Bart, and Els Bogaerts. 2014. "Recollecting Resonances: Listening to an Indonesian-Dutch Musical Heritage." In *Recollecting Resonances: Indonesian-Dutch Musical Encounters,* edited by Bart Barendregt and Els Bogaerts, 1–30. Leiden: Brill.

Barker, Joshua. 2005. "Engineers and Political Dreams: Indonesia in the Satellite Age." *Current Anthropology* 46 (5): 703–727.

Barlow, Tani E. 1997. *Formations of Colonial Modernity in East Asia.* Durham, NC: Duke University Press.

Baud, Michiel, and Willem Van Schendel. 1997. "Toward a Comparative History of Borderlands." *Journal of World History* 8 (2): 211–242.
Bernstein, Jane A., ed. 2004. *Women's Voices across Musical Worlds.* Boston: Northeastern University Press.
Bowers, Jane, and Judith Tick, eds. 1986. *Women Making Music: The Western Art Tradition, 1150–1950.* Urbana: University of Illinois Press.
Brace, Timothy Lane. 1992. "Modernization and Music in Contemporary China: Crisis, Identity, and the Politics of Style." PhD diss., University of Texas.
Brackett, David. 1995. "The Electro-Acoustic Mirror: Voices in American Pop." *Critical Quarterly* 37 (2): 11–27.
Bradby, Barbara, and Dave Laing. 2001. "Introduction to 'Gender and Sexuality' Special Issue." *Popular Music* 20 (3): 295–300.
Bray, Francesca. 2007. "Gender and Technology." *Annual Review of Anthropology* 36:37–53.
Brett, Philip, Elizabeth Wood, and Gary C. Thomas, eds. 1994. *Queering the Pitch: The New Gay and Lesbian Musicology.* New York: Routledge.
Burgess, Chris. 2004. "The Asian Studies 'Crisis': Putting Cultural Studies into Asian Studies and Asia into Cultural Studies." *International Journal of Asian Studies* 1 (1): 121–136.
Butler, Judith. 1990. *Gender Trouble: Feminism and the Subversion of Identity.* New York: Routledge.
Chakrabarty, Dipesh. 2000. *Provincializing Europe: Postcolonial Thought and Historical Difference.* Princeton, NJ: Princeton University Press.
Chen, Kuan-Hsing. 2010. *Asia as Method: Toward Deimperialization.* Durham, NC: Duke University Press.
Chen, Kuan-Hsing, and Beng Huat Chua. 2007. "Introduction: *The Inter-Asia Cultural Studies: Movements* Project." In *The Inter-Asia Cultural Studies Reader,* edited by Kuan-Hsing Chen and Beng Huat Chua, 1–5. London: Routledge.
Chow, Rey. 2007. *Sentimental Fabulations, Contemporary Chinese Films.* New York: Columbia University Press.
Chow, Yiu Fai, and Jeroen de Kloet. 2013. "The Spectre of Europe: Knowledge, Cultural Studies and the 'Rise of Asia.'" *European Journal of Cultural Studies* 17 (1): 3–15.
Chu, Yiu-wai, and Eva Kit-Wah Man. 2010. "Introduction." In *Contemporary Asian Modernities: Transnationality, Interculturality, and Hybridity,* 9–24. Bern, Switzerland: Peter Lang.
Chua, Beng Huat. 2004. "Conceptualizing an East Asian Popular Culture." *Inter-Asia Cultural Studies* 5 (2): 200–221.
———. 2012. *Structure, Audience and Soft Power in East Asian Pop Culture.* Hong Kong: Hong Kong University Press.
Cohen, Matthew Isaac. 2010. *Performing Otherness: Java and Bali on International Stages, 1905–1952.* Basingstoke, UK: Palgrave Macmillan.
Cook, Susan C., and Judy S. Tsou, eds. 1994. *Cecilia Reclaimed: Feminist Perspectives on Gender and Music.* Urbana: University of Illinois Press.
Cooper, Frederick. 2005. *Colonialism in Question: Theory, Knowledge, History.* Berkeley: University of California Press.

Danielson, Virginia. 1997. *The Voice of Egypt: Umm Kulthum, Arabic Song, and Egyptian Society in the Twentieth Century.* Chicago: University of Chicago Press.

Denning, Michael. 2015. *Noise Uprising: The Audiopolitics of a World Musical Revolution.* London: Verso.

Dickinson, Kay. 2001. "Believe? Vocoders, Digitalised Female Identity and Camp." *Popular Music* 20 (3): 333–347.

Dirlik, Arif. 2007. *Global Modernity: Modernity in the Age of Global Capitalism.* Boulder, CO: Paradigm.

———. 2010. "Asian Modernities in the Perspective of Global Modernity." In *Contemporary Asian Modernities: Transnationality, Interculturality, and Hybridity,* edited by Yiu-wai Chu and Eva Kit-Wah Man, 27–54. New York: Peter Lang.

———. 2013. "Thinking Modernity Historically: Is 'Alternative Modernity' the Answer?" *Asian Review of World Histories* 1 (1): 5–44.

Doane, Mary Ann. 1991. *Femmes Fatales: Feminism, Film Theory, Psychoanalysis.* New York: Routledge.

Dolar, Mladen. 2006. *A Voice and Nothing More.* Boston: MIT Press.

Dunn, Leslie C., and Nancy A. Jones, eds. 1994a. *Embodied Voices: New Perspectives on Music History and Criticism.* Cambridge: Cambridge University Press.

———. 1994b. "Introduction." In *Embodied Voices: New Perspectives on Music History and Criticism,* edited by Leslie C. Dunn and Nancy A. Jones, 1–13. Cambridge: Cambridge University Press.

Eisenstadt, Shmuel Noah. 2000. "Multiple Modernities." *Daedalus* 129 (1): 1–29.

Erlmann, Veit. 1999. *Music, Modernity, and the Global Imagination: South Africa and the West.* New York: Oxford University Press.

Farrell, Gerry. 1997. *Indian Music and the West.* Oxford, UK: Clarendon.

Felski, Rita. 1995. *The Gender of Modernity.* Cambridge, MA: Harvard University Press.

Gaonkar, Dilip Parameshwar. 1999. "On Alternative Modernities." *Public Culture* 11 (1): 1–18.

Geschiere, Peter, Birgit Meyer, and Peter Pels, eds. 2008. *Readings in Modernity in Africa.* London: International African Institute; Bloomington: Indiana University Press.

Goh, Beng-Lan. 2011. *Decentring and Diversifying Southeast Asian Studies: Perspectives from the Region.* Singapore: Institute Southeast Asian Studies.

Gold, Thomas B. 1993. "Go with Your Feelings: Hong Kong and Taiwan Popular Culture in Greater China." *China Quarterly* 136:907–925.

Gronow, Pekka. 1981. "The Record Industry Comes to the Orient." *Ethnomusicology* 25 (2): 251–284.

Guyer, Jane I. 2004. "Anthropology in Area Studies." *Annual Review of Anthropology* 33:499–523.

Hall, Stuart. 1981. "Notes on Deconstructing 'the Popular.'" In *People's History and Socialist Thought,* edited by Raphael Samuel, 227–240. London: Routledge and Kegan Paul.

Harding, Sandra. 2008. *Sciences from Below: Feminisms, Postcolonialities, and Modernities.* Durham, NC: Duke University Press.

Hellier, Ruth, ed. 2013. *Women Singers in Global Contexts.* Champaign: University of Illinois Press.

Hsu, Hua. 2015. "The Melancholy Pop Idol Who Haunts China." *New Yorker,* 3 August.
Huotari, Mikko. 2014. "Fostering Methodological Dialogue in Southeast Asian Studies." In *Methodology and Research Practice in Southeast Asian Studies,* edited by Mikko Huotari, Jürgen Rüland, and Judith Schlehe, 1–24. Basingstoke, UK: Palgrave Macmillan.
Inglehart, Ronald, and Christian Welzel. 2005. *Modernization, Cultural Change, and Democracy: The Human Development Sequence.* Cambridge: Cambridge University Press.
———. 2010. "Changing Mass Priorities: The Link between Modernization and Democracy." *Perspectives on Politics* 8 (2): 551–567.
Iwabuchi, Koichi. 2014. "De-Westernisation, Inter-Asian Referencing and Beyond." *European Journal of Cultural Studies* 17 (1): 44–57.
Jameson, Fredric. 2002. *A Singular Modernity: Essay on the Ontology of the Present.* London: Verso.
———. 2001. *Yellow Music: Media Culture and Colonial Modernity in the Chinese Jazz Age.* Durham, NC: Duke University Press.
Kahn, Joel S. 2001. *Modernity and Exclusion.* London: Sage.
———. 2003. "Islam, Modernity, and the Popular in Malaysia." In *Malaysia: Islam, Society and Politics,* edited by Virginia Hooker and Norani Othman, pp. 147–166. Singapore: ISEAS.
Koskoff, Ellen, ed. 1987. *Women and Music in Cross-Cultural Perspective.* New York: Greenwood.
Kraidy, Marwan M. 2015. "The Politics of Revolutionary Celebrity in the Contemporary Arab World." *Public Culture* 27 (1): 161–183.
Kramarae, Cheris. 1988. "Gotta Go Myrtle, Technology's at the Door." In *Technology and Women's Voices: Keeping in Touch,* edited by Cheris Kramarae, 1-11. New York: Routledge and Kegan Paul.
Kumar, Krishan. 2005. *From Post-industrial to Post-modern Society: New Theories of the Contemporary World.* Malden, MA: Blackwell.
Lewis, Martha Wells, and Kären Wigen. 1997. *The Myth of Continents: A Critique of Metageography.* Berkeley: University of California Press.
Lipsitz, George. 1994. *Dangerous Crossroads: Popular Music, Postmodernism, and the Poetics of Place.* New York: Verso.
———. 2007. *Footsteps in the Dark: The Hidden Histories of Popular Music.* Minneapolis: University of Minnesota Press.
Lockard, Craig. 1998. *Dance of Life: Popular Music and Politics in Southeast Asia.* Honolulu: University of Hawai'i Press.
Lohman, Laura. 2010. *Umm Kulthūm: Artistic Agency and the Shaping of an Arab Legend, 1967–2007.* Middletown, CT: Wesleyan University Press.
Majumdar, Neepa. 2009. *Wanted Cultured Ladies Only! Female Stardom and Cinema in India, 1930s–1950s.* Urbana: University of Illinois Press.
Mamula, Stephen. 2008. "Starting from Nowhere? Popular Music in Cambodia after the Khmer Rouge." *Asian Music* 39 (1): 26–41.
Mankekar, Purnima, and Louisa Schein. 2012. "Mediations and Transmediations." In *Media, Erotics, and Transnational Asia,* edited by Purnima Mankekar and Louisa Schein, 1–32. Durham, NC: Duke University Press.

Manuel, Peter. 2001. "Popular Music." *Oxford Music Online*. http://www.oxfordmusiconline.com/public/book/omo_gmo.

Marvin, Carolyn. 1988. *When Old Technologies Were New*. New York: Oxford University Press.

McClary, Susan. 1991. *Feminine Endings: Music, Gender, and Sexuality*. Minneapolis: University of Minnesota Press.

Mee, Wendy, and Joel S. Kahn. 2012. "Introduction." In *Questioning Modernity in Indonesia and Malaysia*, 1–18. Singapore: NUS Press.

Middleton, Richard. 1990. *Studying Popular Music*. Milton Keynes, UK: Open University Press.

Mignolo, Walter D. 2007. "Delinking: The Rhetoric of Modernity, the Logic of Coloniality and the Grammar of De-coloniality." *Cultural Studies* 21 (2–3): 449–514.

Mitchell, Timothy, ed. 2000. *Questions of Modernity*. Minneapolis: University of Minnesota Press.

Miyoshi, Masao, and Harry Harootunian, eds. 2002. *Learning Places: The Afterlives of Area Studies*. Durham, NC: Duke University Press.

Moisala, Pirkko, and Beverley Diamond, eds. 2000. *Music and Gender*. Urbana: University of Illinois Press.

Moskowitz, Marc L. 2010. *Cries of Joy, Songs of Sorrow: Chinese Pop Music and Its Cultural Connotations*. Honolulu: University of Hawai'i Press.

Mrázek, Rudolf. 2002. *Engineers of Happy Land: Technology and Nationalism in a Colony*. Princeton, NJ: Princeton University Press.

Negus, Keith. 1996. *Popular Music in Theory*. Hanover, NH: Wesleyan University Press.

Nieuwkerk, Karin van. 1995. *"A Trade like Any Other": Female Singers and Dancers in Egypt*. Austin: University of Texas Press.

Ochoa Gautier, Ana María. 2014. *Aurality: Listening and Knowledge in Nineteenth-Century Colombia*. Durham, NC: Duke University Press.

Pinches, Michael, ed. 1999. *Culture and Privilege in Capitalist Asia*. London: Routledge.

Pope, Rebecca A. 1994. "The Diva Doesn't Die: George Eliot's Armgart." In *Embodied Voices: Representing Female Vocality in Western Culture*, edited by Leslie C. Dunn and Nancy A. Jones, 139–151. Cambridge: Cambridge University Press.

Prakash, Gyan. 1999. *Another Reason: Science and the Imagination of Modern India*. Princeton, NJ: Princeton University Press.

Protschky, Susie. 2015. "Tracing Trajectories of Modernity in Southeast Asia, 1920s–1970s." Paper presented at the KITLV Workshop on Tracing Trajectories, Leiden, the Netherlands, 12–13 January.

Pykett, Lyn. 1995. *Engendering Fictions: The English Novel in the Early Twentieth Century*. London: Edward Arnold.

Rabinow, Paul. 1989. *French Modern: Norms and Forms of the Social Environment*. Cambridge, MA: MIT Press.

Rofel, Lisa. 1999. *Other Modernities: Gendered Yearnings in China after Socialism*. Berkeley: University of California Press.

Schmidt, Volker H. 2010. "Modernity and Diversity: Reflections on the Controversy between Modernization Theory and Multiple Modernists." *Social Science Information* 49 (4): 511–538.

Scott, James C. 2009. *The Art of Not Being Governed: An Anarchist History of Upland Southeast Asia*. New Haven, CT: Yale University Press.
Shuker, Roy. 2013. *Understanding Popular Music Culture*. 4th ed. London: Routledge.
Solie, Ruth, ed. 1993. *Musicology and Difference: Gender and Sexuality in Music Scholarship*. Berkeley: University of California Press.
Spivak, Gayatri Chakravorty. 1988. "Can the Subaltern Speak?" In *Marxism and the Interpretation of Cultures*, edited by Cary Nelson and Lawrence Grossberg, 271–313. Basingstoke, UK: Macmillan.
Stone, Christopher. 2008. *Popular Culture and Nationalism in Lebanon: The Fairouz and Rahbani Nation*. New York: Routledge.
Stras, Laurie. 2007. "White Face, Black Voice: Race, Gender, and Region in the Music of the Boswell Sisters." *Journal of the Society for American Music* 1 (2): 207–255.
"Superstar Teresa Teng: The Idol of the Idols." 2015. All China Women's Federation, 8 May. http://www.womenofchina.cn/womenofchina/html1/people/celebrities/1505/687-1.htm.
Surawijaya, Bunga. 1991. "Goyang Dangdut." *Tempo*, 25 May, 49–60.
Szanton, David L., ed. 2004. *The Politics of Knowledge: Area Studies and the Disciplines*. Berkeley: University of California Press.
Tavakoli-Targhi, Mohamad. 2001. *Refashioning Iran: Orientalism, Occidentalism, and Historiography*. New York: Palgrave.
Vickers, Adrian. 1996. *Being Modern in Bali: Image and Change*. New Haven, CT: Yale University Press.
Wagner, Peter. 2012. *Modernity: Understanding the Present*. Cambridge, UK: Polity.
Wang Hui. 2007. "The Politics of Imagining Asia: A Genealogical Analysis." Translated by Matthew A. Hale. *Inter-Asia Cultural Studies* 8 (1): 1–33.
Weidman, Amanda. 2003. "Guru and Gramophone: Fantasies of Fidelity and Modern Technologies of the Real." *Public Culture* 15 (3): 453–476.
———. 2006. *Singing the Classical, Voicing the Modern: The Postcolonial Politics of Music in South India*. Durham, NC: Duke University Press.
———. 2014. "Anthropology and Voice." *Annual Review of Anthropology* 43:37–51.
Weinbaum, Alys Eve, Lynn M. Thomas, Priti Ramamurthy, Uta G. Poiger, Madeleine Yue Dong, and Tani E. Barlow, eds. 2008. *The Modern Girl Around the World: Consumption, Modernity, and Globalization*. Durham, NC: Duke University Press.
Weintraub, Andrew N. 2004. "The 'Crisis of the Sinden': Gender, Politics, and Memory in the Performing Arts of West Java, 1959–1964." *Indonesia* 77:57–78.
Whiteley, Sheila, ed. 1997. *Sexing the Groove: Popular Music and Gender*. London and New York: Routledge.
Wimmer, Andreas, and Nina Glick Schiller. 2002. "Methodological Nationalism and Beyond: Nation-State Building, Migration and the Social Sciences." *Global Networks* 2 (4): 301–334.
WuDunn, Sheryl. 1995. "Teresa Teng, Singer, 40, Dies: Famed in Asia for Love Songs." *New Yorker*, 10 May.
Yampolsky, Philip. 2014. "Music on Dutch East Indies Radio in 1938: Representations of Unity, Disunity, and the Modern." In *Sonic Modernities in the Malay World: A History of Popular Music, Social Distinction, and Novel Lifestyles (1930s–2000s)*, edited by Bart Barendregt, 47–112. Leiden: Brill.

Yan, Hairong, and Daniel F. Vukovich. 2007. "Introduction: What's Left of Asia." *Positions: East Asia Cultures Critique* 15 (2): 211–224.
Yue, Audrey. 2006. "Cultural Governance and Creative Industries in Singapore." *International Journal of Cultural Policy* 12 (1): 17–33.
Yuval-Davis, Nira. 1997. *Gender and Nation.* London: Sage.

PART I

Triumph and Tragedies of the Colonized Voice

COLONIAL MODERNITY, COMMODIFICATION, AND CIRCULATION OF WOMEN'S VOICES

CHAPTER 2

Acoustic Ladies

MEDIATING AUDIOVISUAL MODERNITY IN EARLY GERMAN AND CHINESE TALKIES

Yiman Wang

In July 1935, a British newspaper reported, "China's own most famous actress, Miss Butterfly Wu, of Shanghai, shook hands yesterday with Hollywood's most famous Chinese star, Miss Anna May Wong," at a reception in honor of both Wu and Mei Lan-fang, "China's leading stage actor." This report was quickly spotlighted in a Chinese film magazine's recount of Butterfly Wu's European trip *(Dianying huabao)*. These three ethnic Chinese performers visited or sojourned in London—the interwar metropolis—for very different reasons. Both Butterfly Wu (1908–1989) and Mei Lanfang (1894–1961) started with a trip to Moscow (at the invitation of the Soviet Union) and then continued on to their European tour. Anna May Wong (1905–1961) had just returned to London from her one-woman vaudeville performances in northern Europe and within half a year was to embark on her first and only trip to China, where she was to be reunited with Wu in Shanghai and Mei in Beijing. The performers' historical meeting in London was not simply a coincidental convergence. It signaled the beginning of international visibility *and* "audio-ability" accrued to ethnic Chinese performers and Chinese performance arts (including the new medium of film and the traditional Peking opera that was going through significant reconfiguration in the direction of modernization).

By "audio-ability," a term suggested by Rosie Thomas—a coparticipant at the Second Conference of Voices of Asian Modernities (Pittsburgh, Pennsylvania, 2014)—I intend to ask not just what is heard but, more importantly, who are heard, under what circumstances, by whom, how the audiences make sense of what they hear, and in what ways their hearing leads them to understand the subjects of enunciation. These questions echo the postcolonial inquiry as emblematized by Gayatri Spivak's question, "Can the subaltern speak?" (1988). But my critical focus on these ethnic Chinese artists' vocal performance and audio-ability, mediated by the newly developed sound-recording technologies at the turn of the 1930s and the broader interwar geopolitics of coloniality and cosmopolitanism, takes the postcolonial inquiry in a direction that has been so far understudied. That is the issue of the interwar ethnic *female* singing voice, its transnational production, circulation, and consumption, enabled by the performers' labor, skills, performativity, and cinematic technologies, all of which developed in tandem with interwar modernity, cosmopolitanism, and national/transnational geopolitics.

The historical meeting of Wong, Wu, and Mei threw this issue of interwar female vocal performance and audio-ability into relief by highlighting performative "Chineseness"—especially its gendered constructions—to the international gaze. Such gendered "Chineseness" was necessarily heterogeneous, protean, and inconclusive, arising from the interplay of media platforms (film and theater), the cross-fertilization between variant acting techniques (including Mei's operatic female impersonation and Wu's and Wong's ostensibly more realistic gender performance on the screen), and finally, the convergence and divergence of Chinese lingua-culture and its diasporic geopolitics and cultural politics.

The Acoustic Turn

Springing from the diasporic Chinese community in the United States, Wong combined her southern Chinese heritage with her Los Angeles upbringing in pursuit of an unconventional career in acting. Her frequent European trips from 1928 to 1935 further expanded her career scope and acting abilities while enabling her to partake in the interwar cosmopolitanism. Tim Bergfelder argues in his study of the German and British reception of Wong's European films that Wong's Chinese American "complex hybridity" "rendered [her films] more or less acceptable in the different markets that made up the pan-national distribution networks central to the Film Europe project" (2004, 73). Such hybridity and pan-European appeal constituted her cosmopolitan stardom in interwar Europe. Similarly, Patrice Petro's historical study of a set of 1928 photos that feature Wong flanked by Leni Riefenstahl and Marlene Dietrich in Berlin demonstrates that contrary to the late 1930s, which "ushered in an era of intensely nationalist rhetoric," the interwar years represented "an auspicious time for thinking both within and beyond nationalism and for sustaining multiple and flexible attachments to more than one community" (2014, 308). In this context, the convergence of Dietrich, Wong, and Riefenstahl in the photos suggests "a deeply cosmopolitan cultural imaginary, forged in the interwar years and disseminated across various popular, everyday, and quotidian forms" (Petro 2014, 308–309).

Both Petro and Bergfelder make a compelling case for interwar artistic cosmopolitanism that defies the reified nation-centered framework. They also both ground their studies on the *visual* quality of either photography or film. Drawing on *The Modern Girl around the World,* Petro sees interwar cosmopolitanism as promoted via "a gendered aesthetic" that was "fundamentally visual in nature" (2014, 297). Bergfelder compares the German and British reception of Wong's films and concludes that the variant, and sometimes conflicting, discourses surrounding Wong's "cultural hybridity" came to find a common ground in the celebration of Wong's "performance style as an example of a universal art of acting" (2004, 73). This perceived universal art, however, was undermined with the inception of sound, according to some of Wong's reviewers. A German review of Wong's first talkie, *Flame of Love,* lamented that one great "treasure" of the silent film, as embodied by Wong's "incredibly subtle and expressive art, enhanced by her exotic appeal," was unfortunately destroyed by the "introduction of dialogue" (review from *Lichtbildbühne,* quoted in Bergfelder 2004, 66). Bergfelder does not endorse this review but uses it to illustrate the German press's pejorative take on sound film, contrary to the British press's greater confidence in the emerging technology, which enabled enhanced screen realism (66–67).

My analysis of *Flame of Love* in this chapter directly engages with Wong's vocal performance and its contribution to her "cultural hybridity" and, more generally, to interwar modernity and cosmopolitanism with an ethnic reinflection. Following Petro and Bergfelder, I challenge the nation-centered paradigm to reconfigure the "nation" and the continent as being constituted by transnational interactions. Thus, I understand interwar modernity and cosmopolitanism as being coconstitutive with coloniality, both unfolding at the global scale, with Asia as a crucial site and link in the global circuit. Asian modernities, therefore, developed from the necessary encounter, negotiation, and crosscurrents between the contested geopolitical "Asia" and other geopolitical zones that it was in contact/conflict with. The network of economic, cultural, aesthetic, and political contacts, crosscurrents, and intersections not only constituted "Asia" but also powerfully bankrupted this same concept as an a priori "self-evident, self-sufficient, and self-made" essence. Instead, "Asia" was recast as a constantly shifting geopolitical zone of interaction and contention (Yan and Vukovich 2007, 212).[1] With this interactive and intra-active Asian map in mind, I study the Chinese and Chinese-diasporic performers' vocal (in comparison with their visual) performances. In this study, I specifically zoom in on the ways in which Asian modernities developed in a transnational circuit in relation to variegated cinematic and media technological modernities, screen/stage performance techniques, racial/ethnic identities, and the construction of (trans)national cinemas. The historical meeting of three major ethnic-Chinese performers—Butterfly

Wu, Anna May Wong, and Mei Lanfang—in the metropole of London in 1935 offers a productive nodal point for unpacking the multivalent intricacies of Asian modernities during the interwar era.

Wu, Wong, and Mei all occupied pioneering positions in the early twentieth-century new medium of cinema. Whether working in Hollywood and European cinema in roles ranging from an ethnic extra to the exotic star or in Shanghai as leading players in the emerging indigenous Chinese film industry, they foregrounded two key qualities of the new cinema culture, namely, its multiethnic, multicultural, and polylocal constitution from the beginning and its crystallization of the racial/ethnic and national power hierarchies in the global colonial politics referenced above. Just as Wong's participation in the Hollywood and European film industries testified to ethnic performers' constitutive role in constructing the Euro-American film cultures and cosmopolitanism, Wu's and Mei's pioneering film acting contributed to China's cinematic modernity—one that went in tandem with global coloniality, which subjugated China's sovereignty and irrevocably stitched China into the world system.

In this chapter, I specifically focus on these performers' contribution to cinematic modernity at the acoustic turn, or the dawn of the talkie era. Wong starred in an "all talking, singing, and dancing" picture, *Flame of Love* (aka *Hai Tang*; dir. Richard Eichberg, 1930), in all three of its versions—German, British, and French. Hu starred in China's first all-dialogue, all-singing Vitaphone film, *The Singing Peony* (1931), performing Peking opera episodes; she later revealed that her performance was dubbed by Mei Lanfang (more on this later). Both Wong and Hu opened their first talkies with singing and multilingual skills. Both films received enthusiastic publicity that highlighted the two actresses' accomplishments, superb sound-recording effects, and in Wu's case, the film's contribution to Chinese national cinema.[2] Mei Lanfang's direct participation in sound film came later. In fact, when some of his most popular Peking opera repertoire pieces were filmed as silent shorts between 1920 and 1924, he needed to foreground his physical performance and visual choreography while tuning down the vocal performance. As talkies emerged, Mei's vocal virtuosity became a widely sought-after asset. His collaboration with Sergei Eisenstein on a short sound film, *The Rainbow Pass* (*Hongni guan*; 1935), during his Soviet visit is a salient example. Moreover, both Wu and Wong informally apprenticed themselves to Mei, studying the operatic performance in order to better adjust to the new talkie technologies and aesthetics or to expand their repertoires. Wu's apprenticeship led to what was advertised as her operatic tour de force in *The Singing Peony*, while Wong's reunion with Mei in Beijing during her 1936 China trip possibly triggered her operatic costuming in her 1937 stage performance of *Turandot* at the Connecticut Westport Country Playhouse.

Wong's and Wu's contributions to the interwar Film Europe project and Chinese cinema highlight the import of the performative female voice, its audio-ability through technologization, commercialization, and (inter)nationalization in relation to cinematic modernity and global coloniality. In unpacking these issues, I underscore the processes of mediation in the production, circulation, and signification of the female vocal performance. Instead of seeing the female singing voice as spontaneous self-expression or pure virtuoso performance, I examine how the women's singing voices and vocal performances were filtered, reconstructed, rearticulated, rendered audio-able, and even burdened by the technologies of sound recording and audiovisual syncing. I further study another layer of mediation, namely, the performers' (self-) dubbing and imitation. Wong's singing in the German and English versions of *Flame of Love* involved her multilingual training and self-dubbing in performing the female protagonist. Wu's performance (even only through lip-syncing) of Peking opera episodes in *The Singing Peony* required her vocal and physical imitation of Mei Lanfang's art of female impersonation.

The mediation of the performative female voice, therefore, involved three important filters: foreign languages for Wong, a male opera artist for Wu, and new filming and recording technologies at the cusp of the sound era for both. By delineating the acoustic contours and audio-ability of the emerging and heavily mediated female vocal performances, I illuminate their entanglement with and configuration of the dialectics between Asian colonial modernity and cosmopolitanism, national identity, and international aspirations.

Anna May Wong's Ethnocosmopolitan Modernity

My study of Wong's, Wu's, and Mei's vocal performances in *Flame of Love* and *The Singing Peony* is circumscribed by the difficulties posed by the partial or complete loss of the voice per se. The English version of *Flame of Love* has fortunately survived, offering us the most complete view of the picture. The German and French film versions, however, are yet to be rediscovered, to the best of my knowledge. Nevertheless, a gramophone recording of Wong's love song performed in German has survived, offering a precious opportunity for us to start appreciating Wong's vocal performance in a recently acquired foreign language. Unlike the partial survival of Wong's first talkie, Butterfly Wu's Vitaphone talkie, *The Singing Peony*, has no surviving film print. Instead, we have a 150-page special issue on the film (including unnumbered pages of stills and advertisements), published in 1931. This issue, along with film reviews, provides the context for analyzing the film's historical significance at a conjuncture when

Chinese filmmaking was closely imbricated with nation-building discourses while also negotiating the Western-originated film technologies. As my analysis shows, the female voice, its successful recording, and its audio-ability occupy the central position in much of the publicity campaign, which significantly shaped the spectatorial expectations.

Publicity for *Flame of Love* and *The Singing Peony* similarly celebrated the films' technological breakthrough, coupled with the leading actresses' superb acting. The British program of *Flame of Love* emphasized the film as Wong's first talkie. Blurbs enthused over her vocal performance: "Her voice surpasses all expectations"; "Anna May Wong scores a big success—one of the most artistically complete talkies I have seen—pleasing to the eye and ear throughout." The blurbs urge the audience to "see and HEAR the ALLURING ANNA MAY WONG in HER FIRST TALKIE." Finally, the film is summarized as "beautifully and lavishly produced, haunting melodies, magnificent settings, charming singing, talking and dancing," with a small image showing chorus girls kicking legs in unison (publicity for *Flame of Love*, 1930).

To foreground Wong's vocal performance, the film opens in medias res, focusing the audience's attention on a female solo singing voice, before revealing her image. The English script reads,

> **SEQUENCE 1**
>
> 1. Stairway of Hai Tang house, late afternoon, twilight
>
> Sound motif of Hai Tang's love song floats down softly to Lieutenant Boris, becomes more distinct as Boris approaches her room.

With Wong / Hai Tang's singing voice being foregrounded as the first and foremost appeal in this film, the audience is treated to her soprano performance from a distance, off the screen, floating down the staircase. As her lover, the Russian lieutenant, goes upstairs, pauses, continues to approach her room, and then listens outside the door, her singing voice becomes closer and louder. The audience, following the lieutenant, thus vicariously experiences the soundscape as it shifts from a long shot of the voice to a close-up. This sequence is followed by a cut to the interior, a high-angle shot of Wong / Hai Tang singing while gliding her fingers over a Japanese *shamisen* (three-string lute), and then a cut to a medium close-up of Wong / Hai Tang in the same act of vocal performance.

The final anchoring of the soprano voice in the Oriental image of Wong / Hai Tang creates the shocking effect of audiovisual incongruity, undermining the illusory "phantasmatic body" delivered by a conventional sound film. According to Mary Ann Doane, the illusion of a three-dimensional "phantasmatic body" prized in classic Hollywood films is constructed through the coordination of three spaces: the space of the diegesis, the space of the screen made visible through synchronized sound, and the quasi-realist auditory ambience in the theater that "envelops the audience" in sound (1980, 377). This "phantasmatic body" supports the illusion of an imaginary subject and agency (380–382). Conversely, when an actor's speech is separated or alienated from the image of his or her body, an "uncanny" effect results, rupturing the illusion of audiovisual unity, spatial integrity, and as a result, the possibility of an integrated subject position. The opening sequence of *Flame of Love* starts with a disembodied female voice, which is eventually sutured with the body of Hai Tang / Wong. However, the Orientalized visual anchor derails the audience expectation triggered by the previously disembodied soprano voice. By highlighting the chasm between visual Orientalism and acoustic Occidentalism, the opening sequence harnessed the new sound-recording film technology to challenge the mainstream ethnic imaginary of Chineseness, promoting a cosmopolitanism that showed nonwhite ethnicity as coeval with European modernity.

In the next sequence, which spotlights Wong / Hai Tang performing for the Grand Duke, she is again introduced first and foremost as a soft singing voice behind the closed curtain. Cued by this voice, the Duke exercises his voyeuristic vision by peering through his monocle toward the stage. As if to gratify his peering gaze, Wong / Hai Tang is finally revealed on the stage, "slim and delicate, almost ethereal" (*Flame of Love* script, 1929). In the film, we see her sitting cross-legged on an altar, wearing an exotic shining outfit, with silvery tassels draping from her head and bare legs. She sings an opera, her body swaying to music, while being flanked by eight men in Mandarin outfits. Again, a cut to the Duke's point of view frames Wong's performance as gendered, exoticized, vulnerable, and exploitable. Then, two close-up shots, of the Duke and of Wong / Hai Tang, mark a new movement in the performance. In a long shot, Wong / Hai Tang rises to dance to the music, swaying her hips and gyrating in a studied, constrained manner, evoking her dance style in silent cinema. She finishes the scene with an operatic aria, winning the audience's enthusiastic applause.

In the next scene, set in Hai Tang's dressing room, the Lieutenant informs her that the Duke would like to dine with her, the "little Chinese girl." Hai Tang, according to the script, responds, "For you alone did I sing, for you alone did I play" (*Flame of Love*, 1929). In the film, Hai Tang is coerced into meeting the Duke so as not to jeopardize her lover's career. Offering a drink to her, the Duke seeks to compromise her: "I don't command. I simply wish. Sing a song." Importantly, here, Hai Tang's singing voice no longer maintains an independent space that adds a surprising cosmopolitan valence to her visual image. Instead, it is reduced to either a pledge of dedication to her lover or a property that the Duke seeks to expropriate. Insofar as the white men's contention over the ownership of this voice is analogized with their fight over her body and sexuality, her voice becomes as sexualized and racialized as her body is. To possess her voice amounts to possessing her racialized sexuality. Given the hierarchical race and class power structure, her refusal to sing for the Duke along with her rejection of his sexual advances means that both her voice and her sexuality are made inaccessible to the lower-rank Lieutenant; moreover, they are to be annihilated through her suicide at the end.

The formulaic tragic ending is not surprising in an Orientalist melodrama such as this. This formula temporarily accommodates the exotic and the desirable only to render it ultimately inassimilable and disposable, so that the colonial power structure can be maintained and reinforced through rehearsing such narratives of trespassing and containment. What *is* noteworthy, in this particular case, is that before this compulsory containment, Wong's voice and singing style are allowed a degree of "strangeness" that challenges clichéd visual Orientalism, enabling a more disruptive representation of race/ethnic identity.

This "strangeness" is redoubled in the German version of the film, which, like the English version, opens with Wong / Hai Tang's solo, this time in German. The German song, "Einmal kommt das Wunder der Liebe," begins with the striking of a gong and some singsongish notes (figure 2.1). Then we hear a melodious voice delivering the song in German, evoking the nineteenth-century Lieder tradition. Disembodied at the opening of the film, the singing voice expresses pensive meditation and lofty melancholy without conventional Oriental identifiers. The singing voice flows through a wide spectrum of tonalities, flaunting its untethered sentimentality, while playing with different media's capacities and interactions. On the one hand, it draws on the operatic tradition and uses the singer's body as the resonating medium that carries the sound to the distant audience. On the other hand, the film's being a talkie meant that sound recording played a crucial role in mediating the voice. The interactions between the performer's body and the sound-recording mechanism meshed with the self-conscious play between the acoustic and the visual that characterized the emerging talkies.

Aside from the singing style, Wong's German-language rendition added another mediation to her virtuosity. In a 1929 letter to her long-term friends the photographer couple Carl Van Vechten and Fania Marinoff, Wong commented on her work in Germany, "So all I've accomplished since I saw you is speaking German like nobody's business as I have to speak both German and English in the new film [presumably referring to the multiple language versions of *Flame of Love*]. It's been most interesting to master what formerly seemed like an impossibility but we sometimes even surprise ourselves at what we can do" (Wong 1929). Wong's apparently flippant tone in this letter revealed her pride in and excitement with her new ability of speaking German. Moreover, the "impossibility" she managed to master was not just a difficult European language but what this language enabled, namely, a cosmopolitan persona who cruised between different languages in defiance of Orientalist stereotypes.

Figure 2.1. Anna May Wong (as Hai Tang) performs a German song, from the *Flame of Love* film program, in *Illustrierter Film-Kurier* (Berlin), no. 1356 (1930).

In performing the German song "Einmal kommt das Wunder der Liebe" and its English counterpart in the German and English versions of *Flame of Love,* Wong performed a dubbed version of her own voice (between English and German),[3] which was further mediated by the burgeoning sound-recording technology. Wong's multilingual "Chinese" singer-dancer role challenged the trite Orientalist image of the inscrutable Other and foregrounded the character's uncanny resemblance to the Western Self. Her densely mediated vocal performance also signaled her participation in cinematic technological modernity and interwar cosmopolitanism.

It is true that Wong's cosmopolitan, pan-European appeal served the specific production and marketing interests of the Film Europe project. And her audiovisual performative incongruity alone (i.e., her Chinese looks and German singing voice) does not guarantee a deconstructive effect. Some Caucasian actors cast in Oriental roles in the tradition of yellowface also made efforts to acquire just enough Chinese vocabulary to deliver a line or sing a song. Two well-known examples are Warner Oland speaking garbled Cantonese in some *Charlie Chan* films and Katherine Hepburn singing a Chinese song in *Dragon Seed* (dir. Harold S. Bucquet and Jack Conway, 1944).

Nevertheless, there are three significant differences between Wong's European persona and the yellowface actors' "Oriental" persona. First, in the latter, Chinese dialogues and songs are deployed to round out the Orientalist fantasy—a Caucasian performer embodying a full package of aural as well as visual Otherness. Thus, even though the yellowface practice foregrounds the mismatch between the actor and the character, thus calling into question the principle of verisimilitude, the aural-visual consistency in portraying the Oriental character (a heavily made-up character speaking a heavily garbled language) serves to reify the Oriental image as the inscrutable Other. The identity masquerade therefore worked to expropriate the Other for the interest of the Euro-American Self. This leads to yellowface acting's second important difference from Wong's German-language performance. Contrary to Wong's almost flawless pronunciation of the German words and emotional performance of the song, the Caucasian performers' Chinese dialogues and songs tend to be delivered as "yellowfaced" voice, which does not aim to be intelligible; nor are they translated into a language understandable for the mainstream audience. Rather, the "yellowfaced" voice is treated as one more exotic trapping for the Orientalist fantasy.

Finally, the history of the racial/ethnic identity masquerade is by no means neutral or bilateral. Power inequity rooted in colonialism and slavery is amply demonstrated in minstrelsy that casts white entertainers in blackface to portray and exploit black stereotypes, while mulattos who tried to pass for white in real life were labeled as tragic mulattos. White privilege underpinning blackface performance similarly structures other forms of unidirectional racial masquerade, including yellowface, brownface, and redface. According to Richard Dyer, "This property of whiteness, to be everything and nothing, is the source of its representational power" (1988, 45). Seen as "colourless multi-colouredness," whiteness becomes all-powerful yet invisible. While "the invisibility of whiteness colonises the definition of other norms—class, gender, heterosexuality, nationality and so on—it also masks whiteness as itself a category" (46). The unidirectional racial masquerade stems precisely from the unexamined assumption that "whiteness" is unmarked and not a category, which can thus easily appropriate racial/ethnic identities that are marked as different from (and inevitably inferior to) the white racial norm.

This taken-for-granted white privilege and white performers' entitlement to nonwhite roles constitute the larger power geometry that constrained the work opportunities for performers of color. Contrary to the white performers who had the right to freely step in and out of a wide spectrum of roles, performers of color were oftentimes treated as the exotic "atmosphere" or, at best, were funneled into a limited number of trite, racialized stereotypes. Under such circumstances, they were rendered mute and decorative or were required to speak a fake "Oriental" accent (despite their American upbringing). The few American-born, Asian-heritage performers during the first half of the twentieth century who were not always forced to "authenticate" their Oriental roles with a fake "Oriental" accent were Anna May Wong (in all of her talkies), Philip Ahn (as an US government agent playing opposite Wong's Chinese American woman in *Daughter of Shanghai* [dir. Robert Florey, 1937]), and Keye Luke (as Charlie Chan's number-one son, playing opposite Warner Oland). Given mainstream entertainment's investment in a fake "Oriental" accent that continues into the present day,[4] Wong's, Ahn's, and Luke's opportunities to speak idiomatic English on the screen constituted exceptional cases that warrant special attention.

In Wong's vocal performance in *Flame of Love,* she went beyond simple resistance to a fake "Chinese" accent to actively acquire other languages and expand the terms of her audio-ability. By grafting the newly acquired British accent, German, and French onto her Oriental-looking character, she portrayed composite figures that spliced together seemingly discrepant attributes, thus deconstructing the Orientalist fantasy based on a stereotypical visual image matched with an equally stereotypical accent. She further made an effective bid for modernity and cosmopolitanism while reinflecting white-oriented cultural capital with her race-specific experience.

Wong's linguistic versatility continued the Chinese and Chinese American vaudeville culture from the 1850s to the 1920s. As Krystyn Moon's study reveals (2004), turn-of-the-twentieth-century ethnic-Chinese vaudevillian artists were constantly trespassing and unsettling racial/ethnic boundaries by portraying white as well as nonwhite characters through costuming and multilingual vocal performances. However, their largely forgotten legacy (contrary to the white actors' continuous racial masquerade) in the history of American popular entertainment makes it abundantly clear that the right of racial masquerade is ultimately reserved for white performers, whereas performers of color are systemically invisibilized even when they successfully trespass racial boundaries.

In view of the white-dominant history of racial masquerade, Wong's adoption of German as well as other languages went against the white hegemony while reviving the forgotten legacy of Chinese (American) vaudevillians from the 1850s to the 1920s. Her claim to linguistic versatility and cosmopolitanism was not simply the flip side of white racial masquerade, since this reverse direction was systemically ruled out in order to reinforce white entitlement. Nor was Wong's use of German yet another case of white domination, namely, a subaltern woman being colonized by a Western language.[5] Reducing her performance to colonial ventriloquism would miss her constant proactive learning, strategic self-positioning, and integral contribution to building the global idiom of cosmopolitanism and modernity from the diasporic vantage point. Undoubtedly, her indefatigable language cruising (encompassing German, French, King's English, and occasional Italian, Swedish, and Norwegian in her one-woman vaudeville shows when she visited Italy and northern Europe from December 1934 to February 1935) was driven by her career ambitions for more work opportunities and broader transnational appeal. This labor-intensive investment played into and was endorsed by the Film Europe project. But it also registered her self-empowerment vis-à-vis the white-dominant film and theater circles, which in turn enabled her to participate in cinematic modernity and to build her diasporic, racial struggles into interwar cosmopolitanism.

Wong's vocal performance was not confined to Western languages but also encompassed her ancestral Taishan dialect as well as her efforts to learn Mandarin Chinese. Rather than seeing these efforts as straightforward authentication of her Chinese ethnicity or political alignment with China's Nationalist-Party government, I argue that her deployment of Sinitic languages was as performative as her European-language cruising was.[6] In all these performances, what was at stake was not so much the establishment of her *true* racial/ethnic identity as the flexible identity positioning she constructed, flaunted, and strategized to best promote her career and transnational appeal. By eclectically mobilizing "the resources of history, language and culture in the process of becoming rather than being" (Hall 1996, 4), Wong used her identity play to redefine cinematic modernity and interwar cosmopolitanism.

In defying reified racial distinctions, Wong's deliberately bifurcated and mismatched vocal and visual performances yoked together the technological and the physical, the jarring and the titillating, the unsettling and the intriguing. Ultimately, her linguistic cruising and the resulting composite persona injected the ethnic into the cosmopolitan, thus revealing cinematic modernity and interwar cosmopolitanism as being coconstitutive with the interstitial ethnic experience.

The National Voice and Sentimental Modernity: Butterfly Wu's Affective Vocal Performance

As a privileged performer in the Film Europe project in the interwar period, Wong deployed vocal-visual performance to forge a technologized modernity that was simultaneously cosmopolitan and grounded in her diasporic and ethnic experience. In comparison, Butterfly Wu's performance in the first Chinese all-singing, all-talking film, *The Singing Peony,* facilitated a more nation-oriented modernity centered on the strengthening of China's film technology and national cinema, as well as other nation-building campaigns. However, this nationalist emphasis, like the Film Europe project, was mounted to thwart the incursion of Hollywood talkies (among other agendas), and thus, it ultimately grew out of transnational political inequities.

Given the unavailability of the original film, I turn to the 150-page special issue on the film and contemporaneous reviews to ascertain the historical significance of the film, especially the role of the female singer played by Butterfly Wu (figure 2.2). One major emphasis in a large number of theater advertisements of the film consists in its acoustic allure (thanks to technological sophistication), in combination with the melodramatic narrative and powerful performance. One advertisement raved about "Hu Die's [Butterfly Wu's] beautiful singing voice on top of her visual appeal" (*Singing Peony Special Issue*, 1931). Wu's voice and the voice of the entire cast were praised for being crystal clear, beautiful, and intelligible. Such intelligibility hinged on two factors: the technology of sound recording and the nationalist linguistic politics. The technical factor referred to the Vitaphone technology—that is, the sound was recorded on a separate wax disk that was then played back to match with the film reels during projection.

The publicity emphasized the grand experiment—that the film involved over one hundred production crew and cast members, who collaborated for six months and experienced despair when sound recording failed time and again, before it was finally successfully completed. The film's sound recording was in the charge of a Frenchman, Xia gu huai (叚谷槐) (his original French name is not identifiable), who worked for Pathé-Oriental in Shanghai. According to Zhou Jianyun, the publicity manager of Star Motion Picture Company, which shot the film, this French technician made five attempts, and only succeeded the

Figure 2.2. Hu Die (as Singing Peony) on the cover of *The Singing Peony Special Issue,* 80–81.

fifth time, because he initially assumed that the Chinese people did not care about the quality of the picture; and furthermore, his lack of Chinese knowledge (particularly regarding the cadence of Peking opera) led to subpar recording (Zhou 1931, 11–12). Cheng Bugao, a Star Motion Picture Company director, more specifically commented on the skills of sound recording. He discussed ways of solving some common problems, including one actor's voice coming across unevenly as if it belonged to several persons, a woman's voice sounding like a man's, or animals' sounds becoming utterly defamiliarized and unrecognizable (Cheng 1931, 37).

In addition to technical difficulties surrounding sound recording on eleven wax discs that corresponded with eleven film reels, the highly praised intelligible voice was also attributed to the use of Mandarin Chinese as opposed to dialects, especially Cantonese. Given the Nationalist Party's political agenda of linguistic nationalism, it is unsurprising that the new medium of sound film was quickly harnessed to promote Mandarin Chinese as the official language. While both Mandarin and Cantonese films were made in Shanghai at the very cusp of the talkie era,[7] Cantonese cinema was soon banned and subsequently pushed to southern China and then further to Hong Kong, which inadvertently led to the formation of Hong Kong cinema.[8] The publicity of *The Singing Peony* manifestly privileged Mandarin Chinese, praising the film's use of Mandarin Chinese as setting the standard for China's national cinema, thus demonstrating cinema's pedagogical value in promoting Mandarin Chinese all around China. Zheng Zhengqiu, one of the founding members of Star Motion Picture Company, asserted, "Mandarin Chinese must be used in talkies. All actors must be coached to speak Mandarin Chinese. Talkies serve as a vanguard in promoting Mandarin Chinese throughout China. . . . Talkies play an important role in education and cultural building" (Zheng 1931, 8).

In addition to privileging Mandarin Chinese over dialects, the publicity also praised this film for delivering a fatal blow to Hollywood talkies that assaulted Chinese audience with barbarian sounds. One commentator lamented that Chinese theaters showing foreign films "expose[d] Chinese audience to men and women with blue eyes and blond hair, speaking an awkward, unintelligible language. . . . These films also humiliate Chinese characters, [and] thus make us upset." He then switched gears to celebrate *The Singing Peony* for "boost[ing] the Chinese morale and national pride [wei minzu tuoqi, wei dangguo zengguang]" (Fan 1931, 4). Another commentator wrote a poem celebrating the film's triumph over Hollywood. The author compared Mandarin Chinese to the familiar and beautiful singing of the swallow and the nightingale, while English was likened to barbarous sounds made by the carnivorous shrike, sounds that were impenetrable even to Hong Shen, a Chinese playwright who was educated in the United States and who also wrote the dialogue script for *The Singing Peony* (Wu 1931, 8). Since the shrike's barbarous sounds are traditionally associated with southern Chinese dialects, English and southern Chinese dialects became interchangeably barbarous, equally abject and unacceptable in the Chinese national cinema.

Nonetheless, the foreign was not rejected wholesale. The same author of the poem attributed the film's triumph over Hollywood to the sound-recording equipment called *Baimingfeng*, or "Baiming-phone," "Baiming" referring to the combination of Pathé-Orient (known as Baidai gongsi in Chinese) and the Star Motion Picture Company (Mingxing yingpian gongsi). In turning against Hollywood, the poet endorsed the alliance between a Shanghai film studio and Pathé-Orient, a French-Chinese company that both produced and distributed gramophone records, including establishing a reputation for producing gramophone records of Peking opera.

This emphasis on the Sino-French alliance in making the first Chinese talkie found a fuller articulation when the director, Zhang Shichuan, made an analogy between Chinese cinema and a baby less than one year old. For Zhang, the baby was induced to speak prematurely (i.e., making a premature transition to the talkie era) thanks to the collaboration between its Chinese parents, who had done their best to give it proper nourishment, and its French nanny (i.e., Pathé-Orient), who utilized the "scientific method" to make the baby speak (Zhang 1931, 2–3). This familial metaphor, evocative of melodrama and the traditional domestic sphere of femininity, was thus updated with modern scientific methods of child-rearing to ensure proper nutrition and to facilitate physiological and cognitive development (such as making the baby speak prematurely). In this analogy, the Chinese parents' nutrition and the French nanny's science were combined, with a felicitous result. The (semi)colonial power inequity was thus reconfigured, with the France-associated Pathé-Orient and its sound-recording technology seen as a positive foreign presence as opposed to Hollywood's hegemony as the violent colonizer. Technological modernity and nationalist modernity reached a rapport in the making of the first all-singing, all-talking Chinese talkie in the midst of crosscurrents of interwar transnational politics and film/media culture.

It is within this context of aspiring for nationalist and technological modernities that we may start to understand the geopolitical as well as affective significance of Butterfly Wu's vocal performance. Given the discursive emphasis on Mandarin Chinese, Peking opera, which utilizes Beijing dialect—the very basis of Mandarin Chinese—became the prized musical performance in the film. As in *Flame of Love,* the film opens in medias res, showing Peony (played by Butterfly Wu) singing Peking opera on the stage, winning all-around applause. Also as in *Flame of Love,* the performer experiences various melodramatic tribulations, including being married to a dandy boy, being betrayed by him, losing her daughter to a human trafficker, losing her melodious singing voice, and suffering a declining career.

Peony's melodramatic suffering serves two purposes. First, it allows the film to deliver an ideological "ism" or social consciousness by dogmatically attributing her suffering to her lack of education and inundation by "old opera."[9] By labeling Peking opera as the "old opera" (despite its use of Beijing dialect, the basis of Mandarin Chinese), the film codes the female protagonist's vocal performance as backward, conservative, self-destructive, and opposed to modern education that would instill new sociopolitical consciousness in the ignorant working class, especially women, who had traditionally been deprived of socially engaged education. Nevertheless, this "ism" largely remained merely lip service to the political doctrine that binarized the old and the new, while nodding to the contemporaneous cultural debate on the reform of "old opera."

The real interest in the film consisted in Wu's technologized vocal performance and excessive melodramatic sentiments. The intertwining of these two aspects led to the second significance of Peony's melodramatic suffering, that is, the breakdown of her vocal performance under emotional duress, captured by the sound-recording system. The vocal and the affective performances gave rise to a mode of sentimental modernity that was intertwined with nationalist and technological modernities yet different from the dogmatic "ism."

The central importance of the female performer's vocal performance *and* its breakdown was fully registered in contemporaneous reviews and publicity writings. Wu, being a Mandarin Chinese speaker but with no prior training in Peking opera, was praised for her exemplary work ethic and effective performance in making this ambitious Vitaphone talkie. One reviewer, Yi Hua, wrote, "The film opens with Peking opera performance in order to introduce Peony right away while foregrounding China's operatic spirit. Hu Die [Butterfly Wu] started studying opera only a year ago. Her first rehearsal at the Star Operatic Society [Mingxing gejushe] was nothing compared to her performance in the film. Her performance in the film impresses as if she really were an opera artist. While I know Peony is just a fictional character, I cannot help feeling the real impact and forgetting that she is a character played by Hu [Wu]. . . . In the cast, Hu [Wu] gave the clearest dialogue and singing performance. Her voice is gentle and pleasant. Hu [Wu] is really the pride of Chinese cinema" (Yi Hua 1931, 77).[10]

Another reviewer, Su Shaoqing, described Wu as a "talented opera performer, tall and slender, with vivacious features and facial expressions, crystal clear voice, giving a superb performance in her diegetic operatic role as a princess visiting her mother" (1931, 49). He further encouraged all performers to take training classes in singing and elocution. Similarly, a correspondent made the following comments upon "listening to" *The Singing Peony:* the film was "complete with dialogue, singing, and music, just the same as Western talkies, and not at all inferior on any account." Wu's Peking opera performance was singled out for special mention ("After listening to *The Singing Peony,*" 1931).

If Wu's vocal performance was praised for being crystal clear and professional, it was equally celebrated for breaking down into weeping under emotional stress. The scene in which Peony, upon witnessing her husband flirting with another woman in the audience, becomes so despondent and jealous that she stutters and breaks down on the stage was deemed as emotionally powerful as when Janet Gaynor's circus girl sees her lover betraying her (Su 1931, 48). Another comparison was with Lillian Gish, similarly featured in "an appealing sentimental plot" that required the actress's copious crying, cuing spectatorial sympathy (Qi Xi 1931, 80).[11] The reviewer Bing Hua poeticized Wu's weeping, comparing it to the cry of a forlorn goose under the moon, which expressed real emotions, rather than simply playacting. Reportedly, Wu, out of emotional sincerity, broke down into tears even when she was listening to the director introduce the story of the film (Bing 1931, 81).

In emphasizing Wu's vocal and affective performance, characterized simultaneously by eloquence and breakdown, the reviewers understood voice as an unreserved expression of the interior psychic state, while relegating the technology of recording to mere transparent mediation. This naturalizing tendency contradicted the other focus of publicity on the laborious language and elocution coaching of the performers and the repeated experiments with sound recording in making the talkie. If the naturalist, affective expression anchored the integrated subjective body and psyche, for which the recording technology simply served as passive mediation, the physical training and technological difficulty emphasized in some publicity materials signaled the encounter between the performer's material body and the materiality of the recording technology, between the crew and cast's unruly linguistic-cultural diversity and the nationalist ideological homogeneity. This encounter necessitated back-and-forth negotiation, trial-and-error experiment, and cumulative labor. As Wu recalled in her memoir, she and the rest of the cast spent over six hours every day in the recording studio to dub their characters. When the film finally succeeded, and many reviewers praised her Peking opera performance, she jocularly commented, "I'm not Mei Lanfang [the Peking opera artist] but Mei Lanyuan [Wu deliberately conflated "fang" in Mei Lanfang's name with a homonym that means "square," in order to oppose it to "yuan," or the circular shape]. It's the 'yuan pan' [the round wax disc] that was singing for me" (Hu 1988, 57).

Wu's recounting seems to belie the publicity and the reviews that sang high praise for her operatic performance. Yet what is at stake is not the accuracy of Wu's recounting versus that of the 1930s publicity and reviews. Rather, Wu's jocular recounting reveals the complex layering and technological mediation of her vocal performance. First, her voice and all other characters' voices were laboriously dubbed through five attempts of recording (with the fifth recording being successful) by a French technician. In that sense, her voice was mechanically and spatially distanced from, and then sutured back onto, her body. Second, due to the crucial separation, realignment, and remediation via the recording technology, Wu's recounting takes on ambivalent meanings. One could be that she did not sing the opera but was simply lip-syncing the prerecorded opera record (of Mei Lanfang's singing). Yet, even if she did sing, the singing voice did not emanate from her body on the screen and was not recorded in sync but rather came from the wax disk with sound recorded on it at a different time and location. This ambiguity disrupts the audiovisual coherence that the film attempts to present and reveals the "phantasmatic body" (à la Doane) as nothing but an illusion premised on technological stitching together of disparate elements. In celebrating the film's hard-earned technological achievement and Wu's seemingly natural sentimental performance simultaneously, the discourses on the film created a mode of sentimental modernity born out of the dual logic of entertainment and nationalist homogenization.

A comparison of Butterfly Wu's Vitaphone character and Anna May Wong's composite screen persona yields important insights into the two ethnic-Chinese actresses' contribution to building Asian modernities through their vocal performances and audio-ability. Whereas one addressed China's nationalist agenda (which harnessed the new film technology to induce homogeneity) while entertaining the audience's (especially women's) desire for melodramatic sentiment, and the other facilitated the Film Europe project, appealing to transnational audiences through discrepant audio and visual performances, they both fundamentally depended on technological mediation that brought together disparate dimensions, whether they were presented as incoherent elements or merged into an illusory integrity. Like Wong's composite persona in *Flame of Love,* which flaunted acoustic and visual incongruity, Wu's character in *The Singing Peony* similarly yoked together dimensions often presumed to be incongruent (such as technological mediation and physical spontaneity, nationalism and mass entertainment). In ushering the early talkie to local or translocal audiences, Wong's and Wu's vocal as well as visual performances played a pivotal role in developing diasporic and nationalist Asian modernities in relation to the shifting cinematic technologies, the unfolding interwar cosmopolitanism, and its obverse, that is, global coloniality and its circumscription of China.

Wu and Wong's 1935 meeting in London was no coincidence. Their convergence at Mei Lanfang's welcome party and informal apprenticeship to him testified to the significance of Mei's art of female impersonation for performing Chinese femininity both within and outside China, both on the screen and on the stage. Furthermore, their simultaneous spotlighting in interwar London—the international stage—marked a historical moment when Chinese and diasporic Chinese intersected to construct and perform the multiplicity of modern Chinese cultural-ethnic identity for the transnational audience. As my analysis shows, both Wong's and Wu's dramatic personae were densely mediated, through Peking opera or the German language, through the female performer's physical, vocal performance and labor, and finally through the emerging technology of sound recording. Insofar as these personae gestured toward divergent, even conflicting coding of Chineseness and Chinese femininity, they embodied and constructed the heterogeneity of Asian modernities, which must be understood as interrelated, mutually implicating, yet not totalizable. Furthermore, the juxtaposition of Wong and Wu demonstrates the importance of studying Asian modernities from both the outside and the inside of the geopolitical constellation called "Asia."

Notes

1. For a concerted theoretical and sociopolitical inquiry into the historical formation of "Asia" across a spectrum of colonial, neocolonial, and postcolonial projects, see the essays in "What's Left of Asia?" (2007).

2. Bergfelder's study shows that *Flame of Love* was poorly received, as indicated by the German and British press coverage. However, the poor reception does not take away from the importance of Wong's contribution to this key multilingual production under the aegis of the interwar Film Europe project. For a collective historical study of the Film Europe project as a counter-Hollywood strategy, see Higson and Maltby 1999.

3. The French version of the film has not survived, to the best of my knowledge. However, the French reviews suggest that Wong did not sing the love song; nor did she have much dialogue. The marginal vocal performance perhaps had to do with her limited French. According to one review, "she only just speaks—to articulate with difficulty a dozen words in French—and does little more than tremble, sob and scream the rest of the time, without much expression on her face" (*Hai Tang* review, 1930).

4. For a contemporary Chinese American comedian's paradoxical spin on the fake "Asian" accent, see Chu 2014.

5. I thank this book's coeditor Andrew Weintraub for alerting me to this potential interpretation of Wong's German vocal performance. In my analysis, I historicize and contextualize Wong's performance to demonstrate its unique contribution not only to her self-empowerment but also to interwar cosmopolitanism and cinematic modernity.

6. For an in-depth discussion of Wong's strategic deployment of Taishan dialect and Mandarin Chinese, see my "Speaking in a Forked Tongue: Anna May Wong's Linguistic Cosmopolitanism" (forthcoming).

7. The first Cantonese film, *Baijin long* (The golden dragon; 1933), adapted from *The Grand Duchess and the Waiter* (dir. Malcolm St. Clair, 1926), was a Cantonese opera film made in Shanghai and became widely popular both within China and among diasporic Chinese communities overseas (especially Southeast Asia).

8. As Stephen Teo writes, "Hong Kong gained a film industry as sound came in circa 1933–34, . . . whereas in the silent years, a film industry based in the colony always seemed a precarious idea. It could only develop as a center of Cantonese film production" (1997, 19).

9. The film's director, Zhang Shichuan, described the film as a quasi-backstage musical with an "ism" (original English) (1931, 2–3).

10. Other members of the Star Operatic Society, affiliated with the Star Motion Picture Company, also participated in performing Peking opera episodes in this film (Tang 1931, 35). Star Motion Picture Company established two subsidiary organs in response to the inception of the talkie era, one for teaching Mandarin Chinese and the other for teaching dancing, singing, and acting of old Chinese plays ("China's First Talkie Next," 1931).

11. The films featuring Gaynor and Gish were not identified in these sources.

References

"After Listening to *The Singing Peony*" (Tingguo *Genu hongmudan* zhihou). 1931. *Beiyang haubao* (Peiyang pictorial) 13 (631).

Bergfelder, Tim. 2004. "Negotiating Exoticism: Hollywood, Film Europe and the Cultural Reception of Anna May Wong." In *Stars: The Film Reader*, edited by Lucy Fischer and Marcia Landy, 59–76. New York: Routledge.

Bing Hua. 1931. "Hu Die de ku" (Hu Die's tears). In *The Singing Peony Special Issue*, 80–81.

Cheng, Bugao. 1931. "Shouying de jiqiao" (Skills of sound recording). In *The Singing Peony Special Issue*, 37–38.

"China's First Talkie Next: 'Singing Peony' Opens at Strand Sunday." 1931. *Damei wanbao* (Shanghai evening post), 13 March. Reprinted in *The Singing Peony Special Issue*, 84.

Chu, Arthur. 2014. "Breaking Out the Broken English." *Code Switch* (blog), NPR, 31 July. http://www.npr.org/blogs/codeswitch/2014/07/31/336380977/breaking-out-the-broken-english.

Dianying huabao (Screen pictorial). 1935. Vol. 23 (15 July).

Doane, Mary Ann. 1980. "The Voice in the Cinema: The Articulation of Body and Space." *Yale French Studies* 60:33–50.

Dyer, Richard. 1988. "White." *Screen* 29 (4): 44–65.

Fan, Shuhan. 1931. "Guochan yingpian zhi xiongwei tisheng" (A triumphant birth cry of domestic sound cinema). In *The Singing Peony Special Issue*, 4.

Flame of Love (aka *Hai Tang*). 1929. English script. 29 October. British Film Institute.

Hai Tang review. 26 September 1930. *Hai Tang* program and press clippings. Bibliothèque nationale de France.

Hall, Stuart. 1996. "Introduction: Who Needs 'Identity'?" In *Questions of Cultural Identity*, edited by Stuart Hall and Paul du Gay, 1–17. London: Sage.

Higson, Andrew, and Richard Maltby, eds. 1999. *"Film Europe" and "Film America": Cinema, Commerce and Cultural Exchange 1920–1939*. Exeter, UK: University of Exeter Press.

Hu, Die (Butterfly Wu). 1988. *Hu Die huiyilu* (Memoirs of Hu Die). Edited by Liu Huiqing. Beijing: Wenhua yishu chubanshe.

Moon, Krystyn. 2004. *Yellowface: Creating the Chinese in American Popular Music and Performance, 1850s–1920s*. New Brunswick, NJ: Rutgers University Press.

Petro, Patrice. 2014. "Cosmopolitan Women: Marlene Dietrich, Anna May Wong, and Leni Riefenstahl." In *Silent Cinema and the Politics of Space*, edited by Jennifer Bean, Anupama Kapse, and Laura Horak, 295–311. Bloomington: Indiana University Press.

positions: east asian cultures critique. 2007: 5 (2). Special issue on "What's Left of Asia?"

Publicity for *Flame of Love* (aka *Hai Tang*). 1930. British Film Institute.

Qi Xi. 1931. "Tongqing zhi lei" (Tears of sympathy). Review. In *The Singing Peony Special Issue*, 80.

The Singing Peony (Genu hongmudan tekan) Special Issue. 1931. Shanghai: Dadong shuju yinshuasuo. Advertisement no. 7.

Spivak, Gayatri Chakravorty. 1988. "Can the Subaltern Speak?" In *Marxism and the Interpretation of Cultures*, edited by Cary Nelson and Lawrence Grossberg, 271–313. Basingstoke, UK: Macmillan.

Su, Shaoqing. 1931. "Guan Zhongguo yousheng dianying *Genu hongmudan* zhihou" (After watching Chinese talkie *The Singing Peony*). In *The Singing Peony Special Issue*, 48–49.

Tang, Xiumei. 1931. "Jieshao *Genu hongmudan*" (Introducing *The Singing Peony*). In *The Singing Peony Special Issue*, 33–36.

Teo, Stephen. 1997. *Hong Kong Cinema: The Extra Dimensions*. London: BFI.
Wang, Yiman. Forthcoming. "Speaking in a Forked Tongue: Anna May Wong's Linguistic Cosmopolitanism." In *Revisiting Star Studies*, edited by Sabrina Qiong Yu and Guy Austin. Edinburgh, UK: Edinburgh University Press.
Wong, Anna May. 1929. Letter to Carl and Fania Van Vechten, 26 September. Carl Van Vechten Manuscript Collection, Beinecke Library, Yale University.
Wu, Guanli. 1931. "He *Genu hongmudan* chenggong" (Celebrating the success of *The Singing Peony*). In *The Singing Peony Special Issue*, 8.
Yan, Hairong, and Daniel F. Vukovich. 2007. "Introduction: What's Left of Asia." *positions: east asia cultures critique* 15 (2): 211–224.
Yi Hua. 1931. "Guozhi youshengpian chenggong" (Success of a China-made talkie). Review. In *The Singing Peony Special Issue*, 76–77.
Zhang, Shichuan. 1931. "*Genu hongmudan* de chenggong bushi yijian ou'ran de shi" (The success of *The Singing Peony* is not a coincidence). In *The Singing Peony Special Issue*, 2–4.
Zheng, Zhengqiu. 1931. "Wei Zhongguo yousheng yingpian gao ge fangmian" (A public statement on Chinese sound cinema). In *The Singing Peony Special Issue*, 5–8.
Zhou, Jianyun. 1931. "*Genu hongmudan* duiyu Zhongguo dianying jie de gongxian jiqi yingxiang" (*The Singing Peony*: Its contributions to and influences on Chinese cinema). In *The Singing Peony Special Issue*, 9–19.

CHAPTER 3

On Becoming Nora

TRANSFORMING THE VOICE AND PLACE OF THE SING-SONG GIRL THROUGH ZHOU XUAN

Yifen Beus

THE New Culture (新文化) or May Fourth Movement (五四運動), beginning in 1919, is generally recognized by historians as the first conscious modernization movement in China. Led by intellectuals such as Hu Shih (胡適) and Chen Duxiu (陳獨秀), who were influenced by Western modern philosophies, the movement called for political, social, and literary reform (Bary, Chan, and Watson 1960, 151–169). Hu in his unpublished English manuscripts clearly places China's modernity with the new Chinese republic's sociopolitical ideals of freedom, democracy, education, scientific thinking, and intellectual renaissance (2001). One of Hu's key agendas was to liberate Chinese women from the traditionalist confinement of gender roles and to give them a voice and place in modern Chinese society.[1] Enthusiastically referenced by China's modernist writer Lu Xun in a 1923 lecture at the Beijing Women's Normal College on the liberation of Chinese women, the Norwegian playwright Henrik Ibsen's work, likewise, was a timely and influential inspiration to Chinese writers, particularly in advocating gender equality. Ibsen, often referred to as the father of modern drama (Cody and Sprinchorn 2007, 354), in 1879 wrote and premiered *A Doll's House,* which pioneered an open discussion in the theater on the liberation of women. The play's protagonist, Nora, not only has come to symbolize the modern woman's fight for self-determination and identity but also served as the role model for many Chinese women to "walk out" (of household/family bonds) during an era when China looked to the West to reform its society, traditionally governed by Confucian principles. Despite the differences in Hu's and Lu's visions for a liberated Chinese "new woman," Ibsenism provided a model for a gender discourse that was unprecedented and seen as a true manifestation of modernity, often embodied in Shanghai's cosmopolitanism, particularly through its entertainment industry.

"To choose the path of Nora" was a public statement that Zhou Xuan (周璇, 1920–1957) made in 1941 (Zhao 1995, 7), when she announced her "walking out" (出走) of her marriage with her famed composer husband, Yan Hua (嚴華), and solidified her place in Republican China's popular cultural history as a modern, independent performer. As China's pop music diva in the late 1930s and 1940s, Zhou has been credited by cultural historians and musicologists with having popularized a music trend that fused Western jazz and Chinese folk tunes (Hong 2008, 1, 9–10, 87–129, 163–218). Scholarly studies on Zhou have been scarce; at this writing, the most comprehensive scholarly study of Zhou's songs in a single volume is Hong Fangyi's *Wandering Songstress: Zhou Xuan and Her Song* (2008), which focuses on Zhou's career and artistry as a song star through the lens of cultural musicology. However, there has been consistent public interest in her personal life since she rose to stardom in the late 1930s. This is reflected in the six published biographies and a recent publication of her diaries, which have collectively portrayed her as the song queen of the Republican era, with a moving "golden voice," who humbly rejected the title of the "film queen" bestowed by *Shanghai Daily* (in 1941) and is remembered by fans and critics alike for her "natural and lively" acting style.[2] The public's interest in her, besides her music and film performance, has mainly been focused on her unresolved birth identity, her childhood stories, her marriages at the peak of her career, and her "mysterious death" in 1957 at the age of thirty-seven, which supplied topics for newspaper and magazine coverage. Consequently, Zhou's stardom was constructed not only through material conditions of her career (the music, film, and print as well as other mass-media industries) but also through the cultural and historical circumstances, as China was experiencing exchanges and changes caused by Western nations' and Japan's colonial activities in the Far East in the early part of the twentieth century. While the historical underpinnings of her stardom in Shanghai's (colonial) "modern culture" have been identified in relation to her music and film careers by both musicologists and film historians, there has been little discussion of her transmedia performance and the role of musical sequences in her films, which ultimately mobilized the placement of the female singer (songstress, or the traditionally denigrated sing-song girl, 歌女) as a profession and as a role type in the public sphere.

Among all the extramusical and extracinematic discussions about Zhou, film critics, as with her audience and fans, have been highly interested in the resemblance of Zhou's most referenced role, Xiao Hong, a songstress, in *Street Angel* (1937) to her own personal life. This conflation of her on- and off-screen personas, along with one of the title songs of this film, "The Wandering Songstress," established an archetype on-screen, which came to represent an oppressed yet persevering female entertainer. This traditionally "low-caste" screen-role type and real-life profession was rehabilitated in Zhou's performance through the dialectic workings of a soundscape comprising diegetic musical numbers and nondiegetic background songs in her films (both often sung by Zhou herself) and her public performance in theaters and on radio shows. The openly romantic and at times explicit lyrics set in hybridized melodies are often juxtaposed in idealized fantasy sequences of the heroine during her most oppressed moments in the narrative. They also appear, as diegetic segments, when the heroine rejoices in brief yet elated moments apart from the otherwise melancholic or tragic events in the narrative. These repeated images and songs fill the public's imagination of Zhou, along with gossip and news in fan magazines. Through mass (re)production on the gramophone, on the silver screen, and through radio broadcasting of her popular songs, her transmedia performance created a discursive space occupied simultaneously by the performer, the audience, and the media maker. It was not only this "crossover" that allowed Zhou as a performer to traverse the public space, but the "aura" in the Benjaminian sense was also transmitted from the typically "invisible" singer behind the scenes to the mechanically reproduced/projected images of the star. Her stardom legitimized her as a cultured, virtuous, and sympathetic female singer, a profession and public image that was no longer scrutinized as it had been before the 1930s.

Highlighting Zhou's cross-media performance and her "walking out" as a female public figure, this chapter aims to fill the gap between the typical readings of music aesthetics and film narratives by musicologists and film historians by examining the following intertwined aspects of Zhou's life and career as a performer: first, the dialectic workings of the music and film industries in shaping Zhou's stardom; second, the functions of song sequences within sound cinema as structured Utopianism; and third, Zhou's aura in reshaping the public image of the sing-song girl in China since the late 1930s. For this purpose, two relevant song sequences from *Street Angel* are analyzed to illustrate the workings of song montage in her cinema.

Theory and Context

Beijing's BTV program *Files* (档案) credited Zhou with having sung more than 200 songs, among which 114 are screen songs in her films ("Golden Voice Zhou Xuan," 2011). The sheer extent of her output and the broad range of her singing techniques easily secured for her a top place among the stars who had a dual acting and singing career in the 1930s and 1940s (Hong 2008, 163–216).[3] Zhou's image, understood within the framework of Richard Dyer's groundbreaking work on stars, was construed as a sociocultural icon mediated through and inseparable from media (popular music and cinema), biography, and public discourses.

This framework converges the workings of the medium and industry in a discursive paradigm motivated not only by the star's apparent personal charisma and cast type but also by economic terms as a dominant factor of shaping stardom. Her stardom enabled a more democratized role for women in the entertainment industry and normalized in particular the sing-song girl character/profession as an archetype of social outcast who paradoxically must be rescued and would eventually be transformed into a Nora that dares to walk out of her previously prescribed boundaries and become her true self. This narrative represents an idealized national allegory of China facing international aggression in the first half of the twentieth century, a connection between ideology and star role type observed by Dyer (1979, 20–32).

At a time of national crisis during the Japanese invasion, the Kuo Ming Tang (KMT, 國民黨) instigated a "New Life Movement" (新生活運動, 1934–1949). This movement merged Confucian moral ideals with a "counterrevolutionary" tendency, a "modern response to a modern problem" (Dirlik 1975, 945). Numerous measures were implemented to provide citizens with a moral education and to purge decadent sounds, the "yellow music" or *mi mi zhi yin* (靡靡之音), in favor of a kind of wholesome music meant to foster a unified nationalist sentiment. Dirlik argues that this traditional-looking movement must not be seen as a "reaffirmation of traditional Chinese political conceptions"; it "had greater affinity with modern counterrevolutionary movements than with political attitudes inherited from China's past" (945). It was a localized modern movement paradoxically merging moral conservatism and progressive revolution, a KMT version of Cultural Revolution. Regarding the political economy of the popular song of this time, Jacques Attali's (1985) work on music and Susan McClary's (1985) reading of Attali provide an analytical paradigm for the "composition" of the synchronized filmic performance and the recorded songs and the impact of these song sequences. In this purging environment, Zhou's music could have faced censorship. Ironically, thanks to cinematography and sound editing, Zhou's songs on- and offscreen were mechanically mass-produced and helped create an imagined community or an "abstract utopia" (Attali 1985, 145) where ambivalent sounds like Zhou's, which bordered between and at times blended yellow music and local tunes (*xiao diao*, 小調) with occasional patriotic allusions, coexisted with the state mandate and the concurrent leftist nationalism.

However, this unifying appeal was often achieved through an apparent lack of direct political references in Zhou's songs, a result of her unique (mellow and full) yet versatile (from traditional to bel canto methods) singing techniques and her collaboration with various top songwriters and composers of the time.[4] The structural functions of the song sequences within the filmic narrative and their relation to the mise-en-scène also rendered them implicit and politically relevant, read through the Attalian lens in mapping out the "strategic usages of music by power": "When power wants to make people *forget,* music is ritual *sacrifice,* the scapegoat; when it wants them to *believe,* music is enchantment, *representation;* when it wants to *silence* them, it is reproduced, normalized, *repetition.* Thus it heralds the subversion of both the existing code and the power in the making, well before the latter is in place" (Attali 1985, 20, emphases in the original). With such a force in social function and in a political climate fostered by the earlier May Fourth Movement and current Japanese imperialism in East Asia (indeed an "extraordinary moment of cultural climax" in Attali's words; 1985, 145), early twentieth-century Chinese popular music, which existed as coded signs alongside its cinematic applications, essentially went through what Mariam Hansen has called an "Americanization from below" (1991, 69). Patterned after Hollywood's musicals in the 1930s and 1940s, Zhou's performance exemplified a vernacularized modern art form that catered to the popular taste of the urban masses (市井大眾), which in turn shaped her public image as the "queen of song and screen" (Hong 2008, 2, 49, 278) and functioned as a "powerful matrix for modernity's liberatory impulses—its moments of abundance, play, and radical possibility, its glimpses of collectivity and gender equality" (Hansen 1991, 69). Nonetheless, the notion of the "New Woman" (新女性) in 1930s China was a highly politicized one, as indicated by the very title of a 1935 film starring Ruan Lingyu, *New Woman,* which depicts an intellectual woman's independent life after divorce. Unable to overcome the emotional trauma of economic hardships and social prejudice, the heroine commits suicide at the end of the story. Despite this long-existent stigma, the archetype of a wandering songstress was ratified through Zhou's presence as a cultural icon for China's then-modern "New Woman" in the public sphere.

Star as New Woman

Three key factors that shaped Zhou's star image were the sociopolitical milieu of 1930s China, her talents, and her striving for the "new womanhood" in her private and public lives. The characteristics of the "New Woman" under the New Life Movement reflected a "curious East-West ideology fusion of neo-Confucian percepts, thinly disguised New Testament Christianity, YMCA-style social activism, elements of Bushido—the samurai code—and European fascism, along with a generous dose of New England Puritanism," an image best exemplified by Madame Chiang Kai-shek (Li 2006, 102). Right before the New Life Movement was officially inaugurated, Liu Yiqing wrote in 1933 in *Linglong* (玲瓏), a Shanghai-based popular women's fan/fashion magazine, of the following traits of a New Woman, later prescribed by the movement: "Such a modern woman should not be known merely by her chic appearance. . . . The true modern woman must also possess such qualities as 'rich knowledge, lofty thinking, and strong will,' all derived from reading and studying" (quoted in Lee 1999, 94). The female star thus aptly "served to instruct the female viewer on how to become correctly modern," besides modeling fashion and style (Hansen 1991, 120).

As was the case for 1920s Hollywood, as observed by Hansen, this new aesthetic of the feminine in 1930s China derived from women's portraits and photos on magazine covers earlier on, and instead of or in addition to serving "as objects of the male gaze in a patriarchal society," these photos "also helped to project a new persona for Chinese women, that of the 'modern' woman in possession of certain new qualities, who is not ashamed to display her personality in public" (Lee 1999, 94). Zhou's image on- and offscreen simulated such a paradoxically modern cultured woman with traditional virtue and morality, a cinematic desire frequently satisfied through Zhou's diverse yet quite consistent role types—those who long to be independent yet suffer from repression and those who are wronged yet remain patient and faithful. This dialectic between the star and the audience is quite consistently observed by Dyer: "stars as images are constructed in all kinds of media texts other than films [and records, in this case], but none the less, films remain privileged instances of the star's image" (1979, 88). This was particularly the case with singer/film stars, whose screen presence helped to authenticate or create (whether or not the song was sung by a playback singer) an illusion of the star's body identical with the source of the voice, a realism enabled by filmic projection and simultaneous sound recording.

In Zhou's private life, her public nickname, "golden voice" (金嗓子, which accompanied her name on all playbills and film posters), and title, "song queen of the generation" (一代歌后), were a result of her innate talent, humble personality, and hard work. He Luting, one of the composers she worked with, described her as "very serious about learning and art" and as "completely different from those yellow music singers who were coy and lascivious, pretentious and flirtatious" (Zhou and Jing 2007, pt. 1, "Work Hard & Stride Forward, I"). Not only was she well poised and sincere, but she also learned quickly, able to hit the right notes and timber of a new song exactly as the composer had wished. Although growing up in Shanghai's rural suburb and speaking the regional dialect, Zhou was coached to speak standard Mandarin by her first husband, Yan Hua, who also attested to her linguistic skills (Zhou and Jing 2007, pt. 1, "Work Hard & Stride Forward, II"). Eliminating her Shanghai accent was a major step in advancing her film career. The dual effects of cinema, as a vernacular recording medium of the objective world's sound and image, and the state mandate of using standardized Mandarin in the public sphere to nationalize the soundscape during the Republican era provided favorable conditions for Zhou to cross over to sound film with ease; dubbing the dialogue was not a typical practice in China's early sound cinema, while using playback recording of screen songs sung by other singers was relatively common.

In addition to this linguistic talent, Zhou's strong desire for learning and passion for knowledge paid off in gaining recognition and favor from her mentors (such as He Luting and Li Jinhui, two well-known composers of the time). Having only a few years of primary education, she learned to read musical notes and film scripts, play the piano, and later write to fans, "all on her own" (Zhou and Jing 2007, pt. 1, "Work Hard & Stride Forward, II" and "Zhou Xuan on the Battleground"). These personal traits have, since her first film, *Street Angel,* become stock characterization in the roles she played on-screen during a time when the nation was in need of revitalizing humble moral values that seemed to have been drowned in the dazzling neon lights on Shanghai's modern entertainment scene. The New Life Movement's political ideology, which conditioned her stardom, again reflects the stabilizing power of a star's personal charisma (Dyer 1991, 57–59).

Cross-Media Performance

Shanghai's song and dance troupes in the 1930s were the origin and hotbed of China's early popular music. Their top apprentices (mostly female), trained by the troupes' masters, developed their song and screen careers, along with appearances on radio shows (Hong 2008, 2, 7, 21–22, 34). When Zhou debuted her film career, having already established a singing reputation as a youngster in the Ming Yue Troupe (明月歌舞團), the image of "good girls" (who behaved naturally without affectedness) was a socially constructed ideal that met the criteria of the New Life Movement. For instance, the *Shanghai News,* or *Shen Bao* (申報), described her as a "courteous" and "promising" singing star ("Zhou Xuan Named Miss PhD") and later ran a review of the 1939 *Meng Jiang Nü* (孟姜女; "Meng Jiang Nü"),[5] tracing Zhou's past "lively" performance in *Street Angel* and her "well-poised manners" in *Night of the West Chamber* (夜西廂) (February 18, 1939). Again in 1946, the poster for the musical-theater version of *Meng Jiang Nü* emphasized, in big and bold print, the endorsement of Madame Chiang Kai-shek (Hong 2008, 161). However, Michael Chang argues that in film, a bold medium for social realism, being a "true character" and the notion of *ziran* (natural), *tianzhen* (innocent), or *zhen* (genuine) acting had nothing to do with verisimilitude in the theatrical sense but rather was understood in terms of acting/performance skills. It was seen only as appearance (appearing or looking genuine on the screen), a gendered standard for "authenticity" in public performance training because this moralized media image (talent, virtue and innocence, chastity and loyalty), in fact, required separation between the screen character and the real star only for males but not for women (1999, 153).

This expectation for a fusion of life and artifice, reality and representation of actresses, further facilitated character types that best suited Zhou's temperament and life story. Besides her earlier work, the twelve films made during the peak of her film career from 1943 to 1949 all feature characters who have personal traits and life stories full of hardships and trials similar to her own (Hong 2008, 74–75). The notion that "a virtuous hero/heroine of feeling is made to suffer through hardships or struggle against forces beyond his or her control" constitutes one such favorite role type that Zhou often played (Lee 1999, 95). This role type resonated with the Chinese audience also because of a narrative quality (*gushixing*, 故事性) common in Tang and Ming *chuanqi* (唐明傳奇) (Leyda 1972, 49), a romantic and legendary literary genre that has governed much of the popular screen narration and story development patterns. This performative resemblance of the role types associated with Zhou's "real" life elevated them to a level where the audience readily accepted her and her characters as allegorical and reflexive in a time of national crisis during internal civil unrest (between KMT and Mao's Red Flag Army) and external warfare with Japan. Such nationalist rhetoric, commonly used in the print media that advertised and critiqued film, was a standard trope in the hope of building an egalitarian republican society by highlighting existing class differences, allowing the humble and the needy to represent the mass majority from rural China.

Among the roles Zhou played, the songstress and the strong-willed orphan are two types readily recognized by the audience that resembled Zhou's screen persona and her true life story. The "authenticating" process during her vocal (as diegetic singer in the narrative's song sequences) and screen (as actress) performance, in turn, rescued the songstress type from the traditional prejudice against the *chang ling bu fen* (娼伶不分, literally "no difference between songstress/actress and prostitute") stereotype. It mobilized singing and acting into a profession category that in reality mediated between the urban, somewhat modernized masses (as consumers) and the intellectual elites (as song- and filmmakers) in the modern urban culture, even under a very strict militarist political climate in the Republican era.

As the 1930s talkies of China emphasized merit and artistic talent, film advertisement often played up the stars' education, training, and skills through other mass media, such as radios and fan magazines as well as face-to-face interactions with the audience on various promotional appearances and tours (Chang 1999, 149–150). This phenomenon coincided with the rise of an urban consuming "fandom," as defined by John Fiske, in which cultural and economic capital flowed to help shape the image of the star (1992, 30–31). Likewise, the extrafilmic discourse surrounding Zhou's stardom relied heavily on these disappearing media boundaries in maintaining the consistency of her public image. The Guo Hua Company (國華公司), with which Zhou contracted, as well as fan magazines and major newspapers (such as *Shanghai News* [申報], *The Young Companion* [良友畫報], *Pop Star Pictorial* [歌星畫報], and *Phenomena* [萬象]), frequently orchestrated numerous "coincidences," such as the timing of the announcement of her brave "walk out"/divorce and the subsequent joint public statement with Yan Hua in the newspaper in 1941, right before the release of a major feature, *Deep, Dark Night* (夜深沈). That film continued to depict her as an ill-fated yet professional and respectable woman, while at the same time sketching out a glamorous, independent star in public, with pitiable personal stories worthy of infinite public speculation and gossip, particularly those concerning her biological parentage, her childhood hardships, the circumstances of her divorce, and later, her mental illness, many of which were never "proved" with hard evidence (Hong 2008, 28–29, 33, 37–39). Thus, the cultural economy and the "structured polysemy" of stars paralleled the workings of the feminine aesthetic, making these two facets of the public performative culture function in synergy to fashion, for Zhou's stardom, a deterritorialized discursive space, where her private life details, screen persona, and the public's imagination of her became necessarily inseparable.

It was because of the antithetically "mythical" nature of Zhou's personal story gone public that her "authentic" voice (without using a playback singer) through song, on the screen or the gramophone, carried such piercing persuasion in "telling" fictional yet universally "real" and relevant stories of the time, whether it be ordinary people's lives disguised in the decadent-sounding yellow music or idyllic folk tunes depicting simple desires of young gentlemen and maidens. Addressing the musician's responsibility to "be a photograph . . . recording the struggles and aspirations of the proletariat" and to "cry out on behalf of the masses," Nie Er, a patriotic leftist composer and author of the PRC's national anthem, recorded in his journal entry, responding to Guo Rou-mo's essay "The Echo of the Photograph," which describes music's ideology-shaping power among the masses, "The sound emitted from the phonograph comes from the objective world. . . . I can only react in this manner because of its objectivity" (Jones 1992, 107–109). Andrew Jones sees Nie's musico-political praxis through the means of music to be a possible solution for leftist intellectuals to effectively represent the subaltern's life. Jones analyzes that music as a neutral recording medium (the objectivity referred to by Nie) that removes the inevitable subjectivity that taints the depiction of the power relations between the elite and the subaltern ("the lettered and the illiterate, the voiced and the voiceless, the narrating subject and the narrative object"; 109). As mass music, on gramophone records, wireless broadcast, or sound film, then was set in standard Mandarin, it could erase not only bourgeois identity but also class and regional differences (112), a paradoxical effect of the New Life Movement that sought to impose a universal sound by eliminating all other regional dialects in the public sphere and by banning popular music in favor of patriotic song. As Zhou rose from a low-caste song apprenticeship with the Ming Yue Song and Dance Troupe into the limelight, her songs emit such "authentic" sounds from below (particularly folk tunes) with an unassuming aura of a star, a subject position that cannot be emulated by elitist artists or musicians, that it "inspired and comforted its listeners in hard times"; her songs also covered all musical styles and genres of her time in urban Shanghai (Hong 2008, 22), a crossroad where the East met the West and a locale where the lowly songstress, like a photograph, stood as witness and troubadour in recording history through a vernacularized technological medium.

Song Sequences and Star Identity

Despite the dialectic effects of music and film industries against a highly speculative personal background in shaping Zhou's stardom, her song sequences on-screen served as a textualized means to contextualize and condition the material and content of the media. As a result, they oriented the audience as the viewing subject, through the mechanical reproduction of the sound and image, in participating in the discursive space in the star-making process. The song montage as a formal mechanism in film was also "a site of film's utopian impulses . . . [that] represent the most idealized aspects of the star's presence," a site where romanticized, dreamlike, and often nondiegetic narrative inserts take place. This utopianism comes from the construction of the sequence and the emotional appeal of the music, not so much from the songs' content (Majumdar 2011, 175). The audience was well aware that there was no separation of the vocal identity of star and character, on- or offscreen. Only occasionally in Zhou's early career were her song sequences sung by playback singers. After the films ran in theaters, the screen songs were mass-produced into gramophone formats, sung on promotional tours and in theater shows performed by the star herself, thus transmitting this utopianism further outside the film's diegetic space into multiple extrafilmic locales, where she and the public engaged in postcinema encounters. Through this type of systematic, orchestrated effort between the film companies (that regularly contracted well-known stars of song troupes/groups), record companies, performing groups, and the actress herself, who also wrote short pieces in newspaper columns, Zhou's stardom was constructed via a multiplatform/media model, which in turn sustained the audience's willing continuation of belief in the authenticity of song, voice, and songstress during the song montage. Hong contends that it was not Zhou's voice quality or vocal skills that put her ahead of other contemporary dual-career stars (such as Bai Guang [白光], Bai Hong [白虹], Wang Renmei [王人美], Yao Li [姚莉], and Gong Qiuxia [龔秋霞], who in fact had better singing techniques than Zhou). It was Zhou's legendary life and love stories that allowed her tragic roles in film to blend with real-life narratives through other media's convergent workings in creating her stardom (Hong 2008, 4).

By blurring the boundaries between the on- and offscreen spaces in identifying the body and voice of the star, Zhou fostered the continuity of her songstress/star coidentity. When examining the songstress in 1950s and 1960s Mandarin films from Hong Kong, Jean Ma has written on similar issues concerning the separation of the body and voice of the performer as a reflexive reading about the playback process and recording technology used in the film industry. Ma further expounds on the "virtual identity between the live and the technologically mediated voice" through a methodology that dissociates close analysis from the historian's investigation of the empirical conditions surrounding cinema (2013, 2). Similarly, while close analysis is useful in this regard, in Zhou's case, the historian's thick descriptions of the film and recording industries' connection through stars like Zhou could only further illustrate the workings of singing film stars. Although separated temporally and temporarily by the recording and playback processes during filming, the combined identity of the very same film star and singer's body and voice in fact enhanced the affect impressed on the audience through these song sequences and, as a result, generated a desire for the audience to repeatedly listen to these songs, which momentarily displaced their reality through the sequences' utopianism and thus boosted the sales of the LPs (黑膠).

After all, the songs audiences heard in the films were sung by the actresses themselves, prerecorded or remastered outside the diegetic space. But the song sequences served as a nostalgic medium for the diegetic details recollected during moments of listening on the LP or on the radio. Zhou's visible body in the song sequences as both diegetic character in the mise-en-scène and nondiegetic popular singer acted as a necessary connection to bridge the technological separation of the filmed and projected image and the singer/star who often performed live on the radio and in theaters. The authenticity, in Ma's terms, of the voice was never doubted by the (diegetic) audience characters within the film or by the spectators/audience watching the film, as it was usually noted on the film posters featuring Zhou as both the lead actress and singer (主演/主唱).[6] Unlike musicals that use a different singer to dub over the voice of the actress during song sequences, the "dubbing process" for Zhou was, on the contrary, an authenticating one.

The first song sequence in *Street Angel* illustrates how songs were written for films not only as part of the narrative but also to promote the sale of the recording and the stardom of the songstress. It is Zhou's first lead role in a feature, in which she plays an orphan who was sold to a teahouse as a sing-song girl, while her sister is sold into the prostitution business—two clearly separate role types and professions. In this song sequence, Zhou's character, Xiao Hong (which happens to be the same as Zhou's real name, a "coincidence" that is speculated on by some observers; Hong 2008, 45), is asked to sing a song called "Four Seasons Song" (四季歌) to entertain the customers. Xiao Hong reluctantly sings along, and the camera cuts between a medium close-up of her singing with a pouting mouth while playing with her braids (a charismatic character trait), the customers' reactions to her singing, also in medium close-ups, and nondiegetic scenes depicting the content of the song. Ostensibly, she is also the heroine of the nondiegetic inserts with the following lyrics:

> Spring comes, and the window fills with green.
> A maiden sits by the window, embroidering a pair of mandarin ducks.
> Suddenly, a heartless blow
> Splits the ducks apart.
>
> Summer comes, and the willow fronds grow long.
> The maiden has been wandering to the Yangzi River.
> The scenery is lovely north and south of the river.
> But how can it compare with the green gauzy sorghum at home?
>
> Autumn comes, and the lotus flowers are fragrant.
> The maiden dreams of home night after night.
> When she awakes, she does not see the faces of her parents,
> Just the moonlight shining at the foot of the bed.
>
> Winter comes, and snow flurries down.
> When winter clothes are ready, I will send them to my love.
> The Great Wall built with flesh and blood is long.
> I would be the ancient Meng Jiang Nü.

Historical references to war and its cruelty ("heartless blow," "Great Wall built with flesh and blood") are sung between a medium- and high-pitch range frequently with a nasal timbre and with the last two syllables lengthened at the end of each line. This is a typical folk-singing technique that draws the audience to the double biographical reference of the character and of the actress as an orphan. Zhou's performance in this film made her an instant media sensation, and it is this film that she liked best and mentioned most frequently in public (Zhao 1995, 163). This film also began her typecasting as an ill-fated heroine, suffering from social injustice and easily winning sympathy from the audience. The combination of her role type with song sequences as social commentary also con-

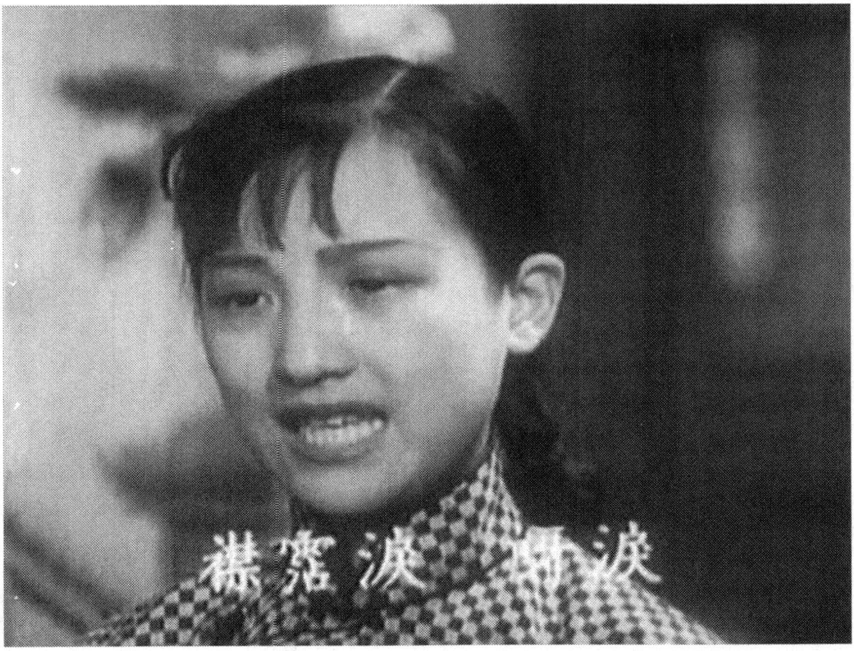

Figure 3.1. Xiao Hong sings "The Wandering Songstress" in the film *Street Angel* (1937).

nected the film industry back to the May Fourth–inspired discourse of nationalism and leftist aesthetics.

Another well-known song in the same film, "Wandering Songstress" (天涯歌女), even inspired the making of a film in 1940 with the same title, also featuring Zhou in the lead role. This song appears in *Street Angel* twice (figure 3.1). It first appears early in the film almost as a duet by the heroine and the young man she is in love with, who accompanies her singing on his *er-hu* instrument. It is a romantic scene without any nondiegetic dramatization, in typical shot/reverse-shot montage, interweaving the sad look of the heroine's sister as she hears the idealistic lyrics that are antithetical to her own circumstance. The staging and movement of Zhou's character coincide with the lyrics, as she does the sewing, sings, and looks affectionately at her love across from her window. This song is sung again by Zhou later in the film at the rude request of her love, now a disrespectful drunkard drinking in the tea house. When she refuses, the owner of the tea house orders her to entertain the guests. During her singing, at a much slower tempo and in a noticeably sadder tone and lower pitch, nonsimultaneous diegetic inserts of the scene from the earlier duet appear as his memories and are edited in with dissolves in a nostalgic mood.

"Wandering Songstress," 天涯歌女 (*tian ya ge nü*, literally "sing-song girl at the ends of the earth")
(Prelude): My love, we are of one heart . . .
I seek, oh, seek at the ends of the earth and the edge of the sea,
One who understands my song.
Young maiden sings songs,
My love accompanies.
My love, you and I are of one heart.
Ai . . . ya, aiya . . . my love, we are of one heart.
Looking northward, towards home mountains,
Tears, oh, tears wet my blouse.
Young maiden misses her love till this day.
My love, our friendship in hard times runs deep.
Ai . . . ya, aiya . . . my love, our friendship in hard times runs deep.
Oh, in this life, who does not treasure youth.
Young maiden is like the thread, and my love is like the needle,
My love, we two are threaded together and will never part.
Ai . . . ya, ai ya, . . . my love, threaded together and will never part.

Interweaving two diegetic sequences of the same song at two story points, performed by the same characters in the narrative, emphasizes the authenticity of the source of the voice. The convergence of the performer's body and her voice, which is projected at recurring diegetic temporal points, further solidifies Zhou's performance as the true voice mediated through filming and song recording for entertainment and social commentary.

The intertextual transformation and translocation of the screen song to another film's title continued to help build Zhou's stardom as a performer whose transmedia performance became an essential link in the "productive symbiotic relationship" between the two cultural industries of China and spectatorship in the first half of the twentieth century (Jones 2001, 96). The "wandering songstress" represented Zhou's personal identity, searching for true love and happiness. From then on, "wandering songstress" also became her professional nickname, which was frequently used in advertising and public relations materials. Of the twelve films in which Zhou had the lead role during the peak of her career, at least five involved a lead role as songstress.[7] This reflexive pattern in her film career path blended reality and fiction, gossip and truth, in the construction of her public image.

Songstress as New Woman

In the same year of the release of the film *The Wandering Songstress* in 1941 came Zhou's public announcement that she would "take after Ibsen's Nora" when she divorced Yan Hua, a move that was both brave and significant as the relationship was not only a personal one but also a professional union (Zhao 1995, 10; Hong 2008, 51). This public display of Ibsenism at this historical juncture of her career was understood not only as a "new definition of realism in the theatre" but also as a true manifestation of the new individual self (Tam 2007, 348). One theatrical example was the play *The Night the Tiger Was Caught* (1921) by the May Fourth–inspired writer Tian Han, who also wrote the lyrics of the two songs mentioned in this chapter. This May Fourth connection is significant in that Zhou, through her role as a film star and popular songstress, transformed female performers' agency from one previously associated with prostitution to one sympathetic and even sanctioned in the public sphere in the post–May Fourth era. Tam Kwok-kan explains, "This [public] speech is the technique of discussion borrowed from Ibsen. However, in the context of modern Chinese culture, they also serve as a public declaration of the new self. The strategy of declaration can be seen, first, in its opposition to authority and, second, in its recognition of autonomy of the self. This new self is characterized by an iconoclastic determination for free will" (2007, 348). Zhou's declaration of divorce not only freed herself from her unhappy marriage but also allowed her to claim, to a certain degree, subjectivity in owning her voice in a real sense, as Yan Hua authored several songs that helped promote her stardom and became an essential part of her known repertoire.

As the Baudrillardian notion of the creation and consumption of popular media (of song, in this case) illustrates "an active mode of relations (not only to objects, but to the collectivity and to the world), a systematic mode of activity and a global response on which our whole cultural system is founded" (quoted in Chow 2007, 112), the relations that Zhou and her audience formed through her cross-media performance placed the dialectics of Zhou's stardom and her fans in a modernized context through the cinematic, recording, and broadcasting machines. Despite being structured either as diegetic musical numbers or nondiegetic montage, song sequences in films made during this era allowed the audience to participate in coproducing the sound offstage, as song lyrics commonly appeared as subtitles, as if on a karaoke screen (at times with a dot bouncing on each word sung), inviting the audience to sing along. Singing here (song and film performance), influenced by the Hollywood musical genre and popularized by Shanghai's burgeoning nightclub and radio scene—both urban bourgeois signs—created singing actresses like Zhou and Bai Guang and film songs that catered to both audiences in and outside the movie theater: the general urban audiences who consumed her songs through mass media like the radio and the better-off audiences who also frequented theaters and nightclubs. The Baudrillardian notion of consumption thus allows for a nuanced look at the synergy in a unified identity in sound and source in both media (film and music) connected in Zhou's dual-career performance, through which intertextual crossings (from song to film, from film to film, and from film to private life) fashioned a clear personalized songstress aura to permeate the space coinhabited by the songwriter, the filmmaker, the audience, and the songstress herself. Zhou's death at age thirty-seven and her life pathos as the fallen but courageous sing-song girl is ultimately appropriated by the discourse of nationalism, in which the image of the wandering songstress became a fixated modern cultural icon that serves only to solidify the dignity of the role type on-screen and the profession offscreen.

Notes

1. Two well-known writings in English by Hu Shih advocating the rights of Chinese women are "A Chinese Declaration of the Rights of Women" (1924) and "A Chinese Gulliver on Women's Rights" (1934).

2. For a full list of Zhou's biographies, consult Cheng 2004, 188–189. Hong's book also lists works in key print media as well as by Zhou's surviving family members that have helped shape her public image and (re)invent her life story (2008, 7–8).

3. Hong counts 242 songs sung by Zhou and forty-four films featuring her (2008, 2, 285–309, 269–284).

4. See Hong 2008, chaps. 3 and 4, for a full analysis of Zhou's singing techniques and musical qualities of her voice (83–216). In particular, Hong meticulously divides Zhou's vocal qualities during her career into five distinct phases (207–216), each of which sees different syntheses of the traditional and Western bel canto vocal methods.

5. The famous folk legend has it that Meng Jiang Nü, a virtuous and chaste woman whose husband had died as a laborer among many others and had been buried at the foot of the Great Wall, crumbled parts of the wall with her tears.

6. Consult the film poster collection at the Shanghai Film Museum or the thirty-six private digital images at Fotoe 图片库, http://fotoe.net/searchid/785766.

7. See Hong's chart of all twelve films made between 1943 and 1949 with role types and character traits (2008, 74–75). All twelve films' lead roles have one thing or more in common with Zhou's life details.

References

Attali, Jacques. 1985. *Noise: The Political Economy of Music*. Minneapolis: University of Minnesota Press.

Bary, W. Theodore de, Wing-tsit Chan, and Burton Watson. 1960. *Sources of Chinese Tradition*. New York: Columbia University Press.

Chang, Michael. 1999. "The Good, the Bad, and the Beautiful: Movie Actresses and Public Discourse in Shanghai, 1920s–1930s." In *Cinema and Urban Culture in Shanghai, 1922–1943*, edited by Yingjin Zhang, 128–159. Stanford, CA: Stanford University Press.

Cheng, Jim (程健). 2004. *An Annotated Bibliography of Chinese Film Studies* (中国电影研究书目提要). Hong Kong: Hong Kong University Press.
Chow, Rey. 2007. *Sentimental Fabulations, Contemporary Chinese Films.* New York: Columbia University Press.
Cody, Gabrielle H., and Evert Sprinchorn. 2007. *The Columbia Encyclopedia of Modern Drama.* Vol. 1. New York: Columbia University Press.
Dirlik, Arif. 1975. "The Ideological Foundations of the New Life Movement: A Study in Counterrevolution." *Journal of Asian Studies* 34 (4): 945–980.
Dyer, Richard. 1979. *Stars.* London: BFI.
———. 1991. "Charisma." In *Stardom: Industry of Desires,* edited by Christine Gledhill, 57–59. London: Routledge.
Fiske, John. 1992. "The Cultural Economy of Fandom." In *The Adoring Audience: Fan Culture and Popular Media,* edited by Lisa Lewis, 30–49. London: Routledge.
Fotoe (图片库). n.d. Guangzhou Integrated Image Company, Ltd. (广州集成图像有限公司). Accessed 17 February 2014, http://fotoe.net/searchid/785766.
"Golden Voice Zhou Xuan (金嗓子周璇)." 2011. *Files* (档案). BTV, 21 February.
Hansen, Miriam. 1991. *Babel and Babylon: Spectatorship in American Silent Film.* Cambridge, MA: Harvard University Press.
Hong, Fangyi (洪芳怡). 2008. *Wandering Songstress: Zhou Xuan and Her Song* (天涯歌女: 周璇與她的歌). Taipei: Show-we.
Hu, Shih (胡適). 1924. "A Chinese Declaration of the Rights of Women." *Chinese Social and Political Science Review* 8 (2): 105–107.
———. (1934) 1995. "A Chinese 'Gulliver' on Women's Rights." *People's Tribune: An Organ of National-Revolutionary Thought and Opinion* 7 (3): 121–127. In *A Collection of Hu Shih's English Writings* (胡適英文文存), ed. Chih-P'ing Chou (周質平). 3 vols. Taipei: Yuanliu.
———. 2001. *Hu Shih's Unpublished English Manuscripts* (胡適未刊英文遺稿). Taipei: Linking (聯經出版社).
Jones, Andrew F. 1992. *Like a Knife: Ideology and Genre in Contemporary Chinese Popular Music.* Ithaca, NY: Cornell University East Asia Program.
———. 2001. *Yellow Music: Media Culture and Colonial Modernity in the Chinese Jazz Age.* Durham, NC: Duke University Press.
Lee, Leo Ou-fan. 1999. *Shanghai Modern: The Flowering of a New Urban Culture in China 1930–45.* Cambridge, MA: Harvard University Press.
Leyda, Jay. 1972. *Dianying—Electric Shadows: An Account of Films and the Film Audience in China.* Cambridge, MA: MIT Press.
Li, Laura Tyson. 2006. *Madame Chiang Kai-shek, China's Eternal First Lady.* New York: Grove.
Liu, Yiqing. 1933. "From the Modern to the Young Women of the Present Era." *Linglong* (玲瓏) 3 (44): 2439–2442.
Ma, Jean. 2013. "Close Reading: The Mise-en-scène of Song Performance." *Cine-Files* 4:1–7.
Majumdar, Neepa. 2011. *Wanted Cultured Ladies Only: Female Stardom and Cinema in India, 1930s–1950s.* Urbana: University of Illinois Press.
McClary, Susan. 1985. Afterword to *Noise: The Political Economy of Music,* by Jacques Attali, 149–158. Minneapolis: University of Minnesota Press.

"Meng Jiang Nü" (孟姜女). 1939. *Shen bao* (申報), 18 February, 22.
Street Angel. 1937. Directed by Yuan Muzhi. DVD. Burbank, CA: Cinema Epoch, 2007.
Tam, Kwok-kan. 2007. "Dramatic Voices of the Self: Ibsen's Ideological Intervention in the Chinese Quest for a Modern Female Identity." In *The Living Ibsen,* edited by Frode Helland et al., 347–351. Oslo: Centre for Ibsen Studies, University of Oslo.
Zhao, Shihui (赵世荟). 1995. *Zhou Xuan's Self-Portrait* (周璇自述). Shanghai: San Lian Books.
Zhou, Wei (周伟), and Jing Chang (常晶). 2007. *Biography of Zhou Xuan* (周璇传). Zhong Guo Shi Dai Jing Ji Publishing Company (中国时代经济出版社). Accessed 5 February 2014, http://lz.book.sohu.com/chapter-7657-110785439.html.
"Zhou Xuan Named Miss PhD" (周璇當選博士小姐). 1935. *Shen Bao* (申報), 25 June, 21.

CHAPTER 4

Malay Women Singers of Colonial Malaya

VOICING ALTERNATIVE GENDER IDENTITY AND MODERNITY

Tan Sooi Beng

BRITISH colonialism brought tremendous sociopolitical and cultural transformations to Malaya in the first half of the twentieth century. Port cities and towns with multiethnic populations developed as people from Europe, China, India, and the Malay archipelago sojourned to trade and to work in the tin mines, the rubber estates, and the construction of roads and railways. Commercial theater from Europe, India, and China, which toured Malaya, provided entertainment for the diverse urban population. In this environment, local commoditized and modern forms of hybrid theater, dance, and music and new spaces of entertainment emerged. New technology such as film, gramophone, radio, and print promoted modern lifestyles and entertainment and the exchange of modern ideas of social reform. With the flow of capital, people, cultures, merchandise, and ideas, a type of vernacular modernity emerged in the colonial port cities, one that was different from the modernity that was being promoted by the British through education and propaganda during the colonial period. The British type of modernity was associated with the Enlightenment, a philosophic movement of eighteenth-century Europe that emphasized rationalism and empiricism over traditional sociopolitical and religious ideas (Tan 1993, 2013). Nevertheless, this chapter illustrates that the vernacular modernity that arose was not a total break with the conditions of the past but developed from the experiences of living in a rapidly changing world where social practices, orders, cultures, and ideas from different regions were constantly assessed, adapted, and transformed (Giddens 1990, 4–6). Vernacular modernity was historically and culturally located and constantly being constructed within the context of colonial Malaya.

It has been pointed out that the project of modernity in non-European countries cannot be studied effectively without considering the hegemonic gender dichotomies intrinsic to the Eurocentric kind of modernity advocated by the

British colonialists. The negative implication of the term "female" in this type of modernity is mainly a consequence of the use of the gender dichotomy male/female in association with other dichotomous categories such as modern/traditional, West/East, rational/emotional, and urban/rural (Stivens 1998; Hayami, Tanabe, and Tokita-Tanabe 2003).

These dichotomies are necessarily patriarchal[1] in nature, as the categories of public/domestic and material/spiritual are superimposed over male/female and modern/traditional (Chatterjee 1993, chap. 6). In colonial Malaya, Malay Muslim women were expected to represent the spiritual and domestic spheres in the village and to maintain aspects of tradition, religion, and morality. In contrast, it was acceptable for Muslim men to play modern and public roles and to earn a living outside the community and in the cities.

This chapter argues that a small group of Muslim women singers in colonial Malaya were able to blur the borders of the dichotomies in this patriarchal modernity through their careers and lifestyles, musical voices, and song texts. Rapid socioeconomic transformations, the development of commoditized entertainment, and emergence of new technology in the colonial cities in the first half of the twentieth century provided the opportunities and sites for them to do so. The women performed in popular urban Malay theater and film; their songs were recorded by gramophone companies such as His Masters Voice, Columbia, and Pathé; and some of them later became film celebrities.

The Malay women singers produced an alternative type of modern identity that embraced hybridity, change, continuity with the past, and colonial difference. Partha Chatterjee (1993) has emphasized that the modernity of non-Europeans is inevitably hybrid as they not only feel the desire to modernize by learning from or mimicking the West but also wish to maintain their local individual identities that distinguish them from the modern West. It is therefore not surprising that heterogeneity and hybridity were integral to the identities and songs of the Malay women entertainers of colonial Malaya. They staged forms of difference through their lives and their music, which intervened in the reproduction of homogeneity (Mitchell 2000).

These Muslim women performers exercised individual cultural agency by creating codes of conduct that were modern yet retaining the traditions, values, and religious morality of Malay Muslim society. These alternative codes of behavior enabled them to move into the public sphere and interact with new kinds of people and contexts in the polyglot urban areas. Musically, they constructed their own hybrid styles of singing by combining the Anglo-American with traditional Malay and other foreign elements and languages of the urban spaces. They were constantly adapting to the global popular music trends and new sound technology of the times. The women singers practiced reflexivity and devised strategies that permitted them to shift the patriarchal notions of womanhood. In the late colonial period, they even ventured into the male domain of public discourse by singing songs about social reform.

The life histories, musical recordings, photographs, recording catalogues, and song texts of some of the women recording artists who were actresses in popular *bangsawan* theater (or Malay opera) and film are useful sources to study the emergence of the women singers' modern identities and gender representations in the first half of the twentieth century. This is because women's histories and voices were seldom scripted, and women played marginal roles in the British colonial state. The data gathered shows that the selected Malay Muslim women singers were able to practice self agency and create a niche for themselves as star performers within the constraints of patriarchal modernity in colonial Malaya. They were not completely liberated, but by shaking up firmly established cultural and religious traditions and dichotomies in the modern, they contested the idea that women were sufferers and docile personalities in patriarchal society.

Alternative Way of Life: Careers as Stars

In Malay village society of the first half of the twentieth century, a young Muslim woman's movements outside the home was restricted. She was occupied with domestic work and helping in the rice fields (Manderson 1980). The daily activities of ordinary village women of the colonial period were associated with the home and village community. On the other hand, men were expected to go out of the home to earn an income and to participate in the public domain.

The development of new forms of commercial urban entertainment such as the *bangsawan* theater, social *ronggeng* dance,[2] gramophone records in the pre–World War II days, and later Malay film in the postwar period contributed to the emergence of a different type of Muslim woman who became a singer, recording artist, film star, and entertainer. These women singers subverted the dichotomies in patriarchal Malay society by moving out of the home and community into the modern public sphere and the urban areas. They went against the norm as they adopted specialized professions or careers, which involved singing, acting, and dancing in and for the public, as well as recording at studios in the city; they had full-time jobs and earned an income from their performances. Both men and women watched their performances in the urban public-entertainment spaces. Gramophone recordings of these singers could be heard in the privacy of the home as well as in the public spaces such as the amusement parks.

The women performers created alternative lifestyles and means of self-expression. They acquired some of the qualities associated with men as they started training and learning to be performers at a young age; they were adaptable and entrepreneurial and changed careers when the situation required. They often grew up on the *bangsawan* stage, became apprentices, and later became stage artists in the opera groups where their parents or adopted parents performed. Well-known recording artists such as Wan Tijah binti Daud and Asiah binti Aman are cases in point. Tijah was one of the early *bangsawan* artists who made recordings with His Masters Voice (HMV) and Chap Kuching (Cat Label), the local sister company of HMV. Born in Pontianak around 1900, she started performing in the *bangsawan* theater at the age of twelve and in the 1920s traveled with the troupe to Singapore, where she joined the Nahar Opera and Star Opera. There, she married Dean, a prominent *bangsawan* hero, and later cofounded the Dean and Tijah Opera, one of the most popular opera troupes in the 1930s and 1940s, which performed all over the Malay Archipelago.

Likewise, Asiah was one of the star singers for the gramophone label Chap Ayam (Cock label, the local name for Pathé), and later for Columbia and HMV. She too began singing in the Malay opera when she was just twelve years old. Born in Singapore in 1931, she was raised in the *bangsawan* troupe. Her mother was the star actress of the Dean and Tijah Opera, while her father played the saxophone and painted the sets and backdrops of the troupe (Asiah oral interview, 2004).

During the colonial days, learning and training can be seen as acts of gaining autonomy for Malay Muslim women. Like most *bangsawan* performers of the early twentieth century, Tijah had no formal education but learned by rote and apprenticeship in the Malay opera. Training for young apprentices then was demanding and rigorous. The apprentice had to acquire skills in acting and dancing in stories adapted from different parts of the world and in singing Malay, Hindustani, Chinese, Arabic, and English songs. Tijah could not go to the formal school as she was constantly traveling from town to town performing in the *bangsawan* troupes (*Straits Echo,* 24 May 1934; Tan 1993). By comparison, Asiah came from a later period and represented one of the few women performers who had the opportunity to study in the primary and secondary Malay schools. Her parents were contracted to perform at the New World Park and stayed permanently in Singapore. Asiah was privileged to learn how to play the piano, music theory, and vocal techniques from Zubir Said, the HMV studio music director in Singapore. She also studied the English language privately by taking night classes on her own (Asiah oral interview, 2004).

Print publications and recording labels created women stage performers as stars, recording artists, and leading media personalities with titles such as Miss or Che next to their names. Tijah was known as Che Tijah in the gramophone catalogues and the press. When she became a star, the title Nona (meaning "Miss") was given to Asiah by her mentor, Zubir Said. Special names were attached to those who were famous. Miss Julia, known for her hit song "Swing dondang sayang," was called the Sophie Tucker of Malaya in the 1950s for her strong voice and strong physical attributes. Saloma, the third wife of the celebrated Malay film star and director P. Ramlee, who achieved stardom singing in the nightclubs and films of the 1950s, was dubbed Marilyn Monroe of Malaya for her beauty and figure. These Malay women singers became public celebrities as their records were bought by the urban elites and were played for all and sundry at the amusement parks.

Adaptability and Entrepreneurship

The Malay Muslim singers were also more versatile and entrepreneurial compared to the Malay village women of the times. To uphold star status, they had to compete with other singers and find ways to be different from each other. Individual women specialized in specific types of musical styles and competed with other vocalists including male singers for fame and financial rewards. Zainab Majid, for instance, was known for her Malay songs, which were sung with the Hindustani beat and flavor. As an artist, she competed with the male singer R. Azmi, who also concentrated on the same genre. Her famous songs included "Kau dihatiku" (You are in my heart) and "Kechantikan" (Beauty).

Women singers were able to maintain control over their lives and income as they were adept in changing with the times. During the Japanese occupation, when Asiah was just fourteen years old, she learned Japanese songs from a Japanese teacher and performed them at the various Japanese army camps in Singapore. She sang these songs at the entertainment shows staged by her family members, who also presented Japanese stories and Malay songs. In return for their services, her family was given rice, bread, and other food and a place to stay by the Japanese.

With the decline of *bangsawan* during the postwar era, some prominent *bangsawan* artists changed careers and ventured into the film industry, which paid higher salaries and provided more security.[3] Normadiah, a famous actress of the Grand Nooran Opera, was an example. She left the Malay opera stage to become a prima donna in Malay films such as *Semerah padi* (1956) and *Panggilan pulau* (1954). She is most remembered for her role as the female Tarzan in the film *Belantara* (1957), in which she fought with a live python and rode on an elephant.

Other *bangsawan* performers like Asiah became film playback singers and band singers and took part in radio programs. After World War II, Asiah became a "freelance" singer. She worked as a playback singer for Malay Film Production (MFP) and later Cathay Keris films. She was the female singer of the band Tiga Serumpun Orkes (comprising famous musicians such as Ahmad Jarr,

Ahmad Wan Yet, Syed Alwi, and her husband, Ismail Kassim). She also sang with the band Kenchanawati (with A. Rahman as conductor), which presented shows for Radio Malaya, the main broadcasting station in Singapore. Asiah acted in only a few films such as *Pelangi* (1951) by the Nusantara Film Company. She recorded many hit songs such as "Miow-miow," "Wak ketok," "Selamat tidor" (Good night), and "Sapu tangan" (Handkerchief) and was famous for her rendition of "Chium lagi" (Kiss me again), a Malay rendition of the Latin hit "Besame mucho." She stressed that she was very "busy" then, as she made recordings for gramophone and film companies and jingles for the radio. She recalled that her life was so hectic that she almost gave birth to her second child at the HMV recording studio. Luckily, the hospital was near the studio and, the ambulance managed to get her to the hospital just in time for delivery (Asiah oral interview, 2004).[4]

Due to Asiah's knowledge of European music, she was called on to teach children how to sing using the solfege system (do, re, mi) in programs aired by Radio Malaya in Singapore in the 1950s. Asiah also sang the practical exercises for lessons on the basic elements of music, such as pitch, scales, note values, rhythm, tempo, and singing using solfege; the exercises were recorded by Columbia in the 1950s over sixteen sides of 78 RPM records titled *Sistem solmisasi* (GEM 1005–1022, late 1950s). Zubir Said, the author of the textbook *Pelajaran menyanyi: Dengan sistem solmisasi* (Singing lessons: With the solfege system) gave the explanations in the records.

Women songsters were naturally multitalented and business minded. Besides singing, Asiah started a fashion business catering to other women artists in the 1950s. She created the design for the *baju seniati,* a type of modern tight-fitting Malay *baju kebaya* (tailored blouse over the *sarong,* a piece of cloth wrapped around the waist), which was worn by other women celebrities such as Siput Sarawak, Latifah Omar, and Kartina Dahari. Maria Menado, the Malayan beauty renowned for her recordings of film songs such as "Arjunaku" (My Arjuna) and "Doaku" (My prayer), became the first woman film producer in Malaya to start her own film company, called Maria Menado Productions. Her company produced films such as *Korban fitnah* (Azlan 2013). She was also famous for her role as a vampire in *Pontianak,* the first local horror movie made in 1957 (*Star,* 31 August 2014).

Mobility and Inclusiveness

As performers, recording artists, and actresses, the women singers of the colonial period mixed with and were inclusive of other ethnic groups. Women recording artists such as Tijah and Asiah lived and traveled with the multiethnic members of the Malay opera troupes they were attached to. The examples that follow further illustrate that the women entertainers were of different ethnic origins; they came from and performed in different parts of Malaya, Singapore, Sumatra, Java, and Borneo. Some even voyaged to China and India with the troupes they were attached to.

Momo Latiff, one of the prominent recording artists and entertainers of the pre– and post–World War II days, was born in Batavia in 1923. Momo was invited to join the Dardanella Dramatic Company from Java as a dancer when she was young and performed dances such as "Bali dance Rhapsody" and "Papua." She toured Hong Kong, Shanghai, Canton, Bombay, and Calcutta with the troupe before arriving in Singapore in 1935. After singing in the extra turns for a while, she was offered a contract with Shaw Brothers to act and sing in films such as *Hang Tuah* (1956) and *Semerah padi* (1956).

Laila Sani, another popular singer and *bangsawan* actress of Singapore, was born in 1927 in Ceylon (now Sri Lanka). She performed in Asian cities such as Istanbul, Tehran, and Baghdad with her parents, who were members of the Kansas Circus. Her mother, Philomena Lauchengo, was a tightrope artist, while her father was known as the "strong man" in the circus. They stayed in Java when her mother started the *bangsawan* troupe Laila Sinaran Bulan Opera, before moving to Singapore in the late 1930s (Azlan 2013).

Mixed marriages often took place. Some non-Malay women singers married Malay men and converted to Islam. Maria Menado, born in Sulawesi in 1932 as Liesbet Dotulong, embraced Islam when she married the script writer A. Razak Sheikh Rahman at the age of nineteen. Another Malay woman performer, Miss Julia Abu Bakar, married the European violinist and conductor David Lincoln, who promoted her as a recording artist. Miss Julia toured Malaya and Java performing in road shows with her husband's Lincoln Orchestra.

The women artists that I have described subverted the dichotomies of men as wage earners and women as homemakers, which correlated with modernist discourses that divided the public and domestic spheres for men and women, respectively. For the women singers, childbirth and domestic work were not their only obligations. They still cooked and took care of the children during the day, but they had careers, underwent training, competed with others to become stars, and even started their own businesses. They were also more independent in that they were able to support themselves and their children financially should the men in their lives abandon them. As they traveled widely in the Asian region performing, learning, acting, singing, marrying, and mixing with diverse peoples, the women stars gained familiarity with people of other races and became more inclusive. Through their interactions, they mediated the binaries of local/global and village/urban. As I discuss in the next section, the women singers were more open to outside influences in the development of their modern identities and songs.

Shaping Individual Identities through Hybridity and Change: New Codes of Conduct

The women entertainers' movements into the public domain created anxiety among the male conservative and religious sections of Malay society. As male/female spheres were explicitly marked, women singers who were mobile were often stigmatized. Working at night in the city also implicated the loss of traditional customs and religious morality for the women. The singers were criticized as women with low morals who performed onstage to be gawked at by men and who sang and danced for the public at night (Tan 1993).

The women performers were further stigmatized because they were caught in a patriarchal and consumer-oriented definition of success and femininity. In order to attract male consumers, female stars were often packaged to be desired by men. Gramophone-company print catalogues published the photographs of women singers who were attractively dressed and who looked feminine with well-made-up faces. Record catalogues printed notes that sought to attract male fans with phrases such as "Brothers do not fret, do not miss hearing the voice of Nancy, buy her records at HMV shops" (HMV catalogue, November 1934).

Nevertheless, in spite of such stigma, women singers acquired a kind of self-reflexive agency. They were resourceful and knew how to negotiate and manage the situation to their advantage. As they moved into the public domain, they continued to embrace gender differences and emphasized that they were also mothers, wives, and devout Muslims who acted in morally appropriate ways. They emulated the modern West by adopting singing careers but did not reject their own traditional roles in society. The women *bangsawan* performers declared that they cooked, washed clothes, and took care of the children during the day but were free to work at night.

More significantly, the women artists continued to engage with conventions of Malay Muslim female propriety and cultural decorum in performance. Unlike the non-Malay women who were held by men as they performed the waltz, tango, and foxtrot in the cabaret, *bangsawan* women of the colonial era danced with men onstage without touching them. This was the custom in Malay folk social dance such as the *ronggeng* or *joget,* which was considered culturally appropriate.[5] Moreover, instead of the shorter European dresses that were worn by non-Malay cabaret girls of the period, the Malay women singers were always featured onstage and in the advertisements of record catalogues and newspapers with their bodies fully covered, which implied local female respectability and tradition (see figure 4.1). If they had to put on knee-length skirts for vaudeville dances during the extra turns, they made sure they wore stockings to conceal their legs and gloves to conceal their hands.

Figure 4.1. Che Tijah in European costume, which covered her body, for *bangsawan* theater. *Berita Film* 2 (December 1960), Oriental and India Office, British Library, London.

Furthermore, the women artists were often dressed in Malay traditional costumes such as the *baju kebaya* with the *selendang* (loose shawl) covering the head and part of the body. The *kebaya* top was often made of see-through or lace material that covered the inner corset, shoulders, and hands of the women (see figure 4.2). The Malay costumes and loose shawl allowed Malay women to perform in the public sphere because they exhibited compliance with the local customs, respectability, and Islamic values. The loose shawl signified moral and cultural appropriateness.

Women film stars of the 1950s adapted to the glamour of the film world and set new fashion trends but maintained cultural decorum. Saloma's big hairdo and new styles of traditional costume such as the *baju kebarung* (a combination of the *baju kebaya* and the *baju kurung*, a loose-fitting knee-length blouse worn by Malay women) earned her much praise in the 1950s. Maria Menado, who was given the title "Malaya's Most Beautiful" by *Times* magazine as well as "Best Dressed Woman in Southeast Asia" by the publisher United Press International, often

Figure 4.2. Nona Asiah wearing a *kebaya* top made of see-through material that covered her shoulders, arms, and corset. *Arena Filem,* 29 April 1960, Malay Heritage Centre Collection; image courtesy of the Malay Heritage Centre, National Heritage Board, Singapore.

Figure 4.3. Maria Menado, film star, producer, and fashion trendsetter of the 1950s. She wears a *kebaya* top with a low neck line but covers her shoulders and arms with a loose shawl. Courtesy of National Archives of Singapore.

wore the traditional Malay *kebaya,* but the ones she wore were tight fitting and had a low neck line (*Star,* 31 August 2014). In figure 4.3, she covers her shoulders and hands with a loose shawl. Even though the women film stars went against tradition as public entertainers, they were admired by moviegoers because they embodied quiet beauty and feminine grace in their appearance, behavior, and clothes, traits that were expected of Malay women of the era. Nevertheless, the images projected by the women singers were often contradictory; they were modern professional performers and iconic beauties who entered the public sphere but wore newly designed Malay costumes and did not touch men onstage; some covered their head with the shawl but donned tight fitting *kebaya* tops.[6]

Through new codes of conduct, fashions, and lifestyles, the women performers exercised individual agency in shaping their own identities. They were modern in their own way, expressing independence from the traditional expectations of how women should live yet maintaining their customs and Islamic values and hence blurring the boundaries of the stark differences between men and women, public and domestic, and modern and traditional in patriarchal modernity. Through self-reflexivity, they were able to act in culturally appropriate ways in diverse contexts.

It should be noted that sound recording facilitated women singers' move into the public sphere in Malay Muslim society. The gramophone record provided a way for Muslim women to sing without being seen onstage; it distanced their voices from the social stigma regarding women singers performing in public. Furthermore, advertisements of the singers with the names of recording companies next to their own titles, such as "Miss Jacoba Reger, Famous HMV Recording Artist" or "Miss Amelia, Respectable Kronchong Singer of Chap Singa Fame" (*Sunday Gazette,* 31 July 1938), brought prestige to the women singers. Malay Muslim women performers were thus able to gain respectability through the gramophone recordings and advertisements.

Modern Musical Styles and Voices

Practices in the gramophone industry during the colonial period were gendered and patriarchal. The music industry was male privileged, and women were excluded from many aspects of music production. In fact, all the recording engineers, talent scouts, music composers, and bandleaders of the colonial era were men. As shown in the catalogues of the recording companies, the established music composers were Jaar, Ahmad Patek, Yusof B., and Kassim Masdor. Well-known studio composers and conductors included Osman Ahmad, Ahmad Jaafar, and Zubir Said, whose names also appeared on the recording labels alongside those of the singers.

Yet women artists helped to build the success of the gramophone industry and an audience base of multiethnic men and women through their recordings. These women were given the freedom and responsibility for developing their own singing styles, which made each one of them distinct and enabled them to attract fans of different races. The voice was also an instrument for self-expression within the male-dominated music industry. The women singers actively incorporated local, European, and other foreign singing styles in their songs and helped to modernize local folk music. They exercised self-agency and mediated between the binaries of traditional/modern and East/West.

Yet there was a constant tension between sameness and difference, local and global. Depending on the particular period different singers lived in and the training they received, they took different positions and developed their singing styles accordingly. The variations in the singing styles of Miss Tijah and Nona Asiah exemplify this tension. Coming from an earlier *bangsawan* era, Miss Tijah kept the traditional singing style as she adapted to the new musical arrangements of the dance band in the 1930s and the three-minute time allotted for each side of the record. In "Anak Tiong" (Chinese child; Chap Kuching, NG 5, 1930s), Miss Tijah was accompanied by a violin, double bass, piano, and Malay drum *(gendang),* a modernized version of the traditional folk *ronggeng* ensemble, which incorporated Western instruments.[7] The new *ronggeng* music was influenced by the Tin Pan Alley music promoted by the gramophone recordings and talkies from Hollywood.

However, Miss Tijah maintained the Malay elements in her vocal rendition of the folk song. She continued to improvise song texts herself using the Malay quatrain verse form *(pantun).* As shown in figure 4.4, she sang in the *asli* style with trills (or wide vibrato) at the long notes and in heterophony with the violin; she used the Malay nasal singing style with a fairly narrow and tense vocal width. Tijah superimposed the folk melody over the characteristic eight-beat *asli* rhythmic pattern played by the Malay drum, double bass, and bass part of the piano (figure 4.4, bars 3–4). The treble part of the piano played triads emphasizing the linear texture and independent lines of the Malay folk music.

Women singers such as Tijah also learned and adapted other foreign modes and singing styles, which they added to the Malay and Anglo-American elements in the recorded *bangsawan* and folk songs of the 1930s and early 1940s. In the example of "Anak Tiong" (Chinese child), Che Tijah used notes that are similar to those of the Javanese mode *pelog pathet nem* (for instance, see the first four notes in figure 4.4). In contrast, Che Tijah employed vocal ornamentations (such as slides between notes) that resembled those used in Indian folk and light classical singing in "Tandi tandi" (HMV, P 16489, 1930s). This song was accompanied by a harmonium, *tabla,* and piano, which showed a blend of Indian and European instruments.[8]

During the postwar period, women singers who became film stars or playback singers adopted the film-song style of the 1950s. What differentiated the film song from the recorded *bangsawan* songs of the prewar days was the increased use of Western musical characteristics such as bigger ensembles, more varied instrumental combinations, western harmony, longer instrumental interludes, and short tuneful melodies, which were considered modern. The trend

Figure 4.4. "Anak tiong" (Chinese child), Miss Tijah, Chap Kuching, NG 5, 1930s.

was also toward scored orchestration, musical arrangements, and lyrics written by the male songwriters.

The women singers of the 1950s began to use the open-throated crooning style of singing associated with Anglo-American popular music, heard on gramophone records and in talkies. Even though some singers already started crooning during the late 1930s and 1940s, this style of singing became the trend in the film songs of the 1950s. The women singers learned to use the microphone, which molded their voices and singing styles. The microphone allowed the women singers to sing with more dynamics and vocal shades, as they did not have to focus on projecting volume. Women with softer voices could also be heard among larger audiences. They shifted from the tense, higher-pitched, nasal traditional-style singing to the softer, lower-pitched crooning. This switch allowed female singers to sing modern forms of music such as jazz and Anglo-American dance music, popularized by the talkie, radio, and gramophone. Gramophone catalogues advertised the singers of the late 1940s and 1950s as having "improved and changed their style of singing" (*telah membaiki dan mengubah gaya suara*; Chap Ayam catalogue supplement, May 1947, Malay records).

"Lihatlah" (Look; sung by Asiah in the film *Bahagia di Singapura,* A. Jaafar Orchestra, Pathé, PTH 181, 1950s) exemplifies this new trend of singing and the film-song style. "Lihatlah" was categorized as a swing reminiscent of "sweet"-style jazz of the big-band era in the United States. The Western drum set and plucked bass maintained a fixed pulse, while the piano played chords with syncopated rhythms against this fixed pulse. The trumpet, saxophone, and piano took turns improvising short solos in between the verses. Texturally, this example sounded more homophonic than Tijah's prewar *bangsawan* song, described earlier. As shown in figure 4.5, Asiah sang short, catchy phrases, which were answered by the trumpet and saxophone. She harmonized with the plucked bass and piano, which produced basic chords and a greater extent of functional harmony. The women singers helped to create through their musical voices a distinct film musical style, which was nationally disseminated.

Both Tijah and Asiah used their musical voices to mediate between East and West and traditional and modern in their own ways, constantly adapting to the musical trends of the times. Tijah employed the traditional singing style and *pantun* texts, which she improvised herself to the modern arrangements of Malay folk songs in *bangsawan* theater. On the other hand, Asiah adjusted to the microphone in the recording studio and used the softer, lower-pitched crooning to sing the Malay modern popular songs created by film-studio composers and musicians. Both recordings were identified with the modern woman who was culturally in tune with tradition. Gramophone catalogues of the 1930s and 1940s described the women's voices as "voices that were sweet sounding" *(suara*

Figure 4.5. "Lihatlah" (Look), sung by Asiah in the film *Bahagia di Singapura* (Prosperity in Singapore), A. Jaafar Orchestra, Pathé, PTH 181, 1950s.

yang merdu) implying their femininity (HMV catalogue, October 1931, November 1934; Chap Ayam supplement, October 1947, Malay records).

Social Change and Progress through Song Texts

In colonial Malaya, song texts were essential in the consumption of popular music. Audiences could often recite or sing the lyrics from memory and used them to communicate with one another. Popular songs were regularly sung to accompany daily routines, as the texts echoed the transformations occurring in the colonial society, the anxieties of urban living, and the search for change. Song lyrics provided a site where performers and audiences (both male and female) could exercise a kind of individual cultural agency by embracing the meanings of the words, becoming emotionally attached to the messages conveyed and engaging in some kind of action in response.

Women performers advocated for change and progress through their recorded songs from the late 1930s till the 1950s. Record catalogues emphasized that the *pantun* song texts of the *bangsawan* songs were created by the women themselves *(karangan sendiri)*. The women entertainers engaged with ideas of reform and progress, which flowed through the wider Malay world as a consequence of Islamic reformism and Malay nationalism in the late colonial period.[9] Not only did they entertain, but they helped to educate and raise the consciousness of the Malay audiences who listened to them. In order to catch the attention of listeners and to sound modern, the songs often had catchy melodies superimposed on upbeat dance rhythms such as the waltz, foxtrot, tango, and rumba or the hybrid *kronchong* from Java, which was made popular through *bangsawan* theater. Women recording artists started to sing about society moving "forward" or "progressing" in the late 1930s and early 1940s. By way of example, Che Eulis' "Bicara gampang, berbuat susah" (Easy to discuss, difficult to do; NS 591, HMV catalogue, September 1939) emphasized that "as long as you are alive, you have to move forward" *(kalau misi ada penghidupan, musti choba maju ke depan).*[10]

However, most of the songs about progress by the women recording artists focused on the need for moral guidance and advice about how to behave. These ideas were circulated by the modernist Islamic reformists, who stressed that the "way forward" was through "individual initiative" and moral values such as *kemanusiaan* (humanness), *kemajuan* (progress), *hak perempuan* (women's rights), *kewajiban* (responsibilities), and *setia* (steadfastness) (Matheson 2000, 5).[11] Songs with these themes became the trend among women singers in the 1940s and 1950s.

A study of the supplementary catalogues for the Malay records of HMV, Columbia, and Pathé of 1947 indicates that the women sang about the moral, social, and spiritual responsibilities that were advocated by the modern Islamic reformists. These were the first recordings produced after the Second World War, and the songs were mainly reissues of the prewar recordings. The keywords *ibarat* (good example, parable), *ajaran* (teaching), and *nasihat* (advice) were used to describe the content of the songs in the three catalogues. Introduced as "a new singer who had hopes of progress" *(penyanyi baharu yang ada harapan maju),* Miss Ining called on audiences to take care of the poor, who were "tortured and suffering" *(azab dan sengsara),* in her song titled "Nasib orang miskin" (The fate of the poor; 61072, Chap Ayam, Kronchong Nasib, May 1947 catalogue). Miss Rambat pronounced that people should be "taught to do good because good deeds would be reciprocated,"[12] in "Yatim yang miskin" (Poor orphan; P. 22936, Kronchong, HMV catalogue, October 1947). Che Na'emah declared, "If poor people were looked down on for a long time, that was the custom in the world,"[13] in "Kehidupan miskin" (Poor life; 61082, Masri, Chap Ayam supplement, October 1947, Malay records).

Moreover, the women singers appealed to audiences to be responsible to Allah (God). In "Berimankan Tohan" (Piety to God; 22928, Lagu, HMV catalogue, May 1947), Che Aminah "advised young people to be loyal to their parents, teachers, and others, and not to drink [alcohol] so that they would not be tempted by the devil."[14] Miss Emma repeated the "Pillars of Islam and the ways to fulfill each one of them,"[15] in her recording of "Rukun Islam" (Pillars of Islam; GE 10091, Kronchong nasihat, Columbia catalogue, May 1947). On the other side of the record, she "reminded listeners not to forget the teachings of Islam so that they can escape the enticement of the devil" ("Zaman sekarang" [This period]).[16]

Women also sang about the demands imposed on them by local customary practices and the traditional Malay Muslim way of life, such as arranged and forced marriages. "Waktu fajar" (Dawn; P. 22936, Hawaiian waltz, Miss Rambat, HMV catalogue, October 1947) is an exemplar about "the fate of a village girl who was tortured daily as she was forced to marry a wealthy man."[17] Other women performers reminded audiences about filial piety and the "difficulties of mothers raising and educating children."[18] Che Aminah instructed listeners to take care of their mothers, in her song "Perasaan tua" (Feeling old; 22928, HMV catalogue, May 1947).

Young girls who were promoted as child stars and novelties in the *bangsawan* theater and by gramophone recording companies often sang about problems concerning children. "Miss Emmy appealed [to the audience to listen to] the sufferings of a girl whose mother had died and whose father had married a woman who was cruel" ("Anak tiri" [Step child], 61073, Chap Ayam, lagu nasib, May 1947 catalogue). On the other side of the same record, Emmy sang a "sad song about how an orphan child yearned for and remembered her parents" ("Anak dagang" [Alien child]).[19]

It was also reported that "Baby Bedah, the cute radio singer" whose "singing was enjoyed by many who listened to the radio broadcasts of Children's Programs," sang "melancholy and sad songs that were mournful,"[20] such as "Ratapan anak tiri" (Laments of a stepchild) and "Bapaku Zaraida" (My father Zaraida; Chap Ayam, 61075, May 1947 catalogue). Girls such as Miss Emmy gave advice about "being kind that will surely be remembered by people"[21] ("Lagu budi bahasa" [Song about kindness]). It was stressed that she "composed her own poetry about kindheartedness *[pantun budi karangan-nya]*. Miss Emmy also urged audiences to follow the teachings of Islam, to fast, do good deeds, and remember God for as long as ever"[22] ("Mesti beringat" [Must remember], 61083, Chap Ayam catalogue, October 1947).

In keeping with the spirit of nationalism and independence in the postwar period, women singers such as Che Juriyah presented new songs such as "Kewajipan pemuda" (Responsibilities of youths; 22927, Kronchong, HMV catalogue, May 1947), advising the youths to work hard, be disciplined, and seek education so that they can assist in the development of the nation and the advancement of the Malay race. On the flip side of the same record, Juriyah sang about the "beauty of the city of Singapore, with intermittent advice to youths regarding the obstacles in the city."[23]

Sitti Aishah "informed all the young people, whether boys or girls, to work hard so that Malaya can become more peaceful and prosperous,"[24] in "Membela Malaya" (Defend Malaya; GE 10094, foxtrot, Columbia catalogue, May 1947). Sitti sang a rumba "advising young people that they should be loyal to their parents, teachers, and . . . not to drink alcohol," in "Nasihat pemuda" (Advice to youths).[25]

A pertinent observation is that most of the songs about "the way forward" and "progress" in the three 1947 catalogues analyzed were gendered: women and girls sang about good morals, virtuous behavior, and Islamic teachings, while men sang about male-oriented issues, which included drinking alcohol and other vices (Mr. Jani, Chap Ayam 61085, May 1947 catalogue); hardships of earning a living in the city (Jaffar, Chap Ayam 61077, May 1947 catalogue); and nostalgia for home and village (Mr. Srik, Columbia Malay records, GE 10088, May 1947). Some male singers such as Ahmad CB and Mohd Yatim urged youths to study hard and strive for unity so that the nation can progress (P 22934 and P 22933, respectively, HMV catalogue, May 1947).

The differences in the themes of the songs about social reform sung by women and men were in tandem with the dichotomies in patriarchal modernity, in which women were the traditional cultural bearers and gatekeepers of spiritual morality in the village, while men went to work in the cities. The women sang about good behavior, good deeds, and spiritual values to gain the empathy of women, youths, and children. Likewise, young girls appealed to the emotions of the listeners regarding the sufferings of orphans and children who were ill treated by their stepmothers.

The women recording artists crossed into the male domain of public discourse by singing songs about social reform, but they accepted gender distinctions by emphasizing texts about moral advice, duties, and good behavior. They gained public acceptance by adhering to Malay customs and Islamic teachings, but some alternative gender imaginations regarding issues such as forced marriages were coded in their lyrics. Consequently, they were able to moderate the gender hierarchies in the music industry and society.

Women, through their musical voices and alternative lifestyles, found the means to promote a type of vernacular modern subjectivity that shook the socially constructed boundaries that separated polarities such as male/female, West/East, village/city, and modern/tradition in colonial Malaya. They challenged the conventional status of women in Malay society but were sensitive to the local customs and Islamic values; they mixed tradition and modernity in their voices and song lyrics; they personified glamour and success as celebrity stars but also advocated for change and progress. The musical voices and codes of behavior reveal the polyvocal and sometimes contradictory experiences and representations of women performers as gendered subjects in colonial Malaya.

The shifting nature of gender roles and identities highlights the complexity and fluidity of identity formation that led to the development of an alternative vernacular modernity in British Malaya. What we observe in this study is a type of gender identity that was emerging but was not fully articulated (Williams 1985, 126). Gender negotiations in the lives of women singers and the popular music they created were not deliberately anticolonial or feminist but signaled a sense of ambivalence toward the hegemonic West and patriarchal society. The women performers did not form organizations to fight for their liberation but exercised a kind of individual cultural agency by negotiating sites of action in which they could express their freedom from the expectations of what their lives should be.

The voices and lifestyles of the women entertainers of colonial Malaya were products of and were shaped by the emergence of rapid social conditions and urban entertainment; new technology such as the gramophone, microphone, and film; and emergent ideas about modernist Islamic social reform in the port cities. Nevertheless, the voices and lifestyles were also vehicles for the individual expressions of the women artists. Women singers were active individuals who strategized and bargained with the forces of patriarchal modernity that confronted them by aligning themselves with Malay customs and Islamic values in their behavior, dress, and singing. They were constantly evaluating, incorporating, or rejecting elements from the East and West in their identities and songs, which they used to construct the modern self. By so doing, they were able to maneuver between two types of social expectations: modernity as necessitated by the entertainment industry and tradition as required by Malay Muslim society.

Acknowledgments

I thank the Singapore National Archives for permission to use the oral interview of Nona Asiah and the photograph of Maria Menado. To the Malay Heritage Centre, Singapore, thanks for providing the photograph of Nona Asiah on the cover of *Arena Film*, 29 April 1960. The 78 RPM recordings transcribed are from the collection of Naina Merican, while the record catalogues are from the British Sound Archives.

Notes

1. Binary contrasts between men and women are based on patriarchal ideology, which defines women as the "other" (de Beauvoir 1978). As a result, women are considered biologically different from men and are believed to be inferior to them. Nevertheless, women are not victims of and often bargain with patriarchy (Kandiyoti 1991).

2. See Tan 1993 and 2013 for information on the development of *bangsawan* and the different types of *bangsawan* songs in the multiethnic stories performed. Popular songs were sung in the *bangsawan* extra turns, which were recorded by gramophone companies. The same songs were also performed in Malay social dancing known as *ronggeng* or *joget*. The Malay *ronggeng* or *joget* is a type of folk social dance that was originally performed during weddings and other celebrations in Malay society. In the early twentieth century, the form was modernized, and male patrons paid a small fee to dance with the female *ronggeng* dancers at the amusement park (Tan 2005).

3. *Bangsawan* began to decline during the Japanese occupation, and many troupes had to close down. After the war, this theater could not compete with the Malay film, which was more realistic in its presentation. For an explanation of the demise of *bangsawan* theater in the 1950s, see Tan 1993.

4. Older *bangsawan* performers such as Tijah retired from performing in the late 1950s. Other less famous women actresses became dancers and singers on the *joget* stage, which was still popular in the amusement parks of the 1950s.

5. Jan van der Putten (2014) has written about Malay anxiety over Malay *ronggeng* social dancing in the first half of the twentieth century and how different nationalist and reformist groups debated these tensions to further their own political and cultural agendas.

6. Timothy Barnard (2009) has written about decolonization in the content of the Malay films of the 1950s. Barnard says that the Malay films began to portray women who were strong and went against tradition. An example is the character Azizah in P. Ramlee's film *Penarek bechak*.

7. For a discussion of the main features of the folk *ronggeng* ensemble and how the music evolved and changed in the twentieth century, see Tan 2005. The folk ensemble comprised a violin, two frame drums, and a gong. The *ronggeng* music and dance formed a big part of the repertoire in Malay opera, recordings, and films of the first half of the twentieth century. Western instruments were added to the modernized ensemble.

8. As in the popular songs of the prewar period, Chinese, Indian, Middle Eastern, and Javanese elements were also added to the film songs of the 1950s. "Tidorlah nanda" (Sleep brother; sung by Noormadiah in the film *Merana*, Osman Ahmad Orchestra, HMV, NAM 206, 1950s) has Indian vocal ornamentations and styles of singing.

9. For discussions about the different ideas of reform and progress by Malay nationalists and Islamic reformists, see Kahn 2006 and Milner 1995. Malay nationalists of differing ideologies were concerned about Malay poverty, backwardness, and the threat from "other," non-Malay immigrants. They debated about how to transform themselves in the vernacular newspapers, journals, cartoons, and new fiction so that Malay society could progress *(maju)* (Khoo 2001).

10. Malay was the lingua franca for the diverse people living in the Malay Archipelago. The spelling of the Malay language was not standardized in the colonial days. The Malay words quoted here use the spelling that was originally found in the catalogues and newspapers.

11. For example, Syed Syekh al-Hadi, a teacher, journalist, and writer who was inspired by reformist Islam from Egypt, wrote a series of stories called "The Moral Trainer" that was published by the Jelutong Press. He advocated morals and values (which included concern for people, responsibility, fidelity, initiative, and education for women) in stories such as "Faridah Hanum" (Matheson 2000, 85).

12. Ajaran orang mesti buat baik, sebat dikalu buat baik belakang hari mesti dapat balasan.

13. Kalau orang miskin memang selamanya di-pandang hina begitulah adat di dalam dunia.

14. Menasihatkan orang orang muda mesti ta'at kepada ibubapa, guru-guru dan lain-lain lagi dan jangan minum arak supaya jangan tergoda shaitan.

15. Rukun Islam dan bagaimana chara-charanya menunaikan tiap-tiap satu-nya.

16. Lain dari itu mengingatkan supaya jangan kita lalai daripada ajaran-ajaran islam supaya terjauh kita dari godaan shaitan.

17. Seorang gadis desa yang sangat sangsara sehari hari terpeksa dinikahkan oleh ayah kepada orang yang berharta tetapi kesudahan jadi chelaka juga nasib gadis itu.

18. Susah payah ibu membela dan mendidik anak.

19. Miss Emmy merayu penderitaan sa-orang perempuan yang kematian ibu-nya dan bapa-nya berkahwin dengan perempuan yang bengis. Sabelah lagu ini Emmy menyanyikan lagu sedih, bagi-mana sa-orang anak yatim piatu rindu dan terkenang kepada ibubapanya.

20. Baby Bedah Penyanyi radio yang chomel. . . . Nyanyiannya menjadi kesukaan ramai dalam siaran radio dalam 'Ranchangan Kanak-Kanak. Kali ini ia menyanyikan lagu yang sayu dan sedih yang memilukan hati.

21. Budi bahasa baik suda tentu dikenangkan kepada orang.

22. Beribadat dan berpuasa membuat pahala ingat kepada Tuhan supaya selamat selama-lama-nya.

23. Kecantikan kota Singapura, diselangi dengan nasihat kepada pemuda-pemuda akan rentangan-rentangan di-kota itu.

24. Memberitahu semua orang orang muda baik laki-laki atau perempuan mesti bekerja lebih kuat lagi supaya Malaya menjadi lagi aman dan ma'amor.

25. Menasihatkan orang-orang muda mesti ta'at kepada ibubapa, guru-guru dan . . . jangan minum arak.

References

Azlan Mohamed Said. 2013. *Malaya's Early Music Scene: Musika Arena Muzik Silam di Malaya.* Singapore: National Arts Council.

Barnard, Timothy P. 2009. "Decolonization and the Nation in Malay Film: 1955–1965." *Southeast Asia Research* 17 (1): 65–86.

Chatterjee, Partha. 1993. *The Nation and Its Fragments: Colonial and Postcolonial Histories.* Princeton, NJ: Princeton University Press.

de Beauvoir, Simone. 1978. *The Second Sex.* Translated and edited by H. M. Parshley. New York: Knopf.

Giddens, Anthony. 1990. *The Consequences of Modernity.* Stanford, CA: Stanford University Press.

Hayami Yoko, Tanabe Akio, and Tokita-Tanabe Yumiko, eds. 2003. *Gender and Modernity: Perspectives from Asia and the Pacific.* Kyoto and Melbourne: Kyoto University Press and Trans Pacific Press.

Kahn, Joel. 2006. *Other Malays: Nationalism and Cosmopolitanism in the Modern Malay World.* Singapore: Asian Studies Association of Australia, in association with Singapore University Press and NIAS Press.

Kandiyoti, Deniz. 1991. "Bargaining with Patriarchy." In *The Social Construction of Gender*, edited by Judith Lorber and Susan A. Farrell, 104–118. Newbury Park, CA: Sage.
Khoo Kay Kim. 2001. *Malay Society, Transformation and Democratisation*. 3rd ed. Selangor: Pelanduk.
Manderson, Lenore. 1980. *Women, Politics and Change: The Kaum Ibu UMNO Malaysia, 1945–1972*. Kuala Lumpur: Oxford University Press.
Matheson, Virginia. 2000. *Writing a New Society: Social Change through the Novel in Malay*. Sydney: Asian Studies Association of Australia, in association with Allen and Unwin and University of Hawai'i Press.
Milner, A. C. 1995. *The Invention of Politics in Colonial Malaya: Contesting Nationalism and the Expansion of the Public Sphere*. Cambridge: Cambridge University Press.
Mitchell, Timothy, ed. 2000. *Questions of Modernity*. Minneapolis: University of Minnesota Press.
Said, Zubir. 1959. *Pelajaran menyanyi: Dengan sistem solmisasi*. Singapore: Pustaka Melayu.
Stivens, Maila. 1998. "Theorising Gender, Power and Modernity in Affluent Asia." In *Gender and Power in Affluent Asia*, edited by Krishna Sen and Maila Stivens, 1–34. London: Routledge.
Tan Sooi Beng. 1993. *Bangsawan: A Social and Stylistic History of Popular Malay Theatre*. Singapore: Oxford University Press.
———. 2005. "From Folk to National Popular Music, Recreating Ronggeng in Malaysia." *Journal of Musicological Research* 24:287–307.
———. 2013. "Negotiating His Masters Voice: Cosmopolitan Modernity in British Malaya in the 1930s and Early 1940s." *Bijdragen tot de Taal, Land-en Volkenkunde* 169:457–494.
van der Putten, Jan. 2014. "'Dirty Dancing' and Malay Anxieties: The Changing Context of Malay Ronggeng in the First Half of the Twentieth Century." In *Sonic Modernities in the Malay World: A History of Popular Music, Social Distinction and Novel Lifestyles (1930s–2000s)*, edited by Bart Barendregt, 113–134. Leiden: Brill.
Williams, Raymond. 1985. *Marxism and Literature*. Oxford: Oxford University Press.

Newspapers and Magazines

Arena Film, 29 April 1960.
Berita Film, 2 December 1960.
Star, 31 August 2014.
Straits Echo, 24 May 1934.
Sunday Gazette, 31 July 1938.

Oral Interviews

Asiah bte Aman oral interview. 2004. By Julianti Parani. 17 April. Reel 1–4. Accession no. 002840. Singapore National Archives.

Gramophone Catalogues

Chap Ayam supplement catalogue of Malay records, May and October 1947; 1 March 1938.

Columbia Malay records catalogue, May 1947.

HMV supplement catalogue of Malay records, October and November 1934; October 1947.

CHAPTER 5

The "Comfort Women" and the Voices of East Asian Modernity

Joshua D. Pilzer

WHAT explains the widespread advent of female screen and pop stars at the dawn of so many Asian modernities? Perhaps it is because women from West to East Asia became prominent public figures in mediated demonstrations of the sloughing off of so-called premodern gender prohibitions, bringing modern technology and gender transformation together in a compelling symbol of modernity and modernizing nation-states.

This triumphant gendered narrative of modernization applies in many cases, but there is a darker side to modernity also represented by the modern female star. The many films and songs of star women in early twentieth-century East Asia are strewn with narratives of women's hardship and suffering, and not all of these stories are about women suffering traces of the "premodern." Many of these narratives are about women suffering due to processes we associate with modernity—the crumbling of political and economic systems, capitalism, industrialization, and colonialism in particular. Prostitutes, bar girls, and urban or colonial émigrés who lose home, family, country, and often their minds and lives pepper the films and songs of the time. In these stories, when girls and women survived the consequences of modernity, their suffering could then be reframed as modern growing pains. Those who did not were often cast as objects sacrificed in the process of modernization, for good or bad.

These suffering women both represented incipient modernity and focused its pain—of rural-to-urban migration, emigration, labor exploitation, social transformation, and so on. It is this dual role that made them such powerful figures in the consolidation of national identities and class sensibilities and in the consolidation of modern masculinities that arise to administer or protect the suffering woman.

These were tragedies of marginal girls and women, and so ironically, in Christine Yano's lovely expression, national imaginaries pulled "the margins in to serve as a version of the center" (2002, 15). At the same time, they often legitimized whole new regimes of gendered domination. In other words, oftentimes the preponderance of women in cinema and song in early East Asian popular culture was not exclusively because women were convenient metaphors, exemplars, metonyms of modernity, or anything else, but because colonial popular culture was in this way engaged in the regulation of the sexes. If these figures were voices of East Asian colonial modernity (its mouthpieces), then these voices were granted only under certain conditions—the conditions of female suffering.

This chapter is about the dependent relationship between this cinematic suffering and real-life female struggles to survive the things that "modernity" euphemistically signifies: aggressive formations of empire and colonization, "late" (and hence quite often brutal) capitalist development, colonial underdevelopment schemes, authoritarianisms, and so on. Mediated narratives of female suffering on screen relied on real-life female suffering to lend themselves credence and to spread.

The brokenheartedness that characterizes modern East Asian national-cultural intimacy circulated via mass media and its stars and was produced in its circulation; but part of that circulation was the panoply of daily rituals that brought these stories both into other women's spheres, including the sex and entertainment world of East Asian modernity—the brothels, the nightclubs, and the "comfort stations"—and back out again, transformed. These two seemingly separate realms—popular culture and sex industries—were connected through the movement of stories and people from films, radio, and records to streets and homes and clubs, and vice versa. The end result was the emplacement of the broken and brokenhearted—yet often resilient and occasionally triumphant—woman as, variously, a metaphor or metonym for modernity, a site for its configuration, and a voice, a sounding medium through which modernity and its subjectivities could be heard and constituted. This voice was a suffering woman's voice, which bore the traces of real-life female suffering. As it elevated real-world sufferers to cinematic heights, it afforded them symbolic power and expressive resources—however partial and constrained—that helped them in the pursuit of survival. It afforded them a voice with which to sing and speak and audiences willing to listen, given that certain conditions were met.

With these ideas in mind, in this chapter, I consider two interconnected features of Korean colonial modernity: the emergence of colonial female pop stars and the development of colonial and wartime sex industries. This sex-industrial development reached its zenith in the "comfort women," a euphemism for the Japanese military's wartime system of sexual slavery during the Asia-Pacific War (1931–1945), which involved between fifty thousand and two hundred thousand girls and young women from across the Japanese empire. The "comfort women" system drew its victims mostly from the colonies of the Japanese empire. It stands as one of the largest coordinated systems of wartime sex trafficking and forced sexual labor in human history; yet it nonetheless shared much in common with the industrialization of sex in the environs of modern militaries and the industrialized, modern city.[1]

I argue that the concurrent rise of popular music's female stars and the rise of colonial sex industries are not the result of opposing forces of modernization and barbarism but deeply intertwined parts of the transformation of the place(s) and the manner of exploitation of women in colonial and wartime modernity. Both are part of a system for the complex emplacement of women—as people, as symbols, and as voices—at the practical and the moral center of modernity and colonial domination. In this chapter, through a detailed analysis of the references to popular music and dance in the testimony and talk of former Korean "comfort women," I consider the remarkable cultural continuities that link the figure of the colonial female pop star and the sexual slave and some of the reasons for and the uses of these connections.

Suffering East Asian Colonial Modernity

Much scholarly opinion locates the beginnings of "modernity" in East Asia either with incipient mercantile activity and the emergence of proto-middle classes or with the unequal treaties that "opened" the various countries throughout the nineteenth century. In any case, by the late nineteenth century, China, Japan, and Korea were so-called modernizing countries, in the midst of a manifestly colonial modernity. Certain places in the region were nexuses of colonial activity, such as Shanghai, with its American, British, French, and Japanese concessions, and the Korean peninsula, the site of a Chinese, Russian, Japanese, and American struggle for domination in Northeast Asia. But trade arrangements made the colonial presence nearly universal. Japan had long been engaged in colonial activity in Hokkaido and Okinawa, but with the Japanese military victories over China and Russia around the turn of the century, Japan became a global colonial power, first through the colonization of Taiwan (1895) and then of the Korean peninsula (1910).

The region's colonial modernity was unique in that while some colonization was by outsiders, Japan and to a lesser extent China were also colonial powers in their own right. Japan's influence grew until the end of the Asia-Pacific War (1931–1945). This colonial modernity meant a highly ambivalent kind of modernization that saw the creation of modern systems of agricultural and industrial production, transportation, commerce, media, education, media, national consciousness, and subjectivities under conditions of colonial domination. Much of the modern transportation systems, for instance, were used for human trafficking—resettlements of work populations, forced military conscription, and forced labor conscription, including the recruitment of girls and women for military sexual labor. All of these ambivalent features of East Asian colonial modernity combined with more typical things we associate with modernity—technological development, urban migration and separation from hometowns, travel abroad, the increased pace of life and its stresses, the alienation and exploitation of labor, and so on—to create an overwhelming sense of sacrifice and woundedness within modernity's promise.

This revelation has something to add to the "cultural intimacy" thesis advanced by the anthropologist Michael Herzfeld that nations are held together through "the recognition of those aspects of a cultural identity that are considered a source of external embarrassment but that nevertheless provide insiders with their assurance of a common sociality" (1997, 3). Woundedness in East Asian national consciousnesses is certainly often a source of embarrassment—for instance, in the case of the persistent embarrassment about the Korean failure to resist colonization, which lends its panicky energy to nationalist projects in both Koreas, or in the case of the embarrassment that surrounded and ratified violence against women as a cornerstone of modern Korean and Japanese masculinities. But perhaps a more important reason why woundedness and the "communally broken heart" (Yano 2002, 3) were such powerful parts of modern East Asian national imaginaries is that they remind us not that nations *have* one another but that they *need* one another to create visions of wholeness—of peoples, of coherent selves, and so on. Hanging together, we might overcome suffering or face it more easily.

That is, whoever the "we" is. This was a wicked point of contention in the context of East Asian colonial modernity. Does "we" refer to Koreans, to Japanese, to men, to women, to classes, to the collective members of the Greater East Asian Co-Prosperity Sphere? This "we" is constantly being drawn and redrawn—in stories of national and transnational love, in stories of the networks of human relations that arise or reveal themselves in response to suffering. In any case, women—from the stars of pop culture to the most humble and ordinary suffering women whom they represented—were among the principal means of circulating these feelings of suffering and injury and the intimate sensibilities and senses of possible futures that arise from them.

Colonial Medias, Migration, and Stories of Women's Suffering

Popular culture and national consciousness in China, Japan, and Korea were essentially born in the nineteenth and early twentieth centuries, with the development of newspapers, radio, and other forms of mass media, with the development of railway systems, and with the progress of universal education in various places. The development of modern media was highly transnational and an inseparable part of the colonial circuitry of East Asia. By the early twentieth century, Japanese popular music and Japanese film were wildly popular throughout the region, and Japan had film- and music-production companies in Manchuria, Shanghai, Korea, and elsewhere throughout the empire. People, expressive forms, technology, and mediated objects moved both in and out of Japan and the colonies; much colonial cultural production and mediation was overseen by Japanese authorities. Complicating the picture, the deeply colonial cosmopolitanism of divided Shanghai enabled a similar circulation of European and American cultural forms to Japan, until wartime censorship largely curtailed it in the midcentury. Music industries, film industries, and other organs of cultural production were systematically interconnected in their very origins, and so it is important not to think of them as series of points in a system connected by channels of cultural movement that moved "culture" around: rather, we must think about cultural production as a process that occurs in the transnational circulation itself (Novak 2013, 17). This means, of course, that more than media was transnational: the whole process of the formation of East Asian national consciousnesses was based in a transnational circulation of cultural forms, ideas, technologies, and human beings, all of which were not simply shuttled around but created in the process. Japan became Japan by way of assuming a place in a global theater of nation-states and vis-à-vis notions of exotic and underdeveloped colonies. Korea became itself through a process of emulating, often forcibly, nations thought to be more advanced and more powerful. And both of these nations became themselves in a transnational economy of human migration and media circulation that brought the image and the voice of the suffering woman as a symbol of the modern into homes and minds throughout the region.

Stories of women's suffering throughout East Asia ebb and flow throughout history with transformations of the gendered balance of power. In Korea, tropes of the suffering woman proliferated during the long neo-Confucian revival of the Joseon Dynasty (1392–1910), which brought with it new rigidity concerning the rightness of women's subordination to men. Korea's most famous story, the legend of Chunhyang, is a paean to the right relations between genders, depicting the daughter of a lowly *gisaeng* (female entertainer) who falls in love with an aristocrat yet remains true to him in his absence despite the threats and advances of a local bureaucrat. Murdered women return from the grave to haunt their murderers, and the archetypal image of a ghost throughout East Asia has long been a woman. The same is true in Japan. Japanese traditional theater and legend are full of instances of wronged women, many of whom return from the dead to haunt or exact revenge on their victimizers as *onry* (vengeful spirits). Pre-nineteenth-century Chinese opera and literature are rife with tales of neglected concubines. And all three places have traditional tales of forlorn or otherwise tragic courtesans and of girls and women in love who die rather than face arranged marriage.

So in the late nineteenth and early twentieth centuries, as the film and music industries emerged, they inherited a stock of traditional stories and story types of women's suffering. The story of Chunhyang became Korea's first sound film (1935). *Yotsuya kaidan,* featuring the vengeful ghost of the murdered wife Oiwa, was filmed more than fifteen times in the early era of Japanese film and paved the way for the modern J-horror genre. The stories of forlorn and abused *geisha* (Japanese professional entertaining women) are perhaps more salient to the argument of this chapter, as they modulated into a significant portion of the repertoire of early Japanese popular song.

These traditional stories gained, rather than lost, traction in the public imaginaries of early twentieth-century Japan and Korea; traditional stories of violence against women were easily reinterpreted to suit the displacements and the violence of East Asian colonial modernity. Nonetheless, they underwent significant transformation, and many new stock characters and narratives arose. The archetypal figure of the courtesan became a bar girl, as in the Korean hit from 1940 "Beonji eobneun jumak" (A bar with no address), about a stranded song-and-dance girl; or she became a prostitute or teahouse girl, as in the Shanghai hit film *Street Angel* (1937). In *Street Angel,* megastar Zhou Xuan (1920–1957) plays a teahouse girl whose sister has already been forced into prostitution in the chaos of Republican China and who is in danger of sharing her fate (see Yifen Beus, chap. 3 in this volume). The film's signature song, "Tianya genü" (The wandering songstress), is about an entertainer who drifts in search of her lover.[2]

These roles were depicted not, or not only, as modern continuations of traditions of women's suffering but as distinctly modern forms. The 1938 Korean pop ballad "Nunmeul jeojeun Dumangang" (The tear-choked Duman river) is often said to be sung from the perspective of a young woman who mourns the absence and likely death of her husband, who has crossed into Manchuria as an anticolonial guerrilla fighter. The bar girls, the orphans, and the wives left behind suffer because of contemporary circumstances—social upheaval, migration, war, and so on.

The suffering woman is ubiquitous in the cinema and music devoted to all sorts of ideological positions, finding a place in Japanese colonial propaganda, in leftist Chinese cinema, and in the subtle anticolonial metaphors of Korean popular culture; but her fate differs depending on whether she is caught up in a narrative of suffering and triumph or of tragic demise. In the left-leaning

Street Angel, the young Xiaoyu, forced into prostitution, is eventually murdered. But the Chinese orphan of the Japanese propagandistic *Shina no yoru* (China night), on the other hand, is ultimately reunited with her Japanese officer husband.

In all events, these suffering girls and women who fall through the cracks into the streets and the dives of the booming sex-and-entertainment industries of 1920s and 1930s East Asia focused the pain of modernity and its various sacrifices, exploitations, tragedies, and promises. In so doing, they helped to consolidate coherent senses of nations and their histories in the midst of modern transformation, along a spectrum of anxiety and celebration about the consequences of all the changes that are lumped under the moniker of "modernity."

Entanglements

The foregoing is the first contention of this essay. Building on it, I go on in the following pages to show the entanglements that connected the worlds of colonial entertainment industries and sexual labor. I investigate how girls and women moved back and forth between the realms of the entertainment world and the world of sex work and even sexual slavery, focusing on the case of Korean women. I also discuss how stories of female suffering that circulated in early twentieth-century East Asian mass media and characterized its colonial modernity were practically entangled with other arenas of female suffering, focusing on the case of the colonial Shanghai film *Shina no yoru* and Korean women's relations to it. I discuss the outcomes of these entanglements, both in terms of the development of popular culture and consciousness and in terms of real-life consequences for particular women. In this context, I discuss the highly conditioned agency afforded by this circulation of suffering women throughout popular culture and vernacular experience: so-called low women were identified with and identified themselves with the suffering female figures of popular media and thus were capable of harnessing the symbolic power of those figures in their own lives.

Migrations

The human interconnections that link sex industries and popular media were a key feature of the circulatory system by which the stories and sentiments of suffering females circulated in the creation of mass consciousness and the disciplining of the sexes. A number of different types of human movement can be distinguished. First, a rather large number of female stars began their professional lives as various types of courtesan throughout East Asia. Many of these roles were traditionally associated with elite culture; some prohibited women from engaging in sex with patrons. But most courtesan institutions in East Asia were gradually assimilated into the burgeoning sex industries of the late nineteenth and early twentieth centuries, which provided entertainment and sex to the emerging capitalist, bureaucratic, and working classes. These industries were dominated by different sorts of drinking houses, of various expense and class patronage, where men gathered to drink, sing, talk with and touch professional women, and (in many places) to negotiate for sex.[3] By the early nineteenth century, these downwardly mobile processes of assimilation were well under way, and the words for courtesan in Korea and China had become nearly synonymous with the words for prostitute. The one exception of a courtesan institution that did not suffer this fate is, fittingly, a Japanese one, that lived on in the embrace of imperial power: the Japanese *geisha* retain high status to this day.

Some courtesans caught in the midst of such processes of sex industrialization sought a way out, and fame and fortune, by pursing careers in popular music; some became stars. Two of Japan's earliest pop stars, Katsutaro Kouta and Matsue Goto (aka Ichimaru), were trained as *geisha*. Wang Subok (1917–2003), who had been educated at the premier Korean courtesan school in Pyeongyang (Pyeongyang giseong gweonbeon), became an early pop icon; Yi Hwaja emerged from the murky world of sex and entertainment—the ambiguous spaces between courtesanship and the sex industry—to become, in her brief life, one of Korea's most beloved early pop stars. Much the same thing occurred in early Republican China, as courtesan culture simultaneously was absorbed by a rationalized sex industry (see Henriot 1994) and produced song-and-dance stars, movie stars, and a host of other prominent cultural figures (see Yu 2012).

The second link in the chain of human movement that concerns us here is the movement out of the courtesan world into modern sex industries, as far afield as the military "comfort women" system. Survivors of the "comfort women" system report meeting both *geisha* and *gisaeng* (Korean courtesans) in the "comfort stations" *(ianjo)* where they were kept and made to provide sexual service to soldiers during the war. In fact, in Korea, where at least half of the victims of the "comfort women" system were from, *gisaeng*-training institutes seem to have played an important role in getting business and military interests the girls and women whom they sought for the sex trade.

During the colonial era, professional female entertainers, deprived of traditional state sponsorship, attempted to perpetuate their traditions and other endangered music and dance genres in *gwonbeon,* private schools/agencies. These institutions were tremendously important in the modern shaping of *pansori* (solo epic story singing with drum accompaniment), *sanjo* (solo instrumental improvisation with drum accompaniment), and many of the other now-famous genres of Korean professional folk music. They were training facilities, but they were also private agencies that sent women out to perform at private homes, restaurants, and the many drinking houses that proliferated in the colonial period in imitation of Japanese drinking-house culture. As the colonial era progressed, *gwonbeon* assimilated more and more into the broader colonial sex-and-entertainment industry.

Many Korean girls and young women in the colonial era found themselves in these institutes. They arrived there searching for income to help their impoverished families; or they came because they had been sold there, or because they were orphaned and sought to trade their talents for livelihood; others sought such training simply out of a passion for music and dance.

In the war era, the *gwonbeon* institutes became hotbeds for recruitment for the "comfort women" system, and many traditional female entertainers and their students were conscripted. "Comfort woman" survivor Jo Yun-ok studied with a *gisaeng* who had been trained at the famous traditional entertainer school in Pyeongyang, who taught her *janggo* (hourglass drum), *sijo* (aristocratic sung poetry), *pansori,* and popular singing, and eventually sold her into sexual slavery (Hanguk jeongsindae yeonguso 2003, 68–69). Yi Sang-ok was fourteen when she took a position cleaning and cooking at a *gisaeng* boarding school; a year later, she was conscripted, together with the other residents of the school, many of whom had been sold to the school by their families (Hanguk jeongsindae yeonguhoe 1995, 185–186). Yi Sun-ok was made a "comfort woman" together with a girl who went by the Japanese name Yoshiko, who had been trained as a *gisaeng* in Daegu (ibid., 171). Kim Haksun trained as a *gisaeng* but had to find other work because she was too young to obtain a license. As she looked for other work in China in 1941, she was forcibly abducted by the Japanese military and made a "comfort woman" near Beijing (ibid., 34–37).

It is crucial to a complete understanding of "comfort women" conscription to know that many Korean girls and young women taken as military sexual slaves had no associations with *gisaeng* schools, drinking houses, or any other establishments in the colonial Korean sex-and-entertainment industry. Many girls were simply abducted or conscripted from their homes, conscripted or taken at meetings in homes and town squares, or transferred to sexual slavery from other kinds of labor for which they had been conscripted or volunteered. The point of this inquiry is not to suggest more of a role for the performing arts and their institutions than they had. Rather it is to demonstrate how the lure of the performing arts was exploited to draw girls into the sex industries, as in the case of girls who were sold into sexual slavery from *gisaeng* schools; to show how sex-and-entertainment-industry establishments were important spheres for conscription; and to illuminate the network of human trafficking dedicated to the exploitation of girls and women and the role that the performing arts played in that systematized trade in human beings.

At the peak of wartime, many *gwonbeon* institutes became part of a network of human trafficking that moved girls and women between its different spheres throughout the war—not only from courtesanship to sexual slavery but also in the opposite direction. The traditional distinctions between *gisaeng* and prostitutes, and the differences between either of these and the new category of "comfort woman," blurred in this circulatory system. Mun Okju related that upon returning from her term as a sexual slave in Manchuria, "I thought, 'After all there's nothing to do but become a *gisaeng*.' When I had first decided to become a *gisaeng* at the age of twelve my older brother had been opposed, beating me and saying 'an aristocrat's daughter wants to become a prostitute?' But (in the interim) I had already become indistinguishable from a prostitute. I knew that if you drank, if you sang, and if you had sexual relations with men you can make money. Anyway ordinary marriage was impossible for this body.[4] No matter how I thought about it, I thought I could have no future other than becoming a *gisaeng*" (Mun with Morikawa 2005, 63). The fact that her brother associated traditional female entertainers with prostitutes is another demonstration of the extent to which private sex industries were drawing in the traditional female entertainer and how sex work was increasingly required of *gisaeng*.

Following Mun's sense of her horizons, she enrolled at a *gweonbeon* and applied herself to learning a variety of traditional performing arts. Her specialty was *pansori*. She learned to sing two hours of the iconic *pansori* epic "Song of Shimcheong," became an accomplished drum accompanist, and was getting closer to receiving her graduation certificate and license. In her testimony, she remembered how happy she felt when she sang *pansori*, cultivating her voice through *pansori*'s erudite historical texts; but her talent and passion for musical performance drew her into a social world where the likelihood of conscription dramatically increased. Soon after, she was promised a job in a restaurant and was instead abducted to Burma as a sexual slave.[5] After the war, she returned to her hometown of Daegu and became a well-known courtesan.

The role of the courtesan and its institutions were a critical link in the chain of human movement that makes up one crucial aspect of the circulation between mass-mediated popular culture and sex-and-entertainment industries. Some women, however, moved rather more directly between the worlds of sex work and popular media. In early twentieth-century China, the popular conception that actresses were prostitutes was at least in part due to the fact that some prominent film actresses had formerly been sex workers (Yu 2012, 227). Many "comfort women" became part of nonwartime sex-and-entertainment industries after the Asia-Pacific War ended in 1945, and this brought them into a social strata where some women went on to become actresses and pop stars. The survivor Yi Okpun recounts working in different bars after the war in Taiwan, wearing a Chinese dress and singing Chinese songs for customers (Hanguk jeongsindae munje daechaek hyobuihoe and Jeongsindae yeonguhoe 1993, 144). The survivor Bae Chunhui sang in a cabaret in Japan for years after the war and even had a brief appearance in the postwar comedy *Chinjarajara monogatari* (A jingle-jingle tale, 1962).[6] The tremendous number of survivors of the "comfort women" system who kept their wartime experiences secret could furnish more links between wartime sexual labor and the world of popular song and film; but we will likely never know. But suffice it to say that there is plentiful evidence that actual women moved between the worlds of East Asian courtesanship, popular music and film, and sexual labor, in many directions, and that these worlds therefore are not as discrete as some people might be disposed to—or wish to—imagine.

Confluences and Identifications

The other link that intertwines mass-mediated stories of female suffering with the real-life experiences of suffering girls and women is the presence, in the environs of sex-and-entertainment industries, of the tropes and materials of the popular culture, the singing of its songs, and the telling of its stories. So now I turn to the musical culture of the "comfort women" system, to demonstrate the ways in which "comfort women" practiced and were identified with and self-consciously identified with at-large stars and stories of female suffering. I discuss the music culture of the "comfort women" system at length in a recent article (Pilzer 2014); so I confine myself here to a brief overview, in order to contextualize the kinds of musical activity that referenced mass-mediated songs and stories of female suffering that circulated during the war and the colonial era.

The network of sex industrial sites that constituted the "comfort women" system was stratified, as it provided sex and (sometimes) entertainment services to all the tiers of the Japanese military and affiliated civilians. Barracks, sheds, caves, and other haphazard structures often served as "comfort stations" for common soldiers, and the girls and young women who were kept in such places were, in average cases, forced to have sex with tens of men every day. Some survivors report having more than fifty "guests"[7] in a single day. Other girls and women, by contrast, worked in officers' clubs or were made the private sexual slaves of particular officers, although some of these women were often eventually turned over to general sexual service for common soldiers.

Sexual violence permeated the "comfort women" system, but there nonetheless were rather pronounced disparities in the tenor of everyday experience of women in the different strata; this has consequences for the musical cultures of the "comfort stations." Women attached to officers often had more mobility than others and were more likely to be expected to sing and dance. But many women from both of the realms—officers' club environments and "comfort stations" for foot soldiers—report being expected to sing and dance with soldiers, in social contexts of drinking and singing, in scheduled dances, or in more formal staged performances on makeshift stages. All of these contexts were conduits through which the "comfort station" channeled the songs, stars, and general trends of Japanese wartime popular culture.

The musical culture of the "comfort women" system was based in imitations of a number of other sorts of social situations. Since girls and women who worked in Japanese and colonial drinking houses were expected to pour drinks, sing, and dance for or with soldiers, this pattern of evening socialization continued. Second, and just as important, was the model of the wartime revue, deeply inspired by early twentieth-century Japanese revue culture and by the variety shows put on by Japanese and other entertainment companies that occasionally visited military bases throughout the empire and the theater of war.[8] Soldiers had been known to put on revue shows by themselves, often in drag; the "comfort women," when present, were often enlisted to create this sort of atmosphere. As I discuss elsewhere (Pilzer 2014), such occasions provided opportunities for performances of the gendered domination of the Japanese colonial project and for the creation of military male solidarity through collective encounters with and spectatorship of subjected colonial girls and young women. All of these occasions were moments in which the "comfort women," who mostly did not read but were intensely orally literate, quickly learned new songs, which then often became tools in their projects of survival.

The viewing of musical films was another important part of the musical culture of the "comfort women" system and a crucial conduit of Japanese colonial popular culture and its suffering divas into the "comfort station." Many of the Japanese popular songs that women testify to singing and hearing in the "comfort stations" had their origins in popular Japanese films of the era, produced both in Japan and in Japan's various colonial film industries throughout occupied China. Several survivors of the "comfort women" system told me about being taken to see such films during their wartime internment and of singing the song hits from these films for soldiers. It is here at the confluence of the "comfort women" system and wartime film that we find the next crucial link in the chain that connects the female colonial pop star to the victims of the "comfort women" system.

Two of the film songs most mentioned by "comfort woman" survivors are "Shina no yoru" ("China Night") and "Soshyu yakyoku" ("Suzhou Nocturne"), both from the late 1930s. They were popularized in part by the 1940 film *Shina no yoru* (*China Night*), which I have mentioned earlier. The film was directed by Fushimizu Osamu and starred the notorious transethnic film star Li Xianglan (1920–2014). Li, born Yamaguchi Yoshiko, was a Japanese national born and raised in Manchuria and Beijing. In the late 1930s and 1940s, she rose to prominence as a singer and was deemed one of the so-called seven great singing stars, the most popular female singers in China. She also became one of the greatest stars of the Japanese colonial film industry through her work for the company Manchuria Film Productions in the production of the so-called Chinese continental friendship films, which promoted the Japanese wartime expansionist ideology of the Greater East Asia Co-Prosperity Sphere (Stephenson 2002, 1). The so-called Continental Trilogy was made up of *Song of the White Orchid* (1939), *China Night* (1940), and *Vow in the Desert* (1940). In these films, Li appears as an ethnic Chinese, who after some resistance falls in love with a Japanese man (played in all three films by Hasegawa Kazuo) and becomes a supporter of the Japanese imperial project. In the course of this common story, she sings Chinese songs or Japanese popular songs that use Chinese instruments and musical features to make exoticist representations of China.

Into the midst of these musical representations comes Li Xianglan's voice, a longing or heartbroken or hopeful female voice of colonial modernity akin to many other such voices in popular film and music of the time. That voice is high, nasalized, and ultrafeminine, in the manner of the Japanese popular music of the time; it glides effortlessly through the glissandos and pentatonicism and all the other melodic references to China. Colonial femininity and exoticism all find concise expression in the voice of Li Xianglan, in the voice of also-transethnic Watanabe Hamako, and in the voices of others.

In *China Night,* Li Xianglan plays Keiran, a Shanghai orphan whose parents have been killed by Japanese bombs and who harbors intense anti-Japanese feelings. She meets a young Japanese naval captain who falls in love with her and attempts to convince her of the rightness of the Japanese imperial cause in China. In an infamous scene, the captain, overcome by Keiran's lack of gratitude and sympathy, slaps her hard across the face. As she falls to the ground, she realizes her love for him and his for her. The film legitimizes colonialism and violence against women with a single blow.

A brief period of courting ensues: Keiran sings "Suzhou Nocturne" as the pair luxuriate in the exotic ruins of nearby Suzhou. Soon they are threatened by a mob. The film paints a Japanese imperial characterization of China as a ruin of ancient civilization overrun by warlords and bandits yet peppered with flowerlike women in need of disciplining and protection.

Marriage follows. Just after the ceremony, Keiran stands on their balcony in her white wedding gown and sings the title song, "China Night," for her new husband.

> China night, China night
> In the purple night of the port lights
> Junks sail up, dream boats.

I can't forget the sound of the kokyu (fiddle)
China night, dreamy night

China night, China night
Lanterns sway in a window by a willow,
A Chinese girl, with a red birdcage,
Inconsolable love songs—
China night, the dreamy—

Keiran's final line is interrupted by an officer who arrives to give the young captain orders to report for duty. The song, an Orientalist painting that promises the totality both of love and of colonial domination, is thus postponed. Keiran's love is then put to the test, as she has to attempt to understand why her husband must go to war to serve his country in its efforts to dominate hers. But in the end, all comes right: they are reunited, the gendered marriage of dominant Japan and subordinated China is secured, and Keiran sings the song through to the end.

The song "China Night" was debuted by Watanabe Hamako in Japan in 1938[9] and appeared in the film two years later. Watanabe herself also traveled to China during the war to raise troop morale, performing this song and others in Chinese dress. Thus, the Japanese imperial representation of China was exported to the Sinophone world, aimed at Japanese colonialists in China and Manchuria. This was the location of the great majority of "comfort stations," and so it is not surprising to hear survivors of the "comfort women" system tell of hearing and performing "China Night." The survivor Han Okseon remembers singing "China Night" at a gathering of troops during her time in Mainland China (Hanguk jeongsindae munje daechaek hyobuihoe and yeoseong gukje beopjeong Hanguk wiwonhoe jeungeon tim 2000, 85). Ji Dori, Bae Chunhui, and many others either sang the song for me or spoke of singing it during the war. The "comfort women" were nodes in the systemic reproduction of that notion of "China" and the other colonies, just as they were nodes in the circulatory system of violence against women that found such a public face in the pivotal slap of *China Night.*

Early modern East Asian film stars were displayed and given voice at one and the same time; the agency of this role was inextricably bound up with the commodification of women in the public sphere and the identification of women's bodies with national bodies. Compounding this dynamic, Japanese colonial film/pop stars such as Watanabe and Li stood for modernity and colonialism at once, so the new opportunities for women that they seized and that they and their voices represented were doubly hedged in by mechanisms of control. It was possible, however, for these Japanese stars to change out of Chinese dress and sing other sorts of songs and become other sorts of stars and public figures. Li Xianglan did, becoming the Hollywood star Shirley Yamaguchi after the war and the Japanese parliamentarian Yoshiko Yamaguchi in the late twentieth century. This transformation is a clue that the fame of that era was translatable into a woman's agency that was not bound to the colonial experience.

But the role was less flexible for colonial nationals. Colonial women who took advantage of such media opportunities presented by colonial modernity were often accused of collaboration, as was so often the case with Korean courtesans, with the famous modern colonial dancer Choe Seung-hui (Sai Sho-ki),[10] and with a host of other stars from across colonial East Asia.

Yet "comfort women" survivors identified with and were identified with Japanese colonial pop and film stars. Why? Whatever agency identifying with such figures afforded seems so profoundly constrained that it is hardly worth mention; yet some of the women remember how popular songs, and in particular the film songs of the Japanese imperial imaginary, played an important role in their survival. Many girls and young women socialized with and sang and danced for or with soldiers hoping to obtain various sorts of help and advantage. Some "comfort women" managed to escape by cultivating the affection of an officer who helped them obtain travel permits and passage home. Mun Okju tried to elicit the sympathy and affections of soldiers by singing songs they liked, such as "China Night" (Mun with Morikawa 2005, 56). She was often rewarded with tips, which helped her to sustain herself (81); eventually, singing and entertaining in a Manchurian "comfort station," Mun Okju became close to an officer; he fell in love with her, asked her to live with him, and obtained a travel permit for her to go back to Korea (Hanguk jeongsindae munje daechaek hyobuihoe and Jeongsindae yeonguhoe 1993, 154). So some "comfort women" seized a small measure of power as they channeled female colonial film and pop stars and their narratives of gendered colonial domination. Love, as it has frequently been noted, has a tendency to backfire like that, to upset its power relationships and the gender and national loyalties that love songs rehearse (see Stokes 2010); in the case of Mun Okju and several other women, the paternalistic love of officers overwhelmed and departed from the colonial agenda to which it was sutured, often through the direct agentive actions of the female love objects.

The way that women looked—and made themselves look—was undoubtedly a key survival strategy in the struggles of these women; and there is every reason to expect that some made an effort to resemble suffering colonial film stars. But their voices, also, played a role in securing the advantages and even freedoms that they sought. These voices were deeply bound up in the sentimental mélange of the star colonial voices that they imitated when they sang; yet they were also etched with the grain of their own sorrows, sentiments, and dreams. The voices of "comfort women" brought the larger-than-life realm of the cinematic screen into the realm of everyday intimacy and made it tangible.

Yet many other women—whether by bad luck or through lacking the ability to look or sound like the suffering stars—sang in vain attempts to elicit sympathy from soldiers. For some military personnel, such expressions of emotion were alienating, transgressions of unspoken rules concerning the boundary between "comfort women" and themselves. Channeling the atmosphere of nonmilitary sex-and-entertainment industries, such performances helped to reinforce that the "comfort women" system was a sphere of social life beyond the normal sphere of family and morality, dooming the girls and young women to temporary status in soldiers' lives and helping soldiers regard "comfort women" as objects for consumption and disposal.

So what can we learn from these confluences? The performances of "comfort women," which confirmed the rightness of gendered colonial domination and enhanced soldier solidarity, also opened up on the paternalistic love relations of colonial film and pop and gave some "comfort women" who channeled these stars a small sliver of social power—the social power of love—and a resonant voice. So the legitimization of colonial modernity, the commodification of women, and new opportunities for women enabled by the figure of the colonial female pop star can also be found among her dystopian sibling, the "comfort woman."

Furthermore, and most importantly, the film and popular-music industries, the world of sex work, and even the "comfort women" system can be thought of as united in a broad system of circuitry in which these processes of legitimization, commodification, and agency circulated, formed, and transformed—a system united by cultural circulation and human migration between worlds. The silver screen and popular music drew both labor and tropes from the world of suffering women. And suffering women elsewhere provided confirmation of the reality of colonial pop-musical and filmic imaginings and perhaps transformed them in the course of reappropriating them. This circuitry that connects popular music and film stars, courtesans, sex workers, and sexual slaves provides a stark example of the deeply ambivalent place of working women in general and entertaining women in particular in emergent East Asian popular cultures and of the particular grain of the colonial voice of East Asian modernity.

Notes

1. See Cynthia Enloe's survey of the deep relations between sex work and militarism (2000, 49–107).
2. "Tianya genü" endures in Chinese popular culture and is often called the Chinese equivalent of *Casablanca*'s "As Time Goes By."
3. On the Korean case, see Pilzer 2006, and for an account of the gradual transformation of the Chinese courtesan institution, see Henriot 1994.
4. She implies that sexual slavery has made her "unclean" and unsuitable for marriage.

5. The process of Mun's removal to Burma is detailed in Mun with Morikawa 2005, 65–77.

6. For an in-depth discussion of Bae Chunhui's move from "comfort woman" life to the cabaret, see the chapter about her in Pilzer 2012.

7. *Seon-nim*, "guest," is the euphemism typically used by Korean survivors to describe soldiers for whom they had to provide sexual services.

8. For an account of the Chosen Music Club, a Korean troupe that performed for Japanese soldiers during the Asia-Pacific War and that involved some of the most prominent Korean singers and film stars of the era, see Maliangkay 2011.

9. gpapscorpion, "China Night—Hamako Watanabe—1938," YouTube, 7 February 2013, https://www.youtube.com/watch?v=S9cCSLucuzE.

10. See Park 2006, 597–632.

References

Enloe, Cynthia. 2000. *Maneuvers: The International Politics of Militarizing Women's Lives.* Berkeley: University of California Press.

Hanguk jeongsindae munje daechaek hyobuihoe and Jeongsindae yeonguhoe. 1993. *Gangjero kkeullyeogan Joseonin gunwianbudeul* (Korean military comfort women forcibly abducted to China). Seoul: Hanul.

Hanguk jeongsindae munje daechaek hyobuihoe and yeoseong gukje beopjeong Hanguk wiwonhoe jeungeon tim. 2000. *Gangjero kkeullyeogan Joseonin gunwianbudeul 4: Gieok euro dashi sseuneun yeoksa* (Forcibly abducted Korean military comfort women, volume 4: Writing history again from memory). Seoul: Pulbit.

Hanguk jeongsindae yeonguhoe and Hanguk jeongsindae munje daechaek hyeobuihoe. 1995. *Junggugeuro kkeullyeogan Joseonin gunwianbudeul* (Korean military comfort women abducted to China). Seoul: Hanul.

Hanguk jeongsindae yeonguso. 2003. *Jungguk euro kkeullyeogan Joseonin gunwianbudeul 2* (Korean military comfort women abducted to China, volume 2). Seoul: Hanul.

Henriot, Christian. 1994. "Chinese Courtesans in Late Qing and Early Republican Shanghai (1849–1925)." *East Asian History* 8:33–52.

Herzfeld, Michael. 1997. *Cultural Intimacy: Social Poetics in the Nation State.* New York: Routledge.

Maliangkay, Roald. 2011. "Koreans Performing for Foreign Troops: The Occidentalism of the C.M.C. and the K.P.K." *East Asian History* 37 (December): 59–72.

Mun Okju with Morikawa Michiko. 2005. *Beoma jeonseon ilbongun "wianbu": Mun Okju halmeoni ildaegi* (Biography of Japanese military "comfort woman" at the Burmese front: Mun Okju). Seoul: Areumdaun saramdeul.

Novak, David. 2013. *Japanoise: Music at the Edge of Circulation.* Durham, NC: Duke University Press.

Park, Sang Mi. 2006. "The Making of a Cultural Icon for the Japanese Empire: Choe Seung-hui's U.S. Dance Tours and 'New Asian Culture' in the 1930s and 1940s." *Positions* 14 (3): 597–632.

Pilzer, Joshua D. 2006. "The 20th-Century 'Disappearance' of Korean Professional Female Entertainers during the Rise of Korea's Modern Sex-and-Entertainment Indus-

try." In *The Courtesan's Arts: Cross-Cultural Perspectives,* edited by Martha Feldman and Bonnie Gordon, 295–311. New York: Oxford University Press.
———. 2012. *Hearts of Pine: Songs in the Lives of Three Korean Survivors of the Japanese "Comfort Women."* New York: Oxford University Press.
———. 2014. "Music and Dance in the Japanese Military 'Comfort Women' System: A Case Study in the Performing Arts, War, and Sexual Violence." *Women and Music: A Journal of Gender and Culture* 18:1–23.
Stephenson, Shelley. 2002. "A Star by Any Other Name: The (After)Lives of Li Xianglan." *Quarterly Review of Film & Video* 19:1–13.
Stokes, Martin. 2010. *The Republic of Love: Cultural Intimacy in Turkish Popular Music.* Chicago: University of Chicago Press.
Yano, Christine R. 2002. *Tears of Longing: Nostalgia and the Nation in Japanese Popular Song.* Cambridge, MA: Harvard University Press.
Yu, Sabrina Qiong. 2012. "Vulnerable Chinese Stars: From *Xizi* to Film Worker." In *A Companion to Chinese Cinema,* edited by Yingjin Zhang, 218–238. Chichester, UK: Wiley-Blackwell.

PART II

Modern Stars and Modern Lives

NATION, MEMORY, AND THE
POLITICS OF GENDER

CHAPTER 6

Diva Misora Hibari as Spectacle of Postwar Japan's Modernity

Christine R. Yano

In 1989, Japan mourned the deaths of two very public persons whose passing marked the end of a historic era. One of these was Emperor Hirohito, whose death officially ended the Shōwa era (1926–1989) that bears his posthumous name. His reign marked a long and tumultuous period in Japan's modern history that spanned colonial expansion, World War II, and postwar economic global ascendancy. Prior to military defeat, Emperor Hirohito was considered literally a god, a distant figure on a pedestal whose subjects could not look directly on him or hear his words. Thus, in August 1945, his weak, wavering voice announcing Japan's defeat, broadcast throughout the nation over crackling air waves startled people as much for its very sound as for his message. This was an aural dismantling of a deity and a nation.

The other very public person whose death was mourned in 1989 was the Japanese songstress Misora Hibari (1937–1989), the "skylark" whose face and voice arose from the masses. The death of Hibari—known widely by her personal name, rather than the more formal family name, or as "Hibari-chan," a term of affection used by many of her friends (affixing the suffix "-chan" is typically reserved for children or very close female junior friends)—at fifty-two years old unofficially ended the Shōwa era as well, some people might say with more direct emotional outpouring and affective force than that displayed for the emperor. Whereas Emperor Hirohito symbolized national defeat, Misora Hibari represented national rebuilding. I contend that the semiotic positions of both public figures may be understood through their voices. His was an older man's voice, most powerful historically in its silence (as the emperor was not supposed to be accessible to the general public) and subsequently marked most weakly by its thin, tinny quality. Speaking stiffly, haltingly, in formal classical Japanese that the common people could barely understand and heard through the imperfect sonorities of a prerecorded phonograph message on a radio broadcast, it was the sound of generations past, representing the patriarchal hierarchy that had sustained Japan in an unbroken line of emperors (Bix 2000; Dower 1999). What that voice expressed—literally and figuratively—was the ultimate failure of a system.

Misora Hibari's voice took up the affective mantle of leadership where Hirohito's left off. Her voice, heard many times over in recordings, concerts, radio and television broadcasts, movies, bars, and restaurants, was the ubiquitous sound of everyday Japan. Whereas the emperor's voice was underexposed as a symbol of remote power, hers was overexposed as a function of her reign as the "people's singer." Her voice arose out of the complex intimacy of postwar Japan that drew the populace in close through their shared experiences of hardship and hard work. In innumerable hits that documented the era, her voice sounded the pulse of the times in all its heady contradictions. Hibari's voice—clear, strong, working class, and female—could be heard as the soundtrack to a new era of wartime reconstruction, a new jazz-inflected flexible modernity. Whereas the emperor's voice was mired in the silencing of careful training in Japanese tradition, hers was set to the populist grooves of circulating sounds, whether from the United States, Japan, or elsewhere. Her voice symbolized the free-for-all sweep of the era, a child star overturning boundaries of decorum. As she grew from child star to adult diva, her voice embraced the trends of the era, helping define what this version of Japanese postwar modernity might sound like.

Hibari sang a variety of songs throughout her career, from jazz to *chanson* to novelty numbers, her voice changing with each aural frame. But the music for which she eventually became best known was *enka*—sentimental balladry reputed to express the heart/soul of Japanese. In her adulthood, she was dubbed the "Queen of *Enka*" and thus the queen of that very public version of heart/soul. Radio stations throughout Japan played her songs constantly, in particular her signature piece, the 1966 tearful hit "Kanashii sake" (Mournful sake). Over forty-two thousand mourners attended her funeral in Tokyo; thirty thousand paid their respects in seven regional centers set up in her honor (Schilling 1997, 130).

In this chapter, I discuss Hibari's voice as public positioning, addressing issues of modernity framed within that mediated space. I ask, what did this version of modernity sound like? What did it represent? How did Hibari help define the era for which she was mourned? How did the very transgressiveness of the era—embodied and sounded through Hibari—characterize the modernity of which it was a part? Indeed, Hibari was not only the Queen of Enka but also, I argue, the Queen of Tears, setting her divahood in motion directly through the range of emotions she spectacularized onstage.

In focusing on the voice as public positioning, I take up the challenge set forth by Nicholas Harkness in his landmark sonic ethnography *Songs of Seoul* (2013). Harkness asks us to consider what he dubs a "phonosonic nexus"—that is, "the voice as an ongoing intersection between the phonic production, shaping, and organization of sound, on the one hand, and the sonic uptake and categorization of sound in the world, on the other" (2013, 12). Although this chapter does not include the detailed inquiry into vocal production of Harkness's gauntlet, I find it productive to consider the semiotic position of voice and voicings, here of a pop diva in postwar Japan. Turning our attention to the voice challenges us to consider the body that produces it, its sonic materiality, and its contextualized meanings. This focus sharpens our own sense of listening. I echo Ana Maria Ochoa Gautier's call for research "about ontologies and epistemologies of the acoustic, particularly the voice, produced by and enmeshed in different audile techniques, in which sound appears simultaneously as a force that constitutes the world and a medium for constructing knowledge about it" (2014, 3). Thus, in examining Hibari as signifier of Japan's postwar modernity, we might do no better than to attend to her voice.

Focusing on the Jet Age of the 1960s and 1970s, when modernity seemed a heady part of the Japanese public's symbolic vocabulary, I examine ways in which Hibari's music contributed to its aural expression. Most media representations of Misora Hibari examine her role as a child star during the late 1940s and 1950s, when she was credited with boosting the Japanese public morale as the spunky singing orphan in the face of wartime devastation and subsequent reconstruction. The voice of that child star seemed preternaturally mature—for some listeners, embarrassingly so—not only for its low register but also for its embrace of both the jazz-inflected, sensual rhythms of boogie-woogie and the more sentimental genres that seemed to arc back to premodern Japan (Shamoon 2009, 134–136). During that period, she symbolized Japan's urban scramble of contradictions that placed old values and practices in flux, while embracing new, sometimes sordid, ways with both enthusiasm and ambivalence (Dower 1999, 148–153). Japan's postwar modernity must be framed within the context of a nation defeated politically, economically, and even to an extent culturally. The Allied occupation (1945–1952) swept in reforms that censored forms of popular culture with any references to feudalism qua militarism. Taken as part of this framework, Misora Hibari represented the optimistic "Tokyo Kid" (after the 1950 film in which she starred and for which she sang the title song) who could sing her way through tough times with an eclectic mix of American jazz-inspired upbeat numbers and melancholic Japanese ballads. Her musical scrappiness was postwar Japan's necessary flexibility for survival (Ōshita 1989).

Hibari's transition from the immediate postwar period of the 1940s and 1950s to the Jet Age of the 1960s and 1970s reflects a slightly different story. The survival mentality and hard work of the previous decades had provided for a degree of material comfort and technological innovation by which Japan could conceive of itself as approaching standards of the rest of the industrial world.

The period itself celebrated mobility and modernity as interlinked strands, symbolized most clearly by jets, which effectively shrank distances between global cities, and jet-setters as glamorous icons of the era (Yano 2013). (Hibari herself had traveled by air as a child star to Hawai'i and California in 1950; she continued to do so as an adult in the decades that followed, eventually purchasing a condominium in Honolulu.)

During the period of the 1960s and 1970s, not only did Hibari have to engineer the shift from child star to young female adult singer, but she also confronted musical shifts that spelled out generational changes: Group Sounds and protest songs inspired by the likes of the Beatles and Bob Dylan filled the Japanese air waves. In many ways, Hibari's musical evolution took place amid a global shift in popular music with the birth of rebel-inspired rock music in the 1950s and the music of a highly politicized counterculture in the 1960s and 1970s as a backdrop. Thus, youth-oriented music, from the Beatles (who toured Japan in 1966) to Bob Dylan, sweeping many parts of the industrial world and student movements and other political protests (e.g., Tokyo University in 1968) form part of the context for musical shifts in Japan. This is not to claim that Hibari was part of the counterculture movement—far from it. Rather, her music represented a complex apolitical swath of Japanese pop music that was part of her persona and the period. The Japanese popular music industry's reaction to these broader changes came amid both left-wing protests and the politically conservative move toward growing cultural nationalism.

Jet Age Hibari of the 1960s and 1970s inhabited this complex mix, symbolized in no small way by the 1964 Tokyo Olympics and the development of the world's fastest train *(shinkansen)*. Both of these gave Japan bragging rights to cosmopolitan achievements, placing Japan on a par with other industrial countries in terms of staging a major international event (the first Olympics held in Asia), as well as dazzling visitors with the technological prowess that surpassed other nations. These elements clearly announced that postwar recovery and reconstruction were over. In their place lay a newfound modernity by which Japan could define itself as not a mere "modernizer" following a Western model but on its own terms through achievements that went beyond other nations. At the same time that foreigners were arriving in Japan for the global stage of the Olympics, the Japanese government allowed more citizens to take part in the stage itself by traveling internationally. As of April 1, 1964, Japanese citizens were allowed to travel abroad freely, and many of them did as part of their newly achieved prosperity. Clearly and dramatically, through jets, bullet trains, and international events, Japan was on the move, upward and outward.

Amid these moves, Misora Hibari's music of the 1960s and 1970s demonstrates the increasing tensions of simultaneously looking outward and inward. In fact, Jet Age Hibari sang of a Japan emplaced within the larger global community far more than displaced by it, through a burgeoning cultural nationalism that created its own homespun version of modernity. I next discuss the contradictions of that emplacement within postwar modernity, analyzing ways in which moving forward engaged a continual remix of looking back.

Rockabilly Geisha: Hibari's Music on the Move

Hibari's Jet Age remix included songs and films that embraced Japan's long-standing consumption and production of American popular song genres. From the beginning of her career as a child star of the late 1940s and 1950s, Hibari, like other popular singers in Japan, sang jazz-inspired boogie-woogie, mambo, samba, and other songs of the American-dominated postwar era. America represented upbeat, dance-inspired, energetic modernity, syncretized in Hibari songs such as "Rockabilly Geisha" (1960). Such a song proved that an American form such as rockabilly—an early style of rock from the 1950s whose name combined rock 'n' roll with hillbilly—could be combined with a Japanese figure such as geisha, as much as that the Japanese figure could find expression in an American form. The achievement for Japanese was their own versatility in taking on any number of Western or, more specifically, American forms as their own. Jet Age Japan thus constituted itself repeatedly in these indigenized versions of America, taking these circulating foreign forms and making them their own.[1]

The music industry created different levels of indigenization. At the minimal level, Japanese singers such as Misora Hibari sang straightforward cover performances of American songs. In fact, Hibari released whole albums of jazz and popular American standards with little change in their arrangement or singing style. The point, in fact, was not to change what had been established as a globally successful standard. Rather, Hibari's recordings were meant to replicate the originals as closely as possible, giving the process of covering a certain triumphal sense for the singer and even the nation. Covering English-language popular songs demonstrated Hibari's versatility: she could successfully mimic, reproducing the syllables of a language that she did not understand or speak. In effect, she could replicate the language of World War II's victors, English-speaking, presumably white, America. As her tongue and lips formed around the foreign words, they represented hours of careful listening and practice of sounds as exotic effects. The voice that resulted from these utterances carried a weight all its own: draped in the finery of global prestige, it enacted a sonic spectacle of wonder that a Japanese could sound so convincingly like an American, at least to Japanese ears. With this, Hibari's voice seemed limitless.

The question arises, what meanings might be given Hibari, as she performs, thus, whiteface, covering American pop songs? And further, what ironies might we fathom, particularly with many of these songs originating as African American–linked music? (Note the inclusion of other songs of foreign origin, such as Spanish, Latin, French, and Hawaiian—also Indonesian popular song; cf. Pope 1993.) This is globalized minstrelsy, doubly or triply embedded: yellowface performing whiteface performing black-/brownface. The racialized effect is as dizzying as the Jet Age itself, shifting perspectives at warp speed. (This racialized minstrelsy also references the early Jazz Age, especially with singers such as the Jewish Lithuanian American singer Al Jolson, 1886–1950, who gained acclaim particularly with his blackface performances.) In Hibari's singing Hoagy Carmichael's "Stardust" or Duke Ellington's jazz standard "Take the 'A' Train" or Harry Belafonte's "Banana Boat Song" (patterned after a Jamaican folk song and popularized as a huge international hit in 1956 by Belafonte), could her mimicry be interpreted as a spectacle of Japan's assimilation in adopting the racialized idioms of the American popular music industry?

Anne Cheng's work on what she calls "the melancholy of race" in assimilationist America is useful here. Cheng proposes a model of identity for minorities in the United States based in "racial melancholia"—"a condition of endless self-impoverishment" by which persons of color coexist under a pervasive, dominant umbrella of whiteness resulting in an internalized sense of grief and loss (2001, 8). Cheng analyzes "the constitutive role that grief plays in racial/ethnic subject-formation" in the United States (xi). Thus, "melancholia alludes not to loss per se but to the entangled relationship with loss" (8). Applying Cheng's formulation to Misora Hibari requires reframing Japan within larger geopolitics of race and nation—a defeated country attempting to assimilate in the image of the victors. If postwar Japan may be interpreted as at least initially assimilationist in its appetite for American idioms, then part of those idioms was the racialized processes of the popular music world. Within this picture, Japan's melancholia is not only racialized (Japanese versus whites, including attitudes toward African American–derived expressive forms) but also nationalized (Japan versus America). In this way, the "melancholia" or grieving through a sense of loss in postwar Japan becomes constitutive of the nation's own subject position framed within the continuing presence of the United States, even well beyond the end of American occupation in 1952. However, the "grief" of which Cheng writes is interpreted in Japan as a public investment not so much in loss (at least at the time) but in exhilarating, even heady, gain—an expanded repertoire of expression within global idioms of pop power that includes Americana (in its eclectic appropriation) while not entirely excluding Japan. This is boogie-woogie as both fraught and fun. Jet Age Hibari (and Japan) went beyond assimilation to double appropriation.

Let us critically examine boogie-woogie and other elements of that expanded repertoire of American expression. In fact, the racial irony of Misora Hibari's (and other Japanese singers') whiteface exists multiply. On the one hand, many American popular hits that Hibari covered happen to represent a highly politicized, historical relationship with peoples of color, whether African Americans (e.g., jazz, rhythm and blues), Latin Americans (e.g., mambo, samba, bossa nova), or even Hawaiians (e.g., Hawaiian songs). America's production and consumption of these popular music forms through movies and recordings became the basis of much of the industrial world's consumption of these musics, including Japan. This was modernity as America's co-optation built into the historical background behind popular songs and their racialized performances. Asian performance of this repertoire engages deeply in such problematic modernity.

On the other hand, Misora Hibari herself represents the irony of the Japanese popular music stage, often populated by hidden Koreans. One of the most persistent rumors that dogged Hibari throughout her career is that of possible Korean ethnicity (cf. Bourdaghs 2012, 79–83). Jean-Noel Kapferer (1990) has identified two critical components to rumor: (1) the importance or significance of an item of information to a community and (2) that item's ambiguity. To these I would add a third component: sensationalism or transgressiveness within the dominant code of the community. The lingering rumors of Hibari's Korean ethnicity provide further irony to reinterpreting her performance as "racial melancholia." This form of melancholia is made poignant through a history of rancorous minority relations within Japan (particularly with *zainichi,* Koreans born and raised in Japan) and processes of passing. This is rumor that has its place as rumor, not as fact to be confirmed or refuted. Shrouded as rumor, this form of racial melancholia carries its own virus-like quality.

This double racial irony—(1) yellowface performing whiteface cum black-/brownface and (2) rumored Korean performing as a Japanese singer—frames Hibari's performances multiply. Racialized mimicry—existing simultaneously at different levels, referencing different countries and circulations of song—makes for a tangled array of meanings and identities for which the Jet Age becomes an apt metaphor. Whereas travel by jets may have shrunk distances and sense of time, this did not mean that these juxtapositions necessarily meant more than superficial rearrangements of nations, cultures, and peoples. The distances traversed by jets in relatively short amounts of time often reproduced hierarchies of capital and power, rather than questioning or dismantling them. Likewise, the many-layered mimicry performances represented by Misora Hibari meant only easy rearrangements rather than more profound shifts of power.

Hibari's performances linked to American popular songs went beyond strict cover versions such as these. At the next level of indigenization, several newly created songs of the 1960s in Japan built on American-inspired themes, such as the Latin dance craze: "Naki warai no mambo" (1960; note that her most famous mambo was "Omatsuri mambo" [1954]), "Bye Bye Beguine" (1966), "Ai no bossa nova" (1968), "Hibari no cha cha cha." Further, Hibari sang more than jazz and pop standards from America's past. Her music followed newer trends that portend an incipient rock-infused culture, as well. For example, the twist, a wildly popular song and dance craze in the United States prompted by Chubby Checker's 1960 hit "The Twist," generated Hibari's own versions only two years later: "Hibari no twist" (1962) and "Blue twist" (1962). The sense of near coevalness, with little time lag between the forefront of popular music in the United States and Japan, became important signposts of achievement not only for the Japanese music industry but also for Hibari as representative of one segment of it. As was appropriate to the Jet Age, some Hibari songs such as "Aloha no minato" (1960) sang of exotic places, especially Hawai'i, where she performed to primarily Japanese American audiences. Hibari thus became part of public bragging rights of the nation's own modernity, demonstrating to Japanese that they could swing like the best of them.

This kind of public achievement gained further traction when one considered who was doing the singing—that is, one of the most central figures of the Japanese popular music world. Hibari's place as a people's singer—from child star to adult songstress—meant that her achievements were those of "the people" and of the time. Arising from their midst, living lives of the postwar period with them, and singing an eclectic mix of American songs (among others) and Japanese ballads, Hibari's performance suggested that this version of modernity belonged not only to the privileged but to the people themselves. She represented the possibility of a domestically wrought, cosmopolitan modernity available even to people from fishmonger families.

These various engagements with the foreign, specifically through covering American songs of a variety of origins as part of the Jet Age, demonstrated some of Misora Hibari's inevitable ties to the era. Hibari may not have been a true jetsetter, but she could cover the songs that spun around the world. Even as she boarded jets and flew them to far-off destinations such as California, Hawai'i, and Brazil, she typically did so within the context of an ethnic bubble of audiences, entourages, and fans of Japanese ancestry. Thus, even when she was not literally home, she was at home. Likewise, Hibari may not have performed at the cutting edge of the avant-garde, but neither was she entirely out of step with the times. Rather, she performed the foreign, including Japanese indigenized forms, as part of her own virtuosity. Her skill lay in the expertise of her versatile range, code-switching genres and voices as the context demanded (Wajima 2010, quoted in Tong 2015, 32). By doing so, she made that range accessible to Japanese themselves, who could play it safe even when dabbling in the borders of the foreign.

Hibari's Gender-Bending Moves

That virtuosic range included constant pulling back to performances of "Japan." The rise of cultural nationalism during the Jet Age pitted centrifugal seductions (pulling away from Japan) against centripetal yearnings (pushing inward to Japan). Here were Jet Age negotiations away from Japan and toward Americana against the nostalgic tug of cultural nationalism, with its countermove back to Japan's core. These negotiations were spatial (outward versus inward), temporal (future/present versus past), transnational (America/the West versus Japan), and finally epochal (labeled as modern versus traditional). They encode divides between what has been labeled *wa-* (Japan originated) versus *yoo-* (Western originated): whole swaths of everyday life in contemporary Japan occupy these divides as consumer choices. Even as these divisions represent monolithic constructions of "Japan" and "the West," they have become part of the semantic code that divides many goods and practices in Japan throughout the twentieth- and twenty-first centuries. What these distinct and ongoing divisions create is a space for both—labeled "Japan" and "the West"—within the contemporary world. In other words, in spite of what might look like a pervasively "Westernized" place, contemporary Japan upholds consumer choices of something called "Japan" as well. Furthermore, the veracity of products and practices within these categories is of less importance than maintaining the categories themselves. Musically, too, the labels and categories have been manipulated for sales purposes. As Misora Hibari came to more closely and consistently inhabit a *wa-* musical space of *enka,* so, too, did her performances include aspects linked to premodern settings.

One such premodern stage practice was cross-dressing. Japanese theater has long embraced the performativity of gender in premodern genres such as Kabuki and Noh in which all actors are male and perform roles whether male or female, as well as modern genres such as *takarazuka* in which all actors are female, performing both male and female roles (cf. Robertson 1998; Mezur 2005). When Hibari was fifteen years old, her mother/manager felt that in order for her to make the successful transition from child to adult star, she should broaden her stage image. Hibari thus performed in period dramas in cross-dressed roles as a young sword-fighting samurai, for which she gained widespread acclaim. Tying Hibari to *jidai-geki* (period drama) by way of cross-dressed (as well as non-crossed-dressed) roles became a significant means to tie Hibari to a premodern past. It was also a way of demonstrating her versatility as a hallmark of virtuosity. Thus, Hibari's cross-gendered, cross-historical performance paralleled her many cross-genre, cross-national performances. Indeed, Jet Age Hibari performed drag multiply and deftly.

Throughout Hibari's career, these cross-dressed roles in period costume became one of her hallmarks. When I have attended yearly fan-club video celebrations of her birthday, among the performances that have received the most enthusiastic response were those in which she played boys or men. In a 2009 interview with three of her female fans, all in their sixties and seventies, the women spoke girlishly, even giddily, about Hibari, miming the way their hearts fluttered when they saw her onstage, especially when she performed as a man. One woman fell backward in her seat on the floor in demonstration of how seeing Hibari onstage "knocked her off her feet." What these women talked about was not the cool, rational appreciation of an accomplished singer so much as, by their own admission, sexual heat, expressed bodily and verbally in Japanese as *horechau* (falling in love, helplessly, rapturously). Jackie Stacey's work on female spectatorship finds parallel here: "The spectator/star relationship significantly concerns forms of intimacy between femininities. These forms of intimacy may not be direct articulations of an 'erotic object choice'; nevertheless, there is an obvious homoeroticism to some of the spectator/star relationships" (1994, 172–173). Furthermore, Hibari is regarded within Japanese male homosexual communities as a particular icon—not unlike Judy Garland in the United States—as what Jonathan Mackintosh calls "the homo cultural sensibility of Misora's iconic personality," finding a place within Japanese men's gay culture magazines (2012, 137–138, 143).

Fan reactions such as these fuel further speculation about Hibari's own sexuality, rumors of which join those of her Korean ethnicity (Mackintosh 2012, 143, 146n14). These rumors come amid a certain normativity in Japan for strong same-sex bonds and intimacy, especially among girls (Shamoon 2012, 35; Imada 2007, 194). Hibari's speculative sexuality is grounded in the fact that she married only briefly and never had a child of her own. It is also grounded in her own persona of straight-talking swagger, from her iconic childhood role as the spunky orphan Tokyo Kid. Social class plays a significant part in interpreting Hibari, from her cross-genderings to her personal life. Somatic and psychosocial cues tie these strands together synergistically: a female with a low, husky speaking voice; speech patterns themselves that encode lower-class, masculine utterances in their clipped, straightforward manner; a range of bodily positions, including a performative physical stance that tends toward broader, planar positions with a low center of gravity specifically when playing men. These elements signal overlapping codes of blue-collar, masculine-coded identities and the crossed interpretations of these. One fan told me of a filmed interview with Hibari enjoying herself at a gay bar, accompanied by a *takarazuka otokoyaku* (female actor who plays men's roles), surrounded by cross-dressing hosts. I want to emphasize that none of this proves or disproves a particular sexual identity, but it does demonstrate the gender play at work in much of the entertainment world in Japan, as well as the acknowledged titillation that gender/sex play invokes. It is the work of rumor—particularly claiming a public-private space—that makes sexuality and ethnicity come alive with the frisson of ambiguity.

Cross-gendering occupied Misora Hibari in both films and songs. What is worthwhile noting is the fact that this crossing, at least in adulthood, is historically embedded as part of the process constantly pulling her to the past. Thus, the crossing in films typically occurs within the context of *jidai-geki;* likewise, her crossing in song often references the past, performed in a kimono worn like a man's, with her obi slung low. These adult crossings set in the past postdate those of her childhood performances, draped with modern sartorial gender ambiguity—whether as the top-hatted, tuxedoed singer in *Kanashiki kuchibue* (1949) or the streetwise orphan in overalls and cap in *Tokyo Kid* (1950). As a prepubescent actress and singer, Hibari could cross easily and broadly, regardless of time period or genre of movie. However, once she reached late adolescence and adulthood, her crossing centered on period pieces, defining and containing possibilities of the "sexual heat" spoken of by her fans.

This is Jet Age Hibari, whose drag mimes not merely men but the iconicity of men past. The samurai that Hibari depicts nostalgically represents the prototypical Japanese warrior, held to a code of honor from a feudal past when Japan did not have to contend with the West. The retro-poignancy of her cross-gendered, Jet Age performance distills Japan as not only premodern but, more importantly, pre-Western. Her signature cross-gendered song and one of her biggest hits is "Yawara" (Judo) from 1964, for which she won the Record of the Year prize in the Japanese music industry in 1965 (Bourdaghs 2012, 69–70). She typically performed this song in a kimono with obi slung low and with short hair styled like a man's, and her gestures during performance flirt with the audience (a mix of men and women) in winking gender play. Her legs positioned stalwartly and slightly apart, one hand tucked into her kimono at the chest as a man would, her eyes looking straight at the camera, she revels in the premodern, *jidai-geki*-inspired stoicism of her masculine performance. Vocally, she embodies a man as well, exaggerating her low register, husky intonation, and guttural utterances. She draws her voice down, emanating from the *hara* (abdomen), as she draws down her center of gravity in her stance. Although the music may be modern (that is, performed on Western instruments in a major key), the sensibility of the song and its performance speak to premodern resources of gendered expression. Here is the sound of modernity on Japan's terms, singing to the simultaneity of *wa-* and *yoo-* that is part of its context.

Singing National Tears

Cross-gendering may pull Jet Age Hibari back in time, but what pulls Hibari closer, centripetally inward, to what is considered Japan's core is emotion and specifically tears. Beginning with a 1949 childhood film, *Kanashiki kuchibue* (Mournful whistle), in which her tears flowed from the onions she peels, through to her final performance months before her death, they never stopped flowing. Known over the course of the Jet Age as the "Queen of *Enka*," Hibari performed to greatest acclaim in Japan as performer of the genre whose hallmark is its emotional expression. Indeed, it is heartbreak that pulls listeners back, individually and collectively, to *enka*, with its reputation as expression of *nihonjin no kokoro* (the heart/soul of Japanese).

Her signature song, "Kanashii sake" (Mournful sake, 1966), written by Japan's leading composer, Koga Masao (1904–1978; also composed "Yawara"), is one in which she is reputed to have cried during every performance. Inasmuch as this song draws on stereotypical *enka* images—alone at a bar, a woman weeps for the man who left her—it may be thought of as the prototypical template of the genre. Besides the sung verses, the song includes a spoken recitative that allows Hibari to step from behind the lyrics and speak even more intimately from the heart. In fact, it is toward the end of the recitative, after she has explained her futile attempts to drown her sorrow in drink, that Hibari stereotypically begins to break down in tears. Once the tears begin, they do not end, leaving the singer's face tear streaked, even amid the performative wonder of never missing a note. Hibari's emotionalism on the concert stage, in fact, became more pronounced as she grew older, as if maturity bred not complacency but heightened, performative angst marked by tears. A comparison of performances of "Kanashii sake," for example, shows that in her later years, she slowed the tempo, pared accompaniment down to solo guitar, and inserted greater rhythmic flexibility (i.e., rubato). In other words, she increasingly milked the performative moment. The result is a more vocally embellished, musically nuanced, dramatically emotive performance.

Time Warp Blues

The tear-streaked face and voice of Misora Hibari in performances of "Kanashii sake" act as mnemonic not only for individual, personal pasts but more importantly for a sense of national pastness. That is, they form part of the *wa-* versus *yoo-* divide, sober Japan versus flashy West, emotion-filled depth versus hedonistic superficiality, tradition versus modernity. These divides structure the conversation asking, who are we Japanese? If Japan during the 1960s and 1970s may be characterized by the mobility and modernity of the heady Jet Age, then that same period incorporated its own self-reflexive reaction to such rapid change, folding back into itself as a form of cultural nationalism. Misora Hibari's performances in song and film demonstrate this juxtaposition as a virtue. Her literal and figurative covers of American popular songs proved that she (and Japan) could do it—that is, Hibari as Japan could perform, among other things, some of the conditions of America's racialized history, without necessarily concerning itself with the significance or depth of that history. Provocatively put, this is "yellowface" (Hibari) in performative admixtures of "blackface" (jazz) and "brownface" (Latin songs) in the context of whiteface America. The literal cover songs became part of Hibari's novelty act as racial-national mimicry. Meanwhile, figurative cover songs (i.e., Japanese songs based in American forms) established her appropriation of foreign genres—or Japanese reinterpretations of those genres. The many songs in Hibari's repertoire titled "Hibari no . . ." (Hibari's . . .) demonstrate the range of her ownership: these include songs based in Japanese genres, such as "Hibari no Sado Jowa" (Hibari's folksong from Sado Island) and "Hibari no komori uta" (Hibari's lullaby), as well as those based in American genres, such as "Hibari no twist" and "Hibari no cha cha cha." "Hibari no . . ." asserts nothing less than "Nihon no . . ." (Japan's songs).

Virtuosity, however, has its limits. Bravado skill does not necessarily tie audiences to performers, except as a kind of rational appreciation for technique. What ties Japanese audiences to Hibari are her ties to them, in particular through the lens of the nation. Tracing the history of postwar Japan through the history of Misora Hibari's career has by now become a common trope of museums, newspaper articles, and television shows in her honor. A collection of Hibari's songs, for example, emphasizes this trope with the title *A—Shōwa. Hibari to tomo ni* (Ah—Shōwa era: Together with Hibari; Hibari Production, 2007). This trope scripts her life alongside that of the Shōwa era and more specifically with postwar Japan, linking events and songs. Within this national spotlight, the jazzy rhythms of covering foreign (American) songs carries only superficial appeal. By comparison, the rhythms of a cross-gendered performance of heroes past or the tears shed over lingering guitar tremolos hold greater depth of emotional ties linking the nation to this performer who could do it all.

This is not to suggest by any means that all of Japan fawned over Hibari's on- and off-stage performances. Indeed, throughout her life, as much as she was acclaimed by many people, she was also denigrated by others. She was dogged by controversy, whether it was for a voice too low for a child singing songs that were too adult-like or for her brother's ties to *yakuza,* which banned her from the Nihon Hōsō Kyokai (NHK) stage. She imparted an air of crude earthiness, rather than refinement. But this is exactly the position from which she could be heralded as the "people's singer," her fans dubbing themselves *Hibari no sedai* (Hibari's generation). Hers is a gendered, classed, generational, and national position. Thus, her tears flow as one whose suffering parades her vulnerability, shared with "the people," an era, and a nation. In fact, tears constitute this particular Asian modernity in song.

These contradictions frame Hibari's Jet Age stage. Challenged by wave after wave of new sounds and images, many from the United States, she eventually became rebranded as a bastion of things Japanese. If Misora Hibari emerged as a poster child of things Japanese in the Jet Age, then that version of Japan included ironic admixtures of racial minority positions and nostalgized retreats into premodern forms. The time warp of Misora Hibari, however, represents more than retreat. Rather, it represents an ongoing conversation, a consumer choice between *wa-* and *yoo-*, a display of virtuosic mimicry amid constant bidding for global prestige. This form of modernity, shaped to suit Japan's ends through global means, is not pre- or post- but neo- in its willful appropriation.

Japan's Modern Diva

In conclusion, let us take a final gendered twist in considering Misora Hibari as a case study in the public voice, with a spotlight on the modern diva. The positionality of the diva points to the interrelationships between gender, social class, public culture, celebrity, media, voice, affect, and modernity. The very stuff of which the diva sings, and often embodies in her life, is that of love—heteronormative in song, sometimes homosexual in fandom (including a significant contingent of gay male fandom). She performs in a heightened manner, even as she lives a life spectacularized by her misdeeds amid the continual media spotlight. Her life transgresses the domestic figure of patriarchal ideology and instead represents the working woman and, even more problematically, the public woman, the woman onstage. She is always, thus, a bad girl—or at least a transgressive one. Melisse Lafrance identifies "disruptive divas" as her field of study, focusing on "creative interrogation of dominant normative systems" and the ability of the female singer's music to "disquiet and unsettle the listener" (2002, 2). Here, by contrast, I am suggesting that the diva by her very public gendered position and spectacularized performance, often against the backdrop of a tumultuous personal life, creates her own inherent "disruption." Even when she sings mainstream, the diva may very well transgress. It is the intensity of the diva and her life—both on- and off-stage, transmitted aurally and figuratively—that makes of Hibari a parable of modernity in contemporary Japan.

That parable crowns Hibari multiply, as the spunky orphan, the adult sufferer, the diva superstar. At the core of these shifting images lies emotion expressed as nostalgized public discourse. Hibari's fandom rests not only on ascribed musical ability but also on the achievements of her personal hardships symbolized by sung tears as the sufferer eternal. Hibari, transgressor with the golden heart, is transfigured posthumously as goddess of mercy. She sheds tears as recipient of public compassion and forgiveness, even as she dispenses support and protection to her public. The source of that compassion, as the consumer of those tears, is those who are bound together through her and to each other—whether as Hibari's rapidly aging generation or more generally that of postwar Japan. The bonds draw her in close, sharing as she does a position and an era simultaneously celebrated for its public, economic, very modern achievements and tainted by its more private, social upheavals. The very position of this child star cum diva—that is, Misora Hibari as postwar Japan—celebrates such a taint of transgression in the glitter of the stage, the melodrama of national sung tears, and the ambivalence of modernity itself.

The virtuosity of the diva's voice suggests the special place of song, culturally embedded as that most elemental of human utterances. If song is positioned as the form of communication that begins where words alone leave off, then the diva who performs song becomes its ultimate bearer. She provides the dopamine-infused high for her audiences, sometimes perceived as at no small cost to herself. She thus becomes the sacrificial sufferer. The virtuosity of the diva's voice contrasts with her off-stage, often less-than-virtuous life. But note that the two are part and parcel of the same gendered phenomenon: here is public achievement that collides with power structures framed within modernity—often resulting in moral, emotional, and personal tragedies. The melodrama of her song parallels the melodrama of her life, whether from alcohol, divorce, or rumor. These elements—virtuosity without virtue, melodrama that pays a price—suggest ways by which the diva holds an inevitably fraught position. She invokes love-hate relationships, challenging while drawing on stereotypes, transgressing while transcending gendered norms. Hers is intimacy as transgressive spectacle—seen through the lens of the close-up, heard through the amplification of the microphone. And that spectacle revolves most critically around the voice, as it whispers, moans, growls, and cries its way to its diva position. Unlike the emperor, who could barely be heard throughout his life, Misora Hibari's voice was heard relentlessly, her voice tracing her own tragic life arc. It was her voice that grabbed the spotlight, plying the air waves through its last vibrato. Misora Hibari, diva of Japan's postwar modernity, understood the centrality of this highly mediated vocal positioning. As she shifted with the times to make the era her own, her voice swelling and dipping, she filled the stage with a larger-than-life presence. In doing so, she performed the era as a litany of her own triumphs and transgressions, vocalizing Japan's fraught modernity.

Notes

1. One two-disc compilation titled *Love! Hibari Misora Jazz and Standard Complete Collection 1955–1966* includes the following songs: CD 1: 1. Love, 2. Lover Come Back to Me, 3. Get Out and Get under the Moon, 4. Torna a Surriento, 5. Core'ngrato, 6. Jeux interdits, 7. I Love Paris, 8. La vie en rose, 9. C'est magnifique, 10. Hymne a l'amour, 11. Ogonek, 12. Love Is a Many Splendoured Thing, 13. Toraji, 14. Bengawan Solo, 15. Sampa guita, 16. Aloha oe, 17. I Can't Tell a Waltz from a Tango, 18. Mack the Knife, 19. Cielito lindo, 20. Cu cu ru cu cu Paloma; CD 2: 1. Take the 'A' Train, 2. Stardust, 3. Walkin' My Baby Back Home, 4. Blueberry Hill, 5. Just One of Those Things, 6. Love Me or Leave Me, 7. Cry Me a River, 8. Love Letters, 9. The Lonely One, 10. La Novia, 11. It's Only a Paper Moon, 12. Dreaming of Home and Mother, 13. Loch Lomond, 14. Danny Boy, 15. Over the Rainbow, 16. Too Young, 17. Red Sails in the Sunset, 18. Pretend, 19. Fascination, 20. Ave Maria, 21. On London Bridge.

References

Bix, Herbert. 2000. *Hirohito and the Making of Modern Japan.* New York: Harper.

Bourdaghs, Michael K. 2012. *Sayonara Amerika, Sayonara Nippon.* New York: Columbia University Press.

Cheng, Anne. 2001. *The Melancholy of Race: Psychoanalysis, Assimilation, and Hidden Grief.* Oxford: Oxford University Press.

Dower, John. 1999. *Embracing Defeat: Japan in the Wake of World War II.* New York: Norton.

Harkness, Nicholas. 2013. *Songs of Seoul: An Ethnography of Voice and Voicing in Christian South Korea.* Berkeley: University of California Press.

Imada Erika. 2007. *Shōjo no shakaishi* [A social history of the shōjo]. Tokyo: Keisō Shobō.

Kapferer, Jean-Noel. 1990. *Rumors: Uses, Interpretations, and Images.* New York: Transaction.

Lafrance, Melisse. 2002. "A Cultural Studies Approach to Women and Popular Music." In *Disruptive Divas; Feminism, Identity and Popular Music,* edited by Lori Burns and Melisse Lafrance, 1–29. New York: Routledge.

Mackintosh, Jonathan D. 2012. "The Homo Cultures of Iconic Personality in Japan: Mishima Yukio and Misora Hibari." In *Idols and Celebrity in Japanese Media Culture,* edited by Patrick W. Galbraith and Jason G. Karlin, 131–149. London: Palgrave Macmillan.

Mezur, Katherine. 2005. *Beautiful Boys / Outlaw Bodies; Devising Kabuki Female-Likeness.* London: Palgrave Macmillan.

Ochoa Gautier, Ana Maria. 2014. *Aurality: Listening and Knowledge in Nineteenth-Century Colombia.* Durham, NC: Duke University Press.

Ōshita Eiji. 1989. *Misora Hibari: Jidai o utau* [Misora Hibari: Singing of an era]. Tokyo: Shinchō Bunko.

Pope, Edgar W. 1993. "Songs of Empire: Continental Asia in Japanese Wartime Popular Music." PhD diss., University of Washington.

Robertson, Jennifer. 1998. *Takarazuka: Sexual Politics and Popular Culture in Modern Japan*. Berkeley: University of California Press.

Schilling, Mark. 1997. *Encyclopedia of Japanese Pop Culture*. New York: Weatherhill.

Shamoon, Deborah. 2009. "Misora Hibari and the Girl Star in Postwar Japanese Cinema," *Signs: Journal of Women in Culture and Society* 35 (1): 131–155.

———. 2012. *Passionate Friendship: The Aesthetics of Girls' Culture in Japan*. Honolulu: University of Hawai'i Press.

Stacey, Jackie. 1994. *Star Gazing: Hollywood Cinema and Female Spectatorship*. New York: Routledge.

Tong Koon Fung Benny. 2015. "A Tale of Two Stars: Understanding the Establishment of Femininity in *Enka* through Misora Hibari and Fuji Keiko." *Situations* 8 (1): 23–44.

Wajima Yūsuke. 2010. *Hajimerareta 'nihon no kokoro' shinwa—'Enka' o meguru sengotaishū-ongakushi* [The created myth of the heart/soul of Japan: Postwar popular music history based on *enka*]. Tokyo: Kōbunsha Shinsho.

Yano, Christine R. 2013. "Jet Age Nationhood: Pan American World Airways in Postwar Japan." In *Japan since 1945: From Postwar to Post-Bubble*, edited by Christopher Gerteis and Timothy George, 208–222. London: Bloomsbury.

CHAPTER 7

Titiek Puspa

GENDERED MODERNITY IN 1960S AND 1970S INDONESIAN POPULAR MUSIC

Andrew N. Weintraub

ALBUM-COVER images of the female pop star Titiek Puspa (1937–) frame the relationship between female bodies, gender, and modernity in 1960s and 1970s Indonesia (figure 7.1). On the *Si kumbang* and *Mengapa harus djumpa* covers, this relationship is presented as a set of contrasting representations. On the *Si kumbang* cover, with hair rolled in a bun *(gelung)* and wearing a distinctly Javanese blouse *(kebaya),* Titiek stares demurely into the distance; in the second pose from the same album cover, with hair piled high and dressed in a form-fitting evening gown and high heels, she fixes her gaze steadily on the viewer. Titiek is presented as both a traditional object of display and a modern subject of action. On the *Mengapa harus djumpa* cover, wearing a *kebaya* (albeit lower cut) and her hair pulled back, she gazes downward with a strong internal focus; while in the second pose, she is wearing her hair down and a shiny blouse, laughing heartily and gesturing actively with her hands. These images suggest a cultural mapping onto two female character types from Javanese mythology: the refined and submissive Sembadra, on the one hand, and the assertive and combative Srikandi, on the other. On the *Taruna djatuh cinta* cover, Titiek has clearly moved closer to Srikandi: standing with legs apart, wearing a pantsuit, arms folded, and hair cut short, she projects a stance of power and unwavering determination. Framed within the shifting political and economic context of 1960s and 1970s Indonesia, Titiek's attire, demeanor, and gaze suggest a range of possible meanings about female agency and power.

The chanteuse and composer Titiek Puspa vocalized the tensions and contradictions of gendered modernity in Indonesia during the socially turbulent 1960s and 1970s. This period of Indonesian history is divided politically by the anti-imperialist "Old Order" (Orde Lama, 1950–1965) of the country's first president, Sukarno, and the pro-Western "New Order" (Orde Baru, 1966–1998) of

Figure 7.1. Left: *Si kumbang* (The ladybug), Mesra Record MP-34; center: *Mengapa harus djumpa* (Why did we have to meet?), Remaco RL-043; right: *Taruna djatuh cinta* (Taruna falls in love), Remaco RL-075.

its second president, Suharto. Titiek cultivated a proximity to male state power—to Sukarno, one of Indonesia's founding fathers, and Suharto, the "Father of Development" *(Bapak pembangunan)*—that amplified her voice and enabled it to circulate more widely and freely than those of other female singers. However, she was not a mouthpiece of these divergent political "orders"; that is, her relatively autonomous voice did not align neatly with either regime. Titiek's voice and body were contested terrain in both presidential regimes, which patronized and celebrated her but also wanted to control her. The patriarchal orders used her as a symbol of proper womanhood in her role as wife and mother, but she developed an image as an independent and successful modern woman who supported her husbands and other family members.

Titiek played an important role in each regime's ideology of modernity, but she also voiced the disjuncture between civil society and the reigning political order. Songs that Titiek composed during Sukarno's anticolonial Old Order point to an emergent soundscape of modernity saturated with American popular music, the specter of capitalism, and female celebrity. In contrast, some of the songs she composed in Suharto's neoliberal New Order period reflect a residual progressive-revolutionary sensibility, a concern for ordinary Indonesians, and a critique of capital-intensive development as the cause of widespread social problems.

In this chapter, I examine Titiek Puspa's songs of the 1960s and 1970s, as they harmonized with and sounded against the two political orders. What musical features defined her as modern? What did this modern woman of the 1960s *sound* like in the transition from the "old" (order) to the "new" (order)? How was she able to survive and flourish as a female artist within the radically contrasting political conditions of the "old" and "new" regimes? How were ideas about gender, culture, and nation projected onto her? How did she vocalize her own agency?

I have chosen to focus on Titiek Puspa's career for several reasons. Singer, composer, film actor, TV star, theater director, cultural ambassador, and advocate for composer's rights, Titiek's career spans virtually the entire history of the republic. Within the history of Indonesian popular music, Titiek is one of a handful of women composers and by far the most prolific (with some five hundred compositions to her credit).[1]

It is important to remember that Titiek did not stand completely alone as an autonomous individual artist. Nor did she always have a "voice" in determining the way she looked or sounded. She composed the lyrics and melodies for her songs, and beginning in 1963, she was credited as the sole composer on nearly all the songs on her albums. However, her male counterparts composed and arranged the instrumental parts to accompany her voice.

In this chapter, I do not show how the songs connected the listener with the "real" Titiek Puspa, nor, conversely, do I examine the constructed nature of her media celebrity.[2] Both of these approaches deserve attention, but I take a different tack. I view Titiek as an individual actor as well as a "figure of modernity," which refers to "persons within a given social formation whom others recognize as symbolizing modern life" (Barker, Harms, and Lindquist 2013, 1). Figures of modernity are not fixed or stable entities; they are "people who loom larger than life because they alternately express and challenge conventional understandings of social types" (ibid.). I am interested in Titiek's career as a social text about gendered modernity, with women at the center. Much has been written about gender ideology in Indonesia, and there is a range of perspectives on the role of women historically. Gender ideology in Indonesia is diverse across the archipelago in terms of ethnicity, religion, and social class, and the meanings attached to gender difference are anything but unitary (Robinson 2009, 11). Throughout this chapter, I utilize the extensive scholarship on gender ideology in Indonesia as a way of situating Titiek Puspa as a symbol of modernity.

Titiek's celebrity status enabled her to express a critique of gendered modernity in a way that the vast majority of women could not. This exceptionalism was due to her status as a celebrity, defined by David Marshall as follows: "In the public sphere, a cluster of individuals are given greater presence and a wider scope of activity and agency than are those who make up the rest of the population. They are allowed to move on the public stage while the rest of us watch. They are allowed to express themselves quite individually and idiosyncratically while the rest of the members of the population are constructed as demographic aggregates" (2006, ix).

Titiek's prolific output of songs and their symbolic meanings in context reveal how she used her voice to narrate themes about women and modernity in

Indonesia. Titiek's life and work are important because women have been historically excluded from narratives about modernity in Indonesia. This is not to say that Titiek's relationship to modernity is singular or totalizing or static. Rather, an analysis of her life and work illuminates the contours of modernity as gendered and in constant flux in Indonesia.

As the center for national media since independence, Jakarta played a dominant role in the production and circulation of texts about gendered modernity. My analysis considers four songs that reflect the social realities of life in Jakarta in the 1960s and 1970s: "Minah gadis dusun" (Minah the village girl, 1964), "Buat adikku" (For my younger sibling, 1966), "Kupu-kupu malam" (Night butterfly, 1977),[3] and "Bimbi" (Bimbi, 1978). All four represent a woman's view of Indonesia's capital city of Jakarta as a gendered space of triumph and tragedy. Three of these songs track the modern girl's passage from the rural province to the city. YouTube contains streaming audio and video of all four songs discussed in this chapter. Readers are encouraged to refer to the recordings while contemplating the points addressed in the text.[4]

Titiek's Biography

Titiek Puspa was born on November 1, 1937, in the district of Tanjung, South Kalimantan, where her Javanese father had taken a job as a hospital attendant. He moved the family to Semarang shortly thereafter. Titiek experienced poverty and hardship as a child. Stories about her childhood in popular print media subsequently captivated audiences who shared the experience of growing up under similar conditions. Her rags-to-riches story demonstrates one of the hallmarks of modernity: the individual ability to transcend one's inherited social and material conditions.

As a young girl, Titiek developed a talent for singing.[5] Singing in public was not considered a reputable profession for a young woman because of its negative associations with hotels, nightlife, dancing bodies, and prostitution. However, despite this unsavory connotation, professional singers were economic actors who often supported husbands, children, and other family members (as Titiek later did). Further, in the 1950s and early 1960s, "[B]eing culturally modern was also to participate in new forms of popular entertainment" (Lindsay 2012, 18). After Indonesian independence, female singers could enjoy greater public media presence, increased economic status, heightened agency, and in some cases, higher social status.

Despite the objections of Titiek's parents, Titiek competed in singing contests in high school. The Semarang branch of the national radio network RRI held regional singing contests to identify talented singers.[6] She won second place in 1954, and she was encouraged by her success to pursue a career as a singer.[7] Throughout the 1950s, she continued to sing at events and for radio broadcasts, shuttling between Semarang and Jakarta. She competed in national singing contests in Jakarta, and although she did not win, she was discovered by Sjaiful Bahri, the director of the national radio ensemble Orkes Studio Djakarta (OSD) from 1954 to 1960, and invited to Jakarta to sing on national broadcasts.

In 1957, at the age of nineteen, Titiek married Kasno, who also disapproved of her being a professional singer. They divorced in mid-1959, while she was two months pregnant with her first child, Petty. Her career continued to prosper; she made her first recording for Lokananta, the national recording company, in 1959.[8] In the same year, Titiek moved to Indonesia's capital city, Jakarta, where she earned a living by performing for parties and radio broadcasts. She gained a reputation as one of the top singers in Jakarta and became a regular member of RRI's Orkes Studio Djakarta in 1960. She worked with the top singers of the era, including Said Effendi, Sri Redjeki, Tuty Daulay, Sam Saimun, and Bing Slamet, the last of whom was especially encouraging and helpful to the young singer.

In February 1960, Titiek married Zainal Ardi, a radio announcer at RRI. That same year, she signed a contract to sing nightly in the lounge at Hotel Des Indes (later renamed Duta Merlin), a top hotel located in the area of Harmoni, Jakarta. Her second daughter, Ella, was born in September 1961. Like Titiek's first husband, Kasno, Zainal did not like her working as a singer, but they had two children to feed. Zainal and Titiek gambled away all her earnings (Endah 2008, 167). They separated in 1963 when he took a job in Germany. In 1964, at the age of twenty-seven, Titiek was already a seasoned professional, performing for radio broadcasts, for parties, on tours (both local and international), and at upscale hotels. She had already been married twice, and she was raising two children on her own.

At RRI, Titiek met Mus Mualim, a talented jazz pianist, composer, and arranger. Mus Mualim (aka Mus Mustafa) became her husband, as well as the arranger of her songs. They made two outstanding albums together, *Si hitam* (Irama LPI 175116) and *Doa Ibu* (Irama LPI 17580). With excellent musicians playing arrangements of jazz and the latest pop music, the music of these two albums was the most sophisticated and modern of its era. The liner notes emphasized the music's complexity as "music that has to be notated," which signaled its modern quality. And like other records produced by the Irama Recording Company, the producers used the most advanced recording technology available in Indonesia. Irama copied the modern practice of the American jazz label Blue Note, which listed the brands and models of the recording equipment and indicated the microphones used for each instrument.

As one of Sukarno's favorite singers, Titiek became a "palace singer" *(penyanyi istana)*, performing at national ceremonies and state functions for visiting foreign dignitaries. She continued as a palace singer in her relationship with Suharto, composing the song "Bapak pembangunan" (Father of development, 1985) for him and becoming friends with the Indonesian first lady Tien Suharto. Titiek's support for these regimes helped to legitimize them, and in exchange, the regimes offered her patronage and freedom from censorship. This quid pro quo relationship was crucial to Titiek's success.

In the 1970s, Titiek continued to perform, compose, and act, appearing in thirteen films. She also created the stories and songs for numerous *operet* (operetta) including *Bawang merah bawang putih* (Red onion, white onion, 1972), *Ketupat Lebaran* (A celebratory food for Lebaran, 1974), and *Kartini manusiawi Kartini* (Kartini's humanity, 1978).[9] In 1972, Titiek organized a group of actors and singers in the capital city (of Jakarta) to perform her *operet*. She named the group PAPIKO, an acronym for the phrase *persatuan artis penyanyi ibu kota* (lit. "the organization of actors and singers in the capital city [of Jakarta]"). These variety shows aired across the country on national television (TVRI) each year on the evening before the end of the fasting month. PAPIKO programs featured new music, dance, elaborate costumes, and impressive sets. Top stars appeared, as well as new talent. The shows were proof, according to Titiek, that "Indonesian artists were capable of performing cabaret as well as those in the West" (Endah 2008, 220). The last program aired in 1985.

Titiek's Music

Modern Western music played an important role in shaping young Indonesian lives during the 1960s and 1970s. During this period, the sounds, images, movements, and gestures from American and British radio programs, recordings, and films became symbolic and material markers of modernity through which Indonesians constructed ideas about their evolving cultural identity.[10] Titiek composed songs in the Western-influenced genre called *hiburan*, which, at the time, was distinguished from other musical genres including *orkes Melayu* (Malay band music), *kroncong* (string-band music) and *seriosa* (semiclassical songs accompanied by Western instruments).[11] *Hiburan* featured songs in the Indonesian language sung by a solo singer or group, structured in Western song forms and accompanied by Western instruments (Yampolsky 1987, 42). The style incorporated elements of Western pop, rock, blues, jazz, and Latin music. Accompaniment was either a small orchestra or a band. It was music for listening, not dancing. *Hiburan* may be analogous to easy listening (also called "orchestral pop"), a genre that was popular in the United States from the 1950s to the 1970s. Songs were composed by (mostly male) professional songwriters and often sung by female singers. The recording company employed producers who worked together with composers, arrangers, singers, and professional accompanying musicians. It was music produced for a national audience and eventually gave way to *pop Indonesia* (Yampolsky 1987, 14).

Although Titiek borrowed liberally from several genres of American music—pop, rock 'n' roll, jazz, Broadway, and blues—her music was not merely a derivative of modern Western sounds. Rather, she appropriated and blended these musics in distinctive and creative ways to define meanings about modern Indonesianness. Being modern was deeply imbricated by Westernization, but Westernization was not a singular or universal practice that embedded itself in non-Western societies. It was the embodiment of a complicated dialogic relationship of power with a long history in colonialism.[12] The important question to ask is, what was the nature of this relationship with Western music, and what did it mean for people in newly independent Indonesia?

In order to understand what a modern Indonesia should sound like and from where it should take its inspiration, I discuss Sukarno's complicated relationship with certain forms of foreign popular music and dance. Sukarno's position was anticolonial and anti-imperialist. In his 1959 political manifesto *(Manipol),* Sukarno used the term *ngak-ngik-ngok* (noisy and grating) to refer to rock 'n' roll, cha-cha, and other forms of music and dance that made people act "crazy" *(gila-gilaan)* (Soekarno 1959b, 62).[13] He believed that young people whose bodies and souls were consumed by those sounds and dances would not be attuned to revolutionary ideals.[14] How could they be true national cultural patriots *(patriot kultural)* if they were consumed by foreign culture *(kebudajaan asing)* (Soekarno 1959a)? How could they imagine completing the revolution if they were consumed by what the national radio station director Soekirman called "sex dream music" ("Kepala Direktorat Radio & TV")?[15] Despite these objections, Sukarno endorsed Western-style musical elements (instruments, song forms, vocal timbres, inter alia), as he himself loved to dance to them (Farram 2007).[16] The sounds of Western pop permeated recordings, even though the lyrics or dance forms were Indonesian. For example, in 1965, Sukarno officially sanctioned an album of songs inspired by Western popular music, performed by Titiek Puspa and a cast of top Jakarta artists (*Mari bersuka ria dengan irama lenso,* Irama LPI 17588). He gave his imprimatur because the songs were in the Indonesian language and accompanied by a dance/rhythm called *lenso* from Ambon.[17]

Why did Sukarno embrace Titiek, while others, like the group Koes Bersaudara, were banned and even jailed?[18] I would suggest that Titiek's personal relationship with Sukarno, as well as other material and symbolic factors, account for this exceptionalism. Titiek was associated with the genre *hiburan,* which had musical elements perceived by national government officials as oppositional to the decadence of Nekolim (neocolonialism, colonialism, and imperialism), particularly American imperialism ("Gerakan Banting Stir," 1965). Instead of weakening the ethical and moral fabric of Indonesian youth, *hiburan* supported the formation of a national culture and spirit (ibid.).

In the 1945 constitution, a woman's status was circumscribed by the principle of *azas kekeluargaan* (family principle), in which the state is likened to a family and each citizen has a defined role. Saskia Wieringa argues that especially during the early years of Sukarno's rule, women were very politically active, but after the tragic events of 1965–1966, they were "re-subordinated" (2002, 1–16). Sukarno "saw the potential power of women as pillars toward nation-building. Because of this, he supported the women's movement, attended women's congresses, gave educational training to women, and, of primary importance, appointed women to his cabinet" (Yulianto 2008, 141). Sukarno loved symbols because they carried on the revolutionary spirit of the times and demonstrated his power and reach. Monuments from this period include the stadium to host the 1962 Asian games (Gelora Bung Karno Stadium, 1962), the Independence Mosque (Masjid Istiqlal), the largest in the world (begun in 1961), and the National Monument (Monumen Nasional, or Monas, begun in 1961). During the early 1960s, Jakarta was full of special days and ceremonies; for example, Sukarno established Kartini Day in 1964 to celebrate Kartini as the model of a progressive woman. He named streets and state enterprises. He also sent artists on missions to perform soft-power diplomacy (Lindsay 2012). For example, Titiek was among a group of artists that participated in a cultural mission *(misi muhibah kebudajaan Indonesia)* to Malaya in 1960[19] and the Netherlands in 1965 (figure 7.2). Sukarno valued music as a symbol of the revolution, and he embraced Titiek's patriotic songs.[20] Further, as my analysis of Titiek's music will demonstrate, she played the symbolic role of the mother, wife, and sister of the national family.

Titiek describes meeting Sukarno in 1960, commenting mostly on his impression of her typically Javanese outfit: "I wore a blouse *[kebaya]* that I had neatly prepared. My skirt *[kain]* was wrapped tightly. I draped a scarf *[selendang]* to hang down over one side of my hips. . . . He praised the way I wore my blouse. 'Good! You really know how to wear a kebaya!' he said seriously" (Endah 2008, 159).

Dressed in a *kain* and *kebaya,* Titiek presented Sukarno with a symbol of Javanese womanhood par excellence. Perhaps because she symbolized an idealized image of a Javanese woman, and due to her status as a "palace singer," Titiek was not censored, even though the Beatles inspired some of her compositions, such as "Marilah kemari" (Irama LPI 175126) and "Potpourri" (Bali BLP 7005)

Figure 7.2. Titiek Puspa (third from left) arriving at Schiphol Airport in Amsterdam as part of a cultural mission with fellow artists (left to right) Jack Lesmana, Bing Slamet, Nien Lesmana, and Munif Bahasuan. On the left is popular Dutch singer Rob de Nijs (June 5, 1965). Photograph by Jac. De Nijs/Anefo. Dutch National Archives 2.24.01.03. Creative Commons 4.0 License, https://na01.safelinks.protection.outlook.com.

(Titiek Puspa, personal communication, 28 April 2016). Further, many of her songs could have been considered *cengeng* (melancholy, overwrought) and subject to censorship due to the sentimentality of their lyrics.[21]

Not only did popular music slip by censors, but composers were clever at masking American-influenced popular songs. Songs with patriotic lyrics *(lagu kebangsaan),* such as Titiek's compositions "Pantang mundur" (Never retreat) and "Kuingin jadi Srikandi" (I want to be [the female warrior] Srikandi) were anything but pure musical expressions of an authentic past. But they were perceived to instill a revolutionary spirit, and so they were encouraged and promoted.[22]

Titiek's Voice and Music in the Sukarno Era

Titiek generally sang in an alto range. Her timbre was warm, husky, and strong, not the restrained soprano voice that would characterize Indonesian pop singers of the late 1960s. Her voice exuded confidence and maturity. She sang with perfect enunciation. The effect was one of elegance, refinement, sophistication, and strength.

Titiek modeled the sound of her voice after recordings of three singers: Anneke Gronloh, Ella Fitzgerald, and Patti Page.[23] She admired Gronloh's vocal power, Fitzgerald's pure tone and tonal accuracy, and Page's lush vocal quality (partly the result of double-tracking). Using a variety of vocal techniques, her singing could deliver a range of emotions. She often inserted a quivering vibrato at key points in a melody to express sadness. She could also generate a whispering quality, and talking in song. Songs of the early 1960s were lyrical, featuring long-drawn-out phrases and gliding melodies.

In the early 1960s, Titiek's songs voiced the concerns of common people *(rakyat)* who were becoming increasingly frustrated with Sukarno. In March 1964, inflation in Indonesia was running at unmanageable highs (100 percent a year), and living standards were at record lows. Indonesia's infrastructure was crumbling, and agricultural production was decreasing. "Minah gadis dusun" (Minah the village girl), released in 1964, expresses these tensions.

"Minah gadis dusun"

In this "pro-rakyat" song, Titiek uses the figure of the young village girl Minah to articulate social class relations between poor rural laborers and rich urban consumers.[24] In a brisk two minutes and forty-eight seconds, the song traces Minah's journey from her village home to the city and back. The city is a visual spectacle beyond her wildest dreams. On the surface, Minah is astounded by the impressive size of the city's tall buildings and monuments, the speed of modern transportation, and the allure of attractive wealthy urbanites. But skyscrapers, cars, and beautiful people cannot satisfy society's material needs. The song argues for the centrality of the periphery (agricultural labor), which provides sustenance for the center (urban consumption). The lyrics are as follows:

Inginkah kawan tahu siapa daku	Friends, do you want to know who I am?
Minah gadis dari dusun di gunung	Minah, a girl from a village in the mountains
Jauh daku berjalan menuruninya	I traveled down from far away
Hanya ingin menjenguk indahnya kota	Only to marvel at the city's beauty
Amboi indah dan megah kotamu kawan	Wow, your city is stunning and wealthy, friends
Rasa daku mimpi di dalam surga	I feel like I'm in a heavenly dream
Jejaka dan gadisnya tampan dan cantik	The young men and women are handsome and pretty

Gedung, tugu dan mobil oh amboi amboi	The buildings, monuments, and cars are awesome
Tapi maaf kawan Daku tak tinggal lama Kekasih hatiku Rindu menanti	But excuse me, friends, I can't stay long The love of my life Is longing for me to come home
Tunggu saja kiriman hasil panenku Daku orang dusun pandai bertani Hanya pesanku kawan jaga negerimu	Just wait to receive my harvest I'm a villager skilled at farming My only request, friends, is to protect your country
Sampai berjumpa nanti salam manisku Salam manisku 3x	Until we meet again, sweet regards Sweet regards

The song begins with the "James Bond theme," the chromatic melody that appears in every James Bond film since *Dr. No* (1962). This musical theme establishes a mood of adventure for Minah, the main character in the narrative. It also puts the story into a dialogue with the West and modernity. Titiek is accompanied by swinging, jazzy lounge music played on piano, guitar, bass, and drums played at a moderate walking tempo. At the end of the song, her voice echoes as it fades into the background, leaving as quickly as it arrived.

Titiek's voice is pitched in a low range, and her articulation is direct and powerful, emphasizing the grounded nature of the main character. Minah does not belong in the city, where no one knows her name ("siapa daku?"). She seemingly has nothing to offer them. She is awestruck as she cranes her neck to take in the beauty of the metropolis that is full of handsome young men and beautiful girls, as well as buildings, monuments, and cars. She expresses her wonderment in the restatement of verse 1 with the word *amboi* (wow!), which she reiterates at the end of the verse.

Verse 2 comes without a break, signaling Minah's desire to return home quickly (to a lover, family, or someone who is waiting for her). Minah has no desire to stay in the city because no one will provide for her there. She makes it clear that it is *her* rice field and *her* skill at farming that produces the food that the city dwellers need to survive. In contrast, the city is useless (for producing sustenance) because all of the land is taken up by buildings, monuments, and cars.

Minah addresses the city dwellers as "friends" *(kawan)*, which was also the word used for "comrade." On the one hand, the text stresses the integration of rural and urban inhabitants as composite parts of the nation, with everyone having a role to play (as members of Sukarno's "National Front"). The celebration of workers and the integration of different functional groups was part of Sukarno's national ideology, which combined the major streams within Indonesian politics: nationalism, religion, and communism (NASAKOM). On the other hand, Titiek expressed the social disparity among the workers and those who exploited them. She states,

> As a child I saw women coming down from the mountains carrying vegetables stacked up high on their heads. It would take months to grow those vegetables. They worked from early morning to afternoon in the hot sun, and they didn't have power tools back then to help them. They would sell their goods at the market for a few bills [money], and that would have to last a month. The city folks would haggle about the price. And they would eat those vegetables quickly without any consideration for the people who grew them. This song expresses the pain of those people [*kepedihan rakyat*]. (Titiek Puspa, personal communication, 29 April 2016)

The disparity between the rural and urban dwellers challenges the idea that they exist in a relationship of harmony and threatens the unity of the nation. As expressed in verse 1, Minah refers to herself as a village girl who lives high up in the mountains, distancing herself from the city. This disunity is even more clear in the last verse; as she is bidding her new friends a "sweet" good-bye, she refers to "your country" *(negerimu),* not "our country" *(negeri kita).* In an interview with the author, Titiek provides the following interpretation of this text in Minah's voice: "Protect your country! You have been given this beautiful country! I have brought food for you. Now you protect it! I am just a simple village girl, after all. You are stunning and wealthy! You should know how to protect it!" (personal communication, 29 April 2016). Titiek invokes the gendered dimension of modernity by contrasting the female space of the village (Minah) with the male space of the city (those who are supposed to "protect" the country). The male protectors, made up of government and military, were not holding up their side of the bargain. As Minah returns home, she tells them to "just wait to receive my harvest" (*tunggu saja kiriman hasil panenku*), as the future of the entire country seems to depend on Minah, a young village girl.

A year after "Minah gadis dusun" was released, the left-leaning anti-imperialism of Sukarno's Guided Democracy was overtaken by the neoliberal hypercapitalism of Suharto's military regime. The change from old to new was ideological, political, economic, and violent, marked by the tragedy of G30S and the subsequent mass murder of somewhere between five hundred thousand and one million citizens.[25] In between the Old and New Orders, Titiek wrote a song titled "Buat adikku" (For my younger sibling), also known as "Arif Rachman Hakim." The song was released on the album *Pita* (Irama LPI 175133, c. 1966).

"Buat adikku"

Arif Rachman Hakim was a medical student at the University of Indonesia who participated in student demonstrations against the government in 1966 ("Arif Rachman Hakim" 1966). The protests were organized around three demands (*tritura,* an acronym for *tiga tuntutan rakyat,* lit. "the people's three demands"): Ritul Kabinet Gestapu (Reorganize the Gestapu cabinet [of ministers]), Bubarkan PKI (Dissolve the PKI), and Turunkan Harga (Lower prices [of rice, fuel]). On February 24, 1966, students carried out a protest against the Old Order. The State Palace (Istana Negara) was heavily guarded by the elite Cakrabirawa regiment made up of military and police personnel. According to official reports, the students ignored the warning shots fired above them, but in the song lyrics, the students were unaware of them. As a result, Arif Rachman Hakim was shot and killed. A mosque at the University of Indonesia and a private radio station (ARH) were named in his honor. He is known as *pahlawan Ampera: Ampera* stands for *am*anat *pe*nderitaan *ra*kyat, "the message of the people's sufferings." The text is as follows:

Gugurmu tujuh pahlawanku	Your deaths, my seven heroes
Menyayat memilukan [?]	Heartbreaking, full of sadness/sorrow
Namun nyala darahmu	Yet the fire in your blood
Jadi penyuluh bangsaku	Became the torch for my nation
Lihatlah yang kau tinggalkan	Look at those you have left behind
Serentak menyusun barisan	Joined together in a line
Membela keadilan	Defending justice
Lenyapkan kelaliman	Eradicating tyranny
Adikku di depan barisan	Younger brother in front of the line
Tak hirau desingnya peluru	Not aware of the warning bullets above
Serukan tuntutan Ampera	Crying out the demands of *Ampera*
Gugurlah tunasku nan mulya	The death of my hope and honor
Kau adikku ini air mata	You, my younger brother, these tears
Mengantar adikku berpulang	Accompany my brother home
Tenanglah kau pahlawan	Be calm heroes
Kami teruskan tujuan	We will continue [fighting for] your goals

"Buat adikku" is in the style of a "pop aria," "a short-lived, rarified genre laden with musical and emotional bombast that can only be described as histrionic and shamelessly manipulative" (Randall 2009, 71). The midsixties British superstar Dusty Springfield made the pop aria famous with songs including "Anyone Who Had a Heart" (1964) and "You Don't Have to Say You Love Me" (1966). Titiek Puspa excelled at these melodramatic ballads, which the musicologist Annie J. Randall describes as having a "compressed musical language—a system of musical signs, a code—through which specific emotions could be telegraphed instantly to [opera] audiences" (2009, 76). Musical devices helped to situate the listener in an emotional story that presents different characters and moods.

In "Buat adikku," Titiek used several devices common to the pop aria, as described by Randall, which are listed here (along with their symbolic associations in parentheses):

- Lengthening or shortening of note values (prolonging or speeding up of action)
- Sudden silence (abrupt break in narrative thread)
- Forceful or delicate attack (startling break with or expected resumption of action)
- Major and minor mode (associated with binaries: positive/negative, happy/sad, joyful/mournful)
- Modulation to a closely related key (move to an expected plot point)
- Acceleration/deceleration (move toward or away from climactic point)
- Gradations of loud and soft (used to intensify or add nuance to other signifiers)
- Chromaticism (complications, uneasiness, a grave situation)

A charging, ascending chromatic passage puts the listener immediately in the mood for the dramatic story that is about to ensue. This passage signifies the Cakrabirawa regiment, the special military unit guarding the palace. It gives way to a plaintive melody played on a violin, with gentle harmonies punctuated on the piano. This passage, only seventeen seconds long, places the song in D minor, but a shift occurs when Titiek's voice enters; this shift emphasizes the related key of F major. However, the first statements of verse 1 defy a clear sense of F major by emphasizing A major and D minor at cadences. The lack of a clear tonal center creates a destabilizing effect that adds to the increasing tension and drama in the story.

The song story begins on a sad note with the deaths of "seven heroes," referring to the seven students who died in student demonstrations of early 1966. It is told from a personal point of view, in the voice of an older sister toward a younger brother (*my* younger brother; *my* nation; *your* blood; *your* death).

A muted drum cymbal establishes the tempo for the first verse. These contrasting statements set the stage for the violent encounter that is about to take place. Titiek enters in a quavering voice with a wide vibrato. Verse 2 is in F major. After verse 2, the tempo slows down right before the word *gugurlah* (death). The momentum builds with a crescendo to the word *mulya* (honor), the crucial point in the narrative, followed by a dramatic pause.

The short interlude restates the melody in the violin part, followed by a rockabilly guitar solo. A military-inspired snare drum leads to a repetition of verse 2 that restates the demands of the people and the honorable and noble deeds of those who fought for them. The song resolves to a major key (D major), signifying that the revolutionary struggle is not over. The violinist ends the song by playing a melodic phrase from "Taps," a piece usually played at funerals for US military personnel.

"Buat adikku" expressed the demands of the people *(rakyat)* against the fallen Sukarno regime, but it is not a pro-Suharto position either. Rather, it is an emotional plea for political and economic change and a comforting sentiment voiced by a woman in a time of national crisis. Titiek Puspa's soft and calming voice may seem inconsonant with the political violence and turmoil of the 1960s. But the song dramatizes the Arif Rachman Hakim killing through a retelling of the story based on specific characters, emotions, and moods. Further, the song emphasizes familial ties and identities—as mother, sister, friend, or lover—that were equally important in the socially tumultuous period of the 1960s.

Music in the Suharto Era

Suharto's economic liberalization policies and openness to the West had significant effects on popular culture. Imports of recordings flowed in easily and helped to shape the sound of popular music. Previously criticized by Sukarno as an imperialist symbol of capitalism, Western rock 'n' roll was encouraged under Suharto. Musicians formed collaborative relationships with the regime. For example, in late 1966, the Army Strategic Command (Kostrad) sponsored a performance tour featuring the Blue Diamonds, a Dutch rock 'n' roll duo, and a group of Indonesian popular artists that included Titiek. The army used the tour to demonstrate its political power against any opposition and to gain the support of Indonesian citizens for the regime by proving that Indonesia was not anti-Western.[26]

The recording industry was relatively dormant during 1965–1966, due to the tragic events of September 30, 1965, and their aftermath, but it picked up in 1967–1968.[27] For example, Suyoso Karsono (aka Mas Jos [Yos]), who founded the Irama Recording Company in 1951, established three new labels in 1967: Elshinta, Jasmine, and J&B (Denny Sakrie, personal communication, 15 June 2014). His counterpart Jamin (Amin) Widjaja established the companies Bali Record and Canary Record in 1968. Expansion in production of recordings corresponded to new markets for middle- and upper-class teenagers *(remaja)* with money.[28]

Another factor in the booming industry of popular music was private radio *(radio amatir)*, which started in the early 1960s and operated illegally, in competition with RRI (Sen 2003, 578). However, some of these stations did not face opposition from the state; for example, Radio Ampera was supported by the military loyal to Suharto. Private radio boomed in the late 1960s (Lindsay 1997, 111). The stations, located in Jakarta and Bandung, were student-run and played Western pop music (Sen 2003, 578).

The emergent genres of *pop Indonesia* and rock were geared primarily to emerging middle- and upper-class youth consumers. *Pop Indonesia* offered accessible lyrics (in Indonesian), sweet and smooth vocal timbres, and sentimental love songs. Recordings of *pop Indonesia* boomed in the late 1960s.

The late 1960s *pop Indonesia* scene showcased a flurry of young teenage starlets with lesser voices and not nearly as much talent or experience as Titiek or her counterpart Lilis Suryani.[29] Titiek stood apart from them in other ways. For example, few of them wrote their own songs, and their songs had little to do with politics.[30] They were seen as cute *(lucu)*, flirtatious *(centil)*, and sexy. They expressed a new kind of freedom based on consumption, Western aesthetics, and romantic love. Occupying an unstable zone between childhood and adulthood, however, these female singers challenged norms of the dutiful wife and mother.

In conjunction with economic exchange, the Indonesian music industry appropriated trends that were popular in the United States. Popular singers went by English-sounding names (for example, Anna Mathovani, Tanty Josepha, Anny Rae, and Ernie Djohan, among others). Comparisons with Western singers were common: Ernie Djohan was called the Brenda Lee of Indonesia (*Aktuil* 47 [1970]: 19), whereas Diah Iskandar had "a voice like Connie Francis" (*Aktuil* 48 [1970]: 34; Leksono 2003, 126; "Ernie Djohan" n.d.). On the one hand, after so many years of Western colonialism, these associations generated disdain from an older generation who saw these "import-minded" and "imitative" practices as another example of colonial mimesis.[31] On the other hand, a younger generation of women welcomed these images of Western fashion, sex before marriage, and urban lifestyles as signs of freedom (from their parents), economic opportunity, and individualism.

There were, of course, popular male singers and bands, but they did not dominate the market until the early 1970s.[32] Girl bands were nearly as popular as male bands. Female singers (and bands) gained prominence in the recording industry during the early New Order, but it was a different sound and image of women than before. Producers had to create a new way of constructing teenage stars, just as they had to construct a way of shaping the new audience of teenagers. The explosion of teen magazines portrayed them as naïve. With their short hair, short dress, and big smiles, they were the "modern girl around the world."

The industry favored complementary arrangements between music (radio, recordings), film, magazines, and fashion (Siegel 1986). Young female singers adorned the pages of the ever-increasing numbers of magazines, where they advertised clothing, makeup, and lipstick, among other products. Singers often appeared in films and on magazine covers, and people could find out intimate details about their personal lives in teenage magazines such as *Topchords.*

James Siegel points out how the discourse of *Topchords* aimed to depoliticize youth by transforming them from politically active youth into passive teenagers, symbolized by the linguistic shift from the term *pemuda* (youth) to *remaja* (teenager). Instead of politics, *Topchords* emphasized taste. According to Siegel, women were symbolic of this depoliticization.[33] However, as others have noted, the idea and celebration of politicized youth *(pemuda)* did not disappear completely (Heryanto 1996, 10; Baulch 2007, 22).

Suharto's Indonesia soon became a phantasmagoria of hope, limitless opportunities, and freedom under the guidance of state-driven capital-induced development *(pembangunan).* In reality, political dissent was dangerous. Artists had to skate on thin ice due to a culture of censorship and self-censorship. Titiek was a friend of the Suharto regime but also expressed her autonomy in songs that mounted a critique of celebrity and the city, as described in the following section.

Titiek's Voice in the Suharto Era

The New Order "promoted a normative vision of women's primary role as wife and mother, taking her place in a family in which the husband wielded patriarchal authority" (Robinson 2009, 5). A woman's role in the family was based on *kodrat,* an "Islam-inspired code of conduct based on women's intrinsic [biological] 'nature'" (Wieringa 1998). Julia Suryakusuma has coined the term "state Ibuism" to emphasize the state's construction of women as wives and mothers (*ibu* means "mother"). State Ibuism defines women as "appendages and companions to their husbands, as procreators of the nation, as mothers and educators of children, as housekeepers, and as members of Indonesian society—in that order" (Suryakusuma 1996, 101). New Order ideology about gender relations operated through two organizations: Family Welfare Guidance (Pembinaan Kesejahteraan Keluarga, 1972) and the Association of Wives of Civil Servants (Dharma Wanita, 1974). Given the structures of these organizations, women's only legitimate access to state power was as wives of powerful male functionaries of the state (Sen 1998, 42).

Susan Blackburn notes that other organizations were active in the New Order, although they were not as prominent as the aforementioned ones. For example, the Ministry for Women's Role/Empowerment formed in 1978 as a junior ministry (Blackburn 2004, 26). Women belonged to LSMs (Lembaga Swadaya Masyarakat; self-reliant social institutions) as well as women's organizations affiliated with NU and Muhammadiyah (ibid., 27). Some women were involved in organizations such as IWAPI, Ikatan Wanita Pengusaha Indonesia, which emphasized economic success for women rather than domestic skills (Suzanne Brenner, personal communication, 1 August 2015). Women in the New Order helped produce gains for women in health (lower infant mortality), education (compulsory education and higher education), and literacy rates (Robinson 2009, 95). The material and symbolic dimensions of women's lives changed over the thirty-two-year history of the New Order. Krishna Sen's work on middle-class women notes a shift from the early New Order refusal of the category of women as workers to the category of "new middle-class working woman" in the 1990s (1998, 39). Women as mothers and wives represented stability, especially in an increasingly unstable environment (Brenner 1999, 35). But while women were lauded for their ability to be progressive *(maju)* and for embracing personal achievement *(budi),* they were simultaneously viewed with suspicion if they appeared too modern (Brenner 1999).

The figure of the modern woman was emergent in 1970s popular culture, even if the New Order state did not promote the progress of women as symbolic of the nation's progress as a whole. Titiek Puspa, among others, embodied the figure of a modern New Order woman. In liner notes and popular print media, Titiek portrayed a sophisticated cosmopolitanism and a sense of engagement with the world. She displayed wealth in expensive clothing and lifestyle as an example of her own artistic labor, not as a sign of her husband's wealth. Her enormous success as a composer, individual career woman, and Jakarta celebrity signified the three hallmarks of Indonesian modernity in the New Order: progress *(kemajuan),* development *(pembangunan),* and individual achievement *(budi)* (Vickers 1996).

In the Suharto era, Titiek wrote several important songs about modern women (for example, "Gadis" and "Apanya dong!" recorded by Euis Dahlia). Her songs of the 1970s maintained a critical edge about modernity, told from the perspective of a woman. In the following section, I focus on "Kupu-kupu malam" (1977) and "Bimbi" (1978).

"Kupu-kupu malam"

Composed in 1977, "Kupu-kupu malam" is arguably Titiek Puspa's best-known song.[34] "Kupu-kupu malam" literally translates as "Night butterfly," a euphemism for prostitute, and in the song, Titiek creates empathy for a female sex worker. Titiek composed the song after hearing from a woman whose husband left her with their young child. The woman had gone into debt and began sleeping with men for money to make ends meet. The backstory of her victimization by a man is not part of the song. Rather, it focuses on the public perception, labor, and internal emotional life of a prostitute.

Ada yang benci dirinya	There are those who hate her
Ada yang butuh dirinya	There are those who need her
Ada yang berlutut mencintanya	There are those who fall in love with her
Ada pula yang kejam menyiksa dirinya	And also those who mistreat her
Ini hidup wanita si kupu-kupu malam	This is the life of a woman of the night
Bekerja bertaruh seluruh jiwa raga	Putting her whole body and soul on the line
Bibir senyum kata halus merayu memanja	Smiling lips, sweet words, flattering and seductive
Kepada setiap mereka yang datang	To everyone who comes
Dosakah yang dia kerjakan	Is what she does a sin?
Sucikah mereka yang datang	Are those who come to her pure?
Kadang dia tersenyum dalam tangis	Sometimes she smiles through her tears
Kadang dia menangis di dalam senyuman	Sometimes she weeps while she smiles
Oh apa yang terjadi, terjadilah	Oh, whatever happens, happens
Yang dia tahu Tuhan penyayang umatnya	All she knows is that God cares for his people
Oh apa yang terjadi, terjadilah	Oh, whatever happens, happens
Yang dia tahu hanyalah menyambung nyawa	All she can do is keep living

In this song/story, Titiek takes the role of a narrator/spectator to illuminate the night butterfly's actions, thoughts, and feelings. The poetry works through a series of oppositions that compel the listener to reflect: love and hate, desire and antagonism, purity and sin, victim and victimizer. Her beauty cannot be seen (at night), and she "cries while she's smiling." These contradictions invite the listener to contemplate the emotional disquiet and physical mistreatment that lurk beneath the night butterfly's smiling face. Moreover, Titiek urges the listener to visualize the fine line that separates strength and weakness through the figure of a butterfly, which can be crushed at any moment. Ironically, it is a figure that everyone needs, and yet one that is never safe or protected.

In the 1970s, prostitutes were blamed for all kinds of social problems, including their perceived immoral behavior, social deviance, the spread of disease, and association with crime and drugs. They were hated by other women, who accused them of luring away their husbands and causing the disintegration of the family unit. The predominant opinion of the time was that it was prostitutes' own fault for being mistreated.

This song reverses the blame by pointing to the narrator's male patrons as unclean and impure. This is important because, as Suzanne Brenner notes, "men's sexual behavior is rarely seen as a matter for genuine public concern; whether or not it should even be the family's concern is open to some debate" (1999, 33). In this song, men are publicly displayed as the ones who need the night butterfly and the ones who fall in love with her. They are the ones who may have sinned, and they are the ones who may need to be purified for what they have done before they came to her. The third stanza is sung with little melodic ornamentation to emphasize the matter-of-factness of the lyrics.

The figure of the prostitute was common in popular culture of the 1970s, especially "prostitution films," in which female sex workers were viewed as passive victims unable to act (Sen 1993; 1994, 145). But unlike the prostitutes in these "prostitution films," the night butterfly does not die in the end or become integrated into the family as a wife or mother.[35] At the end of "Kupu-kupu malam," Titiek expresses the fatalistic attitude that brings prostitution into contact with Islam ("God's will"): "Past or impending disasters are shrugged off with, 'what's done is done' (apa yang terjadi terjadilah) or, 'it's just [my] fate' (nasibnya saya), and the women can usually find something to laugh about in any situation, although they also occasionally sink into exhaustion and despondency. Religious conviction helps them to accept their 'fate'" (Murray 1991, 136). Like the night butterfly, the prostitutes in Murray's study deal with their despair by laughing (through their pain) and, quoting from the lyrics of "Kupu-kupu malam," accepting their fate ("apa yang terjadi terjadilah"). Similarly, "Kupu-kupu malam" does not offer a solution or a narrative conclusion to any of the problems faced by prostitutes. Rather, fate and acceptance provide a temporary respite for the night butterfly's despair that enables her to "keep living."

This shift in narrative voice in the last stanza is curious and may have been added in order to evade censorship, much like the song title, which was changed to please Islamic authorities (see footnote 3). This practice of self-censorship toward the conclusion of a song is similar to practices in filmmaking: "A film can contain (in the sense of both carrying and limiting) contentious images and ideas, as long as it achieves the 'correct' conclusion. And audiences, aware of such conventions, can read the film without or against its narrative closure" (Sen 1991, 145).

"Kupu-kupu malam" ultimately achieved the "correct" conclusion. But the narrative turn at the end allows listeners to identify with the night butterfly's surrender as their own. By reversing the blame from the female to the male (both in its story of origin as well as the song lyrics), the song presents a critique of modern social life in which female sex workers are perceived as "the most abject of victims of the military-patriarchal-capitalist status quo" (Yngvesson 2014, 58). "Kupu-kupu malam" challenges the dominant social order through a series of questions, leaving the problems unresolved. While Titiek also celebrated development, as in the song "Bapak pembangunan" (Father of development), "Kupu-kupu malam" and others in this period present a counternarrative to New Order modernity.

"Bimbi"

The story of Bimbi, from the song of the same name, is different from those of Minah and the night butterfly. Bimbi and Minah are both simple (*sederhana*), sweet (*manis*), and unmarried girls (*gadis*) from the village who want to experience modern life in the city. For Minah, the city is an undesirable place that needs her more than she needs it. In contrast, Bimbi loves the bright lights of the big city. Whereas Minah is able to stand her ground (and leave quickly), Bimbi is easily swayed by the temptations of the city. The text is as follows:

Bimbi nama seorang gadis	Bimbi is the name of a girl
Sederhana tapi manis	Simple yet sweet
Pergi dari kampungnya tujuannya ke kota	She left her village, headed for the city
Ingin hidup coba-coba	To see what life was like there
Cepat dia sesuaikan diri	She adapted quickly
Lagaknya bak p'ragawati	Behaving like a fashion model
Uang entah dari mana segalanya dia punya	Don't know where she got the money to afford everything
Dan langsung ngetop namanya	And quickly her name was known
Bimbi tak mau kenal lagi kampungnya	Bimbi doesn't want to think about her past
Bimbi tak mau kenal lagi saudara	Bimbi doesn't want to think about her family
Tahun ke masa berganti	The years go by
Bimbi tak dikenal lagi	Bimbi has been forgotten
Wajah serupa Bimbi memelas pucat pasi	A face resembling Bimbi's is deathly pale
Menanti di jalan sepi	Waiting on a deserted street

Like the night butterfly in "Kupu-kupu malam," Bimbi "wants to live" *(ingin hidup)* in the city. Their motivations are different: the night butterfly must live in the city to survive, whereas Bimbi desires to try new things *(coba-coba).* Bimbi quickly acclimates to her new surroundings and struts around town "like a fashion model." The bombastic nature of the blaring horns symbolizes her energetic and flamboyant personality. The lyrics suggest that her income, which is abundant, comes from performing disreputable acts. She gains a reputation as a "top name" at performing these acts, probably sex work.

The city transforms Bimbi in negative ways. Money has spoiled her. She no longer remembers her place of origin and forgets about her family. As the years wear on, Bimbi herself is forgotten. Homeless and without money, she is a ghost haunting the streets. Her face begins to lose its luster. She ends up living on the side of the road. The city is no place for a young woman.

Titiek's portrayal of Bimbi mirrors the critique of the gendered city in Indonesian films of the 1970s: "images of the city are often gendered, embodied in the figure of a domineering and sexually loose woman" (Paramaditha 2011, 505). Filmmakers' bleak view of the New Order is expressed through fallen women in the modern city, which represents decline and degradation rather than the state's promise of progress and development (ibid., 501).

Titiek adopts yet another American song style for this song. The arrangement of keyboard, drums, guitar, bass, and horns sounds like a Broadway musical. The swinging rhythm suggests fun and a free and easy attitude. These techniques emphasize Bimbi's desire of wanting to live under the bright lights of the big city, reflecting the ethos and desire for development *(pembangunan).*

"Bimbi" and "Kupu-kupu malam" have similar themes, but they are expressed in different musical styles. The difference in tempo sets a different mood for the two main characters. The slow tempo of "Kupu-kupu malam" portrays the sadness and disappointment of the night butterfly, who feels the burden of providing for children at home (and possibly others). In contrast, Bimbi has just arrived in the city: she is fresh, single, and excited. Borrowing a term from the period, she is an "experimental girl" *(perempuan eksperimen* or *perek),* someone who wants to try prostitution like the latest fashion.

The other interesting contrast is the narrative development of the mood in both songs. In "Kupu-kupu malam," Titiek's voice is restrained at the beginning and full of sighing portamenti to emphasize the despair underlying the conclusion to this story. However, Titiek's voice soars in the second stanza of "Kupu-kupu malam" and gains strength to full voice at the end. Her voice becomes stronger as the story progresses and as the listener empathizes increasingly with her. Titiek takes more liberties with the melody in the restatement of the verse, using vocal breaks and a quivering voice to emulate crying. These vocal techniques point to the night butterfly as a real person with deep and contrasting emotions rather than a commodity.

In "Bimbi," on the other hand, Titiek's vocal production starts out bold and brazen and, by the brief unmetered cadenza, dissipates into a wilted, bluesy, scratchy timbre. An ascending melody, sung with vibrato, articulates the final word of the song, *sepi* (lonely). Accompanied by a resounding seventh chord, the message of the song is clear: a single woman who strikes out on her own (forgetting her past and her family) will eventually be silenced.

All three songs—"Minah gadis dusun," "Kupu-kupu malam," and "Bimbi"—depict young women who venture from a rural past to an urban present, imagining a modern future full of progress. But they quickly find out that modernity has made all sorts of promises to people that it could not keep. Minah escaped just in time, whereas the night butterfly and Bimbi only found loss, suffering, and despair. On one hand, the lyrics metaphorically "put women in their place": women who attempt to succeed alone in the male-dominated space of the city will be crushed. On the other hand, the fact that these songs illuminate women's desires and aspirations highlights the *gendered* modernity of the city and the exclusionary nature of modernity's promise.

In this chapter, I have described Titiek Puspa's music in the context of modernity during the 1960s and 1970s. We may wish to think about the Old and New Order regimes as two ideologies of modernity due to their radically divergent ideological positions and contrasting political and economic realities. Ideologically, the Sukarno period of Guided Democracy (1957–1966) blended nationalism, religion, and communism (NASAKOM). It was wracked by economic hardship, political isolationism, and social upheaval. During the period of the Old Order, Titiek fulfilled her role as a "progressive-revolutionary" artist whose songs advocated national unity and the *rakyat kecil,* the "little people." However, her vocal style (modeled on Anneke Gronloh, Patti Page, and Ella Fitzgerald) and rock-inspired compositions conflicted with Sukarno's anti-Western rhetoric about 1960s popular music, which he characterized as "noisy and grating" *(ngak ngik ngok).*

In a 2008 interview, Titiek stated, "My songs are translations of my feelings as I respond to life and face the problems surrounding [me]" (Endah 2008, 272). Amid the violence and social upheaval of the 1960s, and her own personal struggles, Titiek's soothing and sentimental voice carried messages of love, relationships, everyday life, and patriotism. In the narratives contained in her songs, recited over radio, recordings, and film, Titiek played a mother, a sister, a friend, a lover, and a "progressive-revolutionary artist."[36] Her prolific output of songs expressed a wide spectrum of emotions and accompanied ordinary Indonesians through a period of crisis.

Titiek prefigured depictions of middle-class career women *(wanita karir)* in popular print media of the 1990s, as women who signified "the transition from tradition to modernity" (Brenner 1999, 16). A career woman was a "happy consumer-housewife, devoted follower of Islam, successful career woman, model citizen of the nation-state, and alluring sex symbol" (ibid., 17). Unlike the idealized woman of the New Order, "she is thus a woman with some power—power that is independent of her status as wife or mother, and which establishes her place in a sector of society that is removed from the constraints of 'tradition'" (ibid.).

Several factors account for Titiek's success in the two orders. First, she was a savvy professional who was able to adapt to changing social conditions and top-down power. She cultivated relationships with both Sukarno and Suharto by celebrating the regimes in her compositions and public discourse. Second, her songs projected multiple roles as wife, mother, friend, and heroine. These female "voices" were crucial during a time of crisis in the 1960s, and they were also part of the New Order's regulation of women's behavior in the 1970s.

Titiek's story is not typical of women, nor is it typical of other female entertainers. She achieved tremendous individual success and she did things musically that few women were doing, such as composing and leading her own band (Orkes Puspa Sari). As a composer, she had hits in every decade and wrote songs for many other star singers and bands including Lilis Suryani ("Gang kelinci"), Dara Puspita ("Soal asmara"), and Euis Dahlia ("Apanya dong!"), among others. Her songs have become staples in the *pop Indonesia* genre.[37]

While other singers came and went, Titiek's reputation and celebrity continues to grow. She has been the subject of numerous magazine articles, TV interviews, and two biographies. In celebrity news items, she has been referred to as a "modern Kartini" ("Hari Kartini").

In this chapter, I have chosen to focus on an exceptional life and voice of one woman. Titiek developed an image as an independent modern woman dedicated to the future of the country.[38] She was a professional singer who supported husbands and children and family members. She was a wife, a mother, and a star singer with a career. Titiek's life and work do not represent possibilities for *all* women. However, as the leading female singer of her era, she offers an important gendered perspective on modernity and women in the realm of Indonesian culture and entertainment of the 1960s and 1970s.

Acknowledgments

I am grateful to Bart Barendregt, Suzanne Brenner, Ekky Imanjaya, Jennifer Lindsay, and Philip Yampolsky for reading and commenting on drafts of this chapter. Any errors remaining are my own. I would like to thank Henk den Toom Jr., for providing me with recordings from the period.

Notes

1. Titiek enjoyed a successful career after 1980 and continues to perform as of 2015, but my focus in this chapter is limited to her activities within the shifting political and economic terrain of the 1960s and 1970s.

2. Stories about Titiek proliferate in popular print media. Further, there are two biographies: Leksono 2003; and Endah 2008.

3. The original and preferred title of this song was "Kupu-kupu malam," but due to pressure from Islamic groups, the record company decided to change the printed title on the album to "Aku ingin hidup" (I [just] want to live). The song is commonly known as "Kupu-kupu malam," the title that is preferred by Titiek herself, and I have retained the original title in this chapter.

4. Links to these songs on YouTube are listed at the end of this chapter.

5. Her given name was Sudarwati (Endah 2008, 69). As a child, she was often sick; in step with Javanese custom, her parents changed her name several times.

6. RRI had been sponsoring these contests (*festival bintang radio*) since 1951.

7. She eventually won the award as the top singer in Semarang in 1959.

8. On March 27, 1959, in Semarang, she recorded a version of the popular song "Papaya chacha" (Yampolsky 1987, 107), followed by others in April 1959. Later that year, she did a recording session for Lokananta in Jakarta (18 September 1959).

9. Raden Adjeng Kartini (1879–1904) was a national heroine who advocated for women's rights and education during the Dutch colonial period. She is considered to be Indonesia's first feminist.

10. The United States and Great Britain were not the only models of modernity available in the period 1950–1965. Lindsay cites the strong influence of the USSR and China as well as the Islamic orientation of Egypt (2012, 14). In the realm of popular music, India was also a sign of modernity. Due to the influence of Indian films in the late 1950s and early 1960s, Ellya Khadam, the great *orkes Melayu* singer, adopted Indian clothes and sang Indian-inspired songs that grew into the wildly popular Indonesian national genre of *dangdut* (Weintraub 2010). For more about the nature of Indonesian cultural modernity and progress and their relationship to Western culture in the early Independence period, see Bogaerts 2012, 235–238.

11. The Bintang Radio competition held by RRI Jakarta in 1965 had three categories: *hiburan, kroncong,* and *seriosa* (*Mingguan Radio Televisi* 55 [20 June 1965]). See also Piper and Jabo 1987, 10.

12. Postcolonial scholarship reformulated the encounter between East and West, as described by Lila Abu-Lughod: "[Modernity] is a construct and an organizing trope, especially for the developmentalist successors of colonial regimes. . . . Translation, hybridization, and even dislocation might be more useful metaphors than imitation, assimilation (forced or attempted), or rejection for grasping what happened in the colonial encounter" (1998, 18).

13. I would like to thank Philip Yampolsky for pointing out two different spellings in published speeches by Sukarno: *ngak-ngik-ngèk* (1959b) and *ngak-ngik-ngok* (1959a).

14. The anti-imperialist regime of Sukarno denounced the allegedly harmful influence of American and European commercial culture (Frederick 1982; Hatch 1985; Sen and Hill 2000). He publicly denounced Indonesian musicians playing music by the Beatles and punished citizens for adopting their haircuts. Popular music bands with English-sounding names were compelled to change their names to Indonesian ones to erase any influence of

American music. In a speech in 1965, he declared that "Beatle-ism" was a mental disease, and he ordered the police to cut the hair off anyone found listening to the Beatles. Sukarno even imprisoned members of the American- and British-influenced pop music band Koes Bersaudara (Koes brothers) for one hundred days in 1965 (Piper and Jabo 1987, 11; Farram 2007).

15. See also *Harian Rakjat*, 15 November 1964, as cited in Yuliantri 2012, 430. The reference is to the American teen heartthrob Tommy Sands, who sang two songs about dreaming: "All I Do Is Dream of You" (1959) and "Dream with Me" (1961).

16. Sukarno was also a fan of Hollywood films (Lindsay 2012, 14).

17. In a speech presented on 28 October 1959, he berated youth for favoring rock 'n' roll and cha-cha over local dances and songs of Indonesia (such as *lenso* or Batak songs). He stated that there are lots of bands that play rock 'n' roll but not a single band that performs *(memband-kan)* local Javanese song forms (e.g., Pangkur and Sinom) or *lenso* in a band format (Soekarno 1959a, 19–20).

18. Composers and musicians dealt with the "ban" on popular music in different ways. As reported by Suzan Piper and Sawung Jabo (1987, 10–11), another productive effect of Sukarno's opposition to Western pop in 1965 was to encourage producers, composers, musicians, and singers to create regional pop styles including *pop Jawa* (Javanese); *pop Minang* (Minang); *pop Makassar* (Makassarese); *pop Banjar* (Banjar); *pop Ambon* (Ambonese); and *pop Sunda* (Sundanese).

19. *Berita Indonesia* 4 (15 February 1961) and 4 (1 March 1961).

20. Some of Titiek's songs reflected the revolutionary struggle, while many others did not.

21. For example, Rachmat Kartolo's "Patah hati" (Broken heart, c. 1963) was accused of making people sad and weakening their spirit during a time when the revolution was not yet completed (Piper and Jabo 1987, 11). For more about *cengeng* songs in the New Order period, see Yampolsky 1989.

22. The album *Doa Ibu* contains twelve songs about love, motherhood, friendship, and patriotism. There are three "female-centered Confrontation songs" (Farram 2014, 11). *Konfrontasi* (Confrontation) refers to Indonesia's political opposition to Malaysia from December 1962 to August 1966.

23. She named her two daughters after two of her favorite singers: Petty Tunjung Sari (b. 12 January 1960) was named after Patti Page, and Ella Puspasari (b. 23 September 1961) was named after Ella Fitzgerald (Leksono 2003, 71).

24. The "pro-rakyat" attitude and solidarity with the poor was part of Indonesian modernity of the 1950s, as expressed in literature and paintings (Schulte Nordholt 2011, 390).

25. G30S refers to Gerakan 30 September (30th of September movement). On the morning of October 1, 1965, a group of military officers kidnapped and killed seven generals who were allegedly plotting a coup against President Sukarno. The army responded by blaming the murder of the generals on the Communist Party of Indonesia (PKI, Partai Komunis Indonesia), which was at the time the third-largest communist party in the world. In the ensuing six months, under the leadership of Major General Suharto, the army conducted one of the largest massacres of the twentieth century.

26. The collaboration was organized by BKS-Kostrad (Badan Kerjasama Artis dengan Kostrad) and led by Titiek's husband, Mus Mualim. "For the army, the performances had two functions: to exhibit a *show of force* to its political opponents, and to capture ordinary citizens' sympathies by showing that Indonesia was not anti-Western" (Sasongko and Katjasungkana 1991, 51).

27. From 1961 to 1963, Irama produced as many as thirty thousand discs per month but by the end of 1966 only pressed about one to two thousand per month (and only sold five hundred per month) (MYK 1967).

28. The year 1967 also marked the heightened production and release of Indonesian films (Juliastuti 2002, 4).

29. According to a poll published in the music magazine *Aktuil* (27 [1969]: 6), 7,369 readers voted on the most popular female singers *(biduanita)* of 1968: (1) Ernie Djohan (b. 1951), (2) Vivi Sumanti (b. 1953), (3) Anna Mathovani (b. 1954), (4) Tetty Kadi (b. 1952). Groups included Dara Puspita, Patti(e) Sisters, and Sitompul Sisters. An album cover from that era for a recording by the male singer Bob Tutupoly notes that "there are already many well-known female singers, but what about our male singers?" (Remaco RL-057).

30. Personal communication, Ernie Djohan, 23 August 2016.

31. "Muntjul, berkembang dan hilangnja suatu mode" 1969 and "Kaum muda dan factor meniru" 1970.

32. Male singers and bands included Oma Irama, Gipsy, the Rollies, the Peels, AKA, and Lemon Trees. Indonesian rock music exploded in the 1970s (Panbers, the Mercy's, God Bless, Shark Move, Giant Step).

33. According to James Siegel, celebrity was a phenomenon that emerged for the first time in the New Order (1986, 212); my analysis of Titiek Puspa's celebrity in the Sukarno era suggests otherwise.

34. The song was featured in the 1977 film *Suci sang primadona* (Suci the primadonna; see Sen 1994, 145–147).

35. Similarly, Dag Yngvesson has argued that the character of the prostitute in the 1973 film *Bumi Makin Panas* (The Earth is Getting Hotter) is not "a sign of the Indonesian people's historical silencing and 'circumstantial inability to act'" (Sen 1993, 208) . . . but rather, "a powerful, symbolic weapon" . . . whose "circumstantial ability to become embedded within the structures of Suhartoist patriarchal authority enables her to profoundly convey the 'hidden' amoral drives and strategies that undergird its positivist/capitalist ideological discourse" (2014, 86).

36. Liner notes for *Doa Ibu*. See also Farram 2014, 12.

37. "Bimbi" was covered by the pop band Rollies in the 1970s and the rock band Ungu in the 2000s.

38. In contrast, Ellya Khadam, the leading *orkes Melayu* singer of the 1960s, was the voice of sensuality, fun, naughtiness, and seduction (Weintraub 2010). She was the vamp who portrayed a sexually alluring female in songs and films of the 1960s and 1970s. A comparison of Titiek Puspa and Ellya Khadam in relation to gender, class, and nation would be instructive but is outside the scope of this chapter.

References

Abu-Lughod, Lila. 1998. "Feminist Longings and Postcolonial Conditions." In *Remaking Women: Feminism and Modernity in the Middle East,* edited by Lila Abu-Lughod, 3–32. Princeton, NJ: Princeton University Press.

"Arif Rachman Hakim, pahlawan Ampera." 1966. Djakarta: Dewan Pimpinan Harian Pusat, Kesatuan Aksi Pemuda Peladjar Indonesia.

Barker, Joshua, Erik Harms, and Johan Lindquist. 2013. Introduction to *Figures of Southeast Asian Modernity,* edited by Joshua Barker, Erik Harms, and Johan Lindquist, 1–18. Honolulu: University of Hawai'i Press.
Baulch, Emma. 2007. *Making Scenes: Reggae, Punk, and Death Metal in 1990s Bali.* Durham, NC: Duke University Press.
Blackburn, Susan. 2004. *Women and the State in Modern Indonesia.* Cambridge: Cambridge University Press.
Bogaerts, Els. 2012. "'Whither Indonesian Culture?': Rethinking 'Culture' in Indonesia in a Time of Decolonization." In *Heirs to World Culture: Being Indonesian, 1950–1965,* edited by Jennifer Lindsay and Maya H. T. Liem, 223–254. Leiden: KITLV.
Brenner, Suzanne. 1999. "On the Public Intimacy of the New Order: Images of Women in the Popular Indonesian Print Media." *Indonesia* 67:13–38.
Endah, Alberthiene. 2008. *Titiek Puspa: A Legendary Diva.* Jakarta: PT Gramedia Pustaka Umum.
"Ernie Djohan." n.d. Beranda Ensiklopedi. http://www.jakarta.go.id/web/encyclopedia/detail/540/Ernie-Djohan (accessed December 6, 2016).
Farram, Steven. 2007. "Wage War against Beatle Music! Censorship and Music in Soekarno's Indonesia." *Review of Indonesian and Malaysian Affairs* 41 (2): 247–277.
———. 2014. "Ganyang! Indonesian Popular Songs from the Confrontation Era, 1963–1966." *Bijdragen tot de Taal-, Land- en Volkenkunde* 170 (1): 1–24.
Frederick, William. 1982. "Rhoma Irama and the Dangdut Style: Aspects of Contemporary Indonesian Popular Culture." *Indonesia* 34:102–30.
"Gerakan Banting Stir dibidang musik." 1965. *Mingguan Radio Televisi* 57 (July 4): 16.
"Hari Kartini, Titiek Puspa dapat kado." 2010. Nova, 21 April. http://www.tabloidnova.com/Nova/Selebriti/Aktual/Hari-Kartini-Titiek-Puspa-Dapat-Kado/.
Hatch, Martin. 1985. "Popular Music in Indonesia." In *Popular Music Perspectives 2: Papers from the Second International Conference on Popular Music Studies, Reggio Emilia, September 19–24, 1983,* edited by D. Horn, 210–227. Göteborg, Sweden: IASPM.
Heryanto, Ariel. 1996. "The Student Movement." *Inside Indonesia* 48 (October–December): 10–12.
Juliastuti, Nuraini. 2002. "Media selebritas di Indonesia." *Kunci Cultural Studies Center Newsletter* 11:4–5.
"Kaum muda dan factor meniru." *Aktuil* 57 (1970): 16.
"Kepala Direktorat Radio & TV tentang: Kebidjaksanaan siaran musik di RRI & TVRI." 1963. *Bintang Timur,* 30 October 1963.
Leksono, Ninok. 2003. *Titiek Puspa: Sebuah biografi.* Jakarta: Kompas.
Lindsay, Jennifer. 1997. "Making Waves: Private Radio and Local Identities in Indonesia." *Indonesia* 64:105–123.
———. 2012. "Heirs to World Culture: An Introduction." In *Heirs to World Culture: Being Indonesian, 1950–1965,* edited by Jennifer Lindsay and Maya H. T. Liem, 1–30. Leiden: KITLV.
Marshall, David P. 2006. *Celebrity and Power: Fame in Contemporary Culture.* Minneapolis: University of Minnesota Press.
Mingguan Radio Televisi. Vol. 55, no. 12. 20 June 1965.
"Muntjul, berkembang dan hilangnja suatu mode." 1969. *Aktuil* 27:16–17.

Murray, Alison J. 1991. *No Money, No Honey: A Study of Street Traders and Prostitutes in Jakarta*. Singapore: Oxford University Press.
MYK. 1967. "Produksi Piringan Hitam 'Irama' terpaksa diistirahatkan." *Mingguan Djaja*, 11 February.
Paramaditha, Intan. 2011. "City and Desire in Indonesian Cinema." *Inter-Asia Cultural Studies* 12(4): 500-512.
Piper, Suzan, and Sawung Jabo. 1987. "Musik Indonesia, dari 1950-an hingga 1980an." *Prisma* 16 (5): 8–23.
Randall, Annie J. 2009. *Dusty! Queen of the Postmods*. New York: Oxford University Press.
Robinson, Kathyrn. 2009. *Gender, Islam and Democracy in Indonesia*. London: Routledge.
Sasongko, A. Tjahjo, and Nug Katjasungkana. 1991. "Pasang surut musik rock di Indonesia." *Prisma* 20 (10): 47–66.
Schulte Nordholt, Henk. 2011. "Indonesia in the 1950s: Nation, Modernity, and the Post-Colonial State." *Bijdragen tot de Taal-, Land- en Volkenkunde* 167(4): 386-404.
Sen, Krishna. 1991. "Si Boy Looked at Johnny: Indonesian Screen at the Turn of the Decade." *Continuum: The Australian Journal of Media & Cultural Studies* 4 (2): 136–151.
———. 1993. "Politics of Melodrama in Indonesian Cinema." In *Melodrama and Asian Cinema*, edited by Wimal Dissanayake, 205-217. Victoria, Australia: Cambridge University Press.
———. 1994. *Indonesian Cinema: Framing the New Order*. London: Zed Books.
———. 1998. "Indonesian Women at Work: Re-framing the Subject." In *Gender and Power in Affluent Asia*, edited by Krishna Sen and Maila Stivens, 35–62. London: Routledge.
———. 2003. "Radio Days: Media-Politics in Indonesia." *Pacific Review* 16 (4): 573–589.
Sen, Krishna, and David Hill. 2000. *Media, Culture and Politics in Indonesia*. South Melbourne, Australia: Oxford University Press.
Siegel, James. 1986. *Solo in the New Order: Language and Hierarchy in an Indonesian City*. Princeton, NJ: Princeton University Press.
Soekarno. 1959a. "Amanat Presiden Soekarno pada peringatan kari sumpah pemuda, tanggal 28 Oktober 1959 di Surabaya." Jakarta: Departemen Penerangan R.I.
———. 1959b. "Penemuan kembali revolusi kita: Pidato Presiden Republik Indonesia pada Hari Proklamasi tanggal 17 Agustus 1959." In *Manifesto Politik Republik Indonesia, 17 Agustus 1959*, 27–72. Jakarta: Departemen Penerangan R.I.
Suryakusuma, Julia. 1996. "The State and Sexuality in New Order Indonesia." In *Fantasizing the Feminine in Indonesia*, edited by Laurie Sears, 92–119. Durham, NC: Duke University Press.
Vickers, Adrian, ed. 1996. *Being Modern in Bali: Image and Change*. New Haven, CT: Yale University Southeast Asia Studies.
Weintraub, Andrew N. 2010. *Dangdut Stories: A Social and Musical History of Indonesia's Most Popular Music*. New York: Oxford University Press.
Wieringa, Saskia. 1998. "Sexual Metaphors in the Change from Sukarno's Old Order to Suharto's New Order in Indonesia." *Review of Indonesian and Malaysian Affairs* 32 (2): 143–173.
———. 2002. *Sexual Politics in Indonesia*. New York: Palgrave Macmillan.

Yampolsky, Philip. 1987. *Lokananta: A Discography of the National Recording Company of Indonesia, 1957–1985.* Madison: Center for Southeast Asian Studies, University of Wisconsin.

———. 1989. "Hati yang luka: An Indonesian Hit." *Indonesia* 27:1–17.

Yngvesson, Dag. 2014. "The Earth is Getting Hotter: Urban Apocalypse and Outsider Women's Collectives in *Bumi Makin Panas*." *Plaridel* 11(2): 54–94.

Yulianto, Vissia Ita. 2008. "Consuming Gossip: A Re-domestication of Indonesian Women." In *Popular Culture in Indonesia: Fluid Identities in Post-authoritarian Politics,* edited by Ariel Heryanto, 130–142. London: Routledge.

Yuliantri, Rhoma Dwi Aria. 2012. "Lekra and Ensembles: Tracing the Indonesian Musical Stage." In *Heirs to World Culture: Being Indonesian, 1950–1965,* edited by Jennifer Lindsay and Maya H. T. Liem, 421–452. Leiden: KITLV.

YouTube Links to the Four Songs Discussed in This Chapter

"Bimbi"
https://www.youtube.com/watch?v=bmdzG3isvkg

"Buat adikku"
https://www.youtube.com/watch?v=PRe5Mx83lz4

"Kupu-kupu malam"
https://www.youtube.com/watch?v=M-r8adpVeuY

"Minah gadis dusun"
https://www.youtube.com/watch?v=Mhu0BSkeYi0

CHAPTER 8

The Remarkable Career of L. R. Eswari

Amanda Weidman

THIS chapter examines the career of the South Indian playback singer L. R. Eswari (b. 1939) in relation to the ways female playback singers negotiated their role, as well as how they were constructed in the public imagination as performers and women in film in the 1950s–1970s. Playback, referring to a system in which a singer's voice is first recorded in the studio and later "played back" on the set to be lip-synched by the actors and actresses during the shooting of the film, emerged in the late 1940s. A typology of female voices arose in the later 1950s and 1960s as this system became established in the various South Indian film industries. It was articulated in discourse about playback voices as well as in the division of labor these voices were made to perform in films, a division based on voices that were heard as clean and licit and voices that were considered "husky" or immodest. Within this context, L. R. Eswari started out singing for second heroines and comic characters in the late 1950s and came to be branded as a singer of "sexy" cabaret and "Western" songs in the mid-1960s, primarily in Tamil and Telugu films. She subsequently retreated from playback singing and made a name for herself as a devotional singer in the 1970s and 1980s. Since 2010, defying the usual career path for older playback singers, she has reemerged from retirement to sing several hit "item" songs for Tamil films, in which her voice is matched with the sexually charged performance of the actress on-screen.[1]

A set of conflicting aesthetics came together in the decades following India's independence that shaped the field of playback singing and the possibilities for female singers. The emergence of the new female playback voice in the 1950s, marked by its girlishly high pitch and thin timbre, was not merely a sign of shifting tastes or simply the singular genius of Lata Mangeshkar, the female singer who dominated the Bombay film industry from the 1950s to the 1980s. Rather, this voice and its aesthetic were linked to the larger sociopolitical project of defining women's place within an Indian and specifically Tamil modernity. In Hindi films of the 1950s and 1960s, a national-secular "modern" public sphere, defined in opposition to ties of caste, community, and family—what Kumkum Sangari has called the "Nehruvian episteme of romance"—was evoked by the pervasive trope of romantic love, and it was in this context that the girlish and flirtatious sound of the new female playback voice was cultivated (Sangari 2006, 377; Srivastava 2006).

In the Tamil context, the post-Independence public sphere was additionally shaped by Dravidian cultural and political identity, posed as an alternative to the national. As Eswari and the singers I discuss in this article were beginning their careers in the 1950s and 1960s, the Dravida Munnetra Kazhakam, or Dravidian Progress Federation (DMK), emerged as a force in Tamil Nadu politics, using the medium of cinema to spread its message. Secular modernity in the Dravidian imaginary was inflected by ideas of social reform as a corrective to both the domination of Tamil society by upper castes and the conflation of Indian identity with North India. Tamil films from this period emphasized pride in Tamil language and culture as a way of defining a Tamil modernity against both the West and North Indian hegemony. Anchoring this vision were a series of gendered tropes: the valorization of the self-sacrificing and nurturing mother, elaborated in the concepts of *tāymoḻi* (mother language), *tāynāṭu* (mother land), and *tāykulam* (women as a "community of mothers"); and the elaboration of *kaṟpu* (chastity) and the figure of the *pattini* (a woman loyal to her husband) in contrast to the prostitute or courtesan (Lakshmi 1990, 2008). The phrase *nalla peṇmaṇi* (the good woman) was used in a film song of the 1950s, and thereafter became a shorthand way of describing the attributes of the ideal woman: one who conducts herself according to the ways of Tamil culture and who devotes herself to ensuring the productivity and harmony of the domestic realm.

In many Tamil films of the 1960s, the period when L. R. Eswari became a prominent playback singer, the figure of the Tamil *nalla peṇmaṇi* was juxtaposed with that of women who embodied the modernity and mobility of what Christine Yano has called the "Jet Age" of the 1960s and 1970s, with its bringing together of East and West in "near coevalness" (Yano, chap. 6 in this volume). Although perhaps more central to Japan's postwar modernity than to India's, the Jet Age aesthetic nevertheless entered Tamil films through scenes of airports, jets, and cars but also through the image of a skirt- or pants-clad woman speaking English and dancing wantonly in what came to be called "Western" and "cabaret" songs. Film-music directors of this period liberally used the instrumentation and melodic and rhythmic structure of Latin and rock musics, and Eswari's voice was most often used for these types of songs.

While Eswari's voice acted in many songs as a conduit for bringing in foreign musical elements, as we will see, she also accentuated her rootedness. But

Figure 8.1. A page from a feature on various playback singers from a Tamil magazine. L. R. Eswari's publicity photo (bottom center) features her toothy smile, in stark contrast to the serious-looking photos of the other singers. *Bommai,* March 1982, 57.

this was not rootedness in idealized Tamil culture and the domestic realm in the way of the *nalla peṇmaṇi.* Rather, she became known as a singer of devotional songs about Amman, the sometimes benevolent and sometimes fierce Tamil mother goddess associated with lower-caste and rural Hindu religious belief. Her voice and persona thus presented the public with a complex mix of attributes and associations, like many other singers discussed in this volume who mediated the cultural, racial, and geographic divides of their time (figure 8.1).

Playback Singing as a Cultural and Historical Phenomenon

Playback singing is not merely a technological process; it is a culturally and historically specific phenomenon that involves the production, recording, amplification, manipulation, and circulation of voices. Beginning in the 1950s, playback singers became known figures, some of whom overshadowed on-screen actors in their popularity and longevity as public celebrities. Playback singing carved out a professional realm that was connected to the world of cinema but also separate from it, where singers sang for on-screen characters but maintained a public persona distinct from them. As such, it produced new forms of stardom and opportunities for women to enter the public sphere, while serving as a key site for the creation and circulation of ideologies and aesthetics of gender and voice.

Playback singing was oriented to new schemes of value, distinct from those that underlay established ways that women could perform "classical" arts, particularly Karnatic music. Ideally, a classical singer performs live before an audience who, if not all directly known to the singer, are presorted by their shared knowledge and connoisseurship of classical music; her onstage accompanists are known, and presumed authenticity lies in the uniqueness of the live performance. By contrast, with playback singing, there is no possibility of closing what William Mazzarella has called the "open edge of mass publicity" (2013, 38). Instead, the mobility of the singer's voice is promoted both through its pairing with another's on-screen body and through the mass reproduction and circulation of recordings. The playback singer sings to widely dispersed fans, not to a circumscribed, presorted audience. She sings in many different languages. And for a playback singer of Eswari's generation, rather than musical talent, years of education, or committed discipleship, it was her "god-given voice," its instant recognizability to everyone, including the man on the street, and its reliability—manifested in its ability to sing tens of thousands of songs and in its "evergreen" persistence over the years—that were constantly remarked on. Mobility and mass production translated into money: unlike female classical singers, playback singers often supported themselves by singing and became the main breadwinners in their family, amassing considerable wealth. Although many had little more than a tenth-grade education, they could claim a certain kind of cosmopolitanism through their ability to sing in different languages. For female playback singers of this generation, then, other schemes of value besides education, devotion to a musical lineage, or respectability—most notably fame and money—were at stake.

Beginning in the 1950s, as playback singing became a recognized profession, a certain kind of female playback singer attained iconic status. She was a type who managed to embody seemingly contradictory elements, pairing a high-pitched, girlish voice with a modest, even plain appearance: a woman whose singing voice might be matched with on-screen characters of varying social position and status but whose live persona and demeanor remained that of a nonglamorous, "respectable," middle-class woman. The code of respectability required the playback singer to dissociate herself from the character or emotion she voiced through the song, to present herself as a mere medium (never an author or artistic agent) for songs that others had composed and written and that still others would embody on-screen. Singing and acting were defined as separate activities that placed their practitioners on opposite ends of a moral divide between good "family" women who maintained a modest physical presence in public and women who were of questionable moral standing because they displayed their bodies before the public on-screen.

The aesthetics of the new female playback voice and this respectable persona were shared across the Bombay-based and South Indian film industries. While Lata Mangeshkar and, to a lesser extent, her sister Asha Bhosle dominated the field of Hindi films, in the South Indian context, from the 1950s through the 1970s, the situation was slightly more diversified. Three or four female singers who sang for Tamil, Telugu, and Malayalam films—P. Susheela, L. R. Eswari, S. Janaki, and Vani Jayaram—became dominant, their voices immediately recognizable and well known to the South Indian public.

The enhanced mobility of female voices engendered by playback singing created a certain kind of performative excess: a potential for the singer to be seen as not merely singing but actually feeling, acting, or embodying the emotions or characters she was expressing (Nakassis n.d.). To control these risks, several strategies emerged that involved a series of discursive and performative labors, undertaken both by the singers themselves and by audiences and media surrounding them. First, these singers borrowed prestige from classical vocal traditions; they emphasized their own classical training, adopting certain standards from the classical music world, and were often represented in the media as classically trained singers. Second, they adhered to a particular notion of vocal authenticity that involved cultivating a recognizable and consistent voice. Third, they made sure, through stage appearances, that their "real live" persona was that of a respectable woman, partly through dress and partly through a cultivated ability to dissociate their voice from their body when singing.

As a strategy of containment, this ability to dissociate one's voice from one's body was essential to the live performances of female playback singers of this generation. A woman standing immobile before the microphone, eyes fixed on the music stand or her book of lyrics, using one hand to keep the end of her sari carefully draped over her right shoulder: this is the iconic image of the respectable female playback singer. It is a stance that explicitly distances the singer from the song by emphasizing the idea that she is simply performing a piece of music, that her voice is merely a vehicle for the song.

Playback singers of this generation became exemplars of what Neepa Majumdar has termed "aural stardom," in which "the absence of glamour and the invisibility of playback singers can be regarded as defining features of their star personas. In the context of Indian cinema, aural stardom is constituted by voice recognizability, the circulation of extratextual knowledge about the singers, and the association of certain moral and emotional traits with their voices" (2001, 171).

Voicing the Limits of Respectability

In the context of post-Independence India, the female voice and the persona of the female playback singer took on particular significance as sites for the mapping of oppositions between tradition and modernity, India and the West, morality and debauchery. In the Tamil context, the division between voices that represented "good" women (mothers, wives, chaste girlfriends) and those who represented "bad" women (the overly educated, rich, Westernized, and hypersexualized female characters who were either foils to the heroine or were themselves eventually reformed and brought into the fold) was additionally put to the service of defining ideal Tamil womanhood and, through it, a specifically Tamil identity that was foundational to the emergence of Dravidian party politics in the 1950s and 1960s.

In keeping with this moral dichotomy, a structural position was opened in the 1960s for singers who sang "Western" or "cabaret" songs, sexually charged song-dance sequences in which a female character whose respectability was compromised danced suggestively before a male patron or a male audience within the film narrative. As these kinds of songs became a staple feature of Tamil films in the 1960s, there was a need for singers who would sing them. In the context of a film, these songs were often marked off from the rest of the film by an abrupt aesthetic shift in visual and aural aspects, constituted by performance and singing styles maximally different from respectable genres of female performance. The separation was further reinforced by the fact that the actress and singer featured in these songs were conventionally not the same as the heroine actress and the singer used for her character. The risk of performative excess associated with playback singing in general is seemingly heightened in the case of such songs, in which the act of singing is combined with sexualized bodily performance. Being a singer of "Western" or "cabaret" songs, then, in this generation (as for the present-day version of these songs, known as "item" numbers) required a certain commitment, a willingness to specialize and be branded, for singing these songs renders the voice of the singer unfit for more respectable types of "melodic," "love," or "classical"-based songs.

It was the voice of Eswari that really came to represent female characters beyond the pale of respectability in the 1960s. This role did not present itself immediately but only after she had been a playback singer for nearly ten years. Eswari was born into a poor Tamil Christian-Catholic family as Lourde Mary Rajeswari and was raised largely by her mother; her father died when she was only six years old.[2] She had no training in Karnatic music but learned to sing by listening to Radio Ceylon, which broadcast film songs in the 1950s when All India Radio had banned them. Unlike many other singers of this generation, she was led into the film field not by a father or husband but by her mother, who was a group singer for Gemini studios in the 1950s. After several years of singing in group parts for films, Eswari was discovered in the late 1950s by the director A. P. Nagarajan and the music director K. V. Mahadevan. They changed her name to L. R. Eswari to avoid her being confused with another playback singer whose name was Rajeswari and gave her a solo song in the 1958 film *Nalla idattu sambandam*. Her song from the 1961 film *Paasamalar*, "Vārāy en tō̱li vārāyō" (Come along my friend, will you come?), in which she voices a female friend of the heroine, became a hit and was played and performed at weddings all over Tamil Nadu; a subsequent song, "Manamakaḷē marumakaḷē vā vā" (O daughter of my heart, O bride, come) from the film *Saradha* (1961), also became a favorite at wedding programs. Through the early 1960s, she sang other such songs, rarely for the heroine but certainly not for the sexualized female characters that she later came to be identified with. During this time as well, Eswari gave live performances, first as a girl with her mother at wedding programs, then beginning in the mid- to late 1960s, onstage with a backup orchestra.

A shift in Eswari's singing roles came in the mid-1960s, when a reliable pattern emerged: the voice of P. Susheela for the heroine, juxtaposed with Eswari's voice for the "second woman," comic, or vamp characters. The music director M. S. Viswanathan, who dominated Tamil film music in the 1960s and 1970s, used Eswari's voice for predominantly quick-tempo, racy songs in folk and Western styles. Her voice gained these associations partly through what Viswanathan saw as its natural capabilities and partly through Eswari's "real-life" persona. Equally as important was the association of Eswari's voice with Jayalalitha, who emerged as an actress in Tamil movies in the mid-1960s, often playing the role of an overly educated, rich, spoiled, snobby young woman who must be disciplined. Jayalalitha's image and Eswari's voice were seen as uniquely suited to each other; Eswari's willingness and ability to sing "Western" numbers, peppered with English words, matched Jayalalitha's English-speaking, skirt- and pants-wearing screen characters. The similarity of their life circumstances further cemented the association. Despite stark differences of caste background and education (Jayalalitha came from a Brahmin family and was highly educated; Eswari was from a lower-caste background and did not even study up to tenth grade), they both grew up essentially without fathers and were raised and brought into the film world by their mothers, unlike others who were brought into the film field and chaperoned by fathers or husbands. Both Jayalalitha and Eswari bore the taint of being semiorphaned: having no fatherly presence and a mother who had lowered herself to work in the film industry in order to support the family.

These extratextual details colored both Jayalalitha's screen roles and the way Eswari's voice could be used. For instance, in the 1965 film *Ni,* one of Jayalalitha's first Tamil films, she acted in a double role that played on the ambiguity of her extrafilmic persona. She is both the hero's girlfriend, who has no parents of her own and is taken in by his family as a bride-to-be, and, in the later part of the film, Usha, a woman of loose morals who happens to look just like the heroine, who sings in clubs and works for the film's villain. While the hero's family mistakenly believe the two women are the same person, the use of different playback voices for each "version" of Jayalalitha ensures that the audience is not fooled. While P. Susheela provides the voice for the girlfriend, Eswari sings the drunken "cabaret" number "Enakku vanta inta māyakkam" (This swooning that has come over me), which accompanies the scene in which Usha and the villain attempt to capture the hero. While the film is constructed around the ambiguity of Jayalalitha's persona, on-screen and off, the contrasting playback voices, and in particular Eswari's vocal performance of drunken brazenness, complete with crying, laughing, heightened speech in English, and hiccups, allows for no such ambiguity.

In the later 1960s, Eswari became famous for such songs whose picturization and sound were in various ways excessive. In the 1968 film *Panamaa pasamaa,* she sang for the comedic character of the fruit seller hawking her *elanta paḻam* (a small gooseberry-like fruit), brazenly approaching strangers and dancing in the street. The song is sung with a tremulous tone, open-mouthed "folk" diction, audible moments when the pitch of her voice drops from its "singing" register to one more suggestive of speaking, and a tune that evokes the traditional folk *magudi* or snake-charmer's music. This, in combination with the off-color lyrics (*elanta paḻam* has a double meaning) and the actress's sinuous dancing in the street and drawing attention to her own body, made the song an immediate sensation. In every interview Eswari gave, journalists would comment on the song. In one such interview from 1968, the interviewer, clearly fishing for some way to connect the content of the song with Eswari's persona, starts by asking Eswari what she thought during the rehearsal and recording of the song. She evades the import of the question by replying that she knew immediately that it would be a hit. Later, the interviewer again brings up the song: "The song is famous. But why don't you eat *elanta paḻam*?" "From a young age," Eswari replies, "I had a loathing for it. I was afraid there would be a worm." She goes on to note the peculiar paradox of being so famous for singing a song about a fruit she would not touch in real life but that she is requested to sing at least three times in each stage concert ("El ār īsvari" 1968, 29).

In the 1969 thriller *Sivantha mann,* the hero and heroine stage an elaborate act in order to draw in and trap the villain: the heroine is disguised as a court dancer and must sing as the hero (also disguised) cracks a whip over her. Eswari sings this song, "Pattatu rani," with spectacular hyperventilating effects every time the whip lands on the heroine's body. This too became one of her iconic songs. It showcased what had become her vocal trademarks: strong volume, agility, high pitch, and capacity and willingness to perform special effects. Discourse about Eswari's voice emphasized the very physical effects of her voice on listeners: that is, its performative force, its capacity to move listeners, not in some sentimental way but quite literally to move their bodies. Its sound was variously described to me with the Tamil adjective *gannīr* (ringing), like a "bell," or in words that directly recall the song sequence "Pattatu rani," "like a rubber whip." An article in a film magazine from 1971 described Eswari's voice as suitable for "girls and comedy actresses," praising her "unique voice structure." "For night-time club dances and Western kinds of songs, there is no one equal to her. In those scenes, just as the actress causes her body to be like a coiled metal spring, Eswari causes her voice to be like a snake. . . . There is no one who can sing like this. Even if they wanted to they would not be able to sing a song like 'Elanta Palam.' And she can sing love songs excellently too. . . . All of Eswari's songs make rasikars swoon" ("Mukkani sāro muttamil̲ tēnō" 1971, 102). The text of an award she was given in Chennai in 2009 read, "A husky voice combined with a raspy style made her the talk of the town. Pop Queen L. R. Eswari is amongst the first generation of playback singers to make people shake a leg."

Extrafilmic Persona

Eswari, unlike her contemporaries P. Susheela and S. Janaki, never married and prided herself on her independence, personal and financial. During her active playback and devotional singing years, she supported her younger sister and brother and was proud of having paid for their weddings with her earnings. She would go to the recording studio herself, with no chaperone or assistant, and for some years managed her own musical troupe, which accompanied her in stage performances. With prominent gold jewelry and a large dot of *kumkum* on her forehead, she cut a different kind of figure onstage. Unlike Susheela or Janaki, Eswari was known for moving and gesturing as she sang. And while other singers maintained a downward gaze and closed bodily posture while performing onstage, Eswari regularly acknowledged her audience, raising her hand to receive applause and blowing kisses to the audience.

Eswari was also publicly known to be the long-standing mistress of the music director M. S. Viswanathan, who dominated Tamil film music in the 1960s and 1970s and gave Eswari the vast majority of her singing roles. She made no attempt to hide this; in fact, for a time, her car bore his initials, "MSV," on its license plate. Nevertheless, Eswari also used some familiar signifiers of female respectability. Her careful attention to her public persona, one that had to be guarded because of the type of songs she sang and because she was unmarried, was apparent in her unwillingness to "put a mask on," whether as a singer or an actress. In interviews from the late 1960s and early 1970s, Eswari spoke of offers to act in films, offers that came perhaps because of the skill with which she rendered effects in her songs. Through the years, she had staunchly refused such offers, saying, "My whole inclination is toward music. My soul is not at all involved with acting" ("El ār īsvari" 1968, 29). When I met her in the fall of 2009, she had recently agreed to make a small cameo appearance as a singer in a club in the movie *Thillalangadi*. She told me that for the shooting, they had wanted to put makeup and a special dress on her, but she was adamant that she appear as herself in the movie: "just as I always am onstage." For her, the part in the film was not an acting gig but an important opportunity to project her public persona. More recently, she told me, after singing the hit song "Kalasalā kalasalā" for a 2011 film, some people told her she should start wearing a *churidar* like younger playback singers. "I can wear a *churidar* for recording sessions, but onstage I wear only a silk sari. There should be some respect for my age, no?" In a press meet following the release of this song, Eswari responded to various heckles from the journalists, including the question of whether she would act in films. "If I came to act, would they give me a good character?" she asked rhetorically. "Villain?" called out someone provocatively from the crowd. "No one has asked me to act the role of a villain. But if they did give me a role of a characterless person, I would definitely not act," she replied ("Playback Singer LRE Press Meet").

Concurrent with Eswari's rise as a playback singer, she also had a career in devotional music. Beginning in the late 1960s, she became known for her renditions of Hindu and Christian devotional songs. Through numerous temple concerts and several devotional cassettes that she released in 1985, she developed a large fan following, and her persona came to be identified with the Tamil folk goddess Amman, an incarnation of the mother goddess associated with rural and low-caste Hindu religious practice. Susheela and Janaki have also made devotional albums in their retirement; for them, singing devotional music serves the double function of distancing them from contemporary film music, which they see as increasingly vulgar, and producing appropriate extratextual knowledge about themselves. Appearing in public as a religious devotee is an acknowledged and accepted role for unmarried and older women, precisely because the devotee has renounced her sexuality and attachment to the material world.

Yet for younger women, there is a danger that religious passion displayed in public can be mistaken for uncontrolled sexuality. A younger singer (in her thirties when I spoke to her) explained to me that the issue lies in the mode of performance. In devotional music, you really have to "belt it out"—there has to be *āvēcam* (fury, passion) in your voice. For that reason, she would record devotional songs but would not perform them live; *āvēcam* could not be performed by a young woman, she said, without being mistaken for sexuality.[3] Eswari, however, began recording and performing devotional music as a young woman in her twenties. The excessive energy of Eswari's voice, along with her real-life unmarried status, successfully signified both ways, even when she was younger: as uncontained female sexuality and as the power of the divine.

Eswari's connection to devotional music exceeds the general career path of other playback singers. In the 1990s, she made devotional music videos in which she herself appears singing to the statue of the goddess; many of the videos alternate between close-ups of the goddess statue and of Eswari singing, presenting her simultaneously as an avatar of the goddess, an exemplary devotee, and a privileged intermediary between the goddess and the viewers.[4] Commenting on her career as a devotional singer, she stated that at a young age, a woman has a high voice, but as she gets older, her voice acquires "bass" and "depth," making it "naturally" suited to *Māriyamman pāṭṭu,* the genre of devotional music centering around the benevolent but often fierce and protective mother goddess known for avenging wrongs to lower-caste people and women. Through the years, in recognition of her devotional singing, she was bestowed with titles such as "Eswari who has received the grace of Amman" and "Eswari who has sung the praises of Amman."

In this and other ways, Eswari made the persona of the goddess part of her own image and identity. She capitalized on Jayalalitha's transformation from flirtatious and sassy screen actress to "Amma," her self-appointed name as Chief Minister of Tamil Nadu; drawing on the maternal/divine power that Jayalalitha channeled, Eswari proudly claimed, "I was the first to give voice to Amma" ("LR Easwari on Her Career & 'Kalasala'"). And in a catchy slogan she repeats often in interviews with journalists, Eswari plays on the fact that her name is also one of the goddess Amman's names, thereby identifying herself as a vessel for the divine: "Āntavan coltrān . . . Eswari kēṭkiṟā" (God speaks . . . and Eswari listens/hears).

The Voice

In the 1950s, as the role of the playback singer became professionalized and the film-music world started to be able to support full-time playback singers, singing actresses were mostly phased out. At the same time, the kind of female voice featured in film songs began to change from the relatively lower-pitched voice of Karnatic classical music to the high-pitched female voice that came to dominate Indian film music until the mid-1990s. The girlish character of the new female playback voice was produced in part by the fact that it was not projected but rather dependent on a closely held microphone. The projected voice of a female singing actress like K. B. Sunderambal, with its loud, declamatory style, suggested the presence of the singer's body in a public space and was always associated with older authoritative female characters of historical or mythological significance. The high-pitched, girlish voice that playback singers produced with the closely held microphone did not take up much "vocalic space" (Connor 2000, 12); it became the voice of female characters who moved through but did not command authority in the public sphere. The microphone voice, freed from the association with bodily presence, was thus freed from both womanly sexuality and womanly authority, allowing it to be associated instead with a kind of flirtatious girlish charm (Srivastava 2006, 140).

The timbre of the idealized female playback voice was notably smooth and highly regular. As Sanjay Srivastava has noted, Lata Mangeshkar's voice was characterized by a "stylistic homogeneity" that eliminated the nasality and "heaviness" associated with the voices of Muslim courtesans (2006,139). In South India, the lower-pitched, throatier voice was associated with *devadasi* singing actresses such as T. R. Rajakumari, who sang and acted throughout the 1940s and 1950s; her films of the 1950s, however, met with little success (Guy 1997, 260), partly because the idealized female voice had changed with the emergence of professional playback singers. These new playback voices, in addition to eliminating any marks of courtesan or *devadasi* origins, also excluded any hints of the "folk" or "ethnic," whether in pronunciation of words or in vocal timbre. From the 1950s on, songs that needed to evoke folk characters or village scenes were sung with the same female playback voices, using folk instruments, clapping, folklike vocables, and a particular kind of lilt at the end of phrases but rarely compromising the timbral purity of the voice.[5]

Along with these developments, since the 1950s, female playback voices have been subject to a complex classification based on the breathiness of the voice, a sound associated with available female sexuality and female desire and widely referred to as the "husky voice." The smooth, regular timbre of the idealized "pure" female playback voice was produced in part by an absence of breathiness or, as a voice trainer in Chennai put it to me, "a voice without pixels." Film songs were, however, interrupted occasionally by stylized performances of emotion such as laughter, crying, sighing, or heightened speech. Known as "effects," these were not part of the singing performance; they were interludes to the song, often set apart from the singing voice by a pause or complete stop. The separation of the singing voice from potentially compromising "effects" is particularly noticeable in the song "Pattatu rāni." Each time the whip hits the dancer, Eswari's voice gives a spectacular hyperventilating effect (accentuated visually by a countdown number that appears on the screen) as the dancer recovers from the blow and then returns to her singing voice. The scene produces the illusion of a female body and voice impervious to the physical attacks. The structure of the song, producing a formal separation between the singing voice and voiced expression of bodily feeling/emotion, produces a more general meaning: the imperviousness of the female voice to "effects" but also its fragility, its potential to be compromised by them.

Performing these effects was a liability for female singers not only because they came perilously close to acting but also because they admitted sounds of the body and of breath into the voice. Unlike merely singing about an emotion or feeling, performing "effects" necessitated acting as if one were experiencing or feeling the emotion oneself. Precisely because these effects threatened the ideals of containment and modesty associated with the female singing voice, they had to be strictly and consistently stylized: coded as a performance of someone else's original authorial idea, which the playback singer merely animates. As Eswari told me, "Of course I do effects; that's what gets the claps. But the music director has to teach the effects. Only then I give them. If we [playback singers] give the effects ourselves, they will say we are crazy."

Yet Eswari claimed a certain pride in being the only singer willing and able to perform some kinds of effects. In more than one media interview over the years, she told the story of how she was chosen to sing "Pattatu rāni" after Lata Mangeshkar and Asha Bhosle, the dominant singers in the Bombay film industry at the time, both said they were unable to ("Playback Singer LRE Press Meet"). She talked about how the director, Sridhar, had then suggested Susheela, but M. S. Viswanathan, the music director, said, "It has to be sung without fear. So Eswari must sing it. The character is a woman who does not know fear. Only if Eswari comes it will be good." She recalled that originally the idea was that another person would give the gasping sounds and she would just sing, but then Sridhar said she should give the gasping sound herself. "It took confidence to do that" (Hameed 1979). The effects Eswari performed in the song "Enakku vanta inta māyakkam" included laughing that turns into crying, stopping the song to speak in English, saying "sshhh," and hiccupping. Eswari added, "Everything comes in that song. People asked me, 'kuṭiccittu pāṭininkaḷā?' [Did you get drunk and sing it?] Because it was so realistic. I felt very proud when they asked me that" (Hameed 1979). An actress present at an award function for Eswari in 2009 remarked on how challenging it was to act out the special "effects" Eswari had "mischievously" given with her voice—the sighing, crying, heightened speech, or laughing—as if the actress were merely a puppet manipulated by the playback singer. Effects thus crystallized the performative excess of the playback singer's voice, the excess of voiced emotion or bodily sensations that interrupted the act of singing and sounded so realistic that they caused one listening to wonder about what exactly happened and who exactly was in charge in that profilmic moment.

Iconic Voices

In exploring how a typology of voices emerged in this period, I am interested not only in how particular voices are described and imagined to embody certain qualities but also in how those voices become iconic: how they themselves can be used as potent signifiers. In this regard, it is relevant that Eswari has recently undergone a sort of revival as an item singer, most notably with the hit song "Kalasalā kalasalā" from the 2011 film *Osthi*. The song sequence in the film features the item actress Mallika Sherawat dancing with the villain and then with the hero as he enters to vanquish the villain. The song is a typical item number in all its phatic look-at-me-ness, with lyrics that make multiple references to biting, stinging snakes, chewing, and the constant refrain that "Mallika is calling you." Not only is the item actress playing herself in the song, but Eswari is in a sense as well. There is a palpable self-referentiality to the song; it is built around the assumption that audiences will recognize the voice, and just to make sure they do, the film credits afford her a prominent place and mention her government award, beginning with a statement of "sincere thanks to Kalaimamani L. R. Eswari."

Prior to the film's release, the hero actor, Simbu, declared that the song would become "a youth anthem and an evergreen hit" ("Kalasala Will Be Youth Anthem"), thus giving it two potential meanings that would seek to contain the potentially transgressive fact of an elderly playback singer singing a modern item number with a scantily clad and gyrating Mallika Sherawat lip-syncing her words. But other elements of publicity and the song itself worked against this containment. To hype the song, a "making-of" video was released on YouTube, featuring footage of Eswari, T. Rajendar (the male voice), and the music director in the studio, interspersed with shots of the set during the filming of the song. Such "making-of" videos have become a phenomenon in the past few years, as a tactic for glamorizing the production of songs as part of show business. Interspersing cuts of the singers in the studio with Mallika, Simbu, and the other dancers during the visual shooting of the song sequence, the making-of video accentuates the contact and interaction between two sites of film- and song-making usually assumed to be (and, for playback singers of Eswari's generation, *necessarily*) temporally and spatially separated.

The song itself overflows the boundaries of the "evergreen" category; for although Eswari's voice is meant to be recognizable, it is not presented in the spirit of fidelity to the voice she put forth in so many of her earlier film songs. Not only is there no attempt to disguise or clean up the huskiness of age, but it is ambiguously conflated with the huskiness of youthful sexual desire. In addition, Eswari's voice is heavily embellished with audible Auto-Tune effects, something that it would be unthinkable to apply to the voices of other "respectable" singers such as Susheela. Finally, Eswari's aggressively rolled *r* in the half-English refrain "My dear darling unnai Mallika kūppiṭṟṟa" (My dear darling, Mallika calls you) is an exaggerated folk vocal gesture characteristic of the recently emerged genre of *kuttu* songs, which have become a vehicle for presenting images and sounds considered lower class and vulgar (Weidman 2012).

Using the voice of Eswari in fact ensured that the song could not be positioned within the established categories of a "youth anthem" or an "evergreen hit." The song displayed the edge of Eswari's persona—a persona and voice that seem to evade efforts to gentrify film and film production since the 1990s (Ganti 2012) or to contain the products of earlier decades within a nostalgic frame. Unlike Asha Bhosle, with whom Eswari is sometimes compared, Eswari's claim to respectable evergreenness is shaky at best. Asha also became known for her cabaret and Western songs in the 1950s and 1960s and was often the voice for the "bad" girl characters who were the foil to those "good" girls voiced by Lata Mangeshkar. However, her singing roles within films were mitigated by extratextual details of her life; as Lata's sister, she was of the same caste/socioeconomic background, and her marriage to the music director R. D. Burman in 1980 further increased her respectability.

Following the release of "Kalasalā," Eswari failed to give the proper signals of disavowal, instead appearing in a series of press meets and fielding speculative questions about her next moves. Rather than shying away from the public eye, she embraced the attention, using the opportunity to enter and shape the public discourse on what her singing could mean. Speaking to a group of largely male journalists on one such occasion, she fielded the questions herself, challenging the men to ask the questions straightforwardly instead of catcalling. Rather than confirming that her singing the song "Kalasalā" was just a one-time occurrence, she proclaimed her readiness to sing whatever young music directors might give her, addressing them informally: "Icai amaikkiṟiyā? Kūppiṭu. Vantu pāṭaṟēn" (Are you composing music? Call me. I'll come and sing). And she bemoaned the degraded status of item numbers, suggesting that they deserved a more elevated status. "They used to call them club songs. That is, it was relaxation, entertainment for men to watch the dancer. Now they call it 'item.' Cutting. Small. As if you are going in the car and ask your friend, 'did you bring that item along?' That's the situation of women these days" ("Playback Singer LRE Press Meet").

"Vamps" are professional, working women in the public sphere. Through their voices and embodied performance, they are mediating agents not only in the sense that they are sites for bringing the foreign into contact with local culture and idioms but also in that they inhabit the space between what is accepted and considered "respectable" and what is considered to be transgressive or immoral. They necessarily create new possibilities for female public performance even as they and the media surrounding them negotiate their place within existing structures and expectations. As I have suggested here, Eswari did not just fit into a preexisting spot in the typology of female voices that emerged in the 1950s and 1960s; rather, she enabled the typology to emerge. Her voice and performance defined, and came to iconically represent, a type within this system, a type that could subsequently be performed by others and by Eswari herself.

While Eswari's contemporaries practiced various strategies of containment to counteract the mobility engendered by the mass mediation of sound recording, cinema, and its culture industry, Eswari seems to have cultivated the mobility of her voice through various means: its transformation from being the voice of licit second heroines to that of vamps; its travel between the goddess Amman and the cabaret scenes of 1960s Tamil film; its ability to move easily between singing and voiced "effects"; its conflation of the huskiness of old age and the huskiness of sexual desire; and its admittance of aspects of her extratextual persona through her public speaking voice. What is perhaps most remarkable about the career of this singer who defied expectations for "respectable" singing and performance in the 1960s was not that she was seen as transgressive but that, much of the time, she was not. The provocative aspects of her persona and vocal sound have been managed, contained within her identity as an unmarried woman of lower-caste Tamil Christian background and by the division of vocal labor accomplished by the typology of female voices. Yet she retained—and still retains—a certain edge, a capacity to exceed the systems of meaning within which she has been placed.

Notes

1. These recent songs are, in 2011, "Kalasalā kalasalā" in *Osthi;* in 2012, "Pūntamalli" in *Thadayara thaka;* and in 2013, "Thagadu thagadu" in *Arya surya.*

2. Information in this section is drawn from interviews with L. R. Eswari conducted in November–December 2009 and January 2013.

3. Anuradha Sriram, personal communication, June 2002.

4. Some of these are viewable on YouTube: the Kanaha Valli CD, http://www.youtube.com/watch?v=-cszPBTnPGs&feature=related (posted by omsakthi, 26 October 2007), or "108 Amman," http://www.youtube.com/watch?v=5kCvtGmthmM (posted by omsakthi, 12 September 2007).

5. For example, in "Vāṅka maccān vāṅka," from the film *Madurai veeran* (1956), P. Leela's voice is timbrally pure; the only things that mark the song as a "folk" number are the lilt at the end of the phrase, clapping, and the chorus. In "Nīla sēlai kaṭṭi," a fishing-village song from the film *Tiruvilayadal* (1964), P. Susheela sings the folkish vocables "ye le lai lo" with an otherwise unmarked voice. The song "Maccānai pātēṅkala" from the film *Anakili* (1976), a paradigmatic example of the music director Illayaraja's "folk" style, features S. Janaki's pure voice singing the folkish vocables "lalli lalli lallo," the end-phrase lilt, and folk instruments.

References

Connor, Steven. 2000. *Dumbstruck: A Cultural History of Ventriloquism*. Oxford: Oxford University Press.

"El ār īsvari." 1968. *Bommai*, November, 26–29.

Ganti, Tejaswini. 2012. *Producing Bollywood: Inside the Contemporary Hindi Film Industry*. Durham, NC: Duke University Press.

Guy, Randor. 1997. *Starlight, Starbright: The Early Tamil Cinema*. Chennai: Amra.

"Kalasala Will Be Youth Anthem & Evergreen Hit—Simbu." 2011. *Kolly Insider*, 30 September. http://www.kollyinsider.com/2011/09/kalasala-will-be-youth-anthem-evergreen.html.

Lakshmi, C. S. 1990. "Mother, Mother-Community, and Mother Politics in Tamil Nadu." *Economic and Political Weekly* 25 (43): WS 72–83.

———. 2008. "A Good Woman, A Very Good Woman." In *Tamil Cinema: The Cultural Politics of India's Other Film Industry*, edited by S. Velayutham, 16–28. London: Routledge.

Majumdar, Neepa. 2001. "The Embodied Voice: Song Sequences and Stardom in Popular Hindi Cinema." In *Soundtrack Available: Essays on Film and Popular Music*, edited by Pamela Robertson Wojcik and Arthur Knight, 161–181. Durham, NC: Duke University Press.

Mazzarella, William. 2013. *Censorium: Cinema and the Open Edge of Mass Publicity*. Durham, NC: Duke University Press.

"Mukkani sāro muttamiḻ tēnō." 1971. *Pēcum Paṭam*, September, 99–103.

Nakassis, Constantine V. n.d. "Item Numbers, Performativity, and the Ontology of the Image in Tamil Film." Paper presented at the *Chicago Tamil Forum*, University of Chicago, May 29–31, 2014.

Sangari, Kumkum. 2006. "Love's Repertoire: Qurratulain Hyder's *River of Fire*." In *Love in South Asia: A Cultural History*, edited by Francesca Orsini, 259–285. Cambridge: Cambridge University Press.

Srivastava, Sanjay. 2006. "The Voice of the Nation and the Five-Year Plan Hero: Speculations on Gender, Space, and Popular Culture." In *Fingerprinting Popular Culture: The Mythic and the Iconic in Indian Cinema*, edited by Vinay Lal and Ashis Nandy, 122–155. New Delhi: Oxford University Press.

Weidman, Amanda. 2012. "Voices of Meenakumari: Sound, Meaning, and Self-Fashioning in Performances of an Item Number." *South Asian Popular Culture* 10 (3): 307–318.

Performances, Interviews, and Press Meets

Hameed, B. H. Abdul. 1979. Interview with L. R. Eswari for the Radio Ceylon program *Thiraikadambam*.
"LR Easwari on Her Career & 'Kalasala.'" 2012. Posted by IndiaGlitz Tamil Movies. YouTube, 8 March. http://www.youtube.com/watch?v=BnWgB8XYIA8.
"Playback Singer LRE Press Meet." 2011. Posted by KOLLYTALKvideos. YouTube, 15 September. http://www.youtube.com/watch?v=qlb_BnKaeaU.

Films

Nalla idattu sambandam. Directed by K. Somu. Sri Lakshmi Pictures, 1958.
Ni. Directed by T. R. Ramanna. Sri Vinayaka Pictures, 1966.
Osthi. Directed by S. Dharani. Balaji Real Media, 2011.
Paasamalar. Directed by A. Bhimsingh. Sivaji Productions, 1961.
Panamaa pasamaa. Directed by K. S. Gopalakrishnan. Sharada Productions, 1968.
Saradha. Directed by K. S. Gopalakrishnan. A.L.S., 1961.
Sivantha mann. Directed by C. V. Sridhar. Chitralaya Films, 1969.
Thillalangadi. Directed by M. Raja. Sun Pictures, 2010.

PART III

Silenced Voices and Forbidden Modernities

CENSORSHIP, MORALITY, AND NATIONAL IDENTITY

CHAPTER 9

Gendered and Censored Modernity

TWO FEMALE SINGERS AND THEIR MUSIC IN SOUTH KOREA

Soojin Kim

Two musical performances staged in the 1960s represent contrasting versions of female subjectivity and Korean modernity. In the first performance (1968), the singer Lee Mi-ja, dressed in a traditional Korean costume (*hanbok*), stands in front of two microphones while repeatedly clasping her hands together in a bowing gesture.[1] Her songs are mostly about brokenhearted women in the countryside who had experienced painful suffering and hardship. In the second performance (1967), the singer Patti Kim is dressed in a formal Western-style evening dress and wears her hair in a popular 1960s hairstyle: high on top and ponytail at the back. Accompanied by a band, she dances along with the music.[2] Her song texts reflect hope and optimism for what the future will bring.

The two performances just described demonstrate each singer's typical performance style, while illustrating the very different musical enunciation and images of women that Lee and Kim each came to symbolize. Lee represented calm, virtuous, and obedient women, while Kim signified charming city girls. Lee Mi-ja and Patti Kim each made their professional debut in 1959. Lee got her start through a local audition program, while Kim made her name performing shows for the US military in Korea. Both women achieved enormous popularity in Korea from the 1960s through the 2010s. At first glance, Kim seems like a more modernized and Westernized figure than Lee, as Kim performed a more radical image of women through her use of a more aggressive voice and a more Westernized fashion style. However, I am not suggesting that one singer reflects modernity and the other does not. Rather, both singers symbolized modernity in contrasting ways.

Musical style reflects the particular social structure and historical milieu in which each singer worked. Lee performed *trot,* a new musical genre during the Japanese occupation (1905–1945). *Trot* is a musical genre that combines Korean, Japanese, and Western musical styles. The term *trot* is an abbreviation of the

Korean term for the foxtrot, an American dance style that was popular in Korea and the United States during the 1930s. Although the style existed earlier, the term for the musical style that we now call *trot* crystallized in the 1950s. Lee's music made a huge contribution to gaining *trot* fans in Korean popular music during the 1960s. I argue that Lee represents a kind of modernity that was historically linked to the Japanese colonial period. In contrast to Lee, Kim's music was part of the standard pop genre introduced by US popular music cultures in the 1960s in Korea. I claim that Kim signifies a kind of modernity based on newly introduced elements from the West yet reconstructed within the particular social conditions of Korea.

This chapter examines the ways in which these two singers differed and how the distinctions between them embody representations of modernity in Korean society. Among the many female singers during the same period, I focus on Lee Mi-ja and Patti Kim because these two singers showed quite dissimilar images of gender and music genres reflecting modernity. Exploring Lee's and Kim's music within the larger sociocultural contexts provides a way to understand the collective consciousness of the times.[3]

Modernity in South Korean popular music reflected various tensions that Korean society was facing and seeking to resolve during the 1960s and the 1970s. According to Laurel Kendall (2010), modernity recreates and repackages "tradition," producing new cultural practices. Seung Sook Moon proposes the term "militarized modernity" as a framework to examine "historical circumstances under which modernity has been pursued in South Korea: national division, the civil war and the prolonged military confrontation between the two Koreas, postcolonial ambivalence to modernity, and the extreme sense of urgency about catching up with advanced countries" (2005, 7–8). Following Kendall and Moon, this chapter examines modernity of the 1960s and 1970s in two ways: (1) modernity reshapes the past in the present, and (2) modernity is linked to the military rule of president Park Chung Hee's regime, which mobilized people through government-led industrialization/modernization projects, close relations to US military intervention, and, in the case of culture, music performances as propaganda.

I show that Lee and Kim signified modernity through different music genres (*trot* versus standard pop), morality (East versus West), place (undeveloped countryside versus the city), censorship (censored versus uncensored), and gender identity (dutiful girl versus modern girl). I demonstrate that the morality and places associated with gender identity and music genre connect with state censorship. By analyzing performance venues, makeup, costume, gestures, song titles, and musical styles, I show that Lee's songs described dutiful girls who maintained a kind of morality in undeveloped rural areas. The women in Lee's songs articulated rusticity, as their song titles were often taken from nature or the names of rural villages far away from cities. On the contrary, Kim's music represented the progressive modern city girls whose morality was influenced by the West. Her song titles had neutral implications of place, reflecting the modernized city lives of the women in the songs. I suggest that these distinctive attitudes show how women in this epoch responded to modernized lifestyles in different ways.

Korean cultural politics attempted to sanitize the colonial experience under the government-led modernization project. Thus, the government project structured what the popular music of modernization sounded like. In this vein, a few of Lee Mi-ja's songs were banned due to their Japanese-flavored melodies, while Patti Kim's songs were permitted because her songs derived from American standard pop styles.

As seen from Lee's popularity among the Korean populace, the vestige of modernity from the Japanese colonial period was widely sustained within localized music. While the general public appreciated the music from the earlier period, the military government censored popular music and attempted to create new kinds of music of modernity. Government regulation and censorship generated discourses in favor of Western-focused modernized artifacts. Moreover, the government mobilized entertainers and singers to perform for soldiers at US military camps, which became crucial stages for their success. This chapter examines not only the historical events and the collective consciousness that structured the modernity of the 1960s and the 1970s but also the performance styles that embodied modernity and gender identities in distinctive ways.

Dutiful Girl and Modern Girl

Male and female singers of the 1960s and 1970s exhibited contrasting approaches to modernization. Due to the rapid industrialization of government-led economic development projects, many men left their hometowns in order to work in cities. In this period, names of places, either rural areas or cities, became important material for songs by male singers. On the one hand, male performers often sang about their nostalgia for their hometowns by emphasizing a phrase, a place, or something/someone left behind. In songs including "Meonameon gohyang" (Distant hometown), "Gohyangyeok" (A hometown station), and "Gohyangi joa" (I like my hometown), male singers expressed loneliness and bemoaned their wandering lives away from home (Jeon 2005, 177). On the other hand, songs such as "Doraganeun Samgakji" (Circulating Samgakji) and "Yeongdeungpoui bam (A night in Yeongdeungpo) employed a landmark and the place name of Seoul, the capital of Korea (Jeon 2005, 172; Lee

2006, 215–216). Regardless of the music genre, male singers appeared in similar costumes, either in suits or in Western-style attire.

The women described in female singers' songs showed different stances toward modernization. Lee Mi-ja's songs were nostalgic about the countryside, whereas Patti Kim's songs glorified life in the modernized Western-style city. Lee expressed sorrow and grief after a woman's partner, husband, or son has left to work in cities. A few of Lee's titles that reference rural areas include "Dong-baekseom agassi" (A Carmellia girl), "Seommaeul seonsaengnim" (A teacher of the island), and "Jeongdeun seom" (The island I am attached to). The women in Lee's songs are located in places very far away from the city (usually Seoul). For example, "Heuksando agassi" (A girl left in Heuksando) takes place on an island located to the southwest of Seoul. During the 1960s and the 1970s, travel to the island from the city was difficult due to poor transportation. The woman in this song is left in Hŭksando and misses her partner, who has gone to Seoul. She laments, "Nobody knows that I suffer from many things. The waves have come and gone ceaselessly. I look out inland toward what I desperately miss. My heart is broken while looking inland. Oh, a brokenhearted girl in Hŭksando."[4] The text of this song portrays the social circumstances of the period from the early 1960s to the 1970s, when a massive influx of people from rural areas to cities increased the population of Seoul by approximately four times. Physical landscape features in the song such as the island and the sea suggest the psychological distance between the partner and the woman (Lee 2006, 213) (figure 9.1).

Two of Lee's other songs, "Yeojaui maeum" (The heart of a woman) and "Yeojaui ilsaeng" (The life of a woman), illustrate women who accept emotional heartbreak as their destiny. The text of "Yeojaui ilsaeng" shows that women in this period were expected to sacrifice and endure suffering (Jeon 2005, 170–171): "Although I feel disastrous as if I cannot suffer any longer, I cannot speak out. It is because I am a woman. (. . .) Because I should suffer, I just cry. It is the life of a woman."[5]

Lee's music employed the characteristic sound of the *trot* genre, which involved nasal vocal timbre, frequent syncopation, mournful tunes in duple meter, and a slow tempo. Her voice and the genre of *trot* blended to represent the docile, obedient girl who is left behind. Lee's extensive repertoire represented conservative subjects who follow their destiny and do what they are expected to do. For example, in Lee's song "Seouriyeo annyeong" (Good-bye Seoul), Seoul is the place responsible for deepening a woman's sorrow. In this song, a woman visits Seoul to meet her partner, only to discover that her partner has fallen in love with someone else.

While Lee Mi-ja often brought objects from nature and distant places into her songs, Patti Kim's music was located squarely within Seoul (figure 9.2). Kim's songs such as "Seourui changa" (A song of Seoul) and "Seourui mojeong" (My heart

Figure 9.1. LP cover of Yi Mi-ja's *Hŭksando agassi* (A girl left in Hŭksando), produced by Chigu Record (LM120147).

for Seoul) express a very cheerful and joyful mood. Seoul is not a place where women experience hardship for work. In these songs, Seoul is where women feel comfortable and create good memories. Rather than a place of escape, Seoul is a beautiful place where women want to live forever with their lovers. The lyrics of "Seourui changa" are as follows: "A chime bell rings, and flowers bloom. Birds' songs and your smiling face. I miss you, my darling. Don't leave. I will live in this beautiful Seoul, where we first met and fell in love, where there are amiable streets, and where my heart is."[6] This overall joyful atmosphere is also shown in musical instrumental techniques and arrangements. In "Seourui changa," the string parts use pizzicato (plucked strings instead of bowing), which adds a joyful atmosphere to the song. As the song reaches its conclusion, the tempo gradually accelerates with the repeated word "ra, ra, ra, and ra," and the song ends in a tempo twice as fast as the beginning. The song features repeated dotted rhythms. As a way to add bright and hopeful colors to the song, snare drums and tambourines are added. Also, the long notes at the end of the phrases are full of clapping sounds.

Figure 9.2. LP cover of Patti Kim's *Stereo Highlight Vol. 3,* which includes "Sŏurŭi ch'an'ga" (A song of Seoul), produced by Sin Seki Record (가12233).

Patti Kim also sang songs about love. Kim expressed heartbreaking sorrow in "Ibyeol" (Parting), "Guworui norae" (A song of September), and "Mot ijyeo" (I will never forget you), among others. However, the women described in Kim's songs are not left behind. The women in her songs are in the middle of drastic social changes and accept urbanization and modernization in their everyday lives. In Kim's songs, women do not endure the suffering dramatized in Lee's songs. Rather, Kim's songs depict an attitude of acceptance and moving on after parting.

Kim's performance style reflected a different attitude from Lee Mi-ja. Patti Kim wore colorful makeup and an evening dress onstage. Lifting hands, bending knees, and bending herself forward and backward, she performed expressive body movements as her music climaxed and musical tensions released. She often appeared on stages descending the stairs of the stage while singing.

Kim's song "Sawori gamyeon" (When April goes by), which was the main musical theme of a film with the same title, relates a love story and the theme of unwanted parting because both lovers are engaged to other people. In the

Figure 9.3. LP cover of Patti Kim's *Greatest Hit Album,* which also includes "Sŏurŭi ch'an'ga" (A song of Seoul), produced by HIT Record (HL12378).

film, Patti Kim appears as an entertainer who sings this song with a tango accompaniment. The hero and heroine of the film watch Kim's performance in a Western-style bar. They drink whisky while appreciating the performance. The music and the setting of the film represent Westernized city life.

Kim's embodiment of the Western lifestyle was also expressed in her album covers (figure 9.3). Most of her album covers include a picture of her wearing either an evening dress or another stylish outfit. Whether standing in front of a two-storied European red bus or wearing a large hat and sitting on travel luggage, she symbolizes a modernized city girl on the move.

However, Kim's songs were not exclusively about the big city. Songs including "Neunggeumkkot pineun nae gohyang" (My hometown having Neuggeum flowers) and "Yeonja maeul agassi" (A girl in Yeonja village) make reference to rural areas. The former expresses nostalgia for the hometown, but the atmosphere is not sad. Accompanied by joyful light music, the girl in the song shows that she is full of hope. In "Yeonja maeul agassi," although the music is very calm and peaceful, the girl has confidence that her partner will return soon.

One could say that Lee's music represents subjects who are excluded from modernity, whereas Kim's music depicts subjects of modernity. However, Lee's music also reflects the modernity of the period. First, the tonal quality of Lee's music entails all the aspects of modernity that are linked to the previous period. Given that the subjects in Lee's *trot* music recognize this vestige of modernity from an earlier period and fully appreciate it by incorporating older with newer aspects, the women in her music are not opponents of modernity but subjects of modernity. Second, the women in Lee's music show indirect participation in the government-led modernization projects through patience, waiting, and sacrifice. On the contrary, the women whom Kim sang about show more direct participation in Western-focused modernization and industrialization projects. Through these distinctive musical genres and different attitudes toward modernization, Lee and Kim represented competing markers of Korean modernity.

Media Technology and Performance Venues

Media technology was an important element in the careers of Lee Mi-ja and Patti Kim. They both appeared on televised music variety shows and hosted their own shows. Media such as television and film reinforced the distinctive images of the women whom Lee and Kim sang about. Lee and Kim also sang in Korean films and soap operas, which increased their popularity.

The recording and media technologies that were introduced during the Japanese colonial period had a profound impact on popular music and its circulation (Lee 2010; Jang 2006; Gwon 2004). Since the first radio broadcast in 1927, radio became an important medium for listening to music in private spaces, alongside phonographic recordings. In 1954, the first commercial broadcasting station, CBS, was established, and in 1957, AFKN (American Forces Korean Network) first transmitted its radio programs. Since then, AFKN has been a channel not only for the US military but also for the general public to encounter American popular music, which is neither filtered nor translated. By the mid-1960s, a few more commercial broadcasting stations were founded: MBC in 1961, DBS in 1963, and TBC in 1964. As radio programs thrived, newspapers included advertisements for radio.[7]

The first television program in Korea was aired in 1961, and three TV channels emerged by the end of the 1960s. Music disc jockeys of radio programs and music variety shows flourished on television. Television enabled viewers to see body movements, attire, and performance settings that became key elements in constructing the gender identities of Lee Mi-ja and Patti Kim. The scenery, body movements, and attire in Lee's and Kim's music performance scenes visualized the women depicted in their songs. Reaching the peak of their popularity in this period, Lee and Kim hosted TV music show programs in the early 1970s: *The Lee Mi-ja Show* and *The Patti Kim Show*, respectively.[8]

The huge popularity of film as a new entertainment medium can be seen in newspaper advertisements that constitute three to four half pages. The soundtracks for popular television soap operas and films were fashionable, and many singers appeared in them. Lee Mi-ja sang theme songs including "Assi," "Bingjeom," "Yeoro," and "Seommaeul seonsaengnim" (A teacher of the island), while Patti Kim contributed songs for the films *Chou* and *Sawori kamyeon*. In the soundtracks for televised dramas and films, Lee and Kim sang not only for the soundtracks but also for the interludes in between scenes. Those scenes are similar to music videos, as the singers enact the stories and attitudes of the women described in the song. For example, in the twenty-minute film *Noraeneun jeulgeowo* (I like to sing a song), Lee sang "Heuksando agassi" (A girl in Heuksando) and "Seommaeul seonsaengnim" (A teacher of the island).[9] The image in the scene that Lee sings suggests a virtuous woman. For the scene, Lee wears a traditional costume and appears on an island surrounded by the sea. Looking out to the sea as if she wants to cross it, she displays sad facial expressions and restrained body movements. In contrast, in the film *Naeirui paldogangsan* (Tomorrow's scenery of Korea), Kim sings "Seourui changa" (A song of Seoul).[10] For the scene, Kim wears a neat, colorful dress. Behind her, the scenery of Seoul is depicted by mountains and palaces. In the middle of the song, the camera shows a couple with full smiles in one of the palaces in Seoul. In addition, this song employs a large mixed chorus, and the climax articulates a joyful conclusion. As the melody rises to its climax, Kim performs sweeping movements with open arms.

Despite the differences I have outlined, it is very complicated to make a linear distinction between Lee and Kim according to whether the women in Lee's music are more docile and submissive than those depicted in Kim's music. Considering music performances as propaganda and considering the military gaze involved in those performances, one might say that both Lee and Kim were nothing more than female objects of the entertainment industry. It is noteworthy that the political contexts of the Cold War, the Korean War, and the US war in Vietnam created important performance venues for singers who performed for soldiers in Korea and Vietnam and at the US military camps in Korea. Popular music singers including Lee Mi-ja and Patti Kim participated in spectacular government-supported performance tours whose aims were to encourage Korean and US soldiers and to legitimate "anti-Communist and anti-North propaganda" (Shin and Ho 2009, 86). For example, on September 5, 1962, the *Donga ilbo* (*Donga* daily) reported that Lee and two hundred other entertainers including singers and comedians performed for Korean soldiers. Ten days later, Kim, along with several ensembles, choirs, and traditional instrumental players performed at the theater of the US Air Force camp in Osan.[11] On May 31, 1965, the *Kyeonghyang sinmun* (*Kyeonghyang* daily) stated that thirteen performers including Lee and Gu Bong-seo, a comedian, would visit Vietnam to give a performance for the American and Korean soldiers in Vietnam. Before this performance tour, President Park Chung Hee would meet the troupe and pass on a few daily supplies for the soldiers. The large size of the performance troupes and participation by celebrities demonstrate the ways in which the government worked to mobilize singers and entertainers in its pursuit of propaganda within the contexts of the Cold War and divided Korea.

Korean singers appeared not only for propaganda performances but also in concerts for US soldiers. Shin Hyunjoon and Ho Tung-hung explicitly state that the US military camp was a "cradle of Korean 'pop' musician[s]" and that "American music—and entertainment in general—unconditionally meant [a] 'modern thing' " (2009, 93). The performances at the US military camps, which were executed solely for the US troops in Korea, were variety shows combining dance, band ensembles, songs, magic shows, and short skits (Han 2009, 137; Shin and Ho 2009, 93). After the Korean War, the US government sent American entertainers to Korea. However, the shows at the US military camps often hired Korean entertainers as a way to reduce the cost of bringing American entertainers from the United States (Han 2009, 133). This led a number of Koreans to be involved in the US military club shows. As the shows were for the US soldiers, the musicians played American popular songs that were in vogue during the era. Popular singers including Patti Kim, Kim Sang-hui, and Choi Hui-jun made their debut as singers at US military clubs.

The US military clubs made a big impact on Korean popular music of the late 1960s and into the 1970s. First, the standard pop style provided a prototype for the popular music of the times. All the singers who had performed at the US military camps including Patti Kim were well known for their standard pop music styles. Second, this period gave new importance to the term *syo,* referring to a show, as a replacement for the term *gongyeon,* a generic term indicating a performance. After the US military shows reached their peak in the early 1960s, the term *syo* was gradually accepted among popular musicians including Lee and Kim. For example, a performance by Kim held in 1962 was publicized as the "Patti Kim Show."[12] Third, regardless of the terms used to indicate a music concert, the presence of concerts and their popularity demonstrated that music was appreciated not just through a sound recording or TV show but also in performance onstage. This type of music appreciation created distance between the audience and performer. The term "show" and the presence of music concerts were common in Lee's and Kim's performance. Thus, both singers reflected modernized ways of music appreciation while illustrating contrasting images of modernity during this time.

Government censorship regarding popular music genres also manifested aspects of modernity of the 1960s and 1970s. The following section explores how Lee and Kim reflected modernity through censorship in contrasting ways.

Government Policies to Sanitize Japanese Influences

During the 1960s and the 1970s, the Korean government enacted cultural policies, promulgated regulations, and established relevant administrative organizations to sanitize Japanese influence. Toward this end, the government intervened in shaping the musical sounds, song texts, and political attitudes of composers and lyricists. For example, the government encouraged musicians to create and sing *keonjeon gayo* (healthy songs).[13] Through "healthy" lyrics and tunes, the government manipulated people's emotions toward positive and cheerful moods and subsequently mobilized people to partake in economic development projects (Jeong 2012; also quoted in Kim 2016). For example, "Jal sarabose" (We shall live well), a representative healthy song, encourages people to work hard for the good of the nation.

While healthy songs regulated the process of writing music and its distribution, two government censorship committees were formed to screen all the popular music of the time: the Korea Media Ethics Committee in 1962 and the Broadcasting Popular Music Review Committee in 1965. Through the examination of the lyrics, music styles, and political attitudes of all musicians, including composers and lyricists, hundreds of popular songs were banned from being performed or broadcast once the censorship regulations were enacted. Any texts expressing lascivious, decadent, gloomy, and pessimistic moods were banned, and music created by those who defected to North Korea was forcefully prohibited (Kim 2016, 184).[14] Screening musical styles was an important way to manipulate the popular music soundscape. The committees banned a number of songs due to their Japanese influence and style (*waesaek*). The government worked to expunge all cultural customs and practices appropriated during the Japanese colonial period, and the censorship of Japanese-inflected musical styles was implemented as a way to obliterate cultural relics from the colonial period.

Songs sung by Lee Mi-ja and Patti Kim were banned, but for different reasons, indicating different approaches by the government toward modernity. In many cases, *trot* songs were banned for the Japanese-tinged melodic and rhythmic aspects that were commonly heard in the musical styles of the genre.[15] The criticism that focused on the Japanese musical aspects of *trot* increased in the 1960s. As one of the main singers in the genre of *trot*, a few of Lee's songs were forbidden due to their inappropriate lyrics.[16]

As the genre name *trot* was widely in use, increasing levels of criticism of *trot* emerged during the early 1960s due to the genre's Japanese musical aspects. On November 16, 1968, the *Donga ilbo* reported that twenty-eight songs of the total thirty-eight forbidden songs from January 1, 1968, to July 1, 1968, were Japanese-flavored songs (eleven songs) or imitations of Japanese popular music (seventeen songs).[17] Newspaper columns of the period between 1960s and the 1980s disparaged composers and singers if they did not clean up Japanese-sounding tunes and rhythms. In addition, the criticism suggested that Japanese-flavored cultural products were undeveloped and vulgar.

What musical aspects of *trot* provoked accusations of a Japanese style? Koreans replaced the genre name *trot* with the degrading term *ppongjjak*, a term that described the rhythmic characteristics of *trot* in an onomatopoeic way yet disdainfully. The sound *ppong* displaced the first beat and *jjak* the second beat. In addition, many *trot* songs were composed in a pentatonic scale and have lots of appoggiaturas and syncopations. The *trot* singers typically sing songs with a strong nasal sound and wide vibrato. Although one can argue that these vocal styles were adopted from Korean folk songs (*minyo*) and newly composed folk songs (*sinminyo*), these vocal qualities are also found in Japanese *enka*, a genre of Japanese popular music (see Christine Yano, chap. 6 in this volume). Due to its similar musical style with enka, the government attempted to erase those musical sounds.

On the contrary, the American standard pop style that Patti Kim sang was not censored.[18] Rather, this music style was acclaimed because the American standard pop could add new musical features to preexisting soundscapes.[19] Different from *trot* singers, a few singers in the American standard pop style began their musical careers at the US military clubs and expanded their audiences rapidly among the general public. As stated earlier, the US military camp became a significant place to learn American popular music. Those singers of the American standard pop style sang not only American pop but also other popular song forms, including Italian *canzone* and French *chanson*. Patti Kim often sang popular foreign tunes with texts in Korean.

The cultural policies vis-à-vis censorship show that the government aimed to shape Korean national identity by controlling popular music. The discourse about the Japanese musical aspects heard in *trot* remained a disputed issue in Korean society since government censorship was implemented. The negative discourses about Japanese musical aspects gradually informed the prevailing assumption that Western-style songs were more aesthetically beautiful than the undeveloped Japanese-influenced *trot*. Subsequently, the modernized musical sounds that the government promoted unsurprisingly came to lean toward Western music from the United States. New musical styles from the United States were introduced and gained popularity in Korea (see Hee-sun Kim, chap. 14 in this volume). Despite the presence of an extensive popular *trot* repertoire from the past, this genre is now appreciated by only a small segment of the population of Korea.

The peculiarities of gendered and censored modernity that developed in the 1960s and 1970s structured the ways in which Lee Mi-ja and Patti Kim performed in succeeding decades and how their music was interpreted by audiences. A middle-aged Lee in the 1980s expressed the voices of conservative women in "The Filial Piety Show" (*hyodo syo*) at Parents' Day performances, among other events. The title reminded listeners of the dutiful girl. Since the 1980s, the term "traditional song" (*jeontong gayo*) has been used as an interchangeable term for *trot*, especially among *trot* singers. The term signifies that the singers want to erase the negative attitudes toward *trot* that were imposed by the government. Changing the name emphasizes the genre's Korean features rather than those associated with Japan, eliminating the negative aspects while highlighting the long history of the genre in Korean culture.

Patti Kim officially announced her retirement from all musical activities in 2012, while Lee Mi-ja continues to perform. At a series of special concerts to conclude Kim's musical career, she maintained a performance style that represented women who are fashionable and full of confidence. Lee and Kim maintained their musical styles and images of modernity of the 1960s and 1970s in distinctive ways. The contemporary singers who succeeded Lee and Kim have shown more varied ways to reflect gendered modernity in their musical genres and performance styles. For example, many young female *trot* singers sing in the nasal vocal style of the music genre but perform in highly sexualized ways. Also, the women described in their songs are not obedient any longer.

In this chapter, I have suggested that Lee Mi-ja's and Patti Kim's music reflected the tensions of modernity in this period. Under these circumstances, Lee and Kim formed their musical careers and became celebrities. They are often compared to each other because they debuted in the same year and performed in the same time period, but their performances and the discourses about them are divergent. The differences found in Lee's and Kim's music link to the juxtapositions of modernity in this period.

The censorship of modernity showed that the Korean government manipulated forms of popular music as a way to sanitize colonial-related memories. Censorship emphasized the negative discourses of Japanese-influenced music and encouraged strong Western influences in popular music. While censored modernity was led by the government, gendered modernity was structured by the women who reacted to drastic social changes and interpreted modernization in different ways.

On the one hand, the process of modernity during the 1960s and the 1970s was geared toward Westernized modernization through the rapid pace of industrialization. In the 1960s, newspaper advertisements were full of symbols from the West. For example, one advertisement for a department store used the title "Paris in Seoul" as a way to highlight Western-style goods and nightlife.[20] In addition, during the 1970s, factory machines, cars, and new factory systems appeared in newspaper advertisements. However, modernity was more complicated than Westernization, as demonstrated by the two singers discussed in this chapter. While incorporating traits of modernity from the earlier period, which included different music cultures from Japan and the United States, modernity in Korea also took shape through government censorship of popular music and the ways in which women embodied competing symbols of modernity in music.

Notes

1. Lee Mi-ja's performance was part of a special performance for soldiers in Seoul. The whole program can be viewed at the following URL: http://ehistory.go.kr/page/pop/movie_pop.jsp?srcgbn=KV&gbn=MH&mediaid=10810&mediadtl=23247&quality=W.

2. Patti Kim's performance was produced by the government and was part of her performance at a Korean army camp in Vietnam. It can be viewed at the following URL: http://www.ehistory.go.kr/page/pop/movie_pop.jsp?srcgbn=KV&mediaid=464&mediadtl=4291&gbn=DH&quality=M.

3. Many other singers displayed images similar to Yi and Kim in Korean popular music during the 1960s and 1970s. Yun Bok-hui was a female singer well known for her flamboyant fashion including very short skirts. Kim Chu-jaa was famous for her psychedelic rock music and her sexy and voluptuous dancing style using her upper body. On the contrary, Kim Serena performed Korean folk songs and usually wore traditional Korean costumes. Jeong Hun-hui's image was somewhere between the modern girl and obedient girl in that she performed feminine elegant images of women while singing the new music genres of her time.

4. The song was released in 1967. Bak Chun-seok composed the melody, and Jeong Du-su wrote the lyrics.

5. The song was released in 1968. Baek Yeong-ho composed the melody, and Han San-do wrote the lyrics.

6. "Seourui changa" (A song of Seoul) was published in 1969 by the composer and lyricist Kil okl-kyun.

7. During the Japanese colonial period, newspapers included advertisements for purchasing radios. In the mid-1950s, Zenith and Philips radios were advertised in newspapers, and beginning in the early 1960s, advertisements for radios made by Geumseong, a Korean company, appeared.

8. *Kyeonghyang sinmun*, 4 November 1970.

9. The film *Noraeneun jeulgeowo* (I like to sing a song) was part of the *Munhwa yeonghwa* (Culture film), which, along with the national anthem and "Daehan News" (News of Korea),

were shown in movie theaters before every film. The government-produced *Munhwa yeonghwa* aimed to educate and enlighten Koreans and promote and publicize government-led projects.

10. The film *Naeirui paldogangsan* (Tomorrow's scenery of Korea) was released in 1971. The film, which aimed to promote the Korean government's modernization project, describes a trip around Korea by a mother and father. The middle of the film features performances by Patti Kim, Lee Mi-ja, and other singers.

11. Traditional music was played by Seong Keum-ryeon (*kayageum*, a Korean twelve-stringed zither) and Ji Yeong-hui (*janggo*, a Korean double-headed drum).

12. The website www.ehistory.or.kr includes a short video clip of the "Patti Kim Show" that she performed after her tour in 1962.

13. The government supported and organized healthy-song choir competitions throughout Korea. *Kyeonghyang sinmun*, 18 November 1972.

14. The first forbidden song was "Giroui hwanghon" by the lyricist Jo Myeong-am, who defected to North Korea.

15. Before the term *trot* was fixed in the late 1960s, Lee Mi-ja was often considered to be a *minyo gasu* (folk music singer).

16. For example, Lee Mi-ja's song "Appa, appa, uri appa" (Dad, dad, my dad) was banned due to the cruel content of its text.

17. The titles, composers, lyricists, and singers of the forbidden songs, as well as the reasons for being prohibited, are listed at the following URL: http://theme.archives.go.kr/next/tabooAutonomy/forbidenSongList.do.

18. A few American pop songs were banned for being vulgar and decadent, but not many.

19. Only a few of Patti Kim's songs were forbidden due to their lyrics, as most of her music was considered standard pop based on American music.

20. *Maeil kyeongje*, 20 November 1969.

References

Jang, Yu-jeong. 2006. *Oppaneun punggak jaengiya* (My brother is a wandering singer: Modern landscape as seen through popular music). Seoul: Minŭmin.

Jeon, Ji-yeong. 2005. *Keundaeseongui chimnyakgwa isipsegi hanguk eumak* (Invasion of modernity and Korean music of the twentieth century). Seoul: Puk Korea.

Jeong, Seung-hwa. 2012. "Governing Emotion in the Developmental State of South Korea: Focused on Public Information Activities and Cultural Policies in the 1960s–70s." Paper presented on 9 November 2012 at the Korean Workshop, University of Illinois, Urbana-Champaign.

Han, Ji-su. 2009. "*Mi palgun budaereul tonghan miguk daejung eumakui guknae yuip yangsang* (Introduction of American Popular Music to Korea through US Military Camp Show)." *Eumakgwa munhwa* (Music and Culture) 20 (2): 131–151.

Kendall, Laurel. 2010. "Introduction: Material Modernity, Consumable Tradition." *Consuming Korean Tradition in Early and Late Modernity: Commodification, Tourism, and Performance*, edited by Laurel Kendall, 1–18. Honolulu: University of Hawai'i Press.

Kim, Soojin. 2016. "Controlling or Supporting?: A History of Cultural Policies on Popular Music." *Made in Korea: Studies in Popular Music*, edited by Hyunjoon Shin and Seung-Ah Lee, 181–190. New York: Routledge.

Gwon, Do-hui. 2004. *Hanguk geundae eumak sahoesa* (A social history of Korean modern music). Seoul: Minsokwŏn.
Lee, Yeong-mi. 2006. *Hanguk daejung gayosa* (A History of Korean popular music). 2nd ed. Seoul: Minsokwŏn.
Lee, Yongwoo. 2010. "Embedded Voices in between Empires: The Cultural Formation of Korean Popular Music in Modern Times." PhD diss., McGill University.
Moon, Seung Sook. 2005. *Militarized Modernity and Gendered Citizenship in South Korea*. Durham, NC: Duke University Press.
Shin, Hyunjoon, and Ho Tung-hung. 2009. "Translation of 'America' during the Early Cold War Period: A Comparative Study on the History of Popular Music in South Korea and Taiwan." *Inter-Asia Cultural Studies* 10 (1): 83–102.

Newspapers

Kyeonghyang sinmun
Maeil kyeongje
Donga ilbo

CHAPTER 10

Princess Siti and the Particularities of Post-Islamist Pop

Bart Barendregt

The career of the Malaysian pop diva Dato' Siti Nurhaliza Tarudin illustrates the ambiguities that modern Malay Muslim star performers face, caught as they are between the particularities of local, national, transnational, and global Islamic music industries. This chapter illustrates not only how such performers have challenged more secular definitions of modernities but also how Islamic popular music stirs its own controversies among representatives of both the Malaysian entertainment industry and the broader Muslim orthodoxy. Such controversies have dealt with issues of the assumed hedonism of the industry's new stars, the commercialism of religion, and most important, the gendering qualities of much Islamic popular music. In the process of these controversies, it is predominantly Muslim Malay female artists that turn out to be both subject and agent in defining the fine lines of a newly emergent Islamic chic that is, at once, transnational in character but firmly embedded within local values.

By introducing the dynamic interplay of the global Islamic project with Asian modernities, I aim to show how "pious stardom" (Tartoussieh 2007) is both constructed and constrained by these forces and how new ideas of masculinity and femininity have emerged. Pious stars combine overtly religious messages and assertive commercial marketing and distribution. As a case study, Siti has moved from the archetypal Malay girl next door to national ethnic star, regional pop diva, and Islam's glamour lady. I show how female Muslim superstars are neither duped by the industry nor wholly silenced by religious authorities but have found their own voice and agency with which to carefully navigate the sensitivities of today's Muslim Asian modernity. This case study, more specifically based on a single song produced in the musical interstices of London, the United Arab Emirates, and Southeast Asia, shows how global Islam has been fantasized in one particular locality, Malaysia, more specifically its Klang Valley, which is also the center of the Malaysian entertainment industry. The song, titled "You Came to Me," raises questions about how Muslim artists should navigate increasingly sensitive issues of modest behavior, moral virtue, and normative Islamic definitions of Muslim masculinity and femininity. By unpacking the song's form, content, reception, and meaning, this chapter strives to show how Asian modernities have increasingly come to be articulated within an explicitly Islamic context.

From Ethnic Pop Diva to Religious Singer: The Many Faces of Siti

Siti Nurhaliza (born 1979) is not an Islamic singer per se but a Muslim pop diva who has collaborated with religious performers, released religious albums, and is perceived as one of the new "pious superstars" of Asia.

Siti grew up in small-town Kampung Awah, Temerloh, with her father, a policeman, and her mother, a local singer.[1] Her mother taught her to sing—some people say in order to sell homemade cakes in the neighborhood—and from an early age onward, Siti has performed traditional and patriotic songs at cultural festivities and family gatherings (Alifstyle 2003). Coming from a modest family and hoping to make something more of her life, she decided at the age of fourteen to follow her brother to Kuala Lumpur to audition for the famous *Asia bagus* talent show. Whereas her brother found success, Siti failed to make it to the first round and left, frustrated, for home. However, she returned the following year and won the prestigious local singing contest *Radio TV Malaysia bintang*, which was nationally televised. She earned a record deal with Suria Records (and rejected record deals with other international majors such as Sony). Her first single, "Jerat cinta" (Love's trap, 1995), was an instant success and earned her an award from the national music industry. A year later, Suria Records released her first, self-titled album, which achieved unprecedented sales by Malaysian standards. During the next twenty years, eighteen Siti albums were released, not only in the Malaysian market but also in neighboring countries such as Indonesia and Singapore, where she obtained a similar status. Both the political scientist Farish Noor (2008) and the blogger Jeff Ooi (2007) have recounted how, amid heated debates over which country was entitled to ownership of particular traditional songs and other forms of heritage, Indonesians took to the street yelling, "Crush Malaysia, but save Siti Nurhaliza" (*Ganyang Malaysia, selamatkan Siti Nurhaliza;* Ooi 2007).

Siti's eighteen albums include at least five ethnic pop albums featuring mostly traditional Malay repertory such as the *dondang* and *zapin* genres (Tan 2005). The albums promote her heritage, although she has similarly recorded in both Chinese and Tamil. In live performances, Siti has been known to dress up

Figure 10.1. Siti Nurhaliza performing at the Kuala Lumpur International Film Festival 2008. Courtesy of Irwandy Mazwir. Fair use via Wikimedia Commons.

in the Malaysian flag (see figure 10.1). Siti is portrayed as the voice of a nation yet simultaneously exceeding it as the "true voice of Asia."[2] In 2003, she was voted Asia's best female artist in the annual Planet Muzik Awards (Patrick 2003). A 2011 documentary, *The Legend of CT,* marking Siti's thirty-third birthday, depicts her activities as a producer, TV presenter, and advertising star (for, among other things, her own brand of tea, aptly called *CTea*). Siti remains, generally, true to herself, often conservatively dressed and known for her polite, small-town behavior. In a world of kitsch and glamour, this may not seem the best asset, and Siti initially had many difficulties positioning herself within and through the local media; but it is exactly this modest behavior that became her trademark.

In contrast to the image represented in the documentary video *The Legend of CT,* Siti is an excellent code switcher. She adopts a musical strategy that best can be described as being "used to establish, cross, or destroy group boundaries; to create, evoke, or change interpersonal relations" (Gal, 1988, 247). Not only does she know how to play on nationalist sentiment, as her ethnic performances attest, but she can also switch register and adapt to other musical languages. For example, she portrayed the Southeast Asian Pepsi girl using an R&B-derived image to promote the soft drink throughout the region (2000–2001).

At age twenty-six, Siti had achieved success throughout Southeast Asia, but Malay audiences started wondering when this rich, charming, and righteous woman would find a life partner. When newspapers finally started reporting on her first affair, it was not the fairy-tale romance that many of her fans had hoped for. Instead, she was dating the forty-seven-year-old Datuk Seri Khalid Muhammad Jiwa (a.k.a. Datuk K.), a Malaysian entrepreneur, former UMNO youth-wing member, and also a divorcé with four sons from a previous marriage.[3] Datuk K. reportedly fell in love with Siti while first visiting her home in Kuala Lipis, being much impressed with the celebrity, who was unpretentiously dressed in just a batik sarong and a T-shirt (Simply Siti 2006). Yet in the popular press, Siti was suddenly portrayed as a home wrecker, stealing away another woman's husband, with Siti defending her new relation with Datuk K. as one based on true love. Moreover, the couple referred to themselves as holding onto Muslim regulations, with the Federal Territory Religious Council approving the breakup of Datuk K. and his former wife. When Siti eventually married Khalid in 2006, the event was dubbed the wedding event of the decade and was witnessed by royalty and celebrities in the Southeast Asian world of pop music. The ceremony was staged at the Federal Territory Mosque and watched by over nine million television viewers in Malaysia and neighboring Indonesia. Yet fans and nonfans were heard complaining about the cost of the event, similarly disapproving of Siti no longer living up to the stereotype of the favorite girl next door. Instead she had become the glamorous diva she so long had resisted.

After Siti returned from a pilgrimage with her husband to the Holy Land in 2009, she announced the release of her fourteenth album, *Tahajjud cinta* (The midnight prayer), her first fully religious album, which was released during that year's Ramadan month. For this album, Siti worked with renowned performers of *nasheed,* the most "modern," global, and commercial of Islamic genres to date, who advised her on singing style and the right pronunciation of the Arabic language, which featured prominently in several songs.[4] Among those songs was a cover version of a previously popular song by the Indonesian religious singer Opick as well as the song "Ketika cinta" (Once in love), which was used in the Indonesian film *Perempuan berkalung sorban* (Lady with the turban). The film portrays a daughter's rebellion against her father, a traditionalist preacher, who, according to her, leaves little room to maneuver for young Muslim females. But it also contains religious prose and adoration for the Prophet Muhammad *(Selawat)* and a recitation of the ninety-nine names and attributes of Allah *(Asma al Husna).*

The response of Siti's predominantly Muslim Malay and female audience was enthusiastic, with some likening her to an angelic voice. According to critics, Siti had overstepped the boundaries of a proper Islamic woman, who was not yet able to make a decision about whether to be an Asian pop diva or a proper Muslim singer. Was she able to act as a role model and to publicly perform piety in the manner expected of someone involved in the commercial *nasheed* repertory?

In late 2009, Siti joined forces with another prominent female superstar, the Indonesian singer Krisdayanti.[5] The result was the album *CTKD,* short for *Canda* (joke), *Tangis* (cry), *Ketawa* (laugh), *Duka* (sad) but also an affectionate acronym for two well-known singers who became friends when Siti first started touring Indonesia from 1997 onward. This album showcases the singers for the divas that they had become, complete with glamorous photo shoots and a *CTKD* album launch at Jakarta's Hard Rock Cafe. The cover art for the album and the reviews highlighted the familial relations between the neighboring nations, which do not always get along. Both had recorded festive songs on the occasion of Ramadan or other special religious days. However, the careers of these women following the *CTKD* album signal two entirely different archetypes of the Asian diva. Krisdayanti went through an unhappy marriage and a divorce and is frequently the subject of gossip in popular print media. Siti largely had managed to navigate the complexities and challenges of fame and stardom and decided to show a more spiritual side of herself by regularly appearing at charity concerts and performing with *nasheed* combos such as the renowned Islamist group Rabbani. The more mature and spiritual Siti may have emerged as a result of her father's untimely death in February 2009, which resulted in her retreat from show business for months; but this image was certainly in accordance with Siti's married status and her success as a *halal* entrepreneur. In 2010, she created a cosmetic line (Simply Siti), which the Jabatan Agama Islam Malaysia (JAKIM,

Figure 10.2. Malaysian pop superstar Siti Nurhaliza performing a virtual duet along with a prerecorded track sung by the late Whitney Houston at a concert in Kuala Lumpur in 2016. A screen image of Whitney Houston can be seen in the background. Courtesy of Paulius Staniunas. Fair Use via Creative Commons.

or Department of Islamic Development Malaysia) certified as *halal*. In 2013, Siti was also awarded an annual prize by the national *Halal Journal* for having created a line of products suitable for Muslim women, not least as it reduces the tedious routine of applying makeup. Former prime minister Abdullah Badawi presented the star with the award.

Siti's work as an entrepreneur reflected the ease with which she was able to switch to other registers, with her company Simply Siti offering a "limited gold edition" of products especially for Idul Fitri, the festive end of the fasting season. A month later, she launched a fresh new collection, known as Simply Siti Glam Red, unmistakably showing, once again, the different faces of the diva without tarnishing her steadfast image of purity and piety.[6]

In 2016, Siti worked with music streaming service Yonder, which organized her Datuk Siti Nurhaliza & Friends Concert. This concert featured Siti as the headliner as well as guest artists, among them the late singer Whitney Houston, with whom, enabled by the latest digital technologies, she performed a "virtual duet" (see figure 10.2). The video clip of this song, *Memories*, was released in late 2016 and aimed to promote Siti to a larger international audience (Chaw, 2016). Whereas Siti had long aimed for a more international market, as also attested by a first full-English album, Islam offered her an alternative trajectory to global fame.[7] June 2012 saw the release of the hit song "You Came to Me" (referred to as YCTM hereafter), a song performed by Siti and Islam's highly celebrated rock star, the London-based Iranian Azeri Sami Yusuf. By unpacking its form, content, reception, and meaning, this chapter strives to show how Asian modernities have increasingly come to be articulated within an explicitly Islamic context.

YCTM

The lyrics of YCTM seem, at first glance, to be a secular text about earthly love but are actually a religious expression of love for Islam's last prophet, Muhammad. An Arab-language chorus further enhances the overt religiosity of the song, as do the Middle Eastern melismatic vocal techniques and the sweet accompaniment of the Turkish *ney* flute. The text, sung in English, Arabic, and Malay, is as follows:

[English-language verse]
You came to me in that hour of need
When I was so lost, so lonely
You came to me, took my breath away
Showed me the right way, the way to lead

You filled my heart with love
Showed me the light above
Now all I want is to be with you
You are my one true love
Taught me to never judge
Now all I want is to be with you

[Arab-language chorus]
Allahuma salli 'ala sayideena mustafa
'alaa habeebika nabieeka mustafa
(O God! Send your blessings upon our leader, the chosen one,
upon your beloved, your prophet, and the chosen one)

[Malay-language second verse]
Dikau hadir kala ku sedih sendirian dan hilang
Dikau hadir kala aku mendambakan petunjuk jalan
(You are with me in times when I am sad or when I am lost
You are with me when I need someone to show me the right way)
(Music and English words by Sami Yusuf, Malay words by Yasin Sulayman)

The song, previously released on one of Sami's solo albums, was repackaged for the Southeast Asian market.[8] Initially promoted through YouTube and Vimeo, YCTM was also included on Sami's latest solo album, *Salaam* (2012), which was launched for the lucrative Southeast Asian Muslim market. The duet with the Asian diva Siti was a big part of Sami's campaign to reach Southeast Asian Muslims.

The deliberate choice to perform part of the song in the Malay language is by no means surprising, considering that a large share of the world's Muslim population happens to live in Southeast Asia and that Malay may be included as one of the informal languages of Islam. The Malay language is intelligible to Indonesians, and by singing in Malay, Sami Yusuf and other Muslim superstars (such as the popular Swedish Lebanese singer Maher Zain) have been able to potentially reach the entire Malay-Indonesian world. Further, for decades, Malaysia has been known as the home of contemporary *nasheed*. As a result, many global Muslim pop stars today enjoy more fame in Malaysia than they do in their home countries. Blending the style of ancient spiritual hymns with hip a cappella boy-band music, *nasheed* has been tremendously successful in the Southeast Asian market, addressing questions about what it is to be a modern Muslim youth in this part of the world. It is thus instrumental in reconciling piety with a modern consumerist lifestyle that may be typified as "funky and shariah" or an approach that others have referred to as either post- or more recently "pop Islamist" (Müller 2014; also discussed later in this chapter).

While the history of *nasheed* dates back much further, the genre has been fully embraced by the entertainment industry since the 1970s. Moreover, *nasheed* continues also to serve as a useful interface for the Malaysian state (to some extent) and especially the Islamist movement, in terms of popularizing and propagating its message *(dakwah)*. As a consequence, *nasheed* performers, many of whom are or were previously attached to Islamist groups and promote Islam as a total way of life, now stand at the forefront of an industry that is thriving throughout Muslim Southeast Asia.[9]

All-female ensembles pioneered *nasheed* during its early uptake by the recording industry, and female student activists are still predominant among its listeners. However, today's contemporary *nasheed* is increasingly performed exclusively by young men. According to some of the genre's leading male artists, it is not appropriate for women to raise their voices in public, despite the fact that young women still constitute the majority of *nasheed* aficionados. Nevertheless, women continue to perform *nasheed* but for female audiences only; and mixed ensembles, except for those consisting of young teenagers, are no longer acceptable in the current *nasheed* scene. Even audiences are carefully segregated by gender, demonstrating just how much the genre is geared to Muslim issues.

Gender segregation has a much longer history in Malay public life, and so has the control of what passes as righteous female behavior or not. Based on fieldwork conducted in the late 1980s, Aihwa Ong (1990) observed how Malay customary law *(adat)* and its emphasis on bilaterality gradually was giving way to Islamic tenets that increase male control over domestic resources. Women until recently had been the ones who had maintained kin and neighborly relations, and masculinity had depended on a man's economic power, as well as his moral authority over women in his household. Islamic emphasis on female chastity so far had "imposed restrictions more rigorously on unmarried women (called *anak dara,* or virgins) than on unmarried youths, although promiscuity in either sex was criticized. Young girls were required to be bashful and modest, but the Islamic emphasis on *aurat* ('nakedness' that should be covered) did not, until recently, extend to covering girls' hair (an erotic feature), which they wore loose or plaited. Everyday wear was loose-fitting long tunics over sarongs *(baju kurong)*" (Ong 1990, 261).

However, as Ong argues, state policies and capitalist relations increasingly were creating conditions making the regulation of female sexuality a major issue. Michael Peletz (2012, 2015) likewise describes how in the past two to three decades, Malaysian official culture has seen the rise of a strict, unforgiving heteronormativity. Since the early 2000s, signaling such a trend, the Malaysian *syariah* judiciary has criminalized various kinds of gender nonconformity. The world of entertainment has not been left untouched, with trans performers for over a decade having been banned from Malaysian state radio and television.[10] Also, others such as Maila Stivens (2006) have commented on what is often dubbed a moral project of "family values" (dressed as either "Asian" or "Islamic values"), now occupying a central place in the cultural contests staged by state, religion, and the media alike and more often with them working in tandem. Today, owing largely to trends in neoliberal governmentality and state-sponsored Islamization, the Malaysian state has become more corporate, intrusive, and punitive as it has embraced neoliberal globalization and the forms and norms of Islam and Islamization held to be most compatible with it (Peletz 2015, 144).

Such governmentality offers the state an additional step toward enhancing surveillance, discipline, and control and thus pushes the public to engage in self-governance. It also involves media coverage of guidelines that help the larger public identify persons allegedly inclined toward same-sex relations or other allegedly deviant behavior (Peletz 2015, 155).

Moreover, Peletz observes how the past two decades have seen a change in proper observance of religion by Malays. Such an observance now moves away from Islamist groups and their previous stress on piety and good behavior to what Peletz dubs as a more "punitive turn" and a forbidding of evil: "Malays are not only increasingly on the lookout for behavior falling outside the range of state-defined normativity but are also more likely than in times past to bring real or imagined ethical and other transgressions to the attention of mosque officials, the police, or authorities" (Peletz 2015, 155). Interestingly, he notes that while enhanced gender segregation among the Malay segment of the population is definitely a preoccupation in the current cultural-political climate, there are some unforeseen and "counter-intuitive" trends in gender dynamics that are not captured by this particular trend. For example, the past five years have seen the appointment of Malaysia's first female *syariah* judges (Peletz 2013, 612), and women now outnumber men in institutions of higher learning in the country (Basarudin 2016, 61; see also Smith-Hefner 2007 for the Indonesian context). Not surprisingly, such contrary trends may even heighten the anxiety over currently prevailing gender stereotypes.

It is necessary for YCTM to be read and listened to against such a background of increased gender conformity and the space, little may it be, to maneuver and act otherwise. Indeed, it was the choice for a male-female duet that stirred considerable debate, raising questions about how Muslim artists should navigate ever-sensitive issues of modest behavior, moral virtue, and normative or proper Islamic definitions of Muslim masculinity and femininity. I discuss how the very same *nasheed* songs, and post-Islamist chic more generally, have become one of the more prominent arenas in which such gendered values are currently reframed in the online world of social and musical discourse. YCTM thus triggered a discussion about the proper conduct of important actors, pious superstars, and especially female singers.

Gender Trouble in the Malaysian Blogosphere

The official YouTube video of YCTM resulted in such fierce debate, mostly among Malaysians, that, at a certain stage, the comments section seems to have been shut down by its moderator. The *nasheed* idiom of YCTM blends an ancient Middle Eastern hymn and global R&B with traditional Sufi art and the boy-band imagery of its male protagonist, Sami. The YouTube video of the couple was adapted from an earlier 2009 clip when Sami still performed YCTM in English and Arab only and on his own, without Siti or any other female singer at his side.[11] The clip triggered responses for other reasons, for example, due to the attention-grabbing art of the Chinese master calligrapher Haji Noor Deen Mi Guang Jiang, whose graphic blend of Arab characters with unmistakable Chinese design seemingly added to Sami's image as a truly cosmopolitan Muslim artist eager to work with fellow Muslims from other parts of the world. Muslims in the Middle East and Southeast Asia appreciated Sami's album, as its success was taken to be the (long-awaited) sign of Islam's acceptance in the West. Muslim youth in the West, identifying with Sami's sense of "double remoteness" (Pond 2006, 12), recognized his feelings of being alienated. Coming from elsewhere, they were similarly estranged from fellow Muslims in their countries of origin, with whom they did not grow up and had little to share. In Sami, who like many other self-confessed awakened stars embraced his faith only at the age of sixteen,[12] they found someone who understood and celebrated their spiritual needs. On the occasion of the rerecording of YCTM with Siti Nurhaliza, a new version of the clip was made, showing Sami in a United Arab Emirates studio discussing the song with the Malaysian music producer Yasin. It was Yasin, one of the industry's most talented performers and himself a *nasheed* singer of some fame, who was credited with having triggered this Malaysian-Arab-Iranian-British cooperation.[13]

It was the visual dimension of YCTM, showing Sami and Siti singing together, side by side, that triggered a considerable controversy in the Malaysian blogosphere and beyond.[14] The reasons for condemning the performance are not straightforward and seemingly contradictory, as one quote from the clip's comment section illustrates:

> this kind of music is not at all allowed in Islam [. . .] he's a good singer
> he shud not depends on music *[sic]*. (posted by afshaanization)[15]

This comment may refer to a radical position in Islam that rejects the use of music in propagating religious values, although it also leaves open the possibility that certain musics are merely less appropriate in this respect. And while it clearly blames Sami for apparently holding this view, most other posts (typically in the Malay language) comment on Siti's role as a female singer in the world of Islam: "u r so amazing princess siti" (posted by DaLadyKillers); "To bad . . . Ct tak tutup aurat" (Too bad . . . Siti does not cover her more vulnerable body parts; posted by seera ziya).

In a number of cases, such remarks initiate a more heated debate about Siti's loyalty to both nation and Islam: "why dont u malay people shut the fuck up about how shes covering her head, compare to most of the ppl in that country, she has a good heart. .soft spoken. .rarely angry. .polite. .never backmouth anybody. .respectful. .and shes LOYAL! to Malaysia" (posted by AlanaSofie94); "AlanaSofie94.dont simply talk bout malay people! they all say that to dato siti coz they love her and care bout her eventhought she dont know them. maybe they dont want she got embrass because the song that they sing is bout rasurullah not brad pit ok! *[sic]*" (posted by suesweytz89). YCTM's second release as a male-female duet thus raises questions about how to properly represent an often-elusive notion of modern Muslim Malayness that is yet part of the (alternative) globalizing project that Islam increasingly has become.[16] These representations are continuously rearticulated and contested, not least by various Islamist groups within and outside Malaysian society itself, turning the notion of what is Asian, what is Islam, what is Malaysian, and what is simply fashionable into an increasingly complex picture. The global Islamic project relates itself to other iterations of what I see as modernity throughout the Asian region, iterations that are often more secular and neoliberal in character, such as banking, fashion, the food industry, or the entertainment industry.

On the surface, artists who wish to be successful performing *nasheed* on a global scale must adapt to the pressure of Islamist (and mostly Middle Eastern) norms in order to appeal to people who constitute the worldwide community of Muslims *(ummah)*. As uniform as this re-Islamization may seem to be, the world of Islam is full of variety. In spite of the commonality in Islam and the lure of a single market shaped by religious affiliation, there is tremendous variation across Islamic societies even within more fundamentalist discourse. Beneath the veneer of sameness, there is a complex interplay of marketing and religious values at stake, which forces producers and artists to take notice. Although Sami's albums are released on a worldwide scale through the company ETM International, they are released in various versions. Local partners adapt to local taste and values. For example, the Southeast Asian version of Sami's fourth studio album, *Salaam* (2012), locally distributed by Arteffects International, contained sixteen songs, some of which, such as YCTM, had already been released as singles. The decision to include YCTM, featuring a duet by Sami and Siti, was a strategic decision to reach the large Muslim market in Southeast Asia. Yet audiences in the Middle East would have disapproved of this choice, considering it improper for any *nasheed* artists to record with an artist of the opposite sex. *Nasheed* artists have long been aware of such varying protocols within the Muslim world, and hence their albums are adapted and released in a variety of versions, addressing the often different needs of a Southeast Asian, Middle Eastern and North African (MENA) or, for that matter, European market.[17] However, Middle Eastern Islamist ideology and practice (mostly Salafist in character) stands on morally high ground within Islam, and transnational pious stars must adhere to it if they want to be popular throughout the *ummah*. YCTM's duet of a global Islamic rock star and a Malaysian pop princess has Malays identify with more universal Islamist values, but it simultaneously inserts Malaysian ideas and practices—that is, the more gender-egalitarian approaches that the region is known for (Peletz 1996; Andaya 2007)—into such trajectories, the outcome of which we have not yet witnessed. The work and lives of Sami and Siti but also of other transnational stars thus increasingly become a point of departure for debates about the nature of Islam.

Having now introduced the song and some of its commentaries, I will clarify how *nasheed* has gradually become a strongly gendered business, preferring to prioritize its more masculine side and neglecting its female participants as singers, listeners, or fans. This has resulted in women being seen as lacking the particular masculine assets needed to perform successfully. It is against this background of such enormous forces that Siti has developed her Malaysian and international career as a pop singer, nationalist symbol, and Islamic diva.

Global Islamism Meets Asian Modernities

The ongoing claim for modernity in a Malaysian context has mostly been a battle of "isms" (see also Barendregt 2010). Ever since independence in 1957 of what was then still Malaya, the multiethnic country has been ruled by a single political party, the United Malays National Organisation (UMNO). This party proudly opted for Asian-style neoliberalism as a shortcut to progress, borrowing a capitalist mode from the West, while claiming Asian exceptionalism. Because there are two other ethnic majority groups in the country, namely, Indian and Chinese, and because UMNO depends on other single ethnic parties united in the National Front coalition (Barisan Nasional) for its electoral votes, UMNO has championed an agenda of Malay racial supremacy in an attempt to undo ethnicity as an economic marker (Williamson 2002). Especially during the rule of past prime minister Mahathir Mohamad (1981–2003), Malaysia performed very well economically, as measured in high-status nationalist projects such as a national air carrier, an automobile industry, and even a space program. Comparable to the late Singaporean prime minister Lee Kuan Yew, Mahathir (often praised by his fellow Malaysians as "the Father of Modernization") explained the accomplishments during his reign, based on so-called Asian values, which prioritized socioeconomic well-being over liberty or democracy and stressed loyalty toward country and authorities (Robison 1996). He thus yearned to convince the world that one could indeed be economically successful but without giving in to Western political and economic pressure.

In the process, the Malaysian state, as is the case with most other nation-states, has shaped what it means to be modern. However, its capitalist-driven secular interpretations of modernity have, at times, been haunted by other subdued readings of the modern: traditionalist, multiethnic, and religiously inspired claims. One of the biggest challenges so far, and one that has proven to be most difficult for Malaysia to contain, is the unprecedented rise of a new wealthy Muslim Malay middle class (see Shamsul 1999), which—contra many secularization theorists—prefers a modern yet profoundly orthodox lifestyle.[18] In response to UMNO's previous secular order and its need for the Malay majority vote, Islamic sentiment has increasingly been co-opted by the Malaysian state, often leaving traditional Islamist contenders, including the Islamist political party PAS, puzzled.[19] Mahathir's Malaysian exceptionalism ("Asian values") has, since the early 2000s, increasingly been wedded to newer state-led programs for modernization, now with a strong focus on Islam.[20]

At the same time, another, more global development has taken place, as UMNO's blending of Asian values with Islamic civilizational values coincides with the shift from a previous Islamic revival in the early 1970s—in which religion was largely seen as the antidote to Western colonial values—toward what Asef Bayat (1996, 2013) and Olivier Roy and Amel Boubekeur (2012) have come to define as "post-Islamism": the move beyond an ideology that merely employs Islam as a political tool to confront Western economic and political domination, towards new spaces and new means of expression (Roy and Boubekeur 2012, 4–5). Muslim activists have been experimenting with new forms of activism and new organizational structures in order to realize a true Islamic society in the cultural rather than the political domain. These developments are driven by the twin processes of objectification and fragmentation, in that combination first described by Robert Hefner (2000; see also Eickelman 1992) with regard to some of the recent manifestations of a globally dispersed and highly mediated world religion in the twenty-first century.[21]

In this respect, it is important to note that Islamism as an ideology has, at least since the 1970s, been further complicated due to processes of individualization and disillusionment with its utopian claims, as well as with its entanglement with the global entertainment industry. Islamism also has increasingly turned out to be an alternative trajectory for globalization, which comes with its own templates and its own standards. Once such standards prove successful in one place, they are quickly adopted elsewhere in the Muslim world. As part of such experiments, an ethos of post-Islamist chic has emerged that propagates its values through new and hitherto unconventional modes, including Muslim day spas, Islamic lifestyle glossies, teen lit, *halal* food processing, and modern Muslim entertainment such as Malaysia's *Imam muda* (The young imam) reality soap or the new wave of *hijabinistas* clad in the latest Muslim Malaysian clothing. These new post-Islamist imaginaries come with gendered articulations, as described in the next section.

Two Genders / No Single Islam

The popularity of post-Islamist chic in Malaysia has to do with a newfound religiosity among its fans. However, another equally important explanation is the continuous search for a modern yet appropriate lifestyle and the concomitant question of how to become a young Muslim man or woman in a quickly changing world. Aihwa Ong (1990) has argued that Islamization of public life in the country strengthened Malay male authority, which had been deteriorating during the 1970s and 1980s due to young Malay women increasingly entering the job market and, in particular, their visibility in campus life, where they often performed more successfully than their male peers did. It is questionable whether the Islamization of Malaysian public life should be seen solely as a male response, leaving young women mostly without agency (Frisk 2004); but it seems indisputable that public acts of piety and Islamist behavior have helped shape novel ideas about Muslim masculinity and femininity in both the Malaysian and global context. Nilüfer Göle thus observes that new ways of imagining the collective in Islamic public spaces are underpinned by alternative spatial and corporeal practices (2002, 174); many modern, middle-class women donning the veil are a prime example. Parallel practices have been noticed for Malaysia and Indonesia, where an increasing number of mostly well-educated women have adopted the headscarf or attend religious classes; these actions have become class markers that these women use to explore their modern Muslim identities (Brenner 1998; Mokhtar-Ritchie 2015).

Göle shows how Islamic identities have been primarily constructed in gendered terms and notes that young women have been at the forefront of what she defines as a "second wave of Islamism" (2002, 174). Public Islam challenges both the secular and the orthodox spheres. By recreating the borders of intimate and gendered spaces, these young women have acquired a kind of agency traditionally withheld from them. As a result, women themselves feel somewhat uneasy with their newly acquired status. Göle recognizes the conflicting agendas that young female (and, in her case, Turkish) activists have acquired through participating in secular education and religious politics, on the one hand, and adhering to the principles of Islamic communalism on the other: "While the former necessitates public participation, the latter sanctions the individuation of women, whose morality specifically involves community and Islamist authenticity" (1996, 3). Göle thus hints at the unintended consequences of modernity or what she calls the "forbidden modern," as these Islamic women may be well educated, politically active, and very visible in the public sphere.

The Vulnerable, the Modest, and Modernity Once Forbidden

In Islam, *Ilm al akhlaq* is traditionally the science of ethics and moral virtue. *Akhlaq* either is a natural state, although only few people are born with entirely good character, or is obtained through regular practice; one can discipline one's mind and soul through purifying practices including prayer and recitation. One self-identified *nasheed* musician, a member of the popular Muslim rock band Al-Farabi, defined *akhlaq* as follows: "It's about what we do in the now, all the good things and deeds we seemingly invest in, for which we will get a reward in the after-life" (personal communication, October 2012). Many of the pious superstars described in this chapter practice *akhlaq* by contributing to Islamic charities or taking a stance in Islamic public affairs. Sami has been regularly involved in a wide range of Islamic philanthropic activities including shows for the United Kingdom–based organization Islamic Relief and also contributing to other humanitarian causes.[22] Siti has created Tabung Prihatin Siti (Siti's charity fund), a fund for children's education and medical treatment that is named after her (*Utusan Malaysia* 2004), and is also widely hailed as a former ambassador for the Malaysian Red Crescent Society. She has also contributed to fundraising concerts, including events to raise awareness of Muslim compatriots in Gaza. However, she is careful to avoid an overtly partisan stance, which may be due to the fact that Malay women are expected to behave modestly and often leave political expression to their husbands and, therefore, are less in sync with the way Muslim Malay femininity is currently constructed.[23]

Akhlaq is primarily about modesty, or as most *nasheed* aficionados would argue, it is a matter of *aurat*. *Aurat* (*awrat* in Arabic) is literally about "vulnerability," but more practically it covers a set of rules pertaining to honor, shame, and especially modesty. It concerns both men and women and those intimate parts of the human body that need to be shielded from the view of nonclose relatives and others. In most contemporary Muslim societies, such rules are customarily restricted to the public behavior of young females. Why? Because it is exactly these young women who are commonly seen as the signifiers of the newly emergent public Islam that is integral to the public debate about the nature and meaning of Islam. Such religious attitudes and cultural beliefs explain why many listeners are keen to comment on the singers of YCTM in terms of "intention" and "modesty." Whereas nobody seemed to doubt Siti's sincere intentions, the practice of modesty was still mentioned in Youtube comments relating to her wearing the veil *(tudung)*:[24]

> love siti forever. .the lyrics is so meaningful and i know siti sincere to sing it. may allah bless her and open her heart to wear full 'tudung'. .
>
> (posted by udinlilyasyraf)[25]

In these examples, *nasheed* is not about music; it is not even about text: it is all about intention, as the frequent use of the ideas of *aurat* and *akhlaq* demonstrates. Statements about intention and modesty are no longer limited to traditionally educated scholars using conventional forms of jurisprudence (Eickelman and Anderson 2003). Rather, increasingly large numbers of Muslims give voice to their ideas and opinions in terms of the normative language of Islam. Popular culture is the contested terrain for articulating what is and what is not properly Islamic (Weintraub 2011). Indeed, within Islam, there is a wider discussion about female performance. In Islam, women are often seen as the weaker sex and in need of protection from male desire; this power balance would be reversed if women had the power to seduce men, as some Muslims believe (Van Nieuwkerk 1998). The way the female voice is used, among and with whom and also other bodily practices such as the covering of one's head, face, or hands depend on one's age, culture, and the religious schools within Islam that one is raised in. Among these differences in Islamic practice, and the fragmentation of religious authority, the domain of popular culture has become a privileged site for articulating how the female voice and body is to behave publicly.

YCTM and other emergent forms of Islamist chic are thus narrating how individual Muslims are to behave publicly. YCTM exposes some of the complexities of a new social Islamic imaginary. Some scholars have explained this imaginary in terms of a second, culturally more intense, Islamization of public life, which is presently occurring in a number of majority-Muslim countries worldwide (Göle 2000). Others, such as Roy and Boubekeur (2012), prefer to use the term "post-Islamism" to describe the transformation of what was once predominantly a political ideology into what gradually has become a cultural orientation, in which popular music has a prominent place.[26] Yet the "post-" in post-Islamism may signal very different things. The post-Islamism of *nasheed,* in its readiness to move beyond a simple East-West divide, clearly departs from the postcolonial sentiment of 1970s Southeast Asian Islamist movements. The *ummah* has increasingly become a truly global community, and with an especially affluent Muslim middle class in the emergent markets of Southeast Asia, feelings of backwardness and inferiority seem far less of an issue for today's young Islamists. Today's Islamist chic similarly transgresses traditional values, especially with regard to the desired behavior of young women; at the same time, it is keen to constantly draw new boundaries, as it is defining new codes of gender relations.

With the universalistic and transnational approach of many of the pious stars mentioned throughout this chapter but also with the new market appeal of the *ummah,* Islamist chic is also strongly postnational in character. Sami and Siti may have been born and raised in Tehran and the United Kingdom or in Malaysia, respectively, but they both aspire to an international audience that the *ummah* clearly offers. Yet universalistic approaches are continually challenged by Middle Eastern Salafist teachings that act as a measure of all things Islamic. In the aftermath of such a challenge, public pious behavior aimed at a larger transnational audience may have a potentially serious impact on how a Malay Muslim female singer is to behave, yet such performances also offer an opportunity to highlight the global project of Islamic entertainment.

Post-Islamism, like its predecessor Islamism, seems to lump all sorts of voices and expressions together. But hidden by this term is a hint of plurality, a much-desired alternative to other trajectories of both modernity and globalization, as well as a wide range of more localized tastes and preferences. Most notable are the different impacts that post-Islamist performance may have on male or female artists, whether recently awakened or always pious, who have devoted themselves to post-Islamist performance.

Acknowledgments

I would like to thank the Netherlands Organisation for Scientific Research (NWO) for funding this research and Professor Datuk Dr. Shamsul Amri Baharuddin and his colleagues at KITA, National University of Malaysia, for so generously accommodating my stay in Malaysia while collecting data for this chapter. Earlier versions of this chapter were presented at colloquia at RMIT Melbourne and Heidelberg University. I am grateful to Michael Peletz, Andrew Weintraub, Dominik Müller, and Mohd. Al Adib Samuri for providing further feedback on it. Final thanks also to Anna Yeadell for her thorough copyediting of this chapter.

Notes

1. Details about Siti's life are based on *The Legend of CT,* a 2011 documentary marking Siti's thirty-third birthday. The film's production company, Astro Malaysia Holdings Berhad, according to its own website, is "a leading integrated consumer media entertainment group in Malaysia and Southeast Asia with operations in four key areas of business, Pay-TV, Radio,

Publications and Digital Media. With a customer base of 4.2 million residential customers or approximately 60 percent penetration of Malaysian TV households, Astro offers 172 TV channels, of which its History channel is but one." See http://www.astro.com.my/, last accessed 3 September 2015.

2. See, for example, the top-ten best female Asian singers, voted for by international site visitors, at http://www.thetoptens.com/best-female-singer-asia/ (last accessed 3 September 2015), where Siti, in the eleventh position, ends up contending with the more popular Agnes Monica (Indonesia) or Charice Pempengco (Philippines).

3. Datuk Khalid Muhammad Jiwa began his career in the banking sector before starting his own business. He owes his title as a *datuk* (sometimes spelled *dato*) mostly to his previous marriage with Tengku Zawyah Tengku Izham, a member of Malay royalty.

4. *Nasheed* is a genre of music popular throughout the Islamic world. The word *nasheed* comes from the Arab word for singing *(annasyid)* and even more generally may mean raising one's voice (Barendregt 2010). According to most hardliners, *nasheed* rejects forbidden instruments, and it is primarily considered *dakwah* (proselytizing) rather than performance. Hence, *nasheed* music is all about "intention," as its practitioners, especially in Southeast Asia, commonly say: it is not just taking up morally righteous issues; it is about the will to practice what one preaches, and a good *nasheed* artist (a *munsheed*) serves at all times as role model to his or her audience. In contemporary times, *nasheed* has particularly been taken up by grassroots movements in Yemen, Egypt (primarily by the Muslim Brotherhood), and Palestine, yet *nasheed* aficionados trace the term for the genre to the times when the Prophet Muhammad had to flee from Mecca to Medina and was hailed by a group of women singing him a verse of praise that has come to be known as the first *nasheed*. In spite of its "female roots," *nasheed* has now become the terrain of mostly young men, and in recent years, especially male solo acts have pushed the genre (and importantly its audiences) in other musical directions and with clear international ambitions.

5. Krisdayanti was twice winner (in 1992 and 1997) of *Asia bagus*, an all-Asian talent show created by Fuji Television, and Siti in 2002 was voted as winning the Voice of Asia music festival. Both have portrayed the ideal of womanhood in their music; for example, Krisdayanti's "I Am Just an Ordinary Woman" (*Aku wanita biasa*, 2009) and Siti's "Woman" (*Wanita*, 2007).

6. See "Ten Interesting Facts of Siti's New Project for Simply Siti," last accessed 3 September 2015, http://www.budiey.com/10-fakta-menarik-projek-terbaru-siti-nurhaliza-untuk-simplysiti/.

7. Siti's efforts to "go international" with her performing at the Royal Albert Hall with the London Symphonic (2005) or her release of a full English-language album, *All Your Love* (2011), were not always equally successful.

8. "You Came to Me" had previously been released in 2009 but then was released as a free download to commemorate the holy month of Ramadan. In anticipation of Sami's upcoming third official album (*Wherever You Are*, 2010), YCTM could in that year be downloaded from iTunes as a single sung in four different versions or "language versions": English, English-Arabic, English-Farsi, and English-Turkish.

9. Elsewhere, I use the term "Muslim Southeast Asia" in reference to "a not sharply delimited field of study that is primarily bound by religious affiliation. It connects Muslims living in the majority Muslim countries of Indonesia, Brunei, and Malaysia with smaller factions of populations living in Singapore, Southern Thailand, and the Southern Philippines" (Barendregt 2012, 316).

10. Michael Peletz, personal communication, May 2016.

11. Some of the international audiences that I have shown the clip to wonder why it is that Sami is shown in full color and Siti is depicted in black and white in the video: what are the intentions here, and is this an effort to downplay some of the gender sensitivities set out in the text? The answer is that the YouTube video is adapted from that 2009 clip, as mentioned in the text.

12. In particular, the London-based label Awakening Records is currently home to many of these newborn (or, more aptly, "awakened") pious stars, including Maher Zain, Irfan Maki, and Mesut Kurtis. Sami Yusuf recorded his first three studio albums with Awakening Records, until he decided to split with the label after a contractual dispute in 2009.

13. Yasin Sulayman's family comes from a strict Salafist background, and while he no longer restricts himself to an exclusively religious repertory, he was once the main singer for the renowned Malaysian *nasheed* act Brothers.

14. Most participants to this discussion, judging from the language practiced and pen names used, clearly identified as Malaysians, but others identified as coming from elsewhere. While web services such as YouTube tend to be localized, their reach is unmistakably beyond that of the nation. People of other nationalities, many coming from Muslim-majority countries, obviously participated in these discussions as well.

15. All quotes here are derived from the YouTube comments section of the clip at https://www.youtube.com/watch?v=XiXiCoTZ8BQ (last accessed 20 November 2012).

16. Islam in itself is a global project and regularly invokes the ancient ideal of the worldwide Muslim community, or *ummah*. The ideal of a supranational community of fellow believers irrespective of race, ethnicity, or class is what Ernest Gellner famously portrayed as a "functional equivalent of nationalism" (John Breuilly in his Introduction to Gellner 2006, xxxviii). Here, I cast Islam in its complex entanglement with the global entertainment industry also as a functional equivalent of or alternative trajectory to globalization.

17. Malaysian *nasheed* acts such as Raihan and Rabbani, reputed for their mix of traditional spiritual song with modern pop, have also known this for quite a while. Whenever performing in the Middle East, they resort to a cappella versions of their music, at most incorporating typical percussive instruments known for their association with Islam. Separate albums are rerecorded for the Southeast Asian and Middle Eastern and North African market, the contents of which differ considerably.

18. Indeed, in the quest for self-definition and setting oneself apart from Western peers, a fancy sharia-compliant lifestyle increasingly serves as an identity tool kit for the well-to-do (see also Fischer 2008).

19. But for some of PAS's creative solutions, see Dominik Müller's (2014, 2015) recent work, especially on the PAS youth wing.

20. Examples include Prime Minister Abdullah Badawi's (2003–2009) call for a more civilizational Islam (Islam Hadhari) and for bringing Islam under direct control of the federal state, with eyes and ears in every mosque of the nation, by appointing most of its preachers.

21. The new sort of post-Islamism noted here similarly presupposes more individualized forms of piety in which people are less inclined to cling onto prescriptions and rules as set by traditional authorities, instead opting for a more personalized body of knowledge that covers the nitty-gritty of the everyday that seemingly penetrates all domains of public and private life. It is the religion of which clothes to wear (and how), which books to read, which foods to eat, and what forms of entertainment are deemed suitable and proper. Such new knowledge also comes with its novel interpreters, ranking among them Islamist celebrities such as TV preachers Amr Khaled in Egypt (Haenni and Tammam 2003) and Abdullah Gymniaster in Indonesia (Watson 2005; Hoesterey 2016).

22. Sami's 2010 album *Hear Your Call* was thus dedicated to Save the Children in Pakistan, and the charity single "In Every Tear" called for donations for victims of natural disasters worldwide.

23. Such an observation, however, immediately seems to be contradicted by Siti's more recently turning to Instagram to pledge her support for former prime minister Mahathir after he had questioned the current Najib-led government over allegations of fraud and corruption. Her post quickly received almost twenty thousand likes (*Malaysian Insider* 2015) but was also seriously questioned in other media outlets. On another occasion, Siti personally met with the late PAS icon Nik Aziz in Kelantan, and she wrote him the song "Lelaki" (Man, male; see Müller 2015). Dominik Müller (personal communication) also points out that at a later stage, UMNO social media activists would claim that the "lelaki" actually hinted at was none other than Mahathir, not Nik Aziz, which may, as he suggests, be yet more proof of Siti's strategically being able to switch registers.

24. It is interesting that wearing the veil, as one of the most important tokens of religiosity in public life, is held against Siti by various actors who accuse her of not conforming to proper Islam, despite the fact that she is also hailed for publicly embracing her faith, with blogs and fan sites regularly featuring pictures of her in full veiling. It proves the point of popular music's discursive qualities in mapping out what is and what is not properly Islamic.

25. The quote is from a post in the comments section to the YouTube clip of the song "Tahajjud cinta" (2009), which can be found at https://www.youtube.com/watch?v=QK5TyPLSQmw (last accessed 20 November 2012).

26. Bayat (2013) more recently has recognized the complexities of the term he helped popularize and insists on seeing Islamism and post-Islamism as two analytical categorizations that are in continuous dialogue over the preferred direction of the Muslim modern and the role of female voices such as Siti.

References

Alifstyle. 2003. "Siti Nurhaliza Taruddin." *Stylol* (blog), 23 November. http://stylol.proboards.com/thread/83/siti-nurhaliza-taruddin.

Andaya, Barbara Watson. 2007. "Studying Women and Gender in Southeast Asia." *International Journal of Asian Studies* 4 (1): 113–136.

Barendregt, Bart. 2010. "Pop, Politics and Piety: Nasyid Boy Band Music in Muslim Southeast Asia." In *Islam and Popular Culture in Indonesia and Malaysia*, edited by Andrew Weintraub, 235–256. London: Routledge.

———. 2012. "Sonic Discourses on Muslim Malay Modernity: The Arqam Sound." *Contemporary Islam* 6 (3): 315–340.

Basarudin, Azza. 2016. *Humanizing the Sacred: Sisters in Islam and the Struggle for Gender Justice in Malaysia*. Seattle: University of Washington Press.

Bayat, Asef. 1996. "The Coming of a Post-Islamist Society." *Critique: Journal for Critical Studies of the Middle East* 5 (9): 43–52.

———, ed. 2013. *Post-Islamism: The Many Faces of Political Islam*. New York: Oxford University Press.

Brenner, Suzanne April. 1998. *The Domestication of Desire: Women, Wealth, and Modernity in Java*. Princeton, NJ: Princeton University Press.

Breuilly, John. 2006. "Introduction: Nations and Nationalism." In Gellner, Ernest. *Nations and Nationalism*, xiii–liii. Oxford: Blackwell Publishing.
Chaw, Kenneth. 2016. "Siti Nurhaliza performs a duet with the late Whitney Houston." 1 December. http://www.star2.com/entertainment/music/music-news/2016/12/01/siti-nurhaliza-to-choose-from-300-songs-for-new-album/.
Eickelman, Dale F. 1992. "Mass Higher Education and the Religious Imagination in Contemporary Arab Societies." *American Ethnologist* 19 (4): 643–655.
Eickelman, Dale F., and Jon W. Anderson. 2003. *New Media in the Muslim World: The Emerging Public Sphere*. Bloomington: Indiana University Press.
Fischer, Johan. 2008. *Proper Islamic Consumption: Shopping among the Malays in Modern Malaysia*. Copenhagen: NIAS Press.
Frisk, Sylva. 2004. *Submitting to God: Women's Islamization in Urban Malaysia*. Göteborg: Göteborg University Press.
Gal, Susan. 1988. "The Political Economy of Code Choice." In *Codeswitching: Anthropological and Sociolinguistic Perspectives*, edited by Monica Heller, 245–264. Berlin: Mouton de Guyter.
Gellner, Ernest. 2006. *Nations and Nationalism*. Ithaca, NY: Cornell University Press.
Göle, Nilüfer. 1996. *The Forbidden Modern: Civilization and Veiling*. Ann Arbor: University of Michigan Press.
———. 2000. "Snapshots of Islamic Modernities." *Daedalus* 129 (1): 91–117.
———. 2002. "Islam in Public: New Visibilities and New Imaginaries." *Public Culture* 14 (1): 173–190.
Haenni, Patrick, and Husam Tammam. 2003. "Chat Shows, Nashid Groups and Lite Preaching: Egypt's Air-Conditioned Islam." *Le monde diplomatique*, September.
Hefner, Robert. 2000. *Civil Islam: Muslims and Democratization in Indonesia*. Princeton, NJ: Princeton University Press.
Hoesterey, James. 2016. *Rebranding Islam: Piety, Prosperity, and a Self-Help Guru*. Stanford, CA: Stanford University Press.
Malaysian Insider. 2015. "Pop Singer Siti Nurhaliza Pledges Support for 'Lonely' Dr M." 14 April. http://www.themalaysianinsider.com/malaysia/article/pop-singer-siti-nurhaliza-pledges-support-for-lonely-dr-m.
Mokhtar-Ritchie, Hanita Mohd. 2015. "The Trouble with Modernity: Melodrama and the Independent Heroine in Selected Contemporary Malaysian-Malay Films." In *Women and the Politics of Representation in Southeast Asia: Engendering Discourse in Singapore and Malaysia*, edited by Adeline Koh and Yu-Mei Balasingamchow, 79–100. London: Routledge.
Müller, Dominik M. 2014. *Islam, Politics and Youth in Malaysia: The Pop-Islamist Reinvention of PAS*. London: Routledge.
———. 2015. "Islamic Politics and Popular Culture in Malaysia: Negotiating Normative Change between Shariah Law and Electric Guitars." *Indonesia and the Malay World* 43 (127): 318–344.
Noor, Farish A. 2008. "Siti Nurhaliza, Save Us!" *Malaysiakini Online*, 29 January. https://www.malaysiakini.com/columns/34565#ixzz3ktzLjU6h.
Ong, Aihwa. 1990. "State versus Islam: Malay Families, Women's Bodies and the Body in Malaysia." *American Ethnologist* 17 (2): 258–276.

Ooi, Jeff. 2007. "Ganyang Malaysia, Selamatkan Siti Nurhaliza." AsianCorrespondent .com, 7 November. http://asiancorrespondent.com/5583/ganyang-malaysia-selamatkan -siti-nurhaliza/.

Patrick, Steven. 2003. "APM Show Unites Malay Markets in SE Asia." *Billboard*, 29 March, 51.

Peletz, Michael G. 1996. *Reason and Passion: Representations of Gender in a Malay Society.* Berkeley: University of California Press.

———. 2012. "Gender, Sexuality, and the State in Southeast Asia." *Journal of Asian Studies: Review of Eastern and Southern Asia and the Adjacent Pacific Islands* 71 (4): 895–917.

———. 2013. "Malaysia's Syariah Judiciary as Global Assemblage: Islamization, Corporatization, and Other Transformations in Context." *Comparative Studies in Society and History* 55 (3): 603–633.

———. 2015. "A Tale of Two Courts: Judicial Transformation and the Rise of a Corporate Islamic Governmentality in Malaysia." *American Ethnologist* 42 (1): 144–160.

Pond, Christian. 2006. "The Appeal of Sami Yusuf and the Search for Islamic Authenticity." *Transnational Broadcasting Studies* 16 (1): 1–13.

Robison, Richard. 1996. "The Politics of 'Asian Values.'" *Pacific Review* 9 (3): 309–327.

Roy, Olivier, and Amel Boubekeur. 2012. *Whatever Happened to the Islamists? Salafis, Heavy Metal Muslims and the Lure of Consumerist Islam.* New York: Columbia University Press.

Shamsul, A. B. 1999. "From Orang Kaya Baru to Melayu Baru." In *Culture and Privilege and Capitalist Asia,* edited by Michael Pinches, 87–111. London: Routledge.

Simply Siti. 2006. "It Hurts . . . I Have Done No Wrong." 17 August. http://simplysiti.com /it-hurts-i-have-done-no-wrong/.

Smith-Hefner, Nancy J. 2007. "Javanese Women and the Veil in Post-Soeharto Indonesia." *Journal of Asian Studies* 66 (2): 389–420.

Stivens, Maila. 2006. "Family Values and Islamic Revival: Gender, Rights and State Moral Malaysia." *Women's Studies International Forum* 29:354–367.

Tan Sooi Beng. 2005. "From Folk to National Popular Music: Recreating Ronggeng in Malaysia." *Journal of Musicological Research* 24 (3–4): 287–307.

Tartoussieh, Karim. 2007. "Pious Stardom: Cinema and the Islamic Revival in Egypt." *Arab Studies Journal* 17 (1): 30–44.

Utusan Malaysia. 2004. "Tabung Prihatin Siti—Kanak kurang bernasib baik dibantu." 13 March. http://ww1.utusan.com.my/utusan.

Van Nieuwkerk, Karin. 1998. "An Hour for God and an Hour for the Heart: Islam, Gender and Female Entertainment in Egypt." *Music and Anthropology* 3. http://umbc.edu /MA/index/number3/nieuwkerk/karin_0.htm.

Watson, C. W. 2005. "A Popular Indonesian Preacher: The Significance of Aa Gymnastiar." *Journal of the Royal Anthropological Institute* 11 (4): 773–792.

Weintraub, Andrew N. 2011. "Introduction: The Study of Islam and Popular Culture in Indonesia and Malaysia." In *Islam and Popular Culture in Indonesia and Malaysia,* edited by Andrew N. Weintraub, 1–17. New York: Routledge.

Williamson, Thomas. 2002. "Incorporating a Malaysian Nation." *Cultural Anthropology* 17 (3): 401–430.

CHAPTER 11

Googoosh's Voice

AN IRANIAN ICON IN SILENCE AND SONG

Farzaneh Hemmasi

In July 2009, the Iranian pop icon Googoosh addressed a crowd of expatriate artists, intellectuals, and activists in front of the United Nations building in New York City. Dressed in a tailored white pantsuit and mirrored sunglasses with her blonde hair pulled back from her face, she, along with other participants, announced the beginning of a three-day hunger strike to draw attention to the plight of individuals killed or believed to be imprisoned in Iran as a result of the citizen uprisings following the contested reelection of then-president Mahmoud Ahmadinejad. She opened with a disclaimer: "Please forgive me—I know how to sing, but not how to speak." Then Googoosh began her statement in earnest, reading carefully from the pages held in her hands and occasionally stumbling over the lengthy sentences' multiple clauses. Her intention, she declared, was to "be the voice of the suffering, bereaved, and concerned mothers" whose children had been harmed or had perished in their political quests. She had come to "be the voice of the intellectuals, writers, artists, and sexual, ethnic, and religious minorities" who had been "tortured, imprisoned, and executed" for expressing their beliefs. She had come "to send Iranians' grievances to the ears of the world," because "people are looking to us Iranians outside of the country to be the voice of those within the country."[1]

This foray into political activism was an anomaly in Googoosh's long career as a professional singer and actress. Born in 1950, the charismatic, beloved performer began as a child actor on stage, television, and film; by her twenties, she was the country's primary female interpreter of *musiqi-yi pap* (Western-influenced "pop music") and its biggest female celebrity, appearing on countless magazine covers, performing on state television and radio, acting in numerous feature films, and releasing wildly popular songs. Yet in another sense, Googoosh has been embroiled in politics for much of her life. Following the Iranian revolution and the establishment of the Islamic Republic of Iran in 1980, Googoosh's fame became a liability. The revolutionary project involved purifying Iran of its "colonized" culture; of moral corruption spread through local cabarets, films, dance halls; and of unveiled "lust-inciting" women—the very twentieth-century developments that had produced Googoosh and that she in turn helped shape. There was no place for Googoosh in postrevolutionary Iran's new order: she was charged with propagating moral corruption and retreated from the public eye for the next twenty years. During her period of silence, Googoosh was mourned and memorialized especially by Iranians in diaspora, many of whom connected her disappearance to the loss of the Iran of the 1960s and 1970s (Maghbouleh 2010). Then, in 2000, Googoosh left Iran to restart her career in exile, landing first in Toronto and then settling in Los Angeles. She embarked on a new phase of her career singing her prerevolutionary romantic repertoire but also with a declaration of her intention to "give voice" to herself, to Iran, and to Iranians around the world.

In this chapter, I argue that the metaphorical "voicing" that Googoosh performed on behalf of the people inside Iran in front of the United Nations was an extension of an already-established pattern in which she blurred the line between celebrity as exceptional individual and celebrity as medium of collective expression. In possession of a singular voice, Googoosh presented herself as uniquely capable of reflecting the voices of the multitudes back to themselves. Googoosh acquired this aspect of her current persona, I suggest, in light of her public biography of private victimization, her postrevolutionary period of silence, and through her collaboration with an Iranian transnational media public that has long concerned itself with representing alternative iterations of Iranianness to those promoted by the Islamic Republic. I trace Googoosh's transformation from silenced to sounding female celebrity and attend to how she and her collaborators have incorporated the political metaphoric language of voice, song, and silence into her pre- and postmigration sung performances and public statements, thus drawing a correlation between her sounded vocalizations and the achievement of agentive voice.[2] Yet, like many pop singers, Googoosh does not author her sung texts, nor is she the sole creative force behind her performances, songs, or videos. I am likewise interested in how her persona "animates" the perspectives of others through performance and media (Goffman 1981, 124–59).

Googoosh remains recognizable as "herself" across media formats and decades of diverse professional activity through what Richard Dyer has termed the "structured polysemy" of the star: "the finite multiplicity of meanings and affects [stars] embody and the attempt to structure them so that some meanings and affects are foregrounded and others are masked or displaced" (1998, 3). In Dyer's view, the elements that make up a star's defining characteristics may be "in some degree in opposition or contradiction, in which case the star's image is characterized by attempts to negotiate, reconcile or mask the difference between the elements, or else simply hold them in tension" (63). From the early part of Googoosh's career, these signal tensions have included her victimhood versus her exceptional abilities; the consolidation of "Googoosh" as a recognizable, coherent being versus her manifest talent for sartorial and stylistic self-transformation; and in her postmigration career, the tension between intentionality, agency, and voice, on the one hand, and passivity and silence, on the other.

Discussing Googoosh through the lens of performance is intended to disrupt assumed correlations between voice, identity, and politics inherited from Euro-American modern thought, such as voice as an externalized manifestation of interiority or (unitary) identity, or the notion of "having a voice" as a manifestation of agency (Keane 2000; Kunreuther 2014; Weidman 2014). Googoosh's voice is a privileged medium, and its sounded form indexes her unique identity; but it is not necessarily the vehicle of authentic, unmediated self-expression, nor has she always sung by choice. Focusing on performance is meant to highlight the constructed, premeditated aspects of Googoosh's speech, song, dance, poses, and acting and to see the performance of political commitment(s) as critical to the postmigration persona she has developed in the context of a highly polarized and politicized transnational Iranian public sphere. To that end, the audiovisual examples I analyze in most depth are diasporic productions—a documentary film about Googoosh made before her reemergence and Googoosh's first postmigration music video—that work creatively with the metaphorization of her voice, performances, and persona vis-à-vis Iranian history and nation.

Professional Performers in Twentieth-Century Iran

In both casual conversation and scholarship, Googoosh is often discussed primarily as a singer *(khananda)*. However, she is better understood as a multiskilled performer who, like many of her generation, is also an accomplished actor and dancer in the "interconnected spheres of urban popular culture of the Pahlavi era" (Meftahi 2016, 3), in which performances of singing, dancing, and delivering jokes on cabaret and café stages, music recording, and eventually, acting and singing in films and television programs were part of a continuum of professional activity. This range of talents and environments is rooted in the changing milieu of the mid-twentieth-century *mutrib,* the popular performers whose music and spectacles enlivened parties and social events—and sometimes Tehran's red-light district, taverns, and opium dens (Breyley and Fatemi 2016). In early twentieth-century Tehran, *mutrib* were commonly employed by the upper and middle classes as an essential part of weddings, circumcisions, and other festivities. Because Muslims of good standing did not generally wish to engage in professional singing, music making, and dance—a discomfort that stemmed in part from an understanding of such activities as illicit in Islam—*mutrib* were often Jewish and/or from low-status backgrounds. Men dominated the *mutrib* profession in the twentieth century, but "respectable" female *mutrib* troupes also entertained all-female gatherings in the nineteenth century (Fatemi 2005), while another class of *mutrib* troupes including female members and/or female impersonators *(zanpush)* performed for men and sometimes offered prostitution among their services (on *zanpush*, see Meftahi 2016). With the growth of urban sites of leisure in early and mid-twentieth-century Tehran, *mutrib* began performing on stages in cabarets, cafés, and public theaters, while by the mid-twentieth century, they were also entering television and film—albeit in marginalized roles.

Googoosh (née Faegh'eh Atashin, 1950) was born into this transforming *mutribi* scene: her father was a traveling performer who incorporated her into his acrobatics acts when she was a toddler. Yet the social mobility and societal approval she eventually acquired at the height of her career in the 1970s was something "none could imagine" given the context of her birth and the low social position of the professional performer (Breyely and Fatemi 2016, 124). Twentieth-century Iran was the site of radical and rapid change in the status of performers and many other areas of life, including government, religion, and relations with the outside world. The female vocalist Qamar al-Muluk Vazirizada (1905–1959) opened the door for Googoosh and other female performers in 1924 by being the first Muslim woman not only to sing on a public stage but also to appear unveiled. Urban Shiite women generally covered themselves before unrelated *(namahram)* men so as to protect males from the potentially unsettling effects of their bodies; because a woman's voice was commonly conceptualized as an extension of the female body, women had also avoided public singing (Chehabi 2000; Youssefzadeh 2004). Qamar's vocal and visual unveiling took place a full twelve years before the Pahlavi monarch Reza Khan mandated that all women unveil in public in 1936, a controversial decree intended to "modernize" the nation by reducing the public appearance of Shiite Islam.

Top-down policies were but one of the factors contributing to Iran's twentieth-century transformations. The influence of occupying American, British, German, and Russian forces in the world wars; the development of a modern media industry whose producers were in dialogue with Indian, Egyptian, Russian, American, and western European musical and cinema trends; the aforementioned expansion of urban sites of leisure in which performances were newly accessible; and the growth of a consumer public eager to take part in popular culture that introduced new, foreign, and at times, previously off-limits sounds and images all contributed to changing tastes and attitudes. By the 1950s, Iranian stages, screens, radio broadcasts, and record stores included solo female singing stars who acted, danced, and sang their way into the hearts of their admirers. Mahvash (1920–1960), a voluptuous, sensuous performer surrounded by (unsubstantiated) rumors of a past in prostitution (see Meftahi 2016, 85–87); Dilkash (1924–2004), a vocalist and actress who performed both light classical and popular music with a deep, sonorous voice; and Puran (1934–1990), a singer-actress known for her Afghan and Indian repertoire, were among the best loved singers of the era. These women did not entirely distance themselves from the moral taint of the popular female (or male) performer; however, their performances were no longer exclusively relegated to cabarets or houses of ill repute but were part of public media and everyday social life as never before. At the same time, the 1940s saw the emergence of a grassroots, politically oriented Islamic press that decried female performers' public "eroticism" *(shahvat)* as part of the dissoluteness of a rapidly spreading, Western-influenced "modernity" *(tajaddud)*. As documented by the historian Ida Meftahi (2016), this press developed an influential discourse that condemned the expansion of cabarets, theaters, cafés, cinema houses, and dance halls as "centers of corruption" *(marakiz-i fisad)* while accusing their patrons and participants of contributing to the demise of Iranian civilization. These ideas were later incorporated into religiously motivated revolutionaries' drive to purify Iran not only of the Pahlavi monarchy (1925–1979) but also of the corruption, cultural colonization, and immorality they believed to characterize the era. Thus, the fertile ground from which Googoosh and her generation of performers sprung was also densely sown with controversy.

The "Structured Polysemy" of Googoosh

The commonly related story of Googoosh's early life positions her both as an exceptional talent and a pitiable victim (Chehabi 2000; Zamani 2000; Breyley 2010; Rahimieh 2016). As she has recounted in interviews, Googoosh was raised by her father, a professional entertainer who incorporated his charismatic daughter into his touring acrobatic act from the time she was two years old.[3] She was a talented mimic who developed an act impersonating many of the era's singing stars (for a description, see Breyley 2010, 207–208); she soon became an attraction in and of herself and has said that she was the family's primary breadwinner from three or four years of age. She performed in her first film at age seven and acted in some fifteen films before she was twenty. Googoosh's life was not easy: her parents divorced when she was two, and she attended school only for a few years while continuing to perform at night and taking care of younger siblings born of her stepmother(s). When she was seventeen, she entered her first marriage, to the nightclub impresario Mahmud Qurbani, with whom Googoosh transitioned from child star to film starlet and top singer of *musiqi-yi pap,* a sophisticated Western-Iranian hybrid genre that dominated state-controlled television and radio in the 1960s and 1970s. Though Googoosh has referred to the five-year marriage as "unsuccessful," she has also acknowledged that she acquired more financial success from her partnership with Qurbani than at any other period of her career.

Musiqi-yi pap was a fitting medium in which to develop Googoosh's star persona. A cosmopolitan genre with elements of *chanson,* soft rock, disco, and Middle Eastern and eastern European elements, *musiqi-yi pap* was fresh, young, and modern. The genre included predominantly Western instruments, complex arrangements, romantic lyrics, and high production values, and was performed by attractive young vocalists outfitted in the latest Western fashions on television variety programs such as *Rangarang* (Colorful) and *Mikhak-i nughri'i* (Silver carnation). *Musiqi-yi pap* was also the popular music medium most favored by state radio and television, to the exclusion of *mutrib-* and cabaret/café-associated genres, which, while widely enjoyed, were too vulgar, "traditional," and unrefined (and thus out of step with the image of a modern, westward-looking Iran officially promoted in this period).[4] Googoosh's celebrity in the 1960s and 1970s was born out of conditions shared with other prominent twentieth-century female vocalists with strong links to their nations and governments, such as the Portuguese Amalia Rodrigues (Gray 2013), Japanese Misori Hibara (Yano 2002; see also Christine Yano, chap. 6 in this volume), Egyptian Umm Kulthum (Danielson 1997; Lohman 2010), Lebanese Fairouz (Stone 2008), and Indonesian Titiek Puspa (Andrew Weintraub, chap. 7 in this volume). In the words of the anthropologist Ellen Gray, such women possess(ed) "a musical celebrity shaped by twentieth-century nationalisms broadly writ and particular economies of feeling and state apparatuses in relation to the national" (2013, 187).

Googoosh's ability to transform herself was one of her unique talents: indeed, malleability is a key aspect of her star persona one can trace to her early days as a celebrity impersonator. On one level, Googoosh embodied the options, the flexibility, and the self-fashioning of the individual—and perhaps especially the self-fashioned modern woman—that many Iranians aspired to realize in this period, but she also developed a signature vocal sound that has remained stable in her years on the stage and in the studio. In the majority of her song repertoire, Googoosh applied delicate, florid ornamentation to her melodic lines while tending to avoid the deeply emotive yodeling-style vocal effect *(tahrir)* common to both Iranian art music and popular performance genres. Her renditions of her songs' typically sentimental lyrics were affecting but not excessive; her voice was agile, capable of belting and cooing in equal turn; and she performed both upbeat and sentimental songs with verve. The vocal and performative flexibility exhibited in her childhood acting, singing, and dancing remained a part of her later work. She recorded in English, Spanish, Italian,

French, Azeri, and Arabic, ventured into disco (c.f. the songs "Talaq" [Divorce] and "Nima-yi gumshuda-yi man" [My lost half]) and soul (as in a cover of Aretha Franklin's "Respect," described in Breyley 2010, 224), and was an apt performer of earthy, often bawdy populist *(mardumi)* cabaret-style vocals (e.g., her role as a cabaret performer in the film *Janjal-i 'arusi* [The wedding scheme; Najibzadah 1970]). This is one sense in which Googoosh's "structured polysemy" works to hold opposing elements in tension: she both took on these roles and retained her star identity.

Within Googoosh's films, however, one observes a more consistent portrayal of female victimization that was resonant with her offstage biography. She often played the part of a young woman who dared to explore her sexuality outside of marriage and was then subjected to heartbreak, sexual violence, forced marriage, and/or unwanted pregnancy, while being dishonored in the eyes of her family (see *Bita* [Dariush 1972] and *Hamsafar* [Asadullah 1975], among many others). Yet while a number of other actresses of the period battled public perception of their profession as either synonymous with or one step away from "prostitution" (Talattof 2011; Meftahi 2016), before the revolution and for some Iranians, at least, Googoosh maintained a modicum of dignity and was accepted in polite society (Breyley 2010, 271; Chehabi 2000, 162).

Visual aspects of Googoosh's performance also set her apart from her peers, especially her dancing and physical appearance. Singers in light classical music featured on radio and television were arguably more technically accomplished than Googoosh, but they hardly moved when they sang. At the other end of the spectrum, the popular *filmfarsi* film genre overflowed with cabaret dancers shimmying and gyrating before roomfuls of ogling male patrons. Googoosh combined confident, skilled singing with adept but restrained dancing, changing her movements to match individual songs' musical styles. Finally, many Iranians remember Googoosh's fashion-plate image as just as important to her fame as her voice. A slender beauty with an expressive face, she constantly changed her clothing and hair styles as the periodicals of the day breathlessly documented her fashion experiments: a floor-length beaded gown with matching turban in one performance, denim overalls in a photo shoot, and hair color changing from black to brown to brassy blonde, with eyebrows dyed to match. When she returned from a trip to Europe with her hair cropped short, women rushed to emulate the bold new style, which became known as the *gugushi*.

The icon's early life was almost precisely coterminous with the reign of Mohammad Reza Pahlavi (1949–1979), the second and final Pahlavi monarch. Coupled with her performances at official events, in the Pahlavi court, and on state television and radio, there grew a strong association between Googoosh, the monarchy, and the particular modern milieu of the period. Mohammad Reza Pahlavi was kept in power through the 1953 American- and British-led coup that was initiated to block the rising nationalist and leftist movements potentially hostile to both the monarch and his Western allies' political and economic interests. The national infrastructure and military developed with oil funds and foreign investment; tremendous numbers of Iranian elites were educated in western Europe and the United States; and the state media projected a glitzy, glamorous image of a country in step with the latest global popular culture trends. Yet on the ground, many of the monarchy's promises rang hollow: wealth disparities grew, political repression was rampant, and some Iranians found relentless Westernization tiresome and disorienting and deeply resented Western political intervention. In the 1960s, opposition to the monarchy grew and diversified, incorporating socialists, secular nationalists, and Iranians pursuing novel ways of melding Islam and politics, such as the Marx-inspired Islamic intellectual 'Ali Shar'iati and the cleric Ayatollah Ruhollah Khomeini's concept of the "rulership of the jurisprudent" *(vilayat-i faqih)*. This was a time of simmering unrest, uneasy political alliances, and ideological experimentation across society.

The broad-based revolution succeeded in ousting the Pahlavis and resulted in what was for many Iranians a highly ambivalent outcome: the ascendance of Islamist factions galvanized behind Ayatollah Khomeini and the 1980 establishment of the Islamic Republic of Iran. Khomeini and his followers set out to build a revolutionized, Islamicized society purified of imperialism, moral corruption, Western cultural colonization, and social inequality, a project that entailed the dramatic transformation of law, society, and public and private space. It was critical that women's public roles be transformed as they were understood to be the vehicles through which religion and culture were undermined in the Iranian twentieth century (Najmabadi 2008, 41). Most importantly for this discussion, the veil that had been forcibly removed some forty years prior was now required for all women, while female singing voices were also required to be veiled in public: just as women could not appear uncovered before unrelated *(namahram)* males, women could not sing in public unless their individual voices were "covered" by a chorus or a male "co-singer" *(ham khan)* to neutralize their seductive powers.[5] Female entertainers were banned from performing and recording, cabarets and theaters were shuttered, and dance was restricted for men as well as women. The removal of female performers from radio, stage, and screen—and their replacement by male performers of Shiite lamentation and patriotic marches—institutionalized state-decreed gender segregation and the audiovisual purification *(paksazi)* of the prior regime's influence on Iranian culture and society.[6]

There was no place for Googoosh in this new order. Along with many other popular singers and actors, Googoosh was charged with propagating corruption and asked to sign a document in which she promised to abstain from all forms of performance. She was jailed for around a month, and her passport was revoked. After her imprisonment, she remained in Tehran, became a private individual, and stayed out of the public eye for the next two decades.

"Her Silence Made Her the Voice of a Nation"

As crucial as Googoosh's dominance of prerevolutionary media was to her fame, her silence after the revolution also contributed to her symbolic importance, something especially apparent in diaspora. The 1980s and 1990s saw the growth of an expatriate Iranian popular music industry in the diaspora stronghold of Los Angeles, fed by the many musicians and media workers who fled the revolution, but Googoosh was not among them. Migration afforded other famous prerevolutionary female vocalists the possibility of continuing their careers in exile, but they enjoyed comparatively fewer resources and humbler circumstances than prior to the revolution, which—according to some listeners—led them to produce lower-quality work in California than they had in 1960s and 1970s Iran. Googoosh's withdrawal meant that there was no postrevolutionary present against which to compare her past, which allowed her to remain associated exclusively with Pahlavi Iran, now framed by many expatriates as a golden era.

Media was and is an important way for Iranians to come in contact with the prerevolutionary past. Immediately following the revolution, Iranian expatriate media companies in Los Angeles salvaged collections of Googoosh's (and others') films, music, and television clips and sold them to the growing numbers of Iranians in North America and western Europe, affording audiences the opportunity to access this lost time via media (Khosravi and Graham 1997; Hemmasi 2011). With the advent of the Internet, collectors around the world uploaded newspaper clippings, recordings, and television footage in which Googoosh featured, making the audiovisual fragments of the Pahlavi past available online (Azimi 2005). Thanks to this recorded and online media, second-generation youth in Southern California have "inherited nostalgia" from their parents, a longing for an Iran—often imagined as "freer" and "more fun" than today—that only exists in their parents' memories and audiovisual fragments (Maghbouleh 2010). Within Iran, a similar sense of loss and the scarcity of newly recorded popular music in the two decades following the revolution also contributed to postrevolutionary generations' interest in Googoosh and her contemporaries (Mehran Attaei, personal communication, 30 May 2015; see also Breyley 2010; Breyley and Fatemi 2016).

Farhad Zamani's experimental documentary *Googoosh: Iran's Daughter* (2000) is one of the most elaborate expressions of the diasporic focus on Googoosh. Zamani conceived the film as an exploration of "Googoosh as metaphor" and a reflection from diaspora on Googoosh's persona in the context of the conditions that produced her as a star and led to her silence (Zamani, personal communication, 16 April 2004). Zamani was born in Iran and moved to New Jersey as a child with his parents, from whom he gained exposure to Googoosh; the documentary was his thesis project for an MFA in film at Columbia University and received attention on the documentary film festival circuit.[7] Through interviews with twenty of Googoosh's fans, colleagues, critics, and historians of Iran, Zamani's film conveys a sense of her broad impact on Iranian society, while friends and professional acquaintances reflect on her difficult childhood; her management and manipulation by her father, husbands, and lovers; the surface and deep meanings of her songs; and the way her persona reflected and contributed to the excitement and ambivalences of a rapidly transforming society. The experimental aspect of Zamani's film is the nonlinear, often jarring inclusion of excerpts from her many prerevolutionary songs and feature films, which, dramatically edited and recombined, become a reflection, illustration, and even foreshadowing of the themes under discussion.

Googoosh's manipulation and abuse is a particular point of focus: the film is punctuated with repetitions of a brief scene from the film *Hamsafar* (Fellow traveler; Asadullah 1975) in which her character is slapped across the face by costar Behruz Vosughi, her hair whipping about from the strength of the blow. In some instances, the scene is allowed to continue for a few more seconds so that we see Googoosh's character hanging her head in shame as she obediently follows Vosughi into the woods, a disturbing scene that shows her acquiescing to her male "protector's" violence.[8] In other repetitions, the scene is interrupted by an excerpt of another of Googoosh's films, which shows an audience of children laughing obnoxiously. Zamani, who had watched many of Googoosh's films in preparation for the documentary, commented to me that the star "basically played the same role in every movie": a sexually desirable woman abused by the men she encounters. He incorporated the laughing children to underscore the perversity of Googoosh's on- and off screen suffering as the nation's entertainment (Zamani, personal communication, 16 April 2004). Another repeating clip is from the feature film *Ihsas-i daq* (Hot feeling; Zadurian 1971), in which Googoosh's character passionately tells her man, "I'm a bad woman." While in the original film Googoosh's character is attempting to drive away her lover, through Zamani's placement of the clip next to commentators' discussions of the moral reprobation that female performers have faced in Iran, Googoosh's declaration voices a broad societal condemnation; in a strange twist, she appears to be condemning "herself."

Zamani's film calls into question again the relationship of the icon to her sung and acted performances through contradictory accounts of Googoosh's political associations. While she was constantly featured on state radio and television and performed at the court for Mohammad Reza Pahalvi and his family, Googoosh also released songs that some of her contemporaries interpreted as expressing subtle criticism of Iran under the monarchy (e.g., "Shikayat" [Complaint] 1984). Most controversial was one of Googoosh's last songs released prior to the revolution: "Agha jan-i khub" (My dear, lovable sir, 1984), a statement of Platonic affection and respect for an older man. Interviewees in Zamani's film relate the rumors they have heard or interpretations of their own: according to some, she intended the song as a veiled statement of support for Ayatollah Ruhollah Khomeini, while her son Kambiz Qurbani insists that she sang the song for a friend and that the piece was misinterpreted because of the heightened political sensitivities at the time. According to others, she never had any intentions regarding this song (or any of her repertoire) but just sang whatever was put before her. Googoosh is portrayed as the consummate *performer,* able to convincingly take on any number of roles regardless of their closeness or distance from her actual opinions.

How should we "interpret voices" like Googoosh's "that are highly audible and public but not agentive in a classic sense" (Weidman 2014, 48)? The paradox of voicing and silencing that Zamani presents is succinctly communicated in the film's tagline: "Her Silence Made Her the Voice of a Nation" (figure 11.1). Zamani makes Googoosh's lack of voice the key to her national political metaphorization—when she was silenced in the revolution, so was the nation. He then illustrates this claim by showing how he and his exiled interlocutors fill the emptiness of Googoosh's absence with their interpretations of her life, her choices, and her relationship to Iranian history. By interspersing clips of Googoosh's prerevolutionary performances between others' analyses of her life and significance, Zamani utilizes what fragments of her voice were available to him in her absence. He carefully deploys excerpts, edits, and repetitions to pointedly and intentionally ventriloquize Googoosh: he presses her recorded voice and body into the service of his own commentary, which is itself a commentary on her manipulation by others. We cannot assume a correlation between Googoosh and the roles she plays and sings, Zamani tells us: she is as polyvocal as her interpreters are. In the words of Diana Taylor, "Like so many overloaded icons, [Googoosh] looks so transparent" (2003, 152, quoted in Gray 2013, 273). If "her silence made her the voice of a nation," her ubiquity, malleability, and convincingness—her craft itself—have made her a cipher.

Figure 11.1. DVD cover of *Googoosh: Iran's Daughter.*

Googoosh's Reemergence: From Silenced to Vocal Celebrity

In 2000, Googoosh was granted a passport and given permission to perform publicly outside the Islamic Republic. How Googoosh managed to acquire official permission was a topic of great speculation, but whatever the conditions, she took the opportunity to leave the country and never returned. Googoosh's first performances following her migration were wildly successful—she played the Air Canada Centre of Toronto, which reportedly sold out its fifteen thousand seats with tickets going between $30 and $250 (Moaveni 2001a, 2001b). She held two concerts in Dubai in March 2001, timed to coincide with the Iranian New Year holiday, which brought more than ten thousand Iranian residents to the popular Persian Gulf destination (Moaveni 2001a). Footage from her first concert in Toronto shows her overcome with emotion, weeping as she addresses the crowd, who weep with her in turn.

When Googoosh chose exile over remaining in Iran, she became part of the extensive Iranian diaspora that includes not only multitudes of fans but also highly developed Persian-language media and culture industries concentrated in London, Dubai, Washington, DC, and Los Angeles. Made up primarily of first-generation migrants who maintain great interest in Iranian national affairs and are often critical of the Islamic Republic, this media and popular culture constitutes a transnational public in which diverse opinions are debated and alternative models of Iran and Iranianness are explored (Hemmasi 2011; Hemmasi, forthcoming b; see also Rahimi 2015; Semati 2012). Many of these media outlets are directed toward Iran, clandestinely enter Iranian territory, and generate response within Iran while remaining officially prohibited there. This has led many expatriate media workers to view themselves as expanding the range of discourse and representation beyond what is acceptable in the Islamic Republic. But expatriate media also has its own red lines: it is common for its producers and most vocal consumers to be suspicious or even hostile toward those who express support for the Islamic Republic and its policies.[9]

When Googoosh gave her first press conference in 2000 in Toronto, she was asked whether the government would allow her to return to Iran and sing. "I don't have that information," she replied, "but I do have hope that this could happen one day, because our revolution is moving towards democracy, and I am very optimistic about the future."[10] Googoosh's friend the lyricist Zoya Zakarian remembers that this statement caused controversy and even anger in the Los Angeles music industry. Zakarian, a prolific lyricist who had worked with Googoosh and many other *musiqi-yi pap* stars in Iran and then in Los Angeles after the revolution, was at the time the host of a call-in television program in Southern California. She had contributed an interview to Zamani's film as a former collaborator and friend of Googoosh's and then aired the documentary on her program. When I asked Zakarian what local audience responses to Zamani's film had been, she said she felt that reactions were colored by how people felt about Googoosh now that she had emerged. "Some would love her no matter what she did or said," she commented, "but others were angry that she didn't come out of Iran saying [the slogan] 'Down with the Islamic Republic'" (Zakarian, personal communication, 7 May 2016). Because so many members of the Los Angeles expatriate music industry harbor deep antipathy toward the Islamic Republic of Iran, Googoosh's optimism was viewed with suspicion; some even called into question whether Googoosh was collaborating with the Iranian government. When Googoosh appeared in the flesh from Iran after twenty years of silence and spoke instead of singing, she was unrulier than she had been as a mute figure on whom meanings could be projected.

Yet Googoosh also emerged with an album that moved her persona and career closer to some expatriates' expectations that she condemn the Iranian government. The new album, titled *Zartusht* (Zoroaster 2000), presented an unmistakably sober political agenda and vocalized a subtle critique of the Islamic Republic. The album cover contributes to this perception: over a black background, Googoosh regards the camera somberly, a black "birdcage"-style netted veil covering most of her face, recalling both mourning and captivity. The songs on the album, especially "Khak-i asir" (Captive land) and the title track, are full of poetic references to dissatisfaction with Iran's postrevolutionary transformation. In itself, this is not unique but a common, even clichéd aspect of Iranian expatriate popular music, which has expressed such sentiments for decades (Naficy 1993; Hemmasi 2011). What set Googoosh apart was that she and her collaborators seized on her iconic status, fans' identification with her, and the long-standing national metaphorization of her as a star and as a singer, while asserting her intention to take on and project the voices of the Iranian people. The title track presents this agenda:

> I who became a woman with you, oh women
> I will loan my voice *[sidayam]* to history
> And your cries for justice *[faryad]*, oh young men and women
> Oh sacrificed land
> Grant me permission
> To sing your tears *[garya'at ra man bikhanam]*

"Zartusht" is not addressed to an unnamed beloved, as was typical of Googoosh's prerevolutionary love songs, but to distinct constituencies whom she asks for permission to represent through song. Googoosh gestures toward using her larger-than-life status to become a loudspeaker for her people and her nation. In her emergence, she presents herself as having performed a metaphorical and literal transformation from a silenced to a vocal woman who not only sings for herself but also "loan[s] her voice to history" to project the perspectives of less audible others. Googoosh thereby adds another layer to her polysemous character: the silenced songbird who escapes her cage to find freedom and lift her voice to the skies.

Representing History: "QQ Bang Bang"

Googoosh's most ambitious work representing others' experiences is "QQ Bang Bang" (2003; figure 11.2). This song is perhaps best described as an epic of a particular Iranian exile experience: over the piece's ten minutes, Googoosh recites

Figure 11.2. Cover of "QQ Bang Bang." © Taraneh Records 2003 (used with permission).

and sings over sixty lines of rhyming lyrics chronicling the hopes of a generation that came of age under Mohammad Reza Pahlavi, experienced a political awakening in the 1970s, and was disillusioned and displaced following the revolution. Everything about the production is on a grand scale: in addition to the length of the poem and song, the accompanying Los Angeles Philharmonic Orchestra plays multiple melodic themes and modulations underscoring the shifting narrative, while the video includes a cast of eighteen credited individuals acting out the various scenarios described, 360-degree shots of Googoosh on a craggy cliff overlooking the ocean, and numerous excerpts from

1970s Iranian feature films—including footage of Googoosh herself—to conjure the prerevolutionary past.

"QQ Bang Bang" marks the entrance of Googoosh into the Los Angeles Iranian expatriate popular music industry. In some senses, this collaboration between Googoosh, Zakarian, and the songwriter Mehrdad Asemani was atypical of most Southern Californian Iranian popular music, the majority of which is romantic, dance oriented, and/or expresses longing for the Iranian homeland in a three-minute pop song format that draws on both prerevolutionary popular music conventions and a host of global popular music trends, from hip-hop to trance to Arab pop.[11] Zakarian's lengthy poem, discussed in detail by Nasrin Rahimieh (2016), is full of evocative references to cultural hallmarks of her generation and conveys a complicated ambivalence regarding the path to the revolution as well as its outcome. Asemani's highly varied composition sets each of the poem's stanzas to distinct themes. The packaging is also unusually elaborate for a Los Angeles Iranian production: "QQ Bang Bang" was released as an instrumental version and as a video, along with a version of the video subtitled in English and containing scenes from the making of the video.[12] Also included are a booklet of lyrics and an autographed picture postcard of Googoosh with a handwritten line that employs the metaphorization of voice once more: "In the hope of singing the song of freedom in Iran together" (Rahimieh 2016, 52). Yet for all these distinctive features, the song is in step with the majority of popular music produced in the expatriate music industry, in which prerevolutionary Iran is nostalgically recalled and postrevolutionary Iran is either absent or portrayed as if in a state of destruction (*Iran-i viran*, or "Iran in ruins," is a common rhyme).

The song narrates the story of Googoosh's (and most of the song's cocreators') generation from the heady, hopeful days of their youth to the "winter" of revolution and, ultimately, the "false paradise" of exile. The words "QQ Bang Bang" are a sonic representation of the sound of gunshots made by playing children, a refrain that Zakarian intended to invoke a cycle of violence running throughout Iranian history (Zakarian, personal communication, 18 April 2007). The song also invokes collective memory, signaled in the refrain "Brother, do you remember?" and its frequent use of first-person-plural pronouns. The singer rhetorically asks if listeners remember "our" western-film-genre-inspired childhood games of "Cowboys and Indians," when "we" went to the movies as teenagers, and the "stolen kisses" of "our" adolescence when "Western stars" such as Elvis Presley and James Dean were "our guiding lights." The next verses introduce the growing polarization and ideological experimentation preceding the revolution, in which some people were "intoxicated with [Friedrich] Engels" while others "followed Buddha," and the "confusion" *(sargija)* of "leftist poets in the mosques / drunken puritans in the bars." The revolution tragically marks the era's conclusion, with innocent childhood play suddenly transformed into "real guns" as the lyrics ask listeners to observe how history "repeats itself." Exile does not offer a new beginning or new hope but the continuation of violence: in this "false paradise," "two immigrant kids" play with toy guns hooked up to a video game, shooting at a screen. Googoosh repeats the sounds of gunshots into the fade-out—"QQ Bang Bang . . . one more time—QQ Bang Bang."

Like Zamani's experimental documentary, "QQ Bang Bang" as song and video is a meditation on Googoosh's iconic and indexical relationships to prerevolutionary Iran, interweaving her biography, cinematic portrayals, and a particular version of national history whose glory days end with the revolution.[13] The viewer is invited to remember "our youth" through Googoosh, who is both a part of the generation whose experience the song depicts and whose films, television programs, and songs embodied and propagated important aspects of the era's aspirations. The booklet containing the lyrics repeats this theme: each section of the poem is titled with an age ("At Seven Years Old") and features a photograph of Googoosh as background to the relevant lines of the poem. Each page of lyrics invoking the prerevolutionary era also includes an image of a semitransparent, ghostlike Googoosh from the period under discussion, a literal superimposition of her persona onto history (figure 11.3). Yet unlike Zakarian and many others involved in the Los Angeles music industry who left Iran in the years immediately surrounding the revolution and have never or rarely returned, Googoosh's life story includes twenty years of living in the Islamic Republic and, at least in her first statements after leaving Iran, an optimism about postrevolutionary Iran that is absent from "QQ Bang Bang." Within the song and its collective address, therefore, she is not relating her own biography but voicing the perspectives and experiences of others in diaspora with whom she has worked and, perhaps, of imagined diaspora audiences to whom she hoped to appeal.

As much as "QQ Bang Bang" is a "Googoosh vehicle" that trades on resonances between the star and the prerevolutionary era, Googoosh's persona also overwhelms the contributions and perspectives of those who originated the content she animates in performance. The lyrics to "QQ Bang Bang" predate Googoosh's arrival in Los Angeles; lyricist Zakarian told me she "needed to write [the poem] for [her]self" (Zakarian, personal communication, 18 April 2007). Yet once the song was produced, the poem became indelibly associated with Googoosh. In a recent exchange, Zakarian questioned whether I or other scholars would have paid any attention to her poem had it not been sung by this most influential of Iranian celebrities. She also noted that neither I nor others had grasped what was for her the central point of the song: that "Iranian intellectuals, confused and not so knowledgeable," pursued Islam, Eastern philosophy, and socialism without fully understanding them. Unlike "European intellectuals,

Figure 11.3. Superimposing Googoosh on prerevolutionary Iranian history. "QQ Bang Bang" lyrics booklet. © Taraneh Records 2003 (used with permission).

who tried to enlighten their people, Iranian intellectuals only wanted people to follow them. Well, they were successful. What's the result?" she asked, rhetorically suggesting that the role-playing of the revolution had gone awry (Zakarian, personal communication, 25 May 2016). Meanwhile, the composer Mehrdad Asemani, who is too young to remember most of the events depicted in the lyrics, noted that it was his experience fighting at the front of the Iran-Iraq War in the 1980s that gave him the emotional reservoir needed to write the song (Asemani, personal communication, 27 May 2016).[14] While the very nature of celebrity is its intense focus on the star to the exclusion of the "behind the scenes" work and workers who make her what she is, it is also ironic that Googoosh's collaborators bear some sense of having their voices silenced by her own larger-than-life presence.

Googoosh's Voice as Medium and Metaphor

Since Googoosh's reemergence, she has released eight albums of new material at the rate of about one every two years. She is now a fixture of Iranian diaspora, no longer a figure lost in obscurity but a professional singer who regularly tours North America, Europe, and the Middle East—though not Iran, where she would still likely face consequences if she dared return. After "QQ Bang Bang," Googoosh released a number of other songs that work through connections between the Googoosh of the popular imagination and other Iranian constituencies. Her 2005 song "Ay mardum murdam" (Oh people, I'm dying) decries the abuse of women while drawing subtle connections between her life story and the experiences of Iranian women as a whole (see Hemmasi 2011; Hemmasi, forthcoming). The most audacious melding of Googoosh and nation to date is her 2009 song "Man hamun Iranam" (I am Iran itself). Singing in the first person, Googoosh adopts the voice of a suffering, abandoned Motherland *(mam-i vatan)* who begs her citizens cum "children" to come to her aid. This is not a song to the Iranian people as a whole but is addressed to Iranians in diaspora, who "promised [they] would be back" but have never returned. The juxtaposition of off- and on-screen narratives presents a contradiction: within the song, the Motherland urges her dispersed offspring to come home, while offstage, Googoosh herself elected to leave Iran. Whatever inconsistencies the production conveys, the song also marks another transformation of Googoosh from national sweetheart—the mistreated "daughter" of Zamani's film—to an outspoken (if still victimized) "mother" of Iran.

Online responses to "Man hamun Iranam" on YouTube range from affirmation and adulation to vulgar insults, as is typical of Googoosh's posted videos. Within the five hundred or so comments surveyed for this project, one in particular sums up the main question explored in the chapter: "In the past she sang for the Royal[s], then for Aga Bozorg [Khomeini] and now [she's] singing for Iran. She is confused and doesn't know what way to follow."[15] Who does Googoosh sing for, and why? Can we infer any relationship between her diverse and even contradictory performances and her personal beliefs? What responsibility do her varied and often politically fractious audiences bear in projecting their voices onto hers?

We cannot assume a link between a single voice and a single identity or even a single person, argues Amanda Weidman, because "speakers may have many different kinds of relationships to their own voices or words [and] a single 'voice' may in fact be collectively produced" (2014, 42). Songwriters, video directors, and others involved in "producing" Googoosh all contribute to the icon's public manifestation, but we cannot assume that these actors are necessarily in agreement with each other or even with Googoosh herself in what image and sound she should present. It has been suggested to me by fans and those who know her personally that Googoosh is less interested in politics than relevance and that in order to be relevant in the Iranian diaspora mediascape, one must be political. As she and her collaborators have incorporated the metaphoric language of voice, speech, and song into her sung performances to "sing the nation's tears" as in "Zartusht," to sing the nation itself in "Man hamun Iranam," and in her speech at the United Nations, to use her voice to "send the voices of Iranians . . . to the world's ears," they have linked voice, performance, and now political commitment to Googoosh's persona. As much as Googoosh's commitments to voice and voicing may be constructions, we need not therefore dismiss them as artificial, for "in more complex readings, the constructed is coterminous with the 'real'" (Taylor 2013, 8). Rather than cast her performances as antithetical to the authentic, we should see Googoosh's silences and voice(s) alike as generating real meaning—however unstable and contested—for multiple generations of Iranians.

Acknowledgments

I would like to thank—without in any way implicating—Ida Meftahi, Golbarg Rekabtalaei, Jairan Gahan, Tyler Bickford, Lauren Ninoshvili, Maria Sonevytsy, Farhad Zamani, Zoya Zakarian, Mehrdad Asemani, Vartan Avanessian, Jahangir Tabaraei, and the editors of this volume, Andrew Weintraub and Bart Barendregt. Research contributing to this chapter was funded in part by the Connaught Fund at University of Toronto.

Notes

1. Unite4IRAN, "Googoosh Speaks at the UN," YouTube, 25 July 2009, https://www.youtube.com/watch?v=njmL5X1t3zU.

2. There are several words in Persian commonly translated to the English word "voice": *sida, avaz, ava,* and *nida*. In Googoosh's United Nations speech, she used the formulation *sida-yi X basham,* which translates as "to be the voice of X," with a meaning consistent with the English-language sense of both sounding aloud and speaking on another's behalf. In the same speech, she compared the oppression of intellectuals and artists to the way she had been forcibly silenced *(chu man . . . ka vadar ba sukutishan kardand)*. Persian contains another link between vocalization and demands for justice in the terms *dad* and *faryad; dad* can mean either a shout or cry but also means justice, while *faryad* likewise indicates a loud cry but as a verb *(faryad kishidan)* also means to cry out for justice. Several of Googoosh's songs (e.g., "Zartusht") use the word *faryad,* as do many other pre- and postrevolutionary poems and song lyrics. See Mohaghegh (2010, 2012, 2013) for more on references to "screams," silence, and the political in prerevolutionary Iranian literature.

3. The biographical details presented here are drawn from Googoosh's 2005 interview with Homa Ehsan, one of the more in-depth and personal interviews Googoosh has undertaken since her emergence: "Homa Ehsan's Interview with Diva Googoosh, Part 1," YouTube, 30 November 2015, https://www.youtube.com/watch?v=4uj895XtG1A.

4. For in-depth discussions of Iranian popular music in the 1960s and 1970s, see Breyley 2010; Hemmasi 2013; and Breyley and Fatemi 2016.

5. For more on official policies and practices regarding women's singing in postrevolutionary Iran, see Youssefzadeh 2004; De Bano 2005, 2009; Mozafari 2012; and Hemmasi,

forthcoming b. For more on music in postrevolutionary Iran more generally, see Nooshin 2005a, 2005b, 2009, 2015; Robertson 2012; Siamdoust 2013, 2015; and Breyley and Fatemi 2016.

6. The perceived incompatibility of veiling and public female solo singing is particular to Iranian history. In Indonesia and Malaysia, veiled pop singers are quite common (see Bart Barendregt, chap. 10 in this volume), while in neighboring postinvasion Afghanistan, veiled women singing pop songs have appeared in the televised talent competition *Afghan Star.*

7. *Googoosh: Iran's Daughter* was shown at the Exile Film Festival in Gothenburg, Sweden; it also won a Gold Merit Award at the Vancouver Iranian Film Festival in the same year.

8. Further blurring Googoosh's on- and offscreen lives is the fact that Googoosh and Vosughi were married for a short period in the 1970s.

9. Satellite television and the Internet are the major avenues by which expatriate and Western-government-produced Persian-language media enter Iran. The Iranian government intermittently jams satellite transmissions, filters Internet sites and search results, and keeps Internet speeds low to slow access to streaming media and downloading large files, but satellite dishes, virtual private networks, and filter-breaking software are readily available and in use. For more on expatriate Iranian media and media producers' relationships with homeland audiences, see Naficy 1993; Akhavan 2013; Sreberny and Torfeh 2014; Marchant 2015; and Rahimi 2015; among others. See Hemmasi (forthcoming b) for a discussion of Googoosh Music Academy, an expatriate televised talent competition that generated great response in Iran and diaspora.

10. Nima Bigloo, "Googoosh, press' [sic] conference in toronto [sic], 2000. Part 2," YouTube, 4 May 2012, https://m.youtube.com/watch?v=Jf_kTEcKFs.

11. There are notable exceptions, such as Moein's mournful romantic ballads, Dariush Eghbali's patriotic anthems and dystopic love songs, the works of Ebi and Siavash Ghomeishi, and others. See Hemmasi 2010; and Breyley and Fatemi 2016.

12. Asemani suggested that the instrumental version was included because the composition was not mere accompaniment but rich enough to stand on its own (personal communication, 27 May 2016). This is the only Los Angeles Iranian production that I am aware of being released in this way.

13. In general, younger artists who have come of age in postrevolutionary Iran do not exhibit the same fixation on prerevolutionary Iran: their gaze may be oriented toward a different past, as in the Brooklyn-based exile avant-garde musician Mohsen Namjoo's "Daha-yi shast" (The sixties, which correlates to the first decade following the revolution in the Iranian calendar), or focused on the recent past or present, as in much of the work of the expatriate San Francisco–based rock band Kiosk.

14. In my discussion with Asemani, he specified that he fought in the war for Iran's honor *(namus),* not for the government *(dawlat).* The founding figures of the expatriate Los Angeles music industry left Iran before the war began; this may be why it is so unusual to hear mention of this seminal, traumatic moment in Iranian history in the music produced in Southern California.

15. Fony boy, comment on The Official Googoosh Channel, "Man hamoon Iranam," YouTube, 22 June 2009, https://www.youtube.com/watch?v=9cBwT3H9Wlg.

References

Akhavan, Niki. 2013. *Electronic Iran: The Cultural Politics of an Online Evolution.* New Brunswick, NJ: Rutgers University Press.

Azimi, Negar. 2005. "Private Devotion: Inside the World of Googoosh's Biggest Fan." In "Icons," *Bidoun* 5 (Fall). http://bidoun.org/articles/private-devotion.

Breyley, G. J. 2010. "Hope, Fear and Dance Dance Dance: Popular Music in 1960s Iran." *Musicology Australia* 32 (2): 203–226.

Breyley, G. J., and Sasan Fatemi. 2016. *Iranian Music and Popular Entertainment: From Motrebi to Losanjelesi and Beyond.* Abingdon, UK: Routledge.

Chehabi, H. E. 2000. "Voices Unveiled: Women Singers in Iran." In *Iran and Beyond: Essays in Middle Eastern History in Honor of Nikki R. Keddie,* edited by Rudi Matthee and Beth Baron, 151–166. Costa Mesa, CA: Mazda.

Danielson, Virginia. 1997. *The Voice of Egypt: Umm Kulthum, Arabic Song, and Egyptian Society in the Twentieth Century.* Chicago: University of Chicago Press.

DeBano, Wendy S. 2005. "Enveloping Music in Gender, Nation and Islam: Women's Music Festivals in Post-Revolutionary Iran." *Iranian Studies* 38 (3): 441–462.

———. 2009. "Singing against Silence: Celebrating Women and Music at the Fourth Jasmine Festival." In *Music and the Play of Power in the Middle East, North African and Central Asia,* edited by Laudan Nooshin, 229–244. Farnham, UK: Ashgate.

Dyer, Richard. 1998. *Stars.* New ed. London: BFI.

Fatemi, Sasan. 2005. "Music, Festivity and Gender in Iran from the Qajar to the Early Pahlavi Period." *Iranian Studies* 38 (3): 399–416.

Goffman, Erving. 1981. *Forms of Talk.* Oxford, UK: Blackwell.

Gray, Lila Ellen. 2013. *Fado Resounding: Affective Politics and Urban Life.* Durham, NC: Duke University Press.

Hemmasi, Farzaneh. 2010. "Iranian Popular Music in Los Angeles: Mobilizing Music, Media, and Nation." PhD diss., Columbia University.

———. 2011. "Iranian Popular Music in Los Angeles: A Transnational Public beyond the Islamic State." In *Muslim Soaps, Halal Rap, and Revolutionary Theater,* edited by Karin Van Nieuwkerk, 85–111. Austin: University of Texas Press.

———. 2013. "Intimating Dissent: Popular Song, Poetry, and Politics in Pre-Revolutionary Iran." *Ethnomusicology* 57 (1): 57–87.

———. Forthcoming a. "Iran's Daughter, Iran's Mother: Googoosh and the Political Metaphorization of the Female Voice." *Popular Music.*

———. Forthcoming b. "One Can Sing and be Veiled! Performing Piety on an Iranian Talent Competition." *Journal of Middle East Women's Studies.*

Keane, Webb. 2000. "Voice." *Journal of Linguistic Anthropology* 9 (1–2): 271–273.

Khosravi, Shahram, and Mark Graham. 1997. "Home Is Where You Make It: Repatriation and Diaspora Culture among Iranians in Sweden." *International Journal of Refugee Studies* 10 (2): 115–133.

Kunreuther, Laura. 2014. *Voicing Subjects: Public intimacy and Mediation in Kathmandu.* Berkeley: University of California Press.

Lohman, Laura. 2010. *Umm Kulthum: Artistic Agency and the Shaping of an Arab Legend, 1967–2007.* Middletown, CT: Wesleyan University Press.

Maghbouleh, Neda. 2010. "'Inherited Nostalgia' among Second-Generation Iranian Americans: A Case Study at a Southern California University." *Journal of Intercultural Studies* 31 (2): 199–218.

Marchant, James. 2015. "The Revolution Will Be Televised: State and Satellite TV in Iran." In *Revolution Decoded: Iran's Digital Media Landscape,* edited by Bronwen

Robertson and James Marchant, 28–66. Small Media & Arab Media Report. https://smallmedia.org.uk/revolutiondecoded.
Meftahi, Ida. 2016. *Gender and Dance in Modern Iran: Biopolitics on Stage*. London: Routledge.
Moaveni, Azadeh. 2001a. "Don't Cry for Me, Iran." *Time,* 23 March. http://content.time.com/time/world/article/0,8599,103628,00.html.
———. 2001b. "Sing It Loud and Proud." *Time,* 16 April. http://content.time.com/time/world/article/0,8599,2047515,00.html.
Mohaghegh, Jason Bahbak. 2010. *New Literature and Philosophy in the Middle East: The Chaotic Imagination*. New York: Palgrave Macmillan.
———. 2012. *The Writing of Violence in the Middle East: Inflictions*. New York: Continuum.
———. 2013. *Silence in Middle Eastern and Western Thought: The Radical Unspoken*. London: Routledge.
Mozafari, Parmis. 2012. "Carving a Space for Female Singing in Post-Revolution Iran." In *Resistance in Contemporary Middle Eastern Cultures: Literature, Cinema and Music,* edited by Karima Laachir and Saeed Talajooy, 262–278. London: Routledge.
Naficy, Hamid. 1993. *The Making of Exile Cultures: Iranian Television in Los Angeles*. Minneapolis: University of Minnesota Press.
Najmabadi, Afsaneh. 2008. "(Un)Veiling Feminism." In *Secularisms,* edited by Janet R. Jakobsen and Anne Pellegrini, 39–57. Durham, NC: Duke University Press.
Nooshin, Laudan. 2005a. "Subversion and Counter-Subversion: Power, Control and Meaning in the New Iranian Pop Music." In *Music, Power and Politics,* edited by Annie Janeiro Randall, 231–272. New York: Routledge.
———. 2005b. "Underground, Overground: Rock Music and Youth Discourses in Iran." *Iranian Studies* 38 (3): 463–494.
———. 2009. "'Tomorrow Is Ours': Re-Imagining Nation, Performing Youth in the New Iranian Pop Music." In *Music and the Play of Power in the Middle East, North African and Central Asia,* edited by Laudan Nooshin, 245–268. Farnham, UK: Ashgate.
———. 2015. *Iranian Classical Music: The Discourses and Practice of Creativity*. Farnham, UK: Ashgate.
Rahimi, Babak. 2015. "Satirical Cultures of Media Publics in Iran." *International Communication Gazette* 77 (3): 267–281.
Rahimieh, Nasrin. 2016. *Iranian Culture: Representation and Identity*. Abingdon, UK: Routledge.
Robertson, Bronwen. 2012. *Reverberations of Dissent: Identity and Expression in Iran's Illegal Music Scene*. London: Continuum.
Semati, Mehdi. 2012. "The Geopolitics of Parazit: The Iranian Televisual Sphere and the Global Infrastructure of Popular Humor." *Popular Communication: The International Journal of Media and Culture* 10 (1–2): 119–130.
Siamdoust, Nahid. 2013. "Neither 'Islamic' nor a 'Republic': Discourses in Music." In *Cultural Revolution in Iran: Contemporary Popular Culture in the Islamic Republic,* edited by Annabelle Sreberny and Massoumeh Torfeh, 151–170. London: I. B. Tauris.
———. 2015. "Tehran's Soundscape as a Contested Public Sphere: Blurring the Lines between Public and Private." *Divercities: Competing Narratives and Urban Practices in Beirut, Cairo and Tehran,* OIS 3, edited by Nadia von Maltzahn and Monique Bel-

lan. Berlin: Orient Institute Studies. http://www.perspectiva.net/publikationen/orient-institut-studies/3-2015/siamdoust_soundscape.
Sreberny, Annabelle, and Massoumeh Torfeh. 2014. *Persian Service: The BBC and British Interests in Iran.* London: I. B. Tauris.
Stone, Christopher Reed. 2008. *Popular Culture and Nationalism in Lebanon: The Fairouz and Rahbani Nation.* London: Routledge.
Talattof, Kamran. 2011. *Modernity, Sexuality, and Ideology in Iran: The Life and Legacy of a Popular Female Artist.* Syracuse, NY: Syracuse University Press.
Taylor, Diana. 2003. *The Archive and the Repertoire: Performing Cultural Memory in the Americas.* Durham, NC: Duke University Press.
Weidman, Amanda. 2014. "Anthropology and Voice." *Annual Review of Anthropology* 43 (1): 37–51.
Yano, Christine Reiko. 2002. *Tears of Longing: Nostalgia and the Nation in Japanese Popular Song.* Cambridge, MA: Harvard University Press.
Youssefzadeh, Ameneh. 2004. "Singing in a Theocracy: Female Musicians in Iran." In *Shoot the Singer! Music Censorship Today,* edited by Marie Korpe, 127–134. London: Zed Books.

Filmography

Asadullah, Mas'ud, dir. 1975. *Hamsafar* (Fellow traveler). Iran.
Dariush, Hajir, dir. 1972. *Bita.* Iran.
Najibzadah, Ahmad, dir. 1971. *Janjal-i 'arusi* (The wedding scheme). Iran.
Thomas, Antony, dir. 2010. *For Neda.*
Zadurian, Rubik, dir. 1971. *Ihsas-i daq* (Hot feeling).
Zamani, Farhad, dir. 2000. *Googoosh: Iran's Daughter.* USA.

Discography

"Agha jan-i khub" (My dear, lovable sir). 1984. From *Fasl-i taza* (New season). Lyrics by Muhammad Salih Ala', music by Sadiq Nawjuki.
"Khak-i asir." 2000. From *Zartusht* (Zoroaster). Lyrics by Nusrat Farzanah, music by Babak Amini.
"Man hamun Iranam" (I am Iran itself). 2009. From *Hajm-i sabz* (Green X). Lyrics by Raha Etemadi, music by Farid Zoland.
"QQ Bang Bang." 2003. Lyrics by Zoya Zakarian, music by Mehrdad Asemani. Taraneh Records.
"Shikayat" (Complaint). 1984. From *Fasl-i taza* (New season). Music by Farid Zoland.
"Zartusht." 2000. From *Zartusht* (Zoroaster). Lyrics by Nusrat Farzanah, music by Babak Amini.

PART IV

Body Politics and Discourses of Femininity

IMAGE, SEXUALITY, AND THE BODY

CHAPTER 12

Enacting Modernity through Voice, Body, and Gender

FILIPINA SINGERS FROM THE CLOSE OF THE PHILIPPINE-AMERICAN WAR TO THE ONSET OF MARTIAL LAW (1913–1972)

Ricardo D. Trimillos

MODERNITY in the Philippines has been, and continues to be, bound up with notions of colonialism and nationalism. A historical interrogation of modernity through popular culture and popular singers invites unique ways of knowing and understanding the Philippines. This approach presents a promising undertaking for which the Philippines manifests points of resonance with Insular Southeast Asia as a region. The aspects of modernity relevant to this discussion include the Filipino engagement with notions of democracy (Abinales and Amoroso 2005; Curato 2015; Karnow 1990; Putzel 1999), consumption of technology and industry (Laurel 2010; Rodell 2002; Torres 2010), and appropriation of and competence with globalized "Western" musical genres (Castro 2011; Lockard 1998; Ng 2006; Quirino 2004; Santos 2003).

Two Filipina[1] singers, the late jazz singer Katy de la Cruz and the chanteuse Pilita Corrales, are relevant cases by which to consider interactions of modernity, popular culture, and gender. I frame these three features for the Philippines during the period 1913–1972, which I call "Developing Modernity." I then discuss Katy de la Cruz and Pilita Corrales in relation to the three features and to this time period. To close, I consider the ways in which the three features are enacted in the Philippines and suggest implications for a Southeast Asia sensibility that extends beyond current national boundaries and the historical period of Developing Modernity. Apropos to my ongoing interest in indigenous vehicles for self-reflexivity and cultural critique, I draw on the *sarswela*, a native musical theater or vernacular operetta (Hernandez 1976), for conceptual criteria embedded in indigenous practice. *Sarswelas* in the twentieth century provide insightful commentary on modernity (the first feature), particularly notions of democracy and technology as markers of progress.

In the Tagalog *sarswela* titled *Pilipinas circa 1907* (Tiongson 1985), one of the highlights is the song "Kundi sa Americano" (If not for the Americans, in act 1, scene 7), in which the pro-American character Pardo enumerates the benefits brought by the Americans (emphasis mine).

Amerika'ng nagtayo rito	America built for us
Nitong gobyernong moderno	This *modern* government
May halalanat may boto	With elections and the vote
Totong demokratiko	Truly *democratic.*
Kundi sa Amerikano	If not for Americans
Pilipino'y atrasado	Filipinos would be behind the times

Ensuing verses provide a litany of blessings of American modernity, including ice-making plants, the phonograph, movies, toothpaste, and toothbrushes. The novelty song concludes with a musical reference to Western "classical music," a parody of Handel's "Hallelujah Chorus." Simultaneously, "Kundi" unerringly critiques American colonial preoccupation with physical comfort, technology, entertainment, hygiene, post-Fordist gadgetry, and (perceived) high culture. In this *sarswela,* the intent of the text is ironic, itself constituting critique. In addition, it does express a general Filipino sentiment present in Filipino scholarship that modernity arrived with the Americans (Constantino 1974; Rafael 2000). American modernity institutionalized notions of democracy and made technology widely available in the archipelago.

The onset of this modernity coincides with the US political occupation of the Philippines, which extended from 1898 until 1946, although US economic domination continues well into the post-martial-law Second Republic.[2] As particularly significant for this discussion, I identify the time period of 1913–1972, which I have called Developing Modernity. It is a period of transition for the Philippines from its status as an economic and political colony to constitutional self-rule. I feel the qualifier "developing" is apt, because these years encompass evolving Filipino notions of modernity reflecting at least four phases: initially the successful "civilizing project" through mastery of Western culture as promulgated by the United States (the "little brown brother" image), through struggles over an ambivalent and eclectically derivative identity ("three hundred years in the convent and fifty years in Hollywood"), as a self-proclaimed Asian nation within a community of nations (founding member of ASEAN in 1967), to an "Evolved Modernity" (1986 to the present)[3]—with concomitant alternative modernities such as the infamous Smoky Mountain.[4] By 1972 (my closing date for Developing Modernity), the country under Evolved Modernity had appropriated and domesticated Western culture in general, for example, Jollibee fast food as the Filipino counterpart to McDonald's, and popular music in particular, for example, OPM (Original Pilipino Music), which I discuss shortly as popular culture.

Philippine modernity from America as a trope is presented de facto by the American journalist Stanley Karnow in his signal 1990 book *In Our Image: America's Empire in the Philippines* and is heavily critiqued by the Filipino historian Renato Constantino in *The Philippines: A Past Revisited* (1975). Earlier, Constantino in *Identity and Consciousness: the Philippine Experience* (1974) had called for a Filipino counterconsciousness, and in the final chapter "A Usable Past," he issued a challenge for nationalist historical salvaging.

Relevant to nostalgia for a usable past for the nation, the period of Developing Modernity is highly informative; it encompasses a duration of relative social and political stability (with the exception of the four years of the Pacific War)[5] that from its inception assumed an end goal of sovereignty and nationhood, both by the Filipinos as colonized and the Americans as (often unaware) colonizers. The two bookends for Developing Modernity are significant: the close of the Philippine-American War in 1913 as its beginning and the onset of martial law in 1972 as its ending. Regarding the beginning year of 1913, the United States and the Philippines officially mark the end of hostilities for the Philippine-American War as 1902, the date of the Philippine Organic Act passed by the US Congress. Conflict in the Lowland Philippines for all intents and purposes had ceased by that date;[6] however, it did not stop in the Muslim South until 1913 with the slaughter of Muslim Filipinos by US General John Pershing in the major battle of Bud Bagsak in Jolo, Sulu. The Philippine government subscribes to the earlier 1902 date, a position that continues to problematize the status of Muslim Filipinos for the current nation-state. For most of the Lowland majority, the Muslim South continues to constitute an exotic and problematic domestic Other rather than a statement of diversity within the nation-state. Briefly, the closing bookend of 1972 marks the declaration of martial law by the Marcos regime, which effectively suspended democracy and undermined the stability critical to the continuation of the Developing Modernity period. However, I note meanings of the music and careers of de la Cruz and Corrales that extend beyond 1972 and that have implications for the twenty-first-century present.

Regarding the second feature, popular culture in the Philippines—from the late nineteenth century onward—rarely exists without music, be it stage performance, cinema, literature, or comics. Stage performance included the *komedya* (popularly known as *moro-moro*) of the nineteenth century. It used a brass band to accompany songs, marching formations, and other aspects of the mise-en-scène on outdoor stages as part of town fiestas. It received competition in the early twentieth century from the *sarswela,* a gentrified genre inspired by the Spanish *zarzuela,* performed on a proscenium stage with a pit orchestra that accompanied songs, dances, and production numbers in the vernacular (Hernandez 1976). *Bodabil,* the variety show derived from American vaudeville, provided competition for the more sedate *sarswela* in the early American period, circa 1920. However, these genres went into decline with the increasing popularity of cinema. A vibrant local industry of films in Tagalog and Visayan languages emerged; these films were initially film musicals, drawing heavily on stories, actors, and songs from both *sarswela* and *bodabil* (Tolentino 2000). The Philippine cinema industry competed with Hollywood and Shanghai, for example, productions by the Minxin Corporation and later the Shaw brothers. Literature during this period focused on Filipino themes and often included accounts of music performances or song texts as part of the narrative, such as the celebrated short story "Summer Solstice" by Nick Joaquin (1962). Comic strips *(komiks),* beginning with Ramos' *Kenkoy* in 1929 (Roxas and Arevalo 1984) and continuing with Alcala's *Mang Ambo* (1988) and Marcelo's *Tisoy* (Aviado, Mayuga, and Marcelo 2005), regularly referenced music in their frames.

In the period of Developing Modernity, Filipinos enthusiastically and often uncritically constructed themselves, using Karnow's words, "in our [American] image" (1990), a derivative of colonial mimicry that encompassed both popular and classical music. In the domain of classical music, Filipinos became educators, composers, virtuoso instrumentalists, and opera singers, the latter including spinto soprano Jovita Fuentes in the 1920s and lyric soprano Evelyn Mandac in the 1960s.[7]

The Philippines' entry into popular and commercial music was even more dramatic and global. In the 1930s, Manila was the hub of colonial culture for Asia. The most notable aspect of this role was the reputation of Filipinos as premier pop and jazz musicians throughout Asia, which is ongoing (Appadurai 1990; Ng 2006; Quirino 2004), as well as their significant presence in tourist venues in North America and Europe. Beginning in the 1910s and extending well into the 1960s, bars, nightclubs, and private clubs in Manila abounded, such as the Savoy and the Palace. They were populated by Filipino singers who could replicate recorded performances of Al Jolson and Nelson Eddy, later Frank Sinatra and Pat Boone, and shortly before martial law, Paul Anka and Julio Iglesias.

I remember in the 1960s at Don Jose's on Azcarraga Street drinking beers and listening to a young Filipina unerringly interpret Peggy Lee's "Mister Wonderful." I was waiting for Peggy Lee's giant hit "Fever," but the singer suddenly stopped and left the stage. She explained, "Oh, sir, I have a class at [Philippine] Normal [College]." However, the music did not stop—she was immediately replaced by a well-coiffed *kayamunggi* (olive-skinned) version of Tony Bennett delivering "I Left My Heart in San Francisco."

Vocal impersonators of every possible American singer populated downtown pubs in Escolta, uptown private clubs such as the German Club on San Luis Street and—beginning in the 1960s—the nightclubs on Burgos Street in Makati, an iconic center of Manila modernity. The beginning of the 1970s, the end of Developing Modernity, coincided with the emergence of a new category for the commercial music industry in the Philippines, Original Pilipino Music (OPM). The OPM category was significant as a musical movement of cultural decolonization on the eve of impending national trauma—the 1972 declaration of martial law. This confluence of political suppression and pop culture nationalism still awaits detailed examination.

For the third feature, gender construction, the notion of the feminine in the Philippines is distinctive and complex, informed by a putative matriarchal past, a patriarchal and prescriptive colonial Spanish Catholic ethos, and an imperative for individual agency fostered by American democratic intentions. There is significant research on gender in the Philippines (de la Cruz and Peracullo 2011; Roces and Edwards 2012; Santiago 2002), so here I only touch on points pertinent to the topic at hand. As I have noted earlier, notions of the Filipino feminine are not only complex but also sometimes contradictory. The publication *Being Filipino* (Cordero-Fernando 1981), a landmark of indigenous and reflexive gender scholarship, identifies seven types of the feminine, ranging from the virginal adolescent to the mistress. In an earlier publication (Trimillos 2000), I argue that there are differences between the feminine as an idealized, prescriptive model and the feminine as quotidian, pragmatic performance. Briefly, the idealized model references a nineteenth-century Spanish upper-class type, in which a passive demeanor, refined behavior, a reputation of respectability, overt religiosity, and virginity before marriage were paramount. However, the feminine as performed is in many ways contradictory; women in the Philippines have agency, do have romantic liaisons, and often engage in sensual and sexual behavior that contradicts ideals of refined womanhood and virginity.[8]

Once more returning to the *sarswela* as an indigenous vehicle for self-reflexivity, female representation in the *sarswela* constitutes emic cultural critique and offers insights for this discussion. For the genre, two stereotypical and contrasting female character types are de rigueur, the *bida* and the *contrabida*. Although the two types are generally differentiated by moral criteria—that is, the *bida* is "good" (honest, naive, and proper), and the *contrabida* is "bad" (scheming, worldly wise, and often morally suspect)—the good/bad binary is not my focus here. More relevant is the performativity of the two types: the *bida* inhabits a femininity that is passive and often subject to external control; the *contrabida* performs the feminine as proactive and capable of asserting control.

My discussion of two Filipina vocalists, the jazz singer Katy de la Cruz and the chanteuse Pilita Corrales, draws primarily on the contrasting proactive qualities of the *contrabida* and *bida*, respectively, as frame, rather than their essentialization as "bad" or "good." It also references other aspects of the two character types.

Katy de la Cruz

Born Catalina de la Cruz in Intramuros, Manila, in 1907, Katy de la Cruz comes from an agrarian and lower-class background in Bulacan, a Tagalog province with a rich cultural and historical heritage. De la Cruz traversed a Filipino rags-to-riches path, paralleling in notable ways the American Dream. As a young child in the municipality of Bustos, she emerged as a talented singer in local town fiestas. From a poor family and with minimal education, at age seven she came to the attention of impresarios in Manila, who initially engaged her to sing between films at movie houses. Experiencing great success as an entr'acte singer, she moved on to *bodabil* (vaudeville) as a novelty singer and, by age eighteen, was an established jazz singer known for her ability to scat. The height of her popularity was in the immediate postwar years, when *bodabil* in the Philippines was at its zenith. She also appeared in Tagalog films. In the late 1950s, she toured internationally. She was a headliner at San Francisco's Forbidden City and performed in Las Vegas in 1961. In the late 1960s, she emigrated to San Francisco, where she effectively retired. She visited the Philippines in 1989 to be feted by a musical based on her life, titled *Katy!* She remained in the Bay Area until her death in 2004 at age ninety-seven.

In temperament, de la Cruz corresponds[9] to the *contrabida* type described earlier. Additionally, her physical appearance is relevant here. A foreign journalist described her this way: "Five feet the height, one hundred and five buxom pounds the weight, dark olive the skin, hell's embers the eyes. . . . Katy has *it*. . . . *It* is only potent in womanly women" (Robb 1963, 37; emphasis added). To a foreigner's gaze, de la Cruz could be a highly attractive woman, or as indelicately expressed, "[she is] served hot" (ibid.). A smoldering picture of the Katy reinforces this sensual description (figure 12.1).

For an American and male gaze of the 1930s, de la Cruz's is clearly a racialized attractiveness. However, a Filipino gaze is different; she does not fulfill the Filipino ideal of beauty. In the Philippines, attractiveness is governed by several characteristics: complexion, height, shape of the face, and shape of the nose (Cannell 1999). The ideal beauty is the Spanish or part-Spanish mestiza, an attitude generally attributed to the Spanish colonial past of the Philippines. The complexion is fair, the body is tall and slim, the face is oval, and the nose is aq-

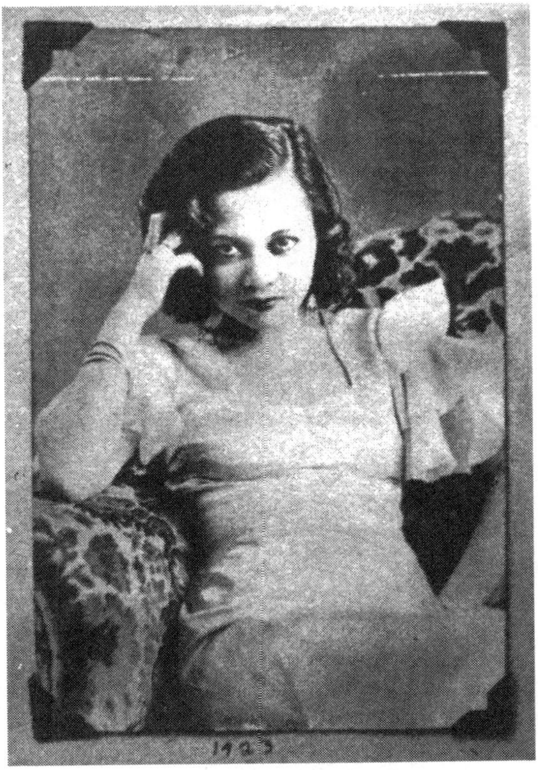

Figure 12.1. The jazz singer Katy de la Cruz, c. 1923: "hell's ember eyes." Alex R. Castro collection.

uiline. In contrast, de la Cruz is *kayamunggi* (olive complexion), short and buxom; her face is round, and her nose is wide ("flat"). By Filipino standards, she is not a beauty.

De la Cruz's onstage persona is one of the "good-time girl," with a flirtatious, sexually naughty streak that approaches but never oversteps the limits of good taste. One of her signature songs is "Ang balut," which refers to a duck egg with a partially formed embryo, a distinctively Filipino delicacy. It is also reputed to increase potency for males, carrying a sexual association similar to oysters for the United States and western Europe. The manner in which it is eaten from the shell also has sexual overtones.

Balut, penoy, balut	Balut, penoy, balut
Bili na kayo ng itlog na balut	Why don't you buy the egg balut
Sapagkat itong balut	Because this balut
Ay mainam na gamut	Is a good medication
Sa mga taong	For people
Nanlalambot ang tuhod	Whose knees are weak

Depending on vocal delivery and the disposition of the auditor, certain words can carry sexual meanings. For example, in the final two lines, the word *taong* (uninflected form *tao*) usually denotes "people" but can also mean specifically "males." The word *nalalambot* usually means "weak" but can also mean "soft"; similarly, *tuhod* denotes the knees but can also refer to the lower part of the body in general. Thus, a sexualized interpretation would be,

Sa mga taong	For males
Nanlalambot ang tuho	Whose lower part is soft

In a 1989 recorded performance, Katy sings a variant of the final line (marked in brackets), which makes a sexual reference even more explicit:

Sa mga taong	For males
[Laging ng lalambot]	[Who are frequently soft]

Clearly double entendre can be further reinforced by delivery. As one fan noted, "Most of the popularity [of "Balut"] was due to the way Katy de la Cruz used to sing it, with her raspy voice and eyes moving along with the naughtiness of the song" (Geocities n.d.). Of course, we must keep in mind that the text of the song and its performance by de la Cruz only allude to the sexual; they are never explicit. As a statement in print, my translation and description in fact constitute a "bold" formulation that crosses the line of Philippine *delicadeza,* that is, good taste. Such directness is to be avoided in normal discourse and if verbalized would probably make Filipinos uncomfortable, certainly in mixed company and perhaps even in an all-male gathering. Thus, de la Cruz's onstage image of femininity is flirtatious, with a suggestion of potential sexual encounter, of a woman knowledgeable, or perhaps of one experienced in "the fast life," but never overtly crude or transgressing the bounds of *delicadeza.*

Regarding issues of sex, good taste, and the "naughty," de la Cruz makes a distinction between her onstage persona and her quotidian femininity. Onstage she takes on the persona of the *contrabida* and the "naughty," especially with a song such as "Ang balut" or "Waray-waray," which in the Tagalog version outlines the attributes of a native Waray woman. However, according to interviews with de la Cruz and observations by others, the onstage persona and the everyday person are not the same. She reportedly flirts onstage but is never promiscuous, for example, dating or sleeping with patrons (Robb [1939] 1963, 38–39). This is corroborated by anecdotal evidence from old-timers who saw her at the Palace and at the Savoy in the pre–Pacific War years. This separation of persona and person was also depicted in the musical *Katy!* based on her life. The onstage persona of the *bida* as flirtatious or naughty constitutes a kind of public *tuksu-*

han or teasing, a recognized Filipino social mechanism (Enriquez 1994). In reality, de la Cruz had a difficult personal life—supporting her children while tolerating a womanizing husband to whom she remained married until his passing.

De la Cruz's vocal stylings reference major American singers of the prewar period, notably Sophie Tucker, Ella Fitzgerald, and Carmen Miranda, whose records she assiduously listened to and performances she copied. Her vocal production is fairly frontal, which produces a bright sound. This timbre is effective for Tagalog-language diction, which has unaspirated consonants and schwa-shaded vowels. She further nuances the texture of the vocal line by singing on the liquids, notably the phoneme */ng/,* which she places fairly forward above the soft palate, producing a bright sound. When singing slow ballads, de la Cruz exploits the microphone, often lending a "bedroom quality" to her delivery.

De la Cruz also introduces silences when parsing the text. This contrasts with her scatting, in which there are no silences. De la Cruz often ends a phrase (either musical or breath) with a drag, a concluding glissando downward from the final note. For example, in the song "Balut," the rare upward glissando occurs only on the word *balut* as mimesis of the actual call of the *balut* vendor.[10] Idiosyncratic to her delivery is a signature raspiness or "growl," reminiscent of Eartha Kitt and other Black blues singers. In up-tempo pieces, such as "Balut," in addition to jazz-style improvisations, de la Cruz often departs from the composed lyrics to address the audience or other musicians *en chantant.* She routinely breaks "the sonic fourth wall" in live and studio renditions, which is particularly effective in her novelty songs, including an unforgettable rendition of "A Tear Fell."

When de la Cruz returned to Manila in 1989 at age eighty-two, the only major change in her performance was singing at a pitch register lower than during her halcyon days of the 1940s and 1950s. During that visit, in a television interview with the composer Ryan Cayabyab, she alluded to the consistency of her styling by saying that on her next visit, the only difference would be that she would probably need to use a cane ("Balut" 1989). Unfortunately, she was unable to return prior to her death in 2004. Consistency in vocal styling is also a feature of the Filipina chanteuse Pilita Corrales.

Pilita Corrales

Pilita Corrales was born Pilar Garrido Corrales in 1939, one generation later than Katy de la Cruz and on the eve of the Pacific War. From an upper-class and mestizo Spanish family,[11] she grew up in Cebu City, with Cebuano being her primary Filipino language in addition to Spanish as a second mother tongue. Cebu occupies an important historical position as the site of the encounter with Magellan, the first known European presence in the Philippines, and as the site of the first conversions to Catholic Christianity for the archipelago.[12] Educated in Cebu's oldest elite parochial school for girls, Corrales was sent to Madrid, Spain, for further education. In contrast to Katy de la Cruz, Corrales exemplifies the *ilustrado* elite, including study in Spain, the former colonizer country. Her career has included concerts, musical theater, films, and television programs as well as recordings. In contrast to "homegrown" de la Cruz, Corrales established her vocal career in Victoria, Australia, beginning in 1958, with successes in concerts, television shows, and recording sales—reportedly the first female to make the Australian pop charts in 1959. Following successes abroad, she returned to the Philippines in 1963 and hosted a radio program featuring Spanish songs. Her reputation as an international chanteuse was established by singing in a number of languages, including her native Cebuano, Spanish, English, and Tagalog, the national language. She toured Asia, Australia, and the United States, including appearances in Honolulu and in Las Vegas with Sammy Davis Jr. in the 1960s. She is still a presence in the entertainment industry, recently as judge for the 2014 second season of *X Factor Philippines,* a pop song competition franchised from the UK property.

Corrales physically embodies the metaphorical *bida* type. In terms of appearance, she more than satisfies the Filipino aesthetic of feminine beauty (figure 12.2). She is fair in complexion, her body type is slim (in effect, tall), her face is oval, and her nose is aquiline ("high"). This visual aesthetic for femininity is strongly reinforced throughout the society by print media advertising and the feature film, in which the romantic female lead is always a light-skinned mestiza. Her media images, when displaying more than the face, emphasize the statuesque gestalt—that is, shooting low and upward to give an appearance of length—as well as her fair complexion. The preoccupation with whiteness is not unique to Filipinos but is widespread throughout Asia (Coté 2009; Mizutani 2006; Rafael 2000). By Filipino standards, Corrales was a beauty in her younger days and is still considered to be beautiful for a mature woman.

Corrales' performance of femininity, particularly in the 1960s and 1970s, projected the idealized femininity of "Ang dalagang Pilipina."[13] The combination of an idealized physical appearance and proper behavior is popularly encapsulated by the label "Maria Clara type," which refers to the female protagonist in the two novels authored by the national hero José Rizal (1887, 1892); Maria Clara was mestiza (the illegitimate daughter of a Spanish priest), raised in a convent, innocent, and virginal. Among sexually active males (bachelors and otherwise), the term "Maria Clara type" in contemporary usage can denote a proper, chaste, and sexually unavailable young woman, often with an older brother who is charged with keeping her that way. In postmodern Filipino feminism, the Maria Clara type is criticized for its qualities of passive objectifica-

Figure 12.2. The chanteuse Pilita Corrales, c. 1967, in traditional attire, from cover of the LP *Filipiniana: Pilita Corrales*. Vicor Music Corporation.

tion, absence of agency, and de facto capitulation to patriarchal control. This image is currently being revisited; some people have looked to other characters in the Rizal novels (Mabanglo 1992) or have posited a "new mestiza" (Uychoco 2012).

Although "cool" and in control as a performer, Corrales was in her personal life a battered wife trapped in an abusive first marriage (Female Network 2012). Although strongly Catholic in a Catholic country, Corrales has one child out of wedlock and has been married twice in a country that does not recognize divorce. Such aspects of her personal life are widely known and openly discussed in the media. Thus, her lived experience departs in major ways from her onstage persona and from the ideal of the Filipino woman.

As a performance persona, Corrales is both proper and classy. Although she developed a comedic side as she matured, her early image is that of the statuesque mestiza who is cool, cosmopolitan, well educated, and with self-control. One of her signature pieces is the Cebuano song "Matud nila" (So they say), composed by Ben Zubiri in 1941 shortly after the Japanese invaded the Philippines. It is often called the Cebuano national anthem. In the 1960s, when the song was achieving commercial popularity, Levi Celerio created lyrics in Tagalog, the national language. Corrales sings the song in both its Cebuano and Tagalog versions.

In general, Corrales' vocal style appears more idiosyncratic than de la Cruz's, although her delivery has similarities to those of Peggy King, Doris Day, and Patti Page. Given sojourns in Spain and in Australia, she had more opportunities to hear live performances of prominent pop vocalists as well as access to a wider range of broadcast music. Her signature vocal production ("sound") is medial rather than frontal, generally located behind the soft palate and with consistent use of head resonation. The result is a rounded, covered quality rather than a bright timbre. The melodic delivery is clean, that is, on pitch with a notable absence of slides, glides, or bending the pitch. As a stylistic feature, Corrales uses a "natural" vibrato for any duration longer than a quarter note; she rarely uses a straight tone or a vibrato that varies in speed or amplitude. She seldom sings on liquids; rather, she holds long durations on the vowel, which reinforces a consistency of vocal timbre. A characteristic ending for a breath or musical phrase is a plosive, unpitched release of air. The "tessitura of comfort" encompasses a tenth, generally with a uniform quality throughout the range—that is, there is no noticeable "break" in her higher range.

In the Philippines, many singers are versatile and change their vocal style and vocal production depending on the genre performed. Corrales' performance is a notable exception to this accommodation to genre—she renders a wide variety of genres with the same sound and styling. Some fans speak of a "Pilita sound" as a musical entity. Notable in this regard is her rendition of the Filipino art song genre *(kundiman),* which normally uses a bel canto vocal production replete with operatic vocal gestures. In contrast, the Corrales version of the concert *balitaw* "Ang dalagang Pilipina" (the Filipina maiden) by the nationalist composer José Santos transforms it into an intimate pop rendition, strikingly different from its usual bel canto, concert-hall delivery.

For Corrales, the microphone enables a relaxed vocal quality with a noticeable absence of back pressure; the overall sound is "cool," an image of aesthetic distance from the listener in both live and recorded performances. As such, her performance remains comfortably behind the proscenium, but without being detached. Notably, the "Pilita sound" has remained consistent and readily recognizable from its inception during the period of Developing Modernity to the present. This consistency may be one of the reasons for her continued popularity among domestic and diasporic Filipino audiences. At seventy, she sings a familiar repertory in a voice that is familiar to an aging overseas population and also to their offspring, for whom the Corrales LP or CD provides a tangible connection with the homeland. Her continuing presence and success in the entertainment industry is testament to her artistry and to the rapport she establishes with generations of Filipinos.

Modernity and Popular Music Performers

The two singers discussed here exhibit different paths in traversing Developing Modernity, both of which reflect general Filipino experiences. Katy de la Cruz through her music career successfully negotiated upward mobility and the American Dream—with all its ironies for a colonized people. Initially she escaped from poverty, low social class, and provincial origins to the Manila metropole. There she successfully engaged the American "civilizing project," becoming adept in jazz, a very American musical genre, as well as a cultural icon. Not only did this transformation allow her to establish a globalized career, but it also ultimately enabled her to escape to the United States and its promise of a "better life," an aspiration held by many Filipinos. Thus, she enacts a typical Filipino pattern of sojourn: initially inhabiting a rural and provincial locale, then relocating to an urban center, and finally establishing residence in a diasporic enclave. Important to the nation and to her own lived experience, she was not resident in the homeland during the upheaval of martial law but rather lived in the relative stability of the United States. Thus, her meaning for the Philippines of the Second Republic is one of nostalgia; she represents the success of Filipinos during the initial phase of Developing Modernity and the personal success of the US-based Filipino. However, her transformation, the putative American Dream, is not one of complete assimilation into the American mainstream. Rather, she remains marginalized, marked phenotypically as a minority American and professionally as a Filipino jazz artist. However, this liminality does not assume social or cultural isolation; rather, it leads to an alternative identity. She settled in California's Bay Area, site of a large and vibrant Filipino community. Indeed, the San Francisco suburb of Daly City is a Filipino enclave (referred to as *DC* in Tagalog). It functions as a "Little Manila" in which Tagalog is often the default language, and its residents move daily among familiar icons of Manila modernity, including Jollibee fast-food outlets, Goldilocks bakeries, and Iglesia ni Cristo churches. All bespeak a Filipino presence if not identity. De la Cruz is known and at home in that locale as well as in the multiethnic jazz community of the Bay Area.

In terms of music, Katy de la Cruz inhabited the space of the "girl singer," standard for American big bands of the 1930s onward and later part of jazz combos of the 1940s and 1950s. That space enabled the sexualized onstage image that de la Cruz clearly considered to be a compartmentalized, onstage persona and from which she distanced herself in her offstage life.

De la Cruz's historical positionality is multifaceted. As is often the case for secondary, transnational participants of a foreign genre (here, American jazz), she was often described as derivative of more authentic American originals—for example, Eartha Kitt or Peggy Lee—although her repertory included Filipino-composed pieces. Her onstage performance of gender contrasted with her consciously articulated "real-life" gendered roles. These corresponded to a number of the categories in the Cordero-Fernando typology: the (female) child, the wife, the mother, and the widow. Moreover, married to a man with a roving eye, she had to contend with an additional "Being Filipino" category: the mistress. As an artist of the Developing Modernity period, she has as one of her meanings for modernity one who mastered the culture of the colonial Other. Further, viewed from the perspective of a twenty-first-century Philippines, she constitutes an icon of nostalgia for the earlier Developing Modernity period with its (imposed) political and cultural stability and during which a positivist sense of progress obtained. The nostalgic image of de la Cruz as the jazz singer remains undisturbed by the turmoil of martial law; she is largely absent from these events. The retrospective musical theater production *Katy!* in 1989 at the Cultural Center of the Philippines invokes a national nostalgia, revalorizing and redefining the earlier colonial age of *bodabil* and jazz for the nation's present. It reinforced her proactive subjectivity, a major quality of the *contrabida* persona.

In contrast to the rags-to-riches narrative for de la Cruz, Pilita Corrales bespeaks the nature of privilege and power, which in the Philippines remains largely in the same hands despite changes or upheavals in political, social, and economic fortunes. As the *bida* figure, Corrales embodies the centrality of *lahi* or lineage in privileging a native elite. Her origins in a province outside the metropole and her mother tongue as regional Cebuano Visayan provide nonconfrontational testimony to a de facto multilinguality and diversity of the Filipino nation that challenges the national claim to "Isang bansa, isang diwa" (One nation, one language). In practice, Filipinos outside the Tagalog-speaking region are at least trilingual, speaking a local mother tongue, Tagalog as the national language, and English as the language of international commerce and global employment. Corrales maintains colonial Spanish as a fourth language. Unlike the Americanization of de la Cruz, Corrales' enculturation perpetuates a nineteenth-century *ilustrado* pattern rehearsed by the historical architects of Philippine independence, including José Rizal, Apollinario Mabini, and Marcelo H. del Pilar. Her fluency in Spanish, her education at an elite Catholic school, and her study abroad replicate this pattern, increasing her already considerable social capital.

Corrales' trajectory as sojourner is not a typical Filipino one: she came from a provincial but privileged locale, went abroad (Spain and Australia), and finally settled in the Manila metropole, where she continues her career and her personal life. Going abroad for Corrales was not a final aspiration; rather, it served as a means for establishing success and an international reputation, again an additional source of cultural capital. Although she toured the United States and other countries during the Developing Modernity period, after 1963, she has been continually based in the Philippines, notably during the difficult years of martial law, when artists often found themselves affected by the *kulturpolitik* of the Marcos regime and implicated in arts projects of the First Lady, Imelda Marcos. For the artist resident in the country during martial law, it was difficult to remain neutral or uninvolved.

Corrales' meaning for Filipinos today is at least twofold. In the Philippines, she is considered a prominent performer rather than a symbol of historical or cultural import. Her major significance in the homeland is artistic. However, for Filipinos in the diaspora, she has symbolic as well as artistic value. She is a Filipina whose vocal stylings continue to remind first-generation émigrés of a Philippines and its burgeoning OPM industry that they left behind. For subsequent generations of overseas Filipinos, her performances offer sonic continuity and an embraceable image defined by physical appearance and vocal style. The significant numbers of diasporic Filipino youth attending her concerts in Chicago (2014), Toronto (2011), and Texas (2007) speak to the latter.

Given Corrales' career experiences in Spain and Australia, she appears less derivative of American pop. During the Developing Modernity period, she presents as a global pop artist similar to Petula Clark and Julio Iglesias, that is, multilingual in lyrics, multinational in repertoire, and idiosyncratic in vocal style. Significantly, the majority of her recorded repertoire consists of Filipino titles, many of them OPM; English and Spanish covers constitute a small minority of this oeuvre. However, evident from her performance tours abroad, she readily controls the English-language pop song "canon," especially repertory from the final three decades of the twentieth century. Recordings typically feature her as solo singer in arrangements using a full (live) orchestra with high studio production values. No backup singers are part of the texture. Modernity in the Philippines also meant a sophistication and expertise with technology, both mechanical and human. During the Developing Modernity period, the Philippine recording industry emerged as the leading producer of high-quality analogue recordings in Southeast Asia and compared favorably with Japan in technical quality. Her recordings are prime exemplars for the technical capacity of the Manila LP recording industry, both sonic and graphic.

Corrales' initial onstage femininity was of the *bida* type described earlier. However, later she underwent a transformation away from this Maria Clara femininity. From the late 1970s onward, her onstage appearance changed. Instead of a Maria Clara persona in the national dress of *terno* with butterfly sleeves, her appearance approached that of the torch singer: dresses are full length, tight, and form fitting, often with a high slit to show some leg. However unlike de la Cruz, Corrales' stage movements and vocal interpretations are not "naughty" or suggestively sexual. Allusions to the sexual are primarily through costume and are not explicit in performance, again a kind of onstage *tuksuhan* (teasing).

Corrales' personal life provides a different narrative, as discussed earlier. These apparent transgressions of an ideal Filipina femininity (the illegitimate child and a second marriage) are of no apparent concern to her audiences or to the community at large, indicating considerable latitude between the feminine as prescribed and the feminine as practiced (Cordero-Fernando 1981; Trimillos 2000).

Because Corrales is still an active performer, her historical significance for the Philippines is synchronically bounded and therefore at this time necessarily provisional. From the perspective of 2016 (the time of this writing), she connects a modern and sovereign Philippines to its heritage of Spanish colonialism, American occupation, and martial law—all parts of a personal and lived experience. Further, she appears as proxy of colonial fantasy to a Filipino population that valorizes the mestizo body, romanticizes Spanish heritage, seeks external and international validation, and admires (if not desires) elite privilege. Finally, her success and high profile validate a technological modernity, including highly produced studio recordings, engagement as hostess for radio and television programs, headliner for television specials and stage shows, numerous international tours, and in 2014 a recognized expert and judge for mediated singing competitions.

I return to the three features mentioned at the beginning of this chapter: modernity, popular culture, and gender. In this chapter, I have argued that popular music in the Philippines is a component of a national trajectory toward modernity, both as harbinger and as causation. I have identified a particular range of years, which I label a period of Developing Modernity, and two female participants within that period whose lives and music reflect both functions—harbinger and causative. I have indicated the importance of mass media in the dissemination and consumption of music, as well as the interrelatedness of the media, that is, recording industry, cinema, broadcasting, and onstage production. I have problematized Philippine modernity in respect to external disruptions to an orderly development of nation as political state and as cultural entity. I have further identified the ways in which cultural identity and the reach of Philippine popular music and musicians comprise interactions beyond the boundaries of the nation-state, leading to engagement with the global and the transnational.

In regard to popular culture as commerce and as social preoccupation, I have suggested that the local music industry has engaged with globalization and transnationalism in a number of different ways that, significantly, are symptomatic for strategies of engagement observable in other domains of the Philippine nation. I have tried to show through a consideration of vocal stylings that processes of assimilation, appropriation, domestication, and invention contribute to a sonic manifestation of this broader engagement.

I claim that gender construction in a Filipino context has both a prescriptive domain (the idealized model) and a performative domain (the lived practice). Although these domains are applicable to all indigenous constructions of gender, here the focus has been on female performing artists and how they play (Tagalog: *maglaro*) with both the prescriptive and the performative, sometimes in a teasing or flirtatious way. These artists critique the prescriptive and the performative as well as their effects on a Filipino way of life—actual, virtual, and imagined. The fact that relationships between onstage and quotidian performance of gender carry inconsistencies and even contradictions speaks to the efficacy of the critique and to the multivalent nature of the prescriptive and the performative in the Philippines.

As final comment, I anticipate that many of the observations for the Philippines presented here have resonance for other parts of Insular Southeast Asia. In terms of the voice, some of the techniques de la Cruz uses, for example, slides, drag, and frontal vocal production, are present in the *kroncong* stylings of Waldjinah (b. 1945; see Russell P. Skelchy, chap. 13 in this volume). In terms of the body, like Corrales, Momo Latif (1921–2015) and Saloma[14] (1935–1983) of Malaya (now Malaysia) had relatively light complexions; they were popular as singers and actresses during the mid-twentieth century.[15] However, in Indonesia and Malay(si)a, pop artists worked against a highly regarded and sophisticated indigenous court music, a genre absent in the Philippines. In arguments for regional correspondences, perhaps Don Handelman's *Logic of Practice* (1998) mitigates such variables and points to a Southeast Asian sensibility suggested earlier. In any case, shared characteristics constitute statements about cultural interconnections and overarching sensibilities that advocate for musical and cultural scholarship that transcends the national and investigates regional cultural coherence as well as diversities.

Notes

1. *Filipina* refers to females. The term *Filipino* usually carries no gender specificity.
2. I use the term "Second Republic" to denote the resumption of democratic rule after the Marcos dictatorship collapsed in 1986.
3. The term is derived from Kaeppler's cultural category of *evolved traditional* (1989).
4. A gigantic dumpsite in metro Manila where thousands of squatters lived under unbelievably abject conditions during the Marcos dictatorship.

5. The war years constitute only 6 percent of the entire period.

6. Except for Macario Sakay and the Tagalog Republic, which ended in 1906.

7. Notably, both are Visayan: Fuentes from the center (Iloilo on Panay) and Mandac from the diaspora (Davao in Mindanao).

8. The informal term *technical virgin* suggests the apparent contradictions and accommodations between the prescriptive and the performative (Cordero-Fernando 1981, 33).

9. Although de la Cruz died in 2004, for ease of making comparisons in this discussion, I use the present tense.

10. The call of the vendor is still heard evenings in most neighborhoods of the Lowland Philippines.

11. Earlier accounts reported the family to be Spanish, although more recent ones describe the family as mestizo, that is, part Cebuano and part Spanish.

12. Magellan was killed in Cebu when the Spanish became involved in an internecine war between two chieftains. Late twentieth-century nationalists consider this the earliest Filipino resistance to foreign invasion, a trope often invoked in discourses of decolonization.

13. The concept is the title of a well-known Filipino art song *(kundiman)*, "Ang dalagang Pilipina" (the Filipino maiden), which I discuss in Trimillos 2000.

14. The stage name of Salmah binti Ismail.

15. In Saloma's later career, she, like Corrales, also appropriated the torch singer image, with form-fitting long dresses, for example, her attire on the CD cover for *Saloma: Bunga Tanjung* (Saloma: Tanjung blossom, 2002).

References

Abinales, Patricio, and Donna J. Amoroso. 2005. *State and Society in the Philippines.* Lanham, MD: Rowman and Littlefield.

Appadurai, Arjun. 1990. "Disjuncture and Difference in the Global Cultural Economy." *Public Culture* 2 (2): 1–24.

Aviado, Pandy, Silvia Mayuga, and Dario Marcelo. 2005. *Huling Ptyk: Da art of Nonoy Marcelo.* Manila: Anvil.

"Balut—Katy de la Cruz (live)." 1989. *Ryan Ryan Musikahan* broadcast. Posted by paomonkey21, YouTube, 14 October 2013. http://www.youtube.com/watch?v=IqbME-OwVAY.

Cannell, Fanella. 1999. *Power and Intimacy in the Christian Philippines.* Cambridge: Cambridge University Press.

Castro, Christie-Ann. 2011. *Musical Renderings of the Philippine Nation.* New York: Oxford University Press.

Constantino, Renato. 1974. *Identity and Consciousness: The Philippine Experience.* Manila: Malaya Books.

———. 1975. *The Philippines: A Past Revisited.* Manila: Insular Packaging Corporation.

Cordero-Fernando, Gilda, ed. 1981. *Being Filipino.* Quezon City: GCF Books.

Coté, Joost. 2009. "Education and the Colonial Construction of Whiteness." *ACRAWSA* 5 (1). http://www.acrawsa.org.au/files/ejournalfiles/39acrawsa512.pdf.

Curato, Nicole. 2015. "Deliberative Capacity as an Indicator of Democratic Quality: The Case of the Philippines." *International Political Science Review* 36 (1): 99–116.

de la Cruz, Noelle L., and Jeane Peracullo, ed. 2011. *Feminista: Gender, Race, and Class in the Philippines.* Manila: Anvil.
Enriquez, Virgilio G. 1994. *Pagbabangong-dangal: Indigenous Psychology and Cultural Empowerment.* Quezon City: Akademya ng Kultura at Sikolohiyang Pilipino.
Female Network. 2012. "Pilita Corrales Reveals She Was a Battered Wife for 10 Years." 4 July. http://www.femalenetwork.com/celebrities/pilita-corrales-reveals-she-was-a-battered-wife-for-10-years.
Geocities. n.d. "Songs: Balut (Duck's Egg)." Accessed 8 February 2014, http://www.geocities.ws/katy_delacruz/songs.html.
Handelman, Don. 1998. *Models and Mirrors: Toward an Anthropology of Public Events.* New York: Berghahn Books.
Hernandez, Tomás C. 1976. "The Emergence of Modern Drama in the Philippines (1898–1912)." Honolulu: University of Hawai'i Asian Studies Program. Philippine Studies Working Paper no.1.
Joaquin, Nick. 1962. "Summer Solstice." In *Nic Joaquin's Selected Stories.* Manila: Albierto Florentino.
Kaeppler, Adrienne. 1989. "Art and Aesthetics." In *Developments in Polynesian Ethnology,* edited by Alan Howard and Robert Borofsky, 211–240. Honolulu: University of Hawai'i Press.
Karnow, Stanley. 1990. *In Our Image: America's Empire in the Philippines.* New York: Random House.
Laurel, R. Kuan. 2010. *Philippine Cultural Disasters: Essays on an Age of Hyper Consumption.* Manila: Willing Ox.
Lockard, Craig A. 1998. *Dance of Life: Popular Music and Politics in Southeast Asia.* Honolulu: University of Hawai'i Press.
Mabanglo, Ruth E. 1992. "Rizal's Sisa and Basilio: Characters as Symbols of National Identity." In *The Age of Discovery: Impact on Philippine Culture and Society,* edited by Belinda A. Aquino and Dean T. Alegado, 13–16. Honolulu: University of Hawai'i at Manoa Center for Philippine Studies.
Mizutani, Satoshi. 2006. "Historicising Whiteness: From the Case of Late Colonial India." *ACRAWSA* 2 (1). http://www.acrawsa.org.au/files/ejournalfiles/85SatoshiMizutani.pdf.
Ng, Stephanie. 2006. "Filipino Bands Performing in Hotels, Clubs and Restaurants in Asia: Purveyors of Transnational Culture in a Global Arena." PhD diss., University of Michigan.
Putzel, James. 1999. "Survival of an Imperfect Democracy in the Philippines." *Democratization* 6 (1): 198–223.
Quirino, Richie. 2004. *Pinoy Jazz Traditions.* Manila: Anvil.
Rafael, Vicente L. 2000. *White Love and Other Events in Filipino History.* Manila: Ateneo de Manila University Press.
Rizal, José M. (1887) 1961. *Noli me tangere.* Manila: José Rizal National Centennial Commission.
———. (1892) 2006. *El filibusterismo.* Charleston, SC: Bibliobazaar.
Robb, Walter. (1939) 1963. *Filipinos: Pre-war Philippines Essays.* Rev ed. Victoneta Park (Malabon, Philippines): Araneta University Press.
Roces, Mina, and Louise Edwards, eds. 2012. *Women's Movements and the Filipina, 1986–2008.* Honolulu: University of Hawai'i Press.

Rodell, Paul A. 2002. *Culture and Customs of the Philippines.* Westport, CT: Greenwood.
Roxas, Cynthia, and Joaquin Arevalo Jr. 1984. *A History of Komiks of the Philippines and Other Countries.* Quezon City: Islas Filipinas.
Santiago, Lila Q., ed. 2002. *In the Name of the Mother: 100 Years of Philippine Feminist Poetry, 1889–1989.* Quezon City: University of the Philippines Press.
Santos, Ramón P. 2003. "Revivalism and Modernism in the Musics of Post-colonial Asia." *Bulawan* 7:12–18.
Tiongson, Nicanor. 1985. *Pilipinas circa 1907: Production Script & Notes Score for Piano and Voice.* Quezon City: Philippine Educational Theater Association.
Tolentino, Rolando B., ed. 2000. *Geopolitics of the Visible: Essays on Philippine Film Cultures.* Manila: Ateneo de Manila Press.
Torres, Cristina E. 2010. *The Americanization of Manila, 1898–1921.* Quezon City: University of the Philippines Press.
Trimillos, Ricardo D. 2000. "Ang Dalagang Pilipina: Representation and Presentation of the Filipino Female in Traditional Musics." In *Feasts and Feats: Festschrift for Doreen G. Fernandez,* edited by Jonathan Chua, 253–267. Quezon City: Ateneo de Manila University.
Uychoco, Marikit T. A. 2012. "Like Water for Chocolate: The Rewriting of the Female Experience and Its Parallels in Philippine History." *Humanities Diliman* 9 (1): 95–110.

CHAPTER 13

Beyond Black and Gray

PORTRAITS AND SCENES OF JAVANESE SINGER WALDJINAH IN INDONESIAN POPULAR PRINT MEDIA

Russell P. Skelchy

> Putri Solo, her beauty is real. Indeed, she's clever in her style. That's Putri Solo. Wearing a silk flowery shawl draped over her shoulder, her hairpin is a jasmine flower, completing her beauty. She moves like a hungry tiger (slow and elegant); thong sandals on her feet make a klinking sound; her earrings sparkle. That's Putri Solo. When she laughs, you'll see her dimples. Dark and sweet is her skin. That's Putri Solo.
>
> —Lyrics to the song "Putri Solo" (Solonese girl, composed in 1940)

WALDJINAH is the most renowned vocalist in *keroncong*, a form of Indonesian national music associated with the era of nationalism and independence in the mid-twentieth century.[1] She is not only a prolific musical artist who has been featured on over two hundred albums but also a beloved public figure. Over the course of her long career, Indonesian media have created an array of gendered representations of Waldjinah. These representations have shaped her public image, but they have not necessarily been imposed on her. Rather, she has had an active voice in advancing certain images of herself, and she has negotiated the parameters of what she is willing to share with journalists. During my interviews with her over a period of eighteen months, I had the opportunity to observe newspaper journalists and radio and television reporters who dropped by her home in Solo (formally known as Surakarta), in central Java. Most interesting to me was the dynamic interplay between subject and interviewer, an aspect of fieldwork that I thought about frequently. The idea of the interview framed as a form of managed self-performance was especially apparent, and I paid close attention to her voice, posture, hand gestures, facial expressions, and style of dress, as well as how she chose to answer questions.

This chapter examines Waldjinah's self-performance and voice in the broader context of how gender identities have been represented in popular print media. I examine what I call "portraits" of Waldjinah in Indonesian print media, referring not only to photographs but also to articles and other written texts. Rather than considering these sources as merely two-dimensional representations, I examine them as temporalized and spatialized "scenes" corresponding to specific places, events, images, and periods in her life. Scenes refer to the broader contexts and interpretive frames of the portraits. Scenes articulate processes of gendering that have created disparate images of Waldjinah ranging from sultry siren to compassionate mother and loyal wife.

These portraits and scenes reveal how rigidly gender has been constructed and how strictly its boundaries are enforced in modern Indonesia, especially during the rule of Indonesia's second president, Suharto—a period known as the New Order (1966–1998). They also highlight the integral role media representations play in establishing gender roles and identities associated with being either "male" or "female." Imaginaries of idealized women (and men) are continuously circulated via mass media, reinforcing state-driven discourses and policies intended to create properly gendered modern citizens. Waldjinah was exemplary in this endeavor as the embodiment of modern Indonesia in the late 1960s and early 1970s. She popularized a Javanized form of *keroncong* known as *langgam jawa* and represented a fresh sound and image that differentiated her from older *keroncong* singers. As a mother, daughter, and wife, she became a symbol for the modern Indonesian woman, especially as her public image was used to espouse ideals about women and gender roles by state and religious authorities. For these and other reasons, Waldjinah commanded a national audience, and Indonesians avidly consumed print media about her, especially if they believed they were acquiring information about her personal life.

Popular print media portraits and scenes used idealized representations of Waldjinah to reinforce an order of gender and sexuality in Indonesia that concealed the complexities of how gender roles were contested, re/interpreted, and re/configured in everyday life. In popular print media, she resembled the patriarchal ideal of a Javanese woman: attractive, docile, and unquestioning. The extended period of time I spent interviewing Waldjinah, however, allowed me to experience both the initial frustration of trying to overcome these parameters and the satisfaction of her eventually becoming more open to filling in the gaps from her more scripted responses. While silences in this story undoubtedly remain, the time I spent was a luxury not afforded to journalists. Furthermore, the somewhat unusual perspective of observing interviews conducted by others provided important insights into what she held back.

Scene One: Arrival

The following excerpt, taken from an article in a local newspaper, describes a journalist's experience meeting Waldjinah for the first time.

> I arrived to find Waldjinah already at the front gate of her home in Mangkuyudan late one afternoon. After explaining that I had come to interview her, I asked if we could chat briefly. Waldjinah smiled, flashing pearly white, evenly set teeth. When I began snapping photos though, she left hurriedly, entering the house and leaving me behind to wait in the beautiful guest parlor room. Five minutes later, she emerged, this time sporting blue jeans and a checkered blouse reminiscent of a cowgirl. For a moment there, I couldn't believe it was really Waldjinah, the true Putri Solo.[2]

I begin with this vignette as a way of discussing how Indonesian popular print media have constructed gendered images of Waldjinah over the course of her career and how she, in turn, has negotiated her own public image. Although brief, this passage is packed with the visual imagery of a young Waldjinah as the archetype of the *Putri Solo* (Solonese girl). *Putri Solo,* a subject I return to later in this chapter, is also the title of a *keroncong* song. Its name is taken from Waldjinah's hometown of Solo, and its lyrics describe the appropriate behavior and appearance of an idealized Solonese girl (as reflected in the lyrics quoted at the beginning of this chapter). Waldjinah's reaction to this reporter is not entirely unusual; she may have been caught off guard by his arrival but was willing to do the interview. When the reporter suddenly began snapping photos, capturing her image seemingly without permission, Waldjinah took advantage of the situation to change her clothes. What she chose to wear, however, surprised the reporter, perhaps because the "cowgirl" look he attributed to her contradicted the established feminine image of her as an iconic *Putri Solo.*

During the early part of Waldjinah's career, she learned how to control her image. Like other public figures, she engaged in a performance of self on various levels and often took on different characteristics depending on context. Richard Bauman argues that performance "sets up, or represents, an interpretive frame within which the messages being communicated are to be understood, and that this frame contrasts with at least one other frame, the literal" (1984, 5). Bauman's observation about performance and framing can be understood in relation to images constructed by and for Waldjinah. Some of these images adhere to common archetypes of Indonesian femininity: the attractive and demure *Putri Solo,* the sexually charged "bombshell," and the responsible, nurturing, and family-oriented mother. Other images show Waldjinah contradicting and complicating stereotypes of femininity—for instance, the "cowgirl" described in the previously quoted passage, her "tomboy" image as a youth, or the professional touring musician who spent much of her time away from home and her children.

Reading between the lines of popular print media is especially important when considering the context of these representations. As Benedict Anderson observes, the vast quantity of "direct speech" (gossip, rumors, public discussion, etc.) in Indonesia is transmuted into illustrations or symbolic representations that can assume documentary status in print form (1990, 154–155). The ephemeral and fluid nature of symbolic representations, according to Anderson, require a close reading as meanings shift, deepen, and invert over time.

Hierarchies of Gender, Discourses of Sexuality

Female performers in Indonesia have generally held a socially ambiguous status, usually conferred by the male audiences they are expected to entertain. Female performers are simultaneously maligned for associations with sexual freedom and prostitution yet revered for having mystical and supernatural powers (Spiller 2010). In actuality, many negotiate desired identities based not only on their own choices but also the agencies of others, which include a host of institutions (media, religious, and government) as well as parents, siblings, spouses, extended family members, and friends.

Although representations of females in Indonesian popular print media are quite diverse, female performers are often represented as sexualized and therefore dangerous and threatening to the patriarchal social order. In *dangdut,* an Indonesian popular music, tabloid stories about sex and scandal attach to singers, especially women, more than in any other genre of music in Indonesia, and the grouping of "female," "*dangdut,*" and "singer" conjures images of sexual pleasure and seduction (Weintraub 2010, 24). While these terms can signify a range of possible meanings including sexual freedom, economic potential, or even Muslim identities, the enduring image of the gyrating, scantily clad, young female *dangdut* singer remains a tool used to market the genre to a nationalized and predominantly male audience.[3]

Sexualization of female performers is not necessarily a new or recent phenomenon in Indonesia. Female vocalists in Javanese gamelan ensembles, known as *pesindhèn,* have long been associated with sexual freedom, prostitution, and other reputed social misconduct (Spiller 2010; Walton 1996; Cooper 1994; Sutton 1987). In certain cases, the overt sexuality associated with dance traditions (for example, *lènggèr, tayuban,* and *ronggèng*) stigmatizes the women well into their old age, affecting relationships within families and their ability to earn income even after they have stopped performing (Lysloff 2002, 4). For these and other reasons, some men remain reluctant to allow their wives and daughters to perform in public settings (Spiller 2010, 10).

From a historical perspective, the "deployment of gender" by the people in power was used as a way of normalizing sexuality first during the Dutch colonial period and later during the New Order era (Blackwood 2010, 36–40, Blackburn 2004). New Order discourses were not directed at sexuality per se but at the creation of properly gendered, reproductive citizens situated within heterosexual nuclear families. "Sex" and "gender" are not distinguished in Indonesia but rather operate in a single discursive framework where gender is conflated with the "nature" of sexed bodies. Deployment of gender during the New Order meant a consistent and comprehensive discourse defining the appropriate positions of women and men in the Indonesian national family *(asas kekeluargaan).* While men were considered the heads of household and leaders of the state, terms left open to wide interpretation, women were narrowly defined according to their nature and subsequently to national duty, interpreted as marrying heterosexually, becoming mothers, raising families, and nurturing others generally.

Sexuality and *Halus*-ness

Bodily movements and dress for female *keroncong* vocalists are considered less overtly sexual than those of other female performers in singer/dancer traditions of Java or popular music genres such as *dangdut.* Many of the performances I observed featured female singers conservatively dressed in *kain kebaya,* a traditional blouse-and-dress combination worn by women in Indonesia (as well as in Malaysia and Singapore).[4] These outfits were well suited to slow, deliberate, and constrained movements considered to be *halus* (refined or genteel).[5] *Halus* female movements required legs to remain relatively close together and arms to remain down and held close to the torso—generally speaking, it was considered unseemly for a woman to have her legs far apart and arms raised to allow a profile view of her torso and breasts.

Waldjinah represented the ideal of a *halus keroncong* vocalist, owing to her coquettish, high-pitched vocal delivery and the way she projected herself both on- and offstage. Part of this *halus*-ness derived from her distinct fashion sense, which nearly always included an ornately decorated *kain kebaya,* a style of dress she has proudly worn her entire career. She explained,

> I wear the *kain kebaya* because it symbolizes Indonesia . . . but also because *keroncong* is considered to be a refined [type of] music. I have to dress in an appropriate and well-mannered way. The *kain kebaya* works

> because it is formal but not overly formal. Some *kain* I wore had a long slit running up the side to expose a portion of the thigh, which really gets people's hearts pounding *[she laughed heartily]*, but you want to make sure you don't expose too much. (personal communication, 22 February 2012)

Waldjinah considered an element of sexuality integral to her live performances. She emphasized, however, that sexuality had to be balanced with an overall *halus* appearance. She mentioned "getting people's hearts pounding" in a tongue-in-cheek manner referring to her reception by male fans and as a way of presenting her sexuality. Part of maintaining this balance is the *kain kebaya* itself. Key characteristics when choosing a good *kain kebaya* are that its colors are striking *(mencolok)*, that its appearance makes you look slim *(langsing)*, and that it is constructed from material with elasticity *(mulur)* so that it wraps well around all areas of the body, especially the chest, waist, buttocks, and legs (Waldjinah, personal communication, 22 February 2012). Waldjinah's loyalty to wearing the *kain kebaya* certainly conveys a sense of "Indonesianness" and "tradition." Batik also has more intimate connections with her own family background, and her choice of batik-themed *kain* may actually have more to do with local Solonese identity and her own upbringing than with expressing national pride or refinement.

Besides Waldjinah's being known for her keen fashion sense, her popularity as a performer and the longevity of her career have made her a model for other *keroncong*, pop, and *dangdut* singers (male, female, and transgender). As a renowned vocalist in Indonesia for some time now, she has not, however, escaped the stereotypes associated with female performers.

Gossip in Popular Print Media

I once asked Waldjinah if she read what was written about her in newspapers, to which she replied, "Sometimes I do, and sometimes I don't. . . . I try to stay clear of gossip." During the year and a half or so I spent regularly visiting Waldjinah, I usually knew when an article about her appeared in a local or national newspaper or magazine. After arriving at her home and sitting down in her foyer, which was ornately decorated with trophies, photos, and plaques of recognition, she would hand me a folded-up newspaper or magazine and gently ask, "So, have you seen this?" Most of the time, I sheepishly grinned, admitted that I had not seen it, and asked if I could possibly borrow and scan it.

Some of these articles were written in a style that could easily be perceived as tabloid gossip by Western standards. Anthropologists have noted that gossip serves as a form of social cohesion intended to assert boundaries between morally acceptable and deviant behavior and how it is used as a tool to foster individual agendas while undermining the interests of others (see Gluckman 1963; Handelman 1973; Gilmore 1978). Gossip is embedded in social relations and symbolic dynamics based on political practices employed in everyday social life (Besnier 2009). Gossip can also provide a political voice or become an instrument of oppression (Brison 1992). Defining the parameters of gossip is particularly difficult given that some languages do not have a word or label comparable to what English speakers term "gossip." In the Indonesian language, terms commonly used include the English-derived *gosip* and *ngomong* (talk). The type of gossip I am referring to here is "public" gossip, namely, celebrity tattler columns, tabloid journalism, and some reality television programs (see Besnier 2009; Gamson 1994), which tend to blur the boundaries between the realms of public and private—a line that has become increasingly permeable because of technologies such as the Internet (Solove 2007).

Gossip in Indonesian popular print media is intended to fan the flames of rumor or speculation about the personal life of a celebrity or some scandalous actions attached to them. Performers are generally aware of the potential for gossip. Throughout Waldjinah's career, she understood the profound and often damaging impact gossip could have on a female performer's career, especially for someone of her stature. In response, she spent much of her life thinking about ways to avoid becoming ensnared in it. In some cases, this resulted in a cautious and vigilant attitude toward socializing in public spaces such as restaurants and nightclubs. Instead she preferred socializing with friends in the privacy of her own home. When she did socialize in public, it was usually in the company of friends or family, so as to avoid being seen with unfamiliar people, especially men. The dramatic consequences of gossip also suggest conditions for what it means to be a woman in Indonesia because it implies that the normative expectation for a woman is to be attached to a man, specifically a husband, father, or in Waldjinah's case, her son. An unaccompanied woman is generally considered sexually available, and the assumption is that she is either an unmarried virgin *(gadis)* or a divorced or widowed woman *(janda)*. Beyond serving as entertainment, gossip in Indonesia is a form of social control over a woman's sexuality, reinforcing a patriarchal order that requires attachment to a man. Waldjinah stated,

> I'm afraid that if I go out, I'll invite "talk" *[ngomong]*. If I'm seen even speaking with a man, later they'll say, "Oh, are they a couple now? Is she with another man?" I don't want to be seen as a woman who likes to go around randomly flirting with men. That's why when I go out, I prefer to travel in my own car, surrounded by my girlfriends or people I know, . . . never alone. If people ask me to go out and socialize with them on my

own, I usually say no. It's not that I don't want to socialize, but I'm afraid of how it may be construed. (personal communication, 17 July 2012)

It is evident that this avoidance had a significant impact on Waldjinah's quotidian life. Hyperawareness about her image influenced mundane choices regarding where, when, and how she was seen in public and even determined her social circle. Potentially most damaging to her reputation were unfamiliar men, namely heterosexual male fans of wealth and political power, who, throughout her career, regularly offered her invitations, gifts, and other enticements. This is not to assume that these offers always concealed unseemly or ulterior (sexually driven) motives or even that most of her male fans resorted to this type of behavior. However, enough have done so to warrant Waldjinah's vigilance. Over the course of her career, she became well aware how the simple act of accepting a gift or a ride home might lead to gossip that could potentially cause irreparable damage to her image. In various ways, these behaviors intended to prevent gossip transformed into naturalized ways of being for her.

Waldjinah was conscious not only of her own behavior in public but also of how journalists would write about it. This concern was especially prevalent earlier in her career, when print media outlets created images that contradicted or challenged her public self-image. These articles created diverse images of Waldjinah showing processes of "gendering," or "representations *about* sex—about the significance of our endowment of sexual difference, about sex-linked regularities in everyday practice" (Smith 1992, 303). Waldjinah's situation suggests that gendering in print media included an array of social processes combining New Order / state and Islamic ideologies of gender as well as localized Javanese ideas about gender roles and aging. I address these in the following sections.

Scene Two: Sex Bomb

A grainy photo in the tabloid *Sinar harapan* (Rays of hope) shows Waldjinah holding a microphone and dressed in an elegant, form-fitting *kain kebaya*. The caption reads, "After causing a commotion at Wisma Indonesia in Singapore, Waldjinah returned to Jakarta for a special performance for her Solo fans. . . . Some have referred to her as a 'sex bomb.' Hopefully there are no objections, especially from Waldjinah herself" (see figure 13.1). Another tabloid newspaper from the early 1970s ran the headline, "Is it true that Waldjinah is an out-of-wedlock pregnant widow? Wait for next week's edition of Eljaya" (see figure 13.2). Yet another tabloid from around this same time featured a photo of her again dressed in form-fitting *kebaya,* this time holding a small video camera. The caption posed the following question: "If the beautiful *Walang Kekek* is

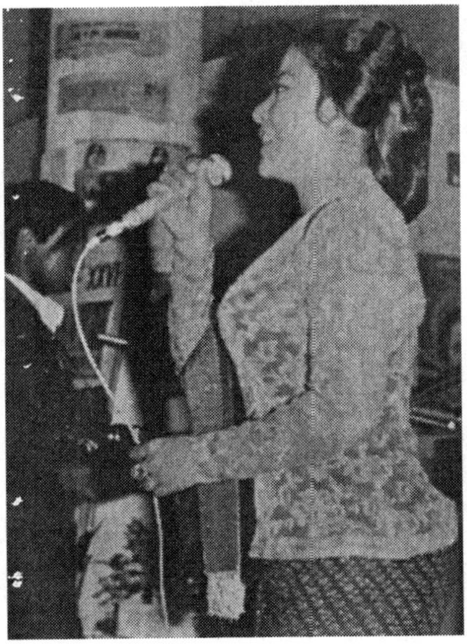

Figure 13.1. Waldjinah performing at a nightclub in Jakarta, early 1970s. Courtesy of *Sinar Harapan*, 1971.

already working behind the camera, will the producers or directors be brave enough to expose her in SEX scenes?"[6]

The sexualized "bombshell" was one of the images attributed to Waldjinah early in her career, as a talented young vocalist. In Indonesia, it is not uncommon for some young female singers, especially in the genres of Indonesian pop or *dangdut,* to be portrayed as "sex bombs." After all, this image reinforces a feminine ideal that simultaneously establishes an identity as a performer and can easily be marketed to male audiences. In today's context, some Indonesians may think that, as a *keroncong* vocalist, the image of Waldjinah as a sex bomb seems unfitting, especially given the sense of refinement and nostalgic "tradition" now attributed to the genre. As the captions in figures 13.2 and 13.3 suggest, however, *keroncong* vocalists were not always perceived this way. When the genre was considered part of the Indonesian pop music milieu in the early 1970s, it was not unusual for an attractive young *keroncong* singer such as Waldjinah to be considered a sex symbol. By the middle of the twentieth century, the music industry, fans, performers, and the Indonesian government successfully rehabilitated *keroncong* by gentrifying it and transforming it into a form of national culture.[7] Being labeled a sex bomb, in this case, had implications far beyond Waldjinah's personal reputation. It extended to the reputation of the genre itself.

These representations, reflecting a brand of sensationalistic coverage associated with certain weekly tabloid newspapers, suggest that Waldjinah could not escape the world of gossip circulating in popular print media. Writing about

Figure 13.2. Tabloid headline about Waldjinah. Courtesy of *Eljaya,* late 1960s.

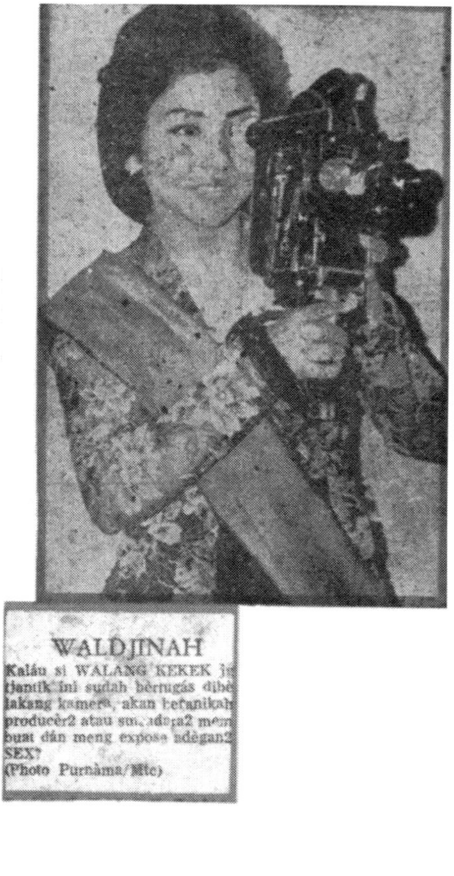

Figure 13.3. Tabloid photo and caption about Waldjinah. Courtesy of *Eljaya,* late 1960s.

eroticized Western female pop stars, Sheila Whiteley observes that what is sold to the public is their image or "a simulacrum which has the power to arouse, but not, in itself, assuage desire. . . . The image and culture of the young are appropriated for the high pleasure quotient they evoke[:] . . . youthful allure and sexual titillation [as] marketable commodities" (2005, 25, 29). Age undeniably factors into the allure of the sex bomb, but for a performer such as Waldjinah, who was already a mother of five in her mid-twenties, blatant allusions to sexuality came in a slightly different context than for other young female performers. In one sense, being a young and attractive performer allowed her to be viewed and marketed as a sexualized "bombshell." Being a mother, however, created a distinctly different set of circumstances that helped balance her public image and shield Waldjinah from any real harm caused by mass-mediated gossip. Selling the image of sexuality was linked to selling her image as a mother and family woman, who despite her age could not be viewed the same way as the average young starlet. As Waldjinah grew older, a shift in how she was portrayed in print media became especially apparent and in certain ways allowed her to transcend the image of "sex bomb" and respond to some of the sexually charged gossip that had been associated with her earlier.

Scene Three: A Mother and Wife

Despite the prevalence of sexually charged gossip, other scenes portraying Waldjinah in print media focus on her roles as a mother and a wife. Unlike other female vocalists of her era, Waldjinah became well-known as a performer only after giving birth. Numerous articles refer to a "comeback" in her late twenties after having put her career on hold to start a family. These articles describe mundane characteristics about her family: her husband, a local high school teacher, and children lived in a "reasonably good" home in a "peaceful" neighborhood. It is rare, however, that the image of the "sex bomb" and the mother of five fit so harmoniously.

Waldjinah presented herself as a good mother/wife first and foremost because she firmly believed that she embodied both. Although being a touring artist and a young mother presented numerous challenges, she never felt her children were neglected at home. Waldjinah instead believed the income she earned from touring provided a better livelihood for her family than if she had only performed locally. Furthermore, the image of the good mother/wife shielded her from gossip and stereotypes associated with some female performers. At the same time, Waldjinah did not adhere to this image entirely, especially since she enjoyed the fame, financial rewards, and freedom afforded to her by touring.

The portrayal of Waldjinah as a modern Indonesian woman incorporated Western ideologies of bourgeois domesticity (woman as a consumer-housewife), local "traditional" ideologies of femininity (woman as self-sacrificing wife and mother), and New Order–era ideas of the ideal Indonesian woman as a dutiful citizen (woman as regime supporter) (Brenner 1996, 678–679). The blending of these characteristics corresponds to what has been referred to as "state Ibuism," an idea institutionalized throughout the New Order bureaucracy defining women's roles according to hierarchy—specifically as appendages and companions to their husbands, procreators of the nation, mothers and educators, housekeepers, and members of Indonesian society (Suryakusuma 1996, 101–102). State Ibuism embraced the "family principle" as an image of the state, incorporating a paternalistic order that combined elements of Javanese feudalistic values with those of military authority. The effect of New Order policies was essentially to legally restrict women from involvement in the public sphere while returning them to domestic roles and constructing an ideal of femininity and masculinity that served the regime's purposes (Yulianto 2008; Wieringa 2002; Dzuhayatin 2001).

Indonesian media played an important role in reinforcing state gender ideologies during the New Order era through an intricate web of security restrictions and draconian legislation controlling the press and moderating messages sent out to the public. Stepping out of line, in most instances, resulted in an uncontestable ban and financial disaster (Hill 1994, 11–12). By the mid-1970s, Waldjinah began performing at campaign rallies for Golkar, the political functional group closely associated with the New Order government, and she continued to do so for approximately twenty years. Although Waldjinah was not formally a civil servant, her involvement as one of the public faces of Golkar placed her directly within its sphere of influence, impacting both her self-presentation and how she was represented by print media. In interviews, she often represented herself as a typical New Order wife and mother despite the fact that she was the breadwinner in the family. For instance, in a 1994 interview with the national newspaper, *Kompas,* she discussed the relationship between a wife and a husband, stating, "Even if a husband has nothing, we still have to respect him because we live under the same roof. . . . For instance, right now, I'm doing well, so I have more money [than him]. However, as a man, he remains the pillar of the household."[8] In another article, she adds, "Even though my husband is younger than me, he is still my husband. . . . As a Javanese woman I view my husband as a prince of the palace, to be respected. I'm afraid of being cursed if I challenge my husband."[9] She echoed similar sentiments in an interview with me: "My mother taught me that a wife must respect her husband. She said that however angry you may be at him, don't ever leave home. Women who leave home are indecent. According to a Javanese proverb, even if he is dumber than you and makes less money, he still has to be respected" (personal communication, 4 May 2012).

Waldjinah's comments about her role as a wife fall firmly within the ideology upheld by New Order policies and contribute to her understandings about respect and deference in a marital relationship. Suzanne Brenner cautions, however, against a simple reading of this relationship that emphasizes certain prevalent, generally male-focused gender ideologies, while paying scant attention to less systematically articulated conceptions of gender, especially those voiced more often by women (1995, 22). Waldjinah was invested in upholding her image as a dutiful, loyal, and obedient Javanese woman, and that is perhaps the reason she remained silent on alternative conceptions of gender. Although her statements appear to fit neatly within the dominant discourse about gender hierarchy, this was not the case in practice. Unlike many other young mothers in her neighborhood, Waldjinah spent long periods of time away from her children while touring or performing outside her hometown of Solo. Although she tried to maintain her responsibilities at home, her career (as the family's main source of income) superseded her role as a mother and as a wife. She did not always conform to the ideal of a subservient Javanese woman. In many instances, it was Waldjinah who acted as head of the household and not her husband. As the primary breadwinner, both her first and second husbands knew that the course of Waldjinah's professional career had a profound impact on their quality of life, and they were acquiescent.

Waldjinah has been married twice. Her first husband, Budi (whom I refer to as Pak Bud), passed away in 1985 from complications due to diabetes. Until then, in addition to being her constant companion on numerous tours, he also managed her and her backing band, Orkes Keroncong Bintang Surakarta (the Surakarta stars *keroncong* orchestra). Pak Bud's death left a sizable void in Waldjinah's life, not only emotionally—she described him as her "one true love" (personal communication, 17 July 2012)—but also because of uncertainty about who would take over as her manager. Although a gifted vocalist, Waldjinah admitted to not knowing much about the business side of her career, and she relied heavily on Pak Bud for his expertise in this area. Anxiety also arose about not having a trusted male companion with her while on tour. She feared that gossipmongers in the media would ruin her image by linking her to various male fans. Anxiety also emerged from a change in status from sexually unavailable married woman to a sexually available widow.

Waldjinah met her second husband, Didit, about four years later, and he fulfilled some of the roles performed by Pak Bud. She did not, however, share the same intense feelings for Pak Didit that she had for Pak Bud. In fact, after Pak Bud's death, she considered remaining a widow for the remainder of her life but eventually got tired of the unwanted attention from suitors and heterosexual male fans, some of whom began referring her to as *janda kwaci,* a term that younger men use to describe an older widowed woman who remains "physically attractive." The *janda kwaci* represents a different scene in Waldjinah's life, returning her, in a sense, to the sexualized imagery of the "sex bomb" earlier on in her career.

Although Waldjinah did not want to drastically alter the way she dressed or behaved, she soon realized that now that she was a widow and popular female performer, the male gaze of fans and media differed. She entered unfamiliar terrain, especially since her career as a performer essentially began as a married woman. These and other considerations led Waldjinah to marry Pak Didit, and she treated him with the respect and obedience associated with a proper Javanese wife. In conversations I had with her, Waldjinah continued to echo some of the same sentiments as the ones published in articles nearly twenty years before. However, it was clear her situation had also changed.

In order for Waldjinah to construct her preferred image in popular print media, she rarely revealed details about her married life to reporters. She felt that any problems or conflicts in her married life would be blamed on her and would reflect negatively on her image as a good wife. Furthermore, there were economic benefits that accrued to the image of a proper wife and a "true Javanese woman." It was only after I visited her regularly for more than seven months that Waldjinah began talking to me about the difficulties in her relationship with Pak Didit. Her accounts of a troubled marriage deeply contradicted the image of a happy couple circulating in the media.

Waldjinah also explained that for most of her second marriage, she had trouble expressing herself openly to Pak Didit, especially when they disagreed over financial issues. "If I wanted to say something, I wouldn't be able to. . . . It was as if he had some sort of power over me, and I would just lose my voice and ability to speak entirely" (personal communication, 17 July 2012). I could not help but consider the irony of associating a renowned vocalist such as Waldjinah with a sense of voicelessness. As scholars have noted, the trope of the "voice" is often deployed as a metaphor for cultural agency, political autonomy, and both individual and collective power (Hellier 2013; Hayes 2006). The voice as metaphor explores the interface between the singing voice and the voice of agency, one that enables the singing voice to be enacted as an instrument of power. The power of Waldjinah's singing voice was connected to economic power, but it did not necessarily translate into a voice of agency, especially over the course of her second marriage. Although not entirely passive in this relationship, she openly discussed the power Pak Didit held over her in determining financial aspects of their relationship. The loss of voice related to these controlling tendencies is particularly compelling given that the dominant representation of how some Javanese conceive of the relationship between husband and wife is in terms of "his authority and her financial control" (Keeler 1987, 52).

Regardless of occupation or social class, women have generally controlled household finances in Java (Brenner 1998; Hatley 1990; Keeler 1987; Siegel 1986). This phenomenon is attributed to men not being especially adept at managing money, and as a result, they are expected to turn over most, if not all, earned income to their wives. Women's control over household finances, however, has not necessarily resulted in higher status—men continue to be seen as having more spiritual potency, based on their "self-control," while women, who purportedly lack self-control, also lack the potency and prestige attributed to males. Conversely, Brenner observes that self-control attributed to men does not always apply, especially in the case of *nafsu* (desire, lust), which can take on various forms but is most dangerous in the form of desire or lust for money and sex (1995, 33).[10] According to Brenner, the Javanese belief that men have an innately greater sexual desire than women do contradicts the ideology of their potency and suggests a possible reason why women manage household finances: men are more likely to squander money away on gambling, sexual indulgence, and other irresponsible acts that create financial burdens for the family. The idea that women lack spiritual resources because they lack self-discipline is also unfounded, given that some women tend to engage in asceticism as much or more than males do. An ability to exercise control over desire is not only vital to safeguarding the family's financial resources but involves a form of asceticism that accrues abstract benefits.

Waldjinah's individual experience poses compelling and complex questions about the generalized ideas attributed to "men" and "women" in these studies. From a young age, Waldjinah has been accustomed to financially contributing to both her immediate and extended family. One of her proudest achievements in life was financially supporting her children through college, as well as doing the same for some of her nieces and nephews. She financially supported each of her husbands for the duration of their married life. After separating from her husband Pak Didit recently, Waldjinah expressed deep regret in having married him, stating that she would be far better off financially had she not supported him for the duration of their marriage. She specifically lamented having to give him 50 percent of her net income over the course of time they were married.

> [Pak Didit] decided on a fifty-fifty split early on in the marriage. I didn't like it at all but stayed silent. I kept it all on the inside for all these years. It was like I was under his control. I couldn't bring myself to say no to him. Despite my close friends telling me I was being used, I didn't want to listen. I never actually sought out the advice of others though. Who could I talk to? Where would I go? If I told him I wanted to meet with someone,

he'd probably end up going too. He'd be the one driving me there. It irritated me that I had to give so much of my money to him. I could sense my growing hatred toward him, but I had to control myself. I had to control myself from telling him to leave . . . to just get out! I couldn't bring myself to utter those words. So I buried it inside. I buried it all until it made me physically ill. (personal communication, 4 January 2013)

A number of complex factors exist in understanding the dynamics of Waldjinah's marital relationship with Pak Didit, and after I extensively interviewed both of them individually, it is evident that their relationship was built around the gendered and economic roles that positioned Waldjinah's career squarely at the center of their marriage. Pak Didit's supporting role as a manager and trusted male companion was crucial to Waldjinah's career. She was aware that her public image as a performer depended on how well he performed his role as a husband (at least publicly). Pak Didit understood his role and believed he performed it to the best of his ability and therefore felt he should reap some of the financial rewards.

The anthropologist Ward Keeler observes that in Java "a man's authority requires a wife defer to him in his expectations and demands, that she address him in some degree of refined language, and that she conduct herself generally in ways befitting his (and therefore their) status" (1987, 53). Waldjinah embraced the idea that respect for one's husband was essential to being a "good wife." However, she also acted in her own self-interest by not instigating conflict within the marriage—after all, a key factor in marrying a second time was having a male figure to deflect the gaze of unwanted (heterosexual male) attention. In Waldjinah's case, control of *nafsu* meant not only managing or conserving the family's financial resources but also protecting the source of that income (i.e., her career), which was directly associated with her public image.

Scene Four: Performing for the Media

Waldjinah thought carefully about her presentation when expecting a visit from a journalist. Rather than the loose-fitting housedress she wore on a regular basis, she put on a batik or floral-print blouse with pants and always wore makeup. Her demeanor around journalists was genuinely cordial, and she was quite expressive and animated when discussing her activities. Often she began talking excitedly before a question was even posed to her; she was adept at establishing the direction of a conversation on the basis of what she determined was worth sharing. As journalists began asking questions, without obvious changes to her demeanor, she spoke slower and more deliberately in her responses, especially when asked about family, health, or other personal issues.

When Waldjinah talked about her personal life, she kept to a very specific script of events and topics, which is not uncommon for someone who has recounted her life story numerous times. This script provided a skeletal framework of important life events that emphasized the challenges she overcame in order to convey a compelling story of survival recognizable to the average Indonesian reader. This accounts for why many articles written about Waldjinah in print media, despite coming from an array of sources and across different periods of time, discuss similar events in roughly the same amount of depth. The script enabled Waldjinah to establish uniformity in each retelling and allowed her to alleviate the potential for gossip, speculation, and misrepresentation. The script not only helped her remember important aspects to address but also established limits for how much she would actually reveal.

As a performer who has endeavored to maintain a reputable public image, Waldjinah employed specific tactics in crafting that image. One such tactic involved having either her son, Pak Ary, or her husband, Pak Didit, present during all interviews (figure 13.4). Waldjinah insisted it was beneficial to have one or both around just in case she overlooked anything important. Her assertion appeared sensible given that both are also involved in *keroncong*—Pak Ary as an accomplished instrumentalist and the leader of Waldjinah's band, and Pak Didit as someone who is knowledgeable about the history and repertoire of *keroncong*.

The presence and participation of Pak Ary and Pak Didit in interviews, however, was not as passive as she made it out to be. During some of our interviews, questions addressed to Waldjinah were frequently intercepted and answered directly by the man accompanying her. In these cases, it was the male voice that delivered the clear and "correct" answers to my questions. Waldjinah willingly followed. This dynamic was not simply a matter of Pak Didit and/or Pak Ary speaking for her. On multiple occasions, Pak Ary casually redirected conversations away from sensitive (or potentially sensitive) topics by interjecting anecdotes to steer the discussion to safer topics. In one such instance, I asked Waldjinah about her relationship with Pak Didit, to which Pak Ary quickly interjected that Pak Didit was away in Jakarta visiting his family. He followed this statement by changing the subject entirely, telling me instead about an upcoming local *keroncong* concert. Pak Ary decided it was a topic that Waldjinah, having only recently separated from Pak Didit, was not ready to (or should not) discuss openly.

Given my regular visits to interview Waldjinah, there were instances when neither Pak Ary nor Pak Didit were present, and I had a chance to speak with her alone. I took the opportunity to ask about the reasons for the men's involvement in her interviews. She reiterated her earlier statement about often forgetting

Figure 13.4. Waldjinah and her son, Pak Ary Mulyono, during an interview with the author (December 16, 2011). Courtesy of Vito Mahaputra.

details and "not getting the story right." My assistant, Hara, once referred to Waldjinah as showing characteristics of "a true Javanese woman," one who masked actual feelings in order to protect her image and stature. After letting her know I was less interested in her being accurate about certain details than her being able to express herself honestly and directly, I requested she conduct interviews with me (and my assistant) alone. She appeared hesitant at first, perhaps wanting to be careful about being alone with two men, but she eventually agreed. These sessions resulted in some of our most productive and revealing interviews, in which Waldjinah openly discussed problems with her marriage, health and financial concerns, and relationships with her children. Each of these discussions brought out issues that complicated and challenged the public image carefully constructed by her (and for her) in print media.

Understanding lived experiences becomes especially valuable in the case of public figures such as Waldjinah, because these figures are known primarily through convoluted webs of two-dimensional images, or "portraits," in print media. The time I spent interviewing Waldjinah helped me better understand how she negotiated her identity and balanced her roles as a professional *keroncong* vocalist, celebrity, mother, and wife. Hearing about the challenges involved in balancing each of these roles, many of which overlapped in complex ways, also suggested reasons why Waldjinah, for the duration of her career, was so consciously focused on controlling her public image.

Ideas about appropriate behavior for women in Indonesia are informed by local traditions, government institutions, and religious teachings. The New Order state was especially influential in developing a rigid ideology of gender relations. These ideas filtered into Waldjinah's thinking about self-performance and the stereotypes attached to female performers in Indonesia. Her position as a performer and public figure created instances in her quotidian life (especially early on in her career) when Waldjinah deviated from established gender norms—most notably as a mother who spent an extended amount of time away from her children.

Portraits and scenes that represented Waldjinah according to normative expectations of the *Putri Solo* did not represent the realities of her life. She confounded gender stereotypes, for instance, by dressing like a cowgirl or by spending long periods of time away from her home and children. These examples provide a counternarrative to the New Order rhetoric of women as wives and mothers who stand behind their husbands. Waldjinah understood that these portraits served a broader function and made her a symbol and model for other Indonesian women. She knew that these representations were not the realities she lived but, rather, the managed performances of self for the media or simulated portraits she wanted others to believe.

On the one hand, Waldjinah had a "voice" in shaping these representations: wearing outfits to complicate the image of a *Putri Solo;* concealing the difficulties of her marriage to keep up appearances of a good wife; and portraying a woman who was sexy (but not *too* sexy). On the other hand, this voice was not entirely hers; it was (1) the voice of the Indonesian state, enforcing its own image of what a properly gendered subject should be; (2) the voice of Javanese tradition and its image of an attractive and charming *Putri Solo;* and (3) the voice of popular print media, which threatened to turn everything into gossip in order to sell newspapers. Waldjinah's many voices, as suggested in these portraits and scenes, reflect the contradictory nature of gendered modernity in Indonesia.

Acknowledgments

My thanks to René Lysloff, Andrew Weintraub, and Bernard Arps for their helpful comments on earlier drafts of this chapter.

Notes

1. I use the spelling *keroncong* (as opposed to *kroncong* or *krontjong*, alternate and older spellings found in Indonesia) because it is the one most commonly used in Indonesia (as well as in Singapore and Malaysia). The *Comprehensive Indonesian-English Dictionary* (Stevens and Schmidgall-Tellings 2010) shows *keroncong* as the standard spelling and *kroncong* as an alternative. *Keroncong* is a string-instrument-based music that came to the north coast of Java on Portuguese ships carrying traders and slaves, and some scholars claim that the first of these ships arrived as early as the sixteenth century (Heins 1975). *Keroncong*'s overall sound is driven by the instruments establishing its foundational interlocking rhythm, namely, two Indonesian ukuleles known as the *cuk* and *cak*. Contrabass and an Indonesian cello (played in a percussive, pizzicato style) add to the overall rhythm. Florid melodic lines, improvised on flute and violin, float in and out as a piece progresses, generally complementing vocal lines. *Keroncong* vocalists in a performance setting are positioned standing alone in front of seated instrumentalists.

2. *Lembaran minggu*, late 1960s (private collection of Waldjinah).

3. Female performers are not necessarily helpless victims in this scheme. Some performers, for instance in *dangdut* and dance traditions such as *lènggèr*, actively collude in their own sexualization, for a variety of reasons, and therefore exploit their sexuality onstage. Weintraub (2010) also observes that although there are actually quite a number of women in the audience for *dangdut* shows, they are not prominent in the public discourse about *dangdut* due to the patriarchal nature of public discourse about women.

4. Specifically, *kain* refers to the cloth worn as a wrap-around, ankle-length skirt, whereas *kebaya* refers to the long-sleeved blouse worn over the *kain* (Stevens and Schmidgall-Tellings 2010, 436–437, 460).

5. Furthermore, Christina Sunardi suggests that musicians used a slower tempo in music accompanying cross-gender dances in East Java because they believed the power of femaleness came from a slower tempo (2015, 55–56). Equating slowness with femininity can also be seen in the refined movements during live performances of *keroncong* vocalists such as Waldjinah.

6. The Indonesian press since early on in Waldjinah's career has referred to her as "Walang kekek" (Grasshopper), also the title of one of Waldjinah's hit songs.

7. Keroncong was marketed on 78-rpm records in the Dutch East Indies, British Malaya, and the Straits Settlements (Yampolsky 2010, 7–10). Before World War I, production of these records was dominated by European companies; in the 1920s and especially the 1930s,

locally run companies entered the market as well. Recordings from this period also highlight stylistic shifts in the keroncong genre and may explain how particular instruments, tempos, and rhythms became codified as "standard keroncong."

8. *Kompas,* 17 April 1994 (private collection of Waldjinah).

9. "Waldjinah berkelit dari gosip-gosip," *Cempaka,* 16–22 October 1991 (private collection of Waldjinah).

10. Brenner explains that the idea of status is always relative and functions within a complex set of considerations, which include, but are not limited to, age and seniority, descent, education, occupation, wealth, ethnicity, place of origin (e.g., urban versus rural), and gender (1995, 25–26).

References

Anderson, Benedict. 1990. *Language and Power: Exploring Political Cultures in Indonesia.* Ithaca, NY: Cornell University Press.

Bauman, Richard. 1984. *Verbal Art as Performance.* Prospect Heights, IL: Waveland.

Besnier, Niko. 2009. *Gossip and the Everyday Production of Politics.* Honolulu: University of Hawai'i Press.

Blackburn, Susan. 2004. *Women and the State in Modern Indonesia.* New York: Cambridge University Press.

Blackwood, Evelyn. 2010. *Falling into the Lesbi World: Desire and Difference in Indonesia.* Honolulu: University of Hawai'i Press.

Brenner, Suzanne A. 1995. "Why Women Rule the Roost: Rethinking Javanese Ideologies of Gender and Self-Control." In *Bewitching Women and Pious Men: Gender and Body Politics in Southeast Asia,* edited by Aihwa Ong and Michael G. Peletz, 19–50. Berkeley: University of California Press.

———. 1996. "Reconstructing Self and Society: Javanese Muslim Women and The Veil." *American Ethnologist* 23 (4): 673-697.

———. 1998. *The Domestication of Desire: Women, Wealth, and Modernity in Java.* Princeton, NJ: Princeton University Press.

Brison, Karen J. 1992. *Just Talk: Gossip, Meetings and Power in a Papua New Guinea Village.* Berkeley: University of California Press.

Cooper, Nancy I. 1994. "The Sirens of Java: Gender Ideologies, Mythologies and Practice in Central Java." PhD diss., University of Hawai'i.

Dzuhayatin, Siti. 2001. "Gender and Pluralism in Indonesia." In *The Politics of Multiculturalism, Pluralism and Citizenship in Malaysia, Singapore and Indonesia,* edited by Robert W. Hefner, 253–267. Honolulu: University of Hawai'i Press.

Gamson, Joshua. 1994. *Claims to Fame: Celebrity in Contemporary America.* Berkeley: University of California Press.

Gilmore, David. 1978. "Varieties of Gossip in a Spanish Rural Community." *Ethnology* 17:89–99.

Gluckman, Max. 1963. "Gossip and Scandal." *Current Anthropology* 4:307–315.

Handelman, Don. 1973. "Gossip in Encounters: The Transmission of Information in a Bounded Social Setting." *Man* 8:210–227.

Hatley, Barbara. 1990. "Theatrical Imagery and Gender Ideology in Java." In *Power and Difference: Gender in Island Southeast Asia,* edited by Jane Atkinson and Shelly Errington, 177–208. Stanford, CA: Stanford University Press.

Hayes, Eileen. 2006. "Theorizing Gender, Culture and Music." *Women and Music* 10:71–79.

Heins, Ernst. 1975. "Kroncong and Tanjidor: Two Cases of Urban Folk Music in Jakarta." *Asian Music* 7 (1): 20–32.

Hellier, Ruth, ed. 2013. *Women Singers in Global Contexts: Music, Biography, Identity.* Urbana: University of Illinois Press.

Hill, David. 1994. *The Press in New Order Indonesia.* Jakarta: Equinox.

Keeler, Ward. 1987. *Javanese Shadow Plays, Javanese Selves.* Princeton, NJ: Princeton University Press.

Lysloff, Rene T. A. 2002. "Rural Javanese 'Tradition' and Erotic Subversion: Female Dance Performance in Banyumas (Central Java)." *Asian Music* 33 (1): 1–24.

Siegel, James. 1986. *Solo in the New Order: Language and Hierarchy in an Indonesian City.* Princeton, NJ: Princeton University Press.

Smith, Stephen. 1992. *Gender Thinking.* Philadelphia: Temple University Press.

Solove, Daniel J. 2007. *The Future of Reputation: Gossip, Rumor and Privacy on the Internet.* New Haven, CT: Yale University Press.

Spiller, Henry J. 2010. *Erotic Triangles: Sundanese Dance and Masculinity in West Java.* Chicago: University of Chicago Press.

Stevens, Alan M., and A. Ed. Schmidgall-Tellings. 2010. *A Comprehensive Indonesian-English Dictionary.* Athens: Ohio University Press.

Sunardi, Christina. 2015. *Stunning Males and Powerful Females: Gender and Tradition in East Javanese Dance.* Urbana: University of Illinois Press.

Suryakusuma, Julia I. 1996. "The State and Sexuality in New Order Indonesia." In *Fantasizing the Feminine in Indonesia,* edited by Laurie J. Sears, 92–119. Durham, NC: Duke University Press.

Sutton, R. Anderson. 1987. "Identity and Individuality in an Ensemble Tradition: The Female Vocalist in Java." In *Women and Music in Cross-Cultural Perspective,* edited by Ellen Koskoff, 111–130. Urbana: University of Illinois Press.

Walton, Susan Pratt. 1996. "Heavenly Nymphs and Earthly Delights: Javanese Female Singers, Their Music and Their Lives." PhD diss., University of Michigan.

Weintraub, Andrew. 2010. *Dangdut Stories: A Social and Musical History of Indonesia's Most Popular Music.* New York: Oxford University Press.

Whiteley, Sheila. 2005. *Too Much Too Young: Popular Music, Age and Gender.* New York: Routledge.

Wieringa, Saskia. 2002. *Sexual Politics in Indonesia.* New York: Palgrave Macmillan.

Yampolsky, Philip. 2010. "Kroncong Revisited: New Evidence from Old Sources." *Archipel* 79:7–56.

Yulianto, Vissia Ita. 2008. "Consuming Gossip: A Re-domestication of Indonesian Women." In *Popular Culture in Indonesia: Fluid Identities in Post-authoritarian Politics,* edited by Ariel Heryanto, 130–142. New York: Routledge.

CHAPTER 14

Mainstreaming Dance Music and Articulating Femininity

SOUTH KOREAN DANCE DIVAS IN THE 1980S

Hee-sun Kim

K-POP groups are in the midst of an ever-changing popular cultural landscape in today's South Korea and beyond (Siriyuvasak and Shin 2007; Ryoo 2009; Shin 2009; Jung and Lee 2009; D. Lee 2010; Cho 2011). Highly gendered all-male and all-female groups, using synchronized dance movements that are prechoreographed to hip-hop and locally articulated pop music, are at the center of the global success of the genre. For the all-female groups especially, as many scholars have pointed out, the highly sexualized and gendered messages of their performances conform to certain notions of femininity, including purity, cuteness, prettiness, glamour, self-assertiveness, and eroticized sexuality. That manufactured sexuality, chosen by forces of the globalized Korean cultural industry to advance the needs of the postindustrial period, directly exposes the contradictions inherent in Korean modernity. With the performance of the all-female K-pop groups, as well as their physical charms, global consumption of them seems to symbolize a male-centered sexuality constructed by the process of Korean modernization. Most studies of Korean pop music focus on current K-pop girl groups' display, objectification, commercialization of sexuality, and construction of a gendered image, both at home and in the global market (Willoughby 2006; Su-ja Lee 2006; Su-an Lee 2008, 2010, 2011; Cha 2009; Zhang 2010; S. Kim 2010; Mungang 2010; Wei 2010; E. Jung 2010; Ye-ran Kim 2011; J. Kim 2011; Y. Jung 2011; Puzar 2011; Epstein and Joo 2012; Saeji 2013).

On the other hand, some K-pop girl groups are considered to have succeeded in establishing their own brand based on their popular image and, by skillfully negotiating discourses on sexuality and gender, to be role models for teenagers and young women in Korea and Asia. Often the practices of K-pop including female girl groups are also seen to provide discursive space for youth to assert their self-identity, to reject older generations' conservatism, to challenge dominant representations of authority, and to resist mainstream norms and values

(Su-an Lee 2011; Zhang 2010; Cha 2012). Furthermore, changes in postindustrial society and consumption patterns have resulted in the singers' sexuality becoming not merely a tool for entertaining men but also a means for expressing the style, taste, symbols, images, and desires of women.

Many scholars have identified the roots of today's "idol" groups in 1990s K-pop (S. Kim 2010; Mungang 2010; Su-an Lee 2008, 2010). However, I maintain that these paradoxical images of femininity based on women's dancing bodies can be traced to solo dancing divas of the 1980s. As a transitional period in Korean society, the 1980s saw large social transformations, most notably in public culture along with the democratization of politics, increasing desire for globalization, and the rise of youth and consumption culture. At the same time, the arrival of the global popularity of disco and dance music in the 1980s helped dance music become a major genre in the Korean popular music scene for the first time.

During the 1980s, dancing divas led to the mainstreaming of dance music within the complex context of a newly emerging consumer culture. At the same time, the female dancing divas of the 1980s articulated notions of modern Korean female womanhood that contradicted previous images of female performers as sentimental, low class, and dependent on men. I argue that they used heightened sexuality in dance movements to represent images of young, urban, sophisticated, stylish, and independent modern women.

In this chapter, I ask how these dancing divas of the 1980s initiated new notions of femininity, which differed from those in previous periods. I examine how dance and its accompanying music became instruments to articulate new notions of femininity. In dealing with the issues of the body in 1980s dance music, I follow the suggestion of Rosi Braidotti (1994) that the body can be understood not only in a biological or sociological context but also as a crossroads of intense forces, both corporeal and symbolic, within specific social conditions. By examining the mainstreaming of dance music by dancing divas during the 1980s, this chapter aims to properly historicize the often paradoxical and conflicting qualities of present-day all-female K-pop groups in the sociocultural context of South Korea. At the same time, it reveals the emergent stereotypes of modern Korean womanhood in a particular time period in relation to the larger transformations especially in public culture. These transformations resulted in a rupture with previous images of the Korean female singers that reflected the stereotypes of womanhood in Korean society in general. Also, this chapter attempts to understand the female dance divas as a social intersection, where the desires and values of Korean society overlapped and where the ideas of freedom and consumer modernity are embodied. Thus, a historical overview is necessary because much of the stereotyped view of Korean female singers and the femininity associated with them also harks back to a Korean entertainment industry of American pop influences and stereotypes of the modern woman.

Historical Overview of Female Singers and Canonical Femininity in Korea

During the Japanese colonial period in the early twentieth century, Korean female singers emerged as major entertainers, both in tandem and in conflict with the roles defined by the nation. The first female popular entertainers in Korea were *gisaeng*,[1] female artists of the Goryeo and Joseon periods and symbols of a feudalistic society. They became the first active participants in the popular music scene of the early twentieth century because they were professionally trained entertainers and ready to function as full-fledged female singers to be discovered by the newly arrived global music industry (Kwon 2001, 2003; Yeong-hui Kim 2006). However, as premodern figures, they were bound by the prescribed roles for women and assigned to the femininity of premodern society. Their popularity was largely restricted to a genre of music called *sinminyo*, newly composed folk songs, which featured traditional forms and a singing style inflected by Western music. Moreover, the genre highlighted singers' personal lives, characterized by poverty, low social standing, and other hardships. These associations, along with songs expressing melancholic emotions, helped to create the stereotype of female singers in Korea. They became symbols embodying the contradictions of colonialism, tradition, modern imperialism, and female sexuality. On the other hand, they were deeply involved in constructing modern concepts of entertainment, pleasure, and sexuality and presented a new prototype of eroticized femininity outside the household.

The activities of popular singers with *gisaeng* backgrounds continued through the 1930s within the genres of *gayo* or *yuhangga*, local terms to designate popular music. Just as a melancholic atmosphere was attached to *sinminyo* and the *gisaeng*, *trot*, a Korean version of Japanese *enka*[2] introduced during the colonial period, articulated a sentimentality associated with its female singers (see Soojin Kim, chap. 9 in this volume).[3] Although *trot* was trendy in its early years, it soon came to represent sentimentality, self-reproaching plaintiveness, and melancholy, all of which were associated with little education and poverty (Yi 2006, 271). Further, the music was attached to the idea of a weak and passive female and the tragic heroine. Songs such as "Mokpoui nunmul" (A tear of Mokpo), by Yi Nan-yeong,[4] were hits, and the female singers who sang *trot* began to represent the traditional femininity of "the mother, the sister, and the benign wife" (Yi 2006, 215).

In the 1940s, live theater performances by *akgeukdan* (music and theater troupes) introduced a new type of popular entertainment that competed with radio and studio recordings. This development, influenced by global American pop culture, led *trot* singers to begin performing onstage; the first all-female *trot* singing group, the Jeogori Sisters—the "first girl-group in Korea" (G. Choi 2012, 443)—was formed in 1939 to suit the new format.

The 1950s saw the immense influence of American popular culture on Korea after the Korean War (1950–1953), and American standard pop and its performance style began to gain popularity in Korea, along with "Mi pal gun" (stationed US armed forces) shows. The majority of early entertainers in these shows were gradually replaced by local entertainers as demand increased. To supply the shows, the entertainment industry was established, along with individual booking agencies, which began to organize packaged programs. A few talented domestic female singers were discovered, and these programs functioned as "an incubator for fostering competent singing groups and solo artists during the barren and hard times after the war" (G. Choi 2012, 445).[5]

The strong influence of American pop culture continued, and packaged show programs developed during the 1960s and into the 1970s along with the introduction of modern popular media such as TV within the context of industrialization, urbanization, economic development, and national rebuilding as part of the official national agenda. The major broadcasting systems (the national broadcaster KBS Television, established in 1961; TBS, the first commercial system, beginning in1964; and MBC TV, launched in 1969) established "the age of image," bringing glamorous female singers from live show stages to television music shows. Owing to various music styles directly influenced by the United States—standard pop, blues, jazz, and soul—glamorous American-influenced female singers gained popularity. Often, they had charismatic styles of performance and dynamic bodily movements, representing the modern, international, and Western, which stood in direct contrast to the former female *trot* singers (Yi 2006, 209).[6]

The 1970s in Korea brought political unrest, with antisocialist sentiment causing severe government intervention and supervision but also an oppositional youth culture that had to maneuver between hedonism and draconianism. The society as a whole still held to conventional femininity based on the hierarchy of gender division and the patriarchal system (Kang 1999, 128–129); thus, many female singers were merely provided as commodities on packaged TV programs, were still mostly considered lowly entertainers for entertainment and pleasure, and were mediated as passive female images by the male gaze. Even though the growth of certain youth cultures met severe censorship under the military regime, female singers generally represented hedonism, as commodities for the pleasure industry of popular entertainment.

Social Contexts for the Mainstreaming of Dance Music during the 1980s

Korea underwent drastic political, economic, and sociocultural change during the 1980s. Politically, the struggle for democracy against the military regime, which lasted more than twenty years, finally succeeded. Economically, the process of industrialization was in its final stages of development, resulting in the prosperity of the conglomerates and the development of several urban centers. Within the city of Seoul, Gangnam district, south of the Han River, underwent rapid development as part of the national economic development project, giving rise to the Gangnam middle class, which soon became the leading class of modern consumption and urban lifestyles. Major national and megaglobal events, such as the Asian Games (1986) and the Olympics (1988), were hosted by the state, resulting in economic prosperity, the rise of entertainment, and global ambitions on the part of both the state and the people.[7]

In previous decades, the national interest took priority over the individual, and mass culture was tightly regulated by the government. However, in the 1980s, individual desires and pursuits could be more freely expressed. Many prohibitions disappeared, the military-regime-initiated late-night curfew was ended, and night life in urban cities thrived. Japanese-influenced school uniforms and regulations for short haircuts were abolished as part of national policy, and the ban on traveling abroad was lifted. A new media environment provided support to the emergence of a modern lifestyle. Color TV was introduced as a national project, and various TV programs were launched to take advantage of color monitors, such as music shows for people of different generations, including youth. The distribution of color TVs increased the need for "video-type" singers and the emergence of music videos. Radio stations also began creating young-adult music programs targeting mostly teenage listeners and college students. For nighttime entertainment in the Gangnam area, disco clubs flourished, and international disco and local dance music became their main sonic resources.[8] The internationally famous film *Saturday Night Fever* (1977) made disco popular, while Michael Jackson turned breakdancing into a new fad among teenagers globally. Following the new worldwide popularity of dance music, the venues for popular music consumption now moved from stage shows to TV programs. These changes—the emergence of color TV, music videos, and disco clubs, with the middle class and middle-class teenagers emerging as consumers during the 1980s—paved the way to make dance music a major genre in South Korea. Teenagers became the major consumers of pop culture, on the basis of the economic success of their parents, and they consumed dance in various ways: as concert-goers, album buyers, club-goers, members of college dance communities such as UCDC (Union College Disco Club), and members of fan cultures. TV programs also developed youth-targeted programs, such as *Jeolmumui haengjin* (March of youth), beginning in 1980 on KBS (Korea Broadcasting System, the public channel), and *Young 11* in 1981 on MBC (Munhwa Broadcasting System). Other popular entertainment forms including motion pictures and sports also flourished during this time (Zhang 2012, 342–345; C. Kim 2010, 167–169; Cha 2012, 159–160).

The 1980s also marked a milestone in the diversification of Korean popular music styles away from the domination of the two major genres of *trot* and American standard pop. This diversification can be seen in the boom of dance music (Yi 2006, 316). In South Korea, "dance music" typically refers to music performed by entertainers who sing and dance onstage and not music produced by a DJ working in a club. The emergence of dance music was, on the one hand, a reflection of changes in the whole society, in which the coexistence of various ideas, discourses, and lifestyles stood in sharp contrast to previous periods. At the same time, it was a reply to social demands, following the growth of youth and consumer culture. Further, the emergence of dance music was a local response to global American pop culture.

Dance music in Korea pop was driven by a few pioneering individual singers and groups. Among them, the leading singers in the dance-music boom were the all-male dance group Sobangcha, the male solo singer Bak Nam-jeong, and several female solo singers. Sobangcha, with three members, performed synchronized choreographed dance movements along with light pop-style music, while Bak Nam-jeong created easily imitated dance movements to accompany his hit songs. The few all-female groups, however, were less empowered than the female solo dance divas. The emergence of these dance divas served diverse expectations and desires of audiences during this period. Their music provided an important source of entertainment in nightclubs for local middle-class youth. They served as heroines for the newly arrived color TV programs. The happy marriage of modern sound and body spectacles in their music made them successful, as I discuss in the following sections.

Dance Divas Articulating Femininity in the 1980s

The 1980s female solo dance divas created contemporary meanings of sound, image, and performance while successfully erasing the earlier stereotypes of female singers in *trot* and standard pop. While their treatment of femininity started from certain features of traditionally defined or previously suggested gender roles in society, female singers articulated new images, styles, and roles that often contradicted those of female singers in Korea in previous periods. In addition, the individualism of their personalities distinguish them from the crafted images of post-1990s all-female K-pop groups, with their childish cuteness and their particular type of girlish and extreme sexuality.

Dance music in the 1980s articulated diverse notions of femininity but, ironically, also paved the way for the new mainstream. While the all-female groups continued to follow an earlier stereotypical image of female singers as commodities for a pleasure industry, the solo dance divas successfully found their own positions within the emerging genre of dance music, articulating femininity in niches between public entertainment and new social demands. In the following sections, I describe three solo dance divas representing the characteristics of self-assertiveness over dependency, eroticism over sentimentality, and glamour over poverty. I demonstrate the ways in which they mobilized song lyrics, performance practices (including dance), fashion choices, and images to express new and diverse femininities (H. Kim 2015).

Self-Assertiveness over Dependency: Nami

Desires that formerly had to be restrained erupted with the advent of consumer society during the 1980s in Korea; representative of these desires was female self-assertiveness. The field of female singers was diverse; I focus on those female singers who presented the image of self-assertive young urban females and whose performances resisted passivity and dependency.

Nami was born in 1958 as the daughter of a record-shop owner, near the US military base in Dongducheon City. Nami was picked up by the Mipalgun entertainment agency in her hometown. She made her debut in 1967 as a child actress in the movie *A Queen of Elegie,* which described the life of the famous Korean female singer Yi Mi-ja (see Soojin Kim, chap. 9 in this volume). The following year, she was featured in another movie, *Mini agassi,* the story of 1960s female singer Yoon Bok-hui. As a teenager, she made her debut as a vocalist in the girl group Happy Dolls and performed frequently in US military shows including overseas shows in Vietnam. When the Happy Dolls disbanded in 1978, she made her debut as a solo singer under the name Nami. Her first song with her band, Nami and Guys, was in the *trot* style. After that, she released mostly dance disco pop music and music in the urban new wave style, including "Yeongwonhan chingu" (Everlasting friend, 1979), "Majimak insa" (Last goodbye, 1982), "Bingle bingle" (Round and round, 1984), "Yuhokhaji marayo" (Please do not seduce, 1985), "Seulpeun inyeon" (Sad affinity, 1985), "Boinae" (I can see, 1985), and "Indian inhyeongcheoreom" (Like an Indian doll, 1989). Her music was accompanied by visually refined and fashionable stage costumes and stage manner, along with backup dancers. Her appearance including clean-cut short hair was a perfect fit for the new medium of color TV (figure 14.1). Her employment of

Figure 14.1. *Nami Vol. 4* (1985), produced by Hyundai Records (HDS-2068).

several male dancers as backup dancers and her use of bodily gestures without sexy overtones helped her to construct an image of an assertive female with the messages of her song lyrics. This odd combination of non-sexually-suggestive bodily gestures by a female singer and male backup dancers was new to Korean audiences and was well received by mostly young female viewers.

The lyrics and themes of Nami's songs are about female self-assertiveness, happiness, and youth, rather than the stereotypical love and departure narratives of a dependent woman. At the same time, her trendy dance movements in light disco and new wave and fashionable stage costumes reinforced the lyrics and mood of her music, which was mostly consumed in nightclubs throughout the 1980s. The lyrics of "Yeongwonhan chingu" are,

Paranhaneul maemdoneun bidulginalgaecheoreom	Like the wings of the dove in the blue sky
Urideului maeumeun haneulul naragayo	Our minds also fly into the sky
Seorodagachi useumyeonseo	Let's smile

Bakeunnaeilui kkumeulkiwoomyeo sarayo	Let's live for tomorrow's dream
[refrain]	
Oh! Yeongwonhan chingu	Oh! Everlasting friend!
Oh! Hangbokhan maeum	Oh! Happy feeling!
Oh! Jeulgeoun Insaeng Yea!	Oh! Joyful Life Yea!

The messages of empowerment and self-expression that Nami conveys in the song, with her soft, whispering, yet powerful and husky voice, helped her to construct her image as a powerful urban woman as opposed to the typical femininity characterized by obedience and powerlessness. Most of her songs were perfect for light dance and have memorable repeated lyrics and hook melodies comfortable for easy listening. Her dance movements did not exaggerate her sexuality but rather embodied the contemporary desires of young modern women who aspired to take control of their lives.

Eroticism Rather Than Sentimentality: Kim Wan-sun

CedarBough Saeji observes that "K-pop has a strong visual component, first because of an emphasis on dance by well-rehearsed young stars" (2013, 341). The importance of visual elements, eroticized bodily gestures, and an emphasis on appearance were pioneered by the entertainer Kim Wan-sun in the 1980s. With her tallness, well-curved body, and eroticized dance choreography, she was a sexy icon of Korean dance divas (figure 14.2).

Kim Wan-sun was born in 1969 and was fortunate to have as her aunt Han Baek-hui, already a big name in the entertainment business as a professional agent. Kim made her successful debut as part of the all-female singing groups In Suni and Rhythm Touch, in which she began her career as a backup dancer. In fact, Kim was her aunt's well-prepared, ready-made commodity, having trained in singing and dancing from an early age. When she made her debut in 1986 at the age of seventeen, she had already spent three years in vocal training, ballet and various dance styles, gymnastics, and even orchestration. The story of her debut, including the fact that she was a teenage girl with a mature, sexy body and her three years of training, was not common in the 1980s. Her debut song, "Oneulbam" (Tonight), a combination of rock and new wave music, has lyrics with strong sexual connotations. She was the first singer who incorporated energetic dancing while singing, earning her the title "dancing queen." Most of her hits were made to suit dancing, as indicated by the titles and lyrics of her songs. Her success as a dance diva continued with her second and third albums, even as she introduced a new style of rock and techno dance music with tracks such as "Naholo ddeulapeseo" (I am alone standing in the yard),

Figure 14.2. *Kim Wan-sun Vol. 4* (1989), produced by Jigu Records (JLS-1202263).

"Rhythmsikui geuchumul" (Dance in the rhythm), and the following year, "Naholro chumeulchugin neomuoerowo" (Too alone to dance).

Kim Wan-sun won several music awards each year, including the gold disc and the KBS Pop Song Great Award following her debut. Although critics attacked her singing voice, she won "Singer of the Year" five times. She had worked with the top composers of the time—Sin Jung-hyeon, Yi Jang-hui, and Ha Gwang-hun—and featured the various hottest dances of the time including breakdance, the hustle, and the robot.

Her erotic and sexualized dance gestures along with the newest choreographed dances emphasized her breasts, waist, legs, exaggerated costumes, and hairstyle, while her strong erotic gaze and erotic lyrics with her unpolished nasal voice led her to be called the "Madonna of Korea." Her exaggerated hairstyle and odd combination of jean jackets with poufy long skirts were reminiscent of the early fashions of Madonna.

Her presentation and performance onstage always contained connotations of "stereotypical fetishized femininity" (Ye-ran Kim 2011, 339), including the dance movements and costumes. Her stage dress—usually with lots of frills or with simple lines and large openings on the upper torso and legs showing cleavage and flesh or with a short jacket and a long and fluffy ballerina skirt—created a fantasy image. She often performed in a long skirt with large openings instead of a short skirt, which made her look more mature than her age. Her strong display of sexuality was highlighted when she was banned from MBC TV programs for about six months for being "too erotic."

The lyrics of her debut and signature song, "Oneulbam" (Tonight), actively hint at eroticism and seduction while still containing connotations of a passive, dependent, and disempowered woman. Even the title carries strong sexual meanings, further reinforced by her stage delivery, with dance using strong sexual gestures and a high-pitched, nasal voice.

Na Oneul Oneul Bameun eodumi museowoyo	I am scared of tonight, tonight's darkness
Musimhan Bamsaesori Guseulpideulryeo	The sound of the night bird sounds very sad
Jeo Haneul dungdeundari oeroweoboyeoyo	The moon in the sky looks very lonely
Jakeunbyeol soksaimdo bujileopseoyo	Whispers of the stars are meaningless
Jeongdaweotdeon yetnari eodumsoke muchigo	Good old days when we were together are covered in the dark
Yijeseoro wooriga namnaminga	Now we are not together anymore
Kkummangatdeon yetnari Angaesokesarajeo	My good old days with you now lost in the fog
Yijenaholrodeoeo namaitnae	Now I am alone, I am left behind

Among Kim's greatest hits are "Namanui geot" (Solely mine, 1990); her first number-one song, "Bbieroneun urilbogo utji" (A clown is smiling at us, 1991); and "Gajang mudohoe" (Masquerade, 1991). She became the first female singer whose album sold more than a million copies, but she retired in 1992 surrounded by much rumor and gossip, until her return in the 2000s.

Kim Wan-sun fulfilled the voyeuristic gaze of males of all ages. Her projected sexuality falls into the standard types of female pop singers, often situated in-between "provocative and active" and "passive and typical" femininity. She became both a "winner and victim" (J. Choi 2012, 216). Kim Wan-sun is considered to have opened a new era as a spectacle and a prototype for sexy female dance divas in Korea.

Glamour Rather Than Poverty: Kim Hye-lim

While Kim Wan-sun was the sexy girl of the time, another female of the same age, Kim Hye-lim, embodied the harmless Gangnam girl following in her parents' footsteps (figure 14.3). Kim Wan-sun was considered a full-time entertainer, whereas Kim Hye-lim was perceived as simply following her mother's career. Kim Hye-lim was the daughter of the female singer and actress Na Ae-sim (b. 1930), who was popular in the 1950s and 1960s. Before Kim Hye-lim made her debut as a singer, she worked as a member of the idol group Tongkeunai, organized by the youth TV show *Jeolmumui haengjin* (March of youth) on KBS in 1988. Her debut song, "D.D.D.," was a huge hit, and she was awarded the Rookie of the Year award at the MBC Top 10 Singer Festival. The simple and repetitive melody featured in "D.D.D." soon gained popularity in nightclubs and Korean karaoke.

In the video for "D.D.D." (an abbreviation for "distance direct dialing," which had just been introduced in Korea), Kim Hye-lim portrays a pretty, cute, and lively young college girl with rich parents; she wears bangs and a short haircut, has a cute smiling face, and wears stylish college-girl fashion. Her dance movements do not feature her body parts, instead using light running motions with cute hand gestures and light foot movements. "D.D.D." employs refrains with repetitive lyrics, and the music constructs an entertaining, fun, and extemporaneous feeling, excluding any serious, painful, sad, or deep emotions, as in songs of female singers from earlier periods.

Kim Hye-lim's cuteness was also highlighted when she was featured as a model in advertisements for ice cream. Her image of "a girl with a family background" was created through media reports about her as a second-generation entertainer, even though she grew up without knowing her father. Kim represented the sophisticated and materialistic younger generation living in Gangnam and the image of a rich and mindless daughter of well-off parents. Kim Hye-lim's family background, with her famous mother, helped to underscore her image as a rich college girl, and her simple, light, and repetitive songs contrasted with the conventional image of female pop singers in Korea as poor, less educated, and lower class. Kim Hye-lim symbolized the elegant consumer culture of the middle class, rather than an object for sexualization.

Female dance singers of the 1980s represented various categories of female subjectivities including self-assertive, sophisticated, urban, sexy, young, lively, and middle class, and they projected the image of independent modern women through the genre of dance pop. Their treatment of the female body was less restricted than in previous eras regarding issues of sexuality and was more open to diverse types of representation. With the emergence of dance music as the new mainstream, female bodies returned to a focus on desires, tastes, and im-

Figure 14.3. *Kim Hye-lim Vol. 1* (1989), produced by Jigu Records (JLS-1202272).

ages of seduction as symbols for the transition of Korea into a consumer society in the 1980s. Furthermore, they spoke for the diverse desires of contemporary females in Korea, as shown in their female fan base. While keeping their distance from their male counterparts, these female dance singers articulated contemporary womanhood.

Although such emphasis on showing the body and sexuality was an important element in female dance music, the femininity they constructed, when combined with the multilayered modernity of the 1980s, helped create a new femininity to represent modern Korean society. When compared with the uniform sexuality and the emphasis on the body in current Korean K-pop, manipulated systematically by the global management industry, it is safe to say that female dance singers in the 1980s, while dancing vigorously onstage, were in fact less influenced by the traditional stereotype of femininity and challenged gender politics by representing a more complex and multilayered image of womanhood. At the same time, their employment of various images prior to the reorganization of the Korean entertainment industry into a global and systematic one anticipated roles for later girl groups and other dance divas. These female dance divas during the 1980s, many of whom continued their activities until 2000, reappeared or saw their images copied and redefined by later solo female dance divas and girl groups.

The female dance singers discussed in this chapter created strong and progressive urban-modern images and became new role models for their contemporaries in Korea and elsewhere in Asia. These dance divas, as symbols of the modern urban soundscape, articulated a new, consumption-based lifestyle, youth, and the sophistication of modern Korea. They constructed new performance styles and reflected new roles for female singers and female fandom culture that were distinct from those of earlier eras. They laid the groundwork for the K-pop girl groups of the 1990s and 2000s. They challenged gender stereotypes in Korean society and became targets of severe criticism for emphasizing their sexuality. They created a diversity of female images in modern Korean society and an ambivalence that both supported and resisted gender stereotypes. In reexamining this ambivalence, this chapter has sought to reveal these female dance singers as active agents and pioneers of a new style, creating their own positions in the contemporary national and transnational entertainment industry, as major figures in the tapestry of modern South Korea. In twenty-first-century Korea, gendered sexuality is interwoven with Korean modernity and manifested in the bodies of Korean female dance divas, whose influence can be felt in the global cultural industry of K-pop.

Notes

1. The system of *gisaeng* was established to officially provide female entertainers during the Goryeo Dynasty (918–1392) and continued until the Joseon Dynasty (1392–1897) under the label *yeoak* (female + music). In traditional society, *gisaeng* served as dancers, singers, and instrumentalists for court, local governments, and private-sector functions such as banquets. They belonged to the lower class but were considered professional artists and entertainers and were famous for their skills in literature, fine arts, and performing arts. After Joseon was annexed by Japan, *gisaeng* formed the *gwonbeon johap,* an association that became the center of the popular industry.

2. *Enka* is a popular musical genre of Japan (see Christine Yano, chap. 6 in this volume).

3. During the colonial period, popular music consisted of *yuhaengga, sin minyo, manyo,* and *jas* (jazz) songs, of which *yuhaengga* and *sin minyo* were favored by most *gisaeng* singers.

4. Yi Nan-yeong (1916–1965) was born in Mokpo in Jeolla province in 1916. As a daughter in a poor family, she entered Taeyang Theater Troupe in 1930 when she was fifteen, and later she became the representative singer of Oke record company. She was adept at various singing styles of the time, from *sin minyo* to *trot,* and her hit song "Mokpoui nunmul" was released in 1935. She married the popular music composer Kim Hae-song and actively performed at his KPK Theater. Her two daughters and a niece later formed the famous girl group Kim Sisters in 1953.

5. This mostly involved inviting American entertainers; however, with the increasing need for entertainment among American troops, more and more Korean entertainers began filling in. This inspired the formulation of entertainment agencies whose job was to provide entertainers chosen through auditions sponsored by the US Army. These agencies organized show groups in a package program, which naturally included many female singers. This offered a good opportunity for domestic female singers who had been unemployed since the war. The Kim Sisters, the first official girl group in the history of Korean popular music, made their debut in the Sudo Theatre in 1953. Performing both for Korean audiences and also for American soldiers, they were the representative group of the KPK orchestra founded by Yi Bong-yeong and Yi Nan-yeong (former member of the Jeogori Sisters and singer of "Mokpoui nunmul"). They even appeared in a motion picture and became the first female group ever to perform in the United States (G. Choi 2012).

6. Gyu-seong Choi (2012) also defines the 1960s as "the age for girl groups" because it is in this period that the number of girl groups performing for the US Army increased enough to became the mainstream in the realm of popular music in South Korea.

7. The second Seoul construction plan was announced in December 1969, and the development project of the southern part of the Han River (called Yeongdong, east to the Yeongdeungpo area) was initiated. Later, Yeongdong district was renamed Gangnam (lit. "south of the Han River"), and investment was begun for a foundation to make the new district vibrant. Following the planning and investment, famous high schools and major public institutions moved to Gangnam. Major apartment complexes shot up. At the same time, various facilities for the Olympic Games (1988) were built, and Gangnam became a symbol of prosperity; Gangbuk (lit. "north of Han River") remained old and backward (An 2010, 63–97).

8. After the late-night curfew was ended, the night life of the Gangnam district flourished. Sinsadong was full of nightclubs, cafés, restaurants, and salons for adults and Seochodong discotheque for young adults and teens (Cha 2012, 161).

References

An, Chang-mo. 2010. "Gangnam gaebalgwa bangbukui tansaenggwajeong gochal" (The birth of Gangbuk in the process of making the Gangnam). *Seoulhakyeongu* (Journal of Seoul studies) 41:63–97.

Braidotti, Rosi. 1994. "Toward a New Nomadism: Feminist Deleuzian Tracks: or Metaphysics and Metabolism." In *Gilles Deleuze and the Theater of Philosophy,* edited by Constantin V. Boundas and Dorothea Olkowski, 159–186. London: Routledge.

Cha, Woo-jin. 2009. "Girl group jeonseonggi" (Boom of girl groups). *Munhwagwahak* (Journal of culture and science) 59:270–283.

———. 2012. "Daejung eumakgwa sedae" (Popular music and generation). In *Daejung eumakui ihae* (Understanding popular music), edited by Chang-nam Kim, 152–176. Seoul: Hanul.

Cho, Younghan. 2011. "Desperately Seeking East Asia amidst the Popularity of South Korean Pop Culture in Asia." *Cultural Studies* 25 (3): 383–404.

Choi, Gyu-seong. 2012. "Hanguk daejungeumak girlgroup gyebohak" (The lineage of girl groups in Korean popular music: From Jeogori Sisters to Sonyeo Sidae). *Daejungeumak Sound* 5:442–457.

Choi, Ji-seon. 2012. "Daejung eumakgwa yeoseong" (Popular music and women). In *Daejung eumakui ihae* (Understanding popular music), edited by Chang-nam Kim, 204–236. Seoul: Hanul.

Epstein, Stephen, and Rachel Miyoung Joo. 2012. "Multiple Exposures: Korean Bodies and the Transnational Imagination." *Asia-Pacific Journal* 10 (33): 1–18.

Jung, Eun-young. 2010. "Playing the Race and Sexuality Cards in the Transnational Pop Game: Korean Music Videos for the US Market." *Journal of Popular Music Studies* 22:219–36.

Jung, Min-woo, and Na-yeong Lee. 2009. "Stareul gwallihaneun fandom, fandomeul gwallihaneun: Saneop-isedae idol fandom munhwasilcheonui teukjing mit hamui" (Fandom that manages stars, industry that manages fandom: Characteristics and connotation of cultural practice of second-generation idol fandom). *Media, Gender & Munhwa* (Media, gender & culture) 12:191–240.

Jung, Yoon-su. 2011. "Girl groupeuldulreossan moheom: Wiheomsahoeeseo saranamgi" (How to survive in a dangerous society: Adventure surrounding girl groups). *Daejung Eumak* (Korean journal of popular music) 8:99–125.

Kang, I-su. 1999. "Geundae hanguk baengnyeongwa yeoseongui Sam" (One hundred years of modern Korea and the lives of women). *Gyeongjewa Sahoe* (Economy and society) 44:116–145.

Kim, Chang-nam. 2010. *Daejung munhwaui ihae* (Introduction to popular culture). Seoul: Hanul.

Kim, Hee-sun. 2015. "Multiplying Femininity: Diversification of Sexualized Bodies in Korean Dance Divas in the 1980s." *Ewha Eumaknonjip* (Ewha journal of musicology) 19 (1): 1–21.

Kim, Jung-won. 2011. "'Hey, Look at Me Now, Mister': 2000 yeondae hanguk girl groupui sigakhwawa seongaehwae gwanhan gochal" (An examination of visualization and sexualization of K-pop girl groups in the 2000s). *Daejung Eumak* (Korean journal of popular music) 8:46–78.

Kim, Su-a. 2010. "Sonyeo imageui bolgeorihwawa sobibangsikui guseong: Sobyeo groupsui samchonfan damronguseong" (Spectacularizing girl images and the construction of consumption patterns: Construction of discourses of uncle fan for girl groups). *Media, Gender & Munhwa* (Media, gender & culture) 15:79–119.

Kim, Yeong-hui. 2006. *Gaehwagi daejungyesului kkot Gisaeng* (The flowers of popular entertainment during the early modern period, Gisaeng). Seoul: Minsokwon.

Kim, Ye-ran. 2011. "Idol Republic: The Global Emergence of Girl Industries and the Commercialization of Girl Bodies." *Journal of Gender Studies* 20 (4): 333–345.

Kwon, Do-hee. 2001. "20segi gisaengui eumaksahoesajeok yeongu" (The activities of the *gisaeng* of the early twentieth century). *Korean Music Research* 29:319–344.

———. 2003. "The Female Musicians Activity since the Dissolution of Gisaeng Guilds." *Tongyang Eumak* 25:129–165.

Lee, Dong-yeon. 2010. "Idolpopiran mueotinga, jinghujeok dokhae" (What is idol pop? A symptomatic reading). *Munhwa Gwahak* (Journal of culture science) 62:210–227.

Lee, Su-an. 2008. "Sobimunhwasaneopui mom image-wa gender hwadeon eungsi" (Body image and gendered gaze in the culture industry). *Handok Sahoegwahak Nonchong* (Journal of Korea German social science) 18 (2): 185–208.

———. 2010. "Daejungmunhwa yeonyesangpuneseo munhwajeok sahoejeo jaonui dongwon mechanism—Idol starui gyeonjejabonhwa gwajeongul jungsimuro" (Mobilizing cultural and social capital in popular culture entertainment—The process of economic capitalization of the idol star mechanism). *Sahoegwahak Yeongu* (Journal of social science) 18 (2): 206–242.

———. 2011. "Daejungmunhwaeseo gihogashiroseoui mom Image-ui sobiyangsik—idol groupeul jungsimuiro" (Consumption patterns of body image as semiotic value—focused on idol groups). *Munhwawa Sahoe* (Journal of culture and society) 11: 193–235.

Lee, Su-ja. 2006. "Global munhwasaneopgwa genderyeokhakui jinghujeok dokhae" (Symptomatic reading of global culture industry and gender dynamics). *Gyeongjewa Sahoe* (Journal of economy and society) 70:38–62.

Mungang, Hyeong-joon. 2010. "Woosangui hwanghon: Hangulsahoeeseo idoleun otteokae sobidoeneunga" (Twilight of the idols: How idols are consumed in Korean society). *Simingwa Sahoe* (Journal of citizens and the world) 17:281–296.

Puzar, Alijosa. 2011. "Asian Dolls and the Westernized Gaze: Notes on the Female Dollification in South Korea." *Asian Women* 27 (2): 81–111.

Ryoo, Woongjae. 2009. "Globalization, or the Logic of Cultural Hybridization: The Case of the Korean Wave." *Asian Journal of Communication* 19 (2): 137–151.

Saeji, CedarBough. 2013. "Juvenile Protection and Sexual Objectification: Analysis of the Performance Frame in Korean Music Television Broadcasts." *ACTA Koreana* 16 (2): 329–365.

Shin, Hyun-joon. 2009. "Have You Ever Seen the Rain? And Who'll Stop the Rain? The Globalizing Project of Korean Pop." *Inter-Asia Cultural Studies* 10 (4): 507–523.

Siriyuvasak, Ubonrat, and Hyun-joon Shin. 2007. "Asianizing K-pop: Production, Consumption and Identification Patterns among Thai Youth." *Inter-Asia Cultural Studies* 8 (1):109–136.

Wei, Jie. 2010. "How Chinese Young People Read the Characteristic of Post-feminism in Korean Girl Hip-Hop Music Videos." Master's thesis, Korea University.

Willoughby, Heather A. 2006. "Images Is Everything: The Marketing of Femininity in South Korean Popular Music." In *Korean Pop Music: Riding the Wave*, edited by Keith Howard, 99–108. Folkstone, UK: Global Oriental.

Yi, Yeong-mi. 2006. *Hanguk daejung gayosa* (History of Korean popular music). Seoul: Minsokwon.

Zhang, Eu-jeong. 2010. "2009 nyeon yeoseonggroupsui hwaldonggwa jakpumedaehab gochal" (A study of girl group's activity and song texts in 2009). *Daejung Eumak* (Korean journal of popular music) 6:164–197.

———. 2012. "Boneun eumak, momui eumak, dance eumak" (Music to see, music of body, music of dance). In *Daejung eumakui ihae* (Understanding popular music), edited by Chang-nam Kim, 335–361. Seoul: Hanul.

CHAPTER 15

The Ideal Idol

MAKING MUSIC WITH HATSUNE MIKU, THE "FIRST SOUND OF THE FUTURE"

Jennifer Milioto Matsue

SINCE debuting in 2007, the Japanese singer Hatsune Miku (初音ミク) has sung over one hundred thousand songs and appeared in more than 250,000 videos online. She has released more than four thousand professional recordings, including the song "World Is Mine," which reached number 7 on the US iTunes charts. She has successfully sold out 3-D concerts around the world and is now recording collaborations with major pop stars (Itoh 2013b). More than one million "derivative artworks" including numerous dolls, games, cars, and even sex toys feature her big violet eyes, floor-grazing turquoise pigtails, and futuristic schoolgirl uniform. She is so popular now, with in excess of two million fans worldwide, that Google Chrome used her image in 2011 to represent global interconnectivity in a marketing campaign (Google 2012). In "live" performances, her ten-foot-tall body confidently strides across the stage, commanding the audience—or does it?

Hatsune Miku is actually a type of vocal synthesizer software developed by Crypton Future Media, Inc. using "Vocaloid" technology produced by Yamaha Corporation. Based on samples of the Japanese voice actress Saki Fujita,[1] Hatsune Miku, or simply Miku, is the personification of Vocaloid 2 (Japanese) and Vocaloid 3 (Japanese and English),[2] initially depicted on the product packaging in the style of a manga character that continues to resonate with fans globally today. Indeed, according to Hiroyuki Itoh, the CEO of Crypton, fans hungrily devour the image of Miku, using her as a "collaborative hub" for their creativity, resulting in copious numbers of songs and video posted on Piapro, a website that Crypton developed precisely to allow the creative chain of shared work to continue to flourish (Itoh 2013b).[3] It was Miku's ever-increasing popularity and global presence that inspired Crypton to project her avatar as a 3-D hologram "live" in concert. Other vocal synthesizer software has come before and since, but none has enjoyed the same success as Hatsune Miku.

But despite Miku's global presence, she still remains uniquely Japanese; no performer captures the modern if not postmodern ethos of contemporary Japan more than she does. She sits firmly at the forefront of Japanese music history, embracing, in her synthesized voice, everything from the wide timbral possibilities of art, folk, and traditional Japanese music to the fascination with technology that has infused much popular culture in Japan since World War II (Milioto Matsue 2016). Today she is widely considered one of the most successful Japanese idols of all time. Idols, or *aidoru* in Japanese, developed in the 1960s, referring to young performers who sing, dance, pose for photographs, and appear in diverse media (Galbraith and Karlin 2012). Idols boomed in the 1970s and 1980s as Japan enjoyed unprecedented economic prosperity, then suffered briefly in the 1990s in the aftermath of the bubble bursting as real estate prices plummeted and Japan entered into a long recession. Idols soon surged once again to the top of the J-pop[4] pile in the 2000s and today dominate not just popular music but the popular culture industry as a whole in Japan.

There are many successful male and female human idols, but as a result of Hatsune Miku being a virtual character who exists only in the minds and creations of her fans, she is by far the most ideal of all idols currently on the market. The following discussion introduces the origins of the Hatsune Miku phenomenon before exploring her position as an ideal idol in greater detail. As will be seen, her virtualness enhances her ability to function in the intertextual media that define human idols' existence. Gender permeates all the ways in which Hatsune Miku serves as an ideal idol, both in how she plays with gender through her own performance and especially in the quality of her voice, revealing a fluidity of what it means to be male and female in contemporary Japan, as well as how Japanese fandom speaks to gender relations in society more broadly. Although Miku most certainly means different things to her male, female, and transgender fans globally,[5] within the context of Japan, as an ideal idol, she serves the needs of many of her predominantly middle-age male fans in particular, offering alternatives to strict expectations of appropriate social behavior. Throughout this exploration, however, Miku will reveal herself to be a complicated and contradictory idol at every turn. She is both an active actor and passive participant, limiting and liberating, perfect in her imperfections, female but also male, Japanese and devoid of ethnic identity at the same time.

Itoh adds that Vocaloid software ultimately creates a "democracy of singing," providing an opportunity for an amateur songwriter to promote his or her own music (2013b), and as such solidifies Miku's position as the ideal idol. Although arguably other types of democratic technology exist in applications such as YouTube or Facebook, assuming one has a computer and account, Itoh focuses on Miku's ability to democratize musicking, here meaning to give access to nonmusicians and musicians alike to compositional tools and performers, as well as to facilitate the creation and dissemination of new works by amateur artists, albeit problematically so. As Itoh summarizes, "One can't always afford a singer, but they can purchase Miku at $149" (2013b). She is a woman for sale at an extremely reasonable rate, but through her, a democratic, even utopian vision for equitable music production may be realized. She is a contradiction yet again—both a commodity and a conduit for changing how we make and hear music.

A Star Is Born

Itoh proudly described the global success of Hatsune Miku during a public lecture at the Japan Foundation in New York City on October 8, 2013.[6] He established his company in 1995 in Sapporo, and Crypton has since become the number-one distributor of music software in Japan.[7] Crypton began marketing Vocaloid, a "singing voice synthesis technology developed by Yamaha Corporation and the name of its application software," in 2004 (Itoh 2013a). There had long been different types of "virtual instruments" available on the computer, but Itoh "wanted to use a 'singing voice' as a virtual instrument, and VOCALOID was a perfect fit for that": "That's how a 'singing voice' became part of our product lineup [with the release of Meiko in 2004] and eventually led the way to the birth of Hatsune Miku" in 2007 (ibid.). Itoh's desire fits well within a long history of obsession with the potential of the artificial voice, dating back to when Thomas Edison first experimented with creating a talking doll featuring a female voice (Black 2012, 211–212). And as will be seen shortly, it is no surprise that Crypton's most successful Vocaloid to date is rendered as a girl.

Miku's name merges the Japanese words for "first" (初, hatsu), "sound" (音, ne), and "future" (ミク, miku), signifying her position as the first of the Vocaloids in the "Character Vocal Series" (Wikipedia 2014). Though fans determine her personality traits, Crypton provided her personal data.[8] Born on August 31 but with no year, she remains forever a youthful sixteen years old. She is an appropriately petite 158 centimeters, or five foot two, and a slim forty-two kilograms, or ninety-three pounds. Miku enjoys performing pop, rock, dance, house, techno, or cross-over, between 70 and 160 beats per minute, with recommended ideal ranges that vary depending on the desired vocal quality.

Miku's now iconic image on the packaging (see figure 15.1) was designed "to appeal to consumers with the idea of a singing persona—[Crypton] thought the concept of 'a singer inside the computer' would be easier for people to understand" (Itoh 2013a). However, "using the visual image of the 'real' person who supplied . . . the voice samples would have been too vivid," and Crypton decided instead to anthropomorphize Miku as a manga character (Itoh 2013a).[9]

Figure 15.1. Hatsune Miku (Japanese version).

Though Miku was not the first software released by Crypton, which markets both male and female packages,[10] she remains the most popular—so popular in fact that Crypton released "Hatsune Miku Vocaloid 3" in English[11] in August 2013, truly propelling her to global stardom.[12]

The fact that the most successful Vocaloid to date was rendered female makes perfect sense, given the roles that women play in Japanese popular music in general. Both male and female idols in Japan, for example, often are perceived as necessarily shaped and even controlled by a male-dominated industry. But Itoh further adds that in the current Japanese music industry, there are more female than male background singers and more singles released by female artists than by male artists, indicating an abundance of female vocalists and comfort with the female voice in the processed popular musical styles that dominate. In addition, most Vocaloid consumers are MIDI (musical instrument digital interface) users, who are predominantly men who in general prefer to work with female rather than male characters (Takahashi 2008). Though interest in male characters is increasing, Crypton seems to be doing all it can to ride the wave that is Hatsune Miku.

A Hub for Collaborative Creation

Several additional factors have fed into the immense success of Miku, many of which can be traced back to Crypton's expert handling of her marketing. Her image was originally depicted on the packaging for the software only, but in a brilliant move, the company allowed this caricature to be manipulated within diverse media platforms, resulting in her becoming a "hub for collaborative creation" among her fans (Condry 2013; Itoh 2013b). "Prosumers," or fans "who produce, modify, or personalize media in various ways to produce mash-ups, remixes, and so on" (Black 2012, 216), initially uploaded works featuring Miku to Niko Niko (formerly known as Niko Niko Douga), a video-sharing website in Japan, launching the "Vocalo-music boom."[13] To ensure that the chain of creation can continue, Crypton subsequently created Piapro to host fans' work, with the understanding that others can use anything posted on the site freely, therefore resulting in extensive collaborations and enhancing the democratic musicking that Itoh idealizes. There is a Piapro Character License (PCL) agreement that allows anyone to make derivative works based on Miku, as long as there is no financial gain and no one is defamed. Crypton also established Miku's own YouTube channel and the virtual community Mikubook.com.[14]

Prosumers, nevertheless, may engage with Miku in different ways, with some drawn to her musical capabilities and the original Crypton software and others to her visual imagery, creating videos that tell Miku's story. Ian Condry, for example, argues that within the context of anime, "the phenomenon around Miku shows that the character, more than the music software, is the platform on which people are building" (2013, 63). He further explains that in anime, the characters and premises are central, rather than the story lines (Condry 2009). And this focus allows for "transmedia" collaborative creation—in which each medium enacts the character, whether creating costumes or choreographing dances in the case of Miku. Therefore, among anime fans, Miku's popularity is grounded in her character and the basic details supplied by Crypton on which prosumers project their own creativity, and people in turn are connecting with the community behind her (Condry 2013, 63; Bell 2016, 225).

Today fans do not even have to engage with Crypton software at all to consume Miku, as she exists on multiple platforms. Nonetheless, Condry acknowledges that "her existence [originally] comes from the energy of a community of people who created her songs and her music" (2011, 12). Her character inspires "fans to develop images, stories and videos around the synthetic voice" (Condry 2009, 15). So although her character may be motivating the continued creation of all things Miku, it is her voice that launched the phenomenon. Indeed, Sarah Bell argues, "it is more accurate to think of Miku as an instrument, a means whereby something is achieved, performed, or furthered, and, especially, as a musical instrument" (2016, 225).

Hamasaki, Takeda, and Nishimura mapped a social network that developed through the collaborative creation of new content through shared interest in Miku and discovered that songwriters may lie at the center of the chain (or chains), confirming the centrality of the music in the collaborative creation of Miku works (2008, 1). As the number of prosumers grows, even if they are primarily interested in her as a character, the need for the original music synthesizer system expands. So by allowing Miku's image to be freely circulated and manipulated, Crypton continues to increase the potential for sales of the actual Vocaloid software. Both V2 and V3 broke software sales records at the time of release, with well over sixty thousand units sold, and Miku's stardom continued to soar with the release of the Vocaloid 4 engine. The source of the collective interest in Miku that has generated the transmedia boom therefore is music synthesizer software and the songwriters who use it. Users of the vocal synthesizer software enter lyrics and melody, and Miku essentially "sings" for them. She thus is passive, open for input, and existing only through someone else's creativity and control. But "what she can become is emergent, dynamic, and malleable in the hands of musicians and fans alike" (Bell 2016, 237). As such, Miku, although arguably at the expense of her own agency, can provide creative autonomy and independence for her prosumers.

On the one hand, Miku thus functions in the same way as well-known human Japanese idol performers (Aoyagi 2005) who inspire fans primarily through an attractive visual and constructed personality but who sing other people's songs (despite often having limited vocal skills), perform predetermined dance moves onstage to synthetic music, appear as guests on variety shows (in Miku's case, in anime or projected as a 3-D hologram), and work as models pitching everything from face cream to fantasy vacations. On the other hand, Miku is not just any old idol, as of course she is a virtual persona rather than an actual person. But it is precisely because she does not actually exist as a living human that Miku has the potential to be the ideal idol.[15]

Intertextuality and Japanese Idols

> On her own, Japanese pop superstar Hatsune Miku can't sing. Nor can she rap, dance or DJ. She is drug- and alcohol-free because she can't indulge in either, and she can't have affairs or engage in offstage shenanigans fit for YouTube scandals or tabloid headlines. Now entering her sixth year as a beloved idol with a global fan base, she looks as youthful and demure as she did when she debuted. She can't even get old. (Kelts 2012)

Patrick Galbraith and Jason Karlin (2012) argue that although idols are an important category in the contemporary production of popular music, they are often dismissed because of a noticeable lack of musical talent and an inability to translate outside Japan given the intensive intertextual construction of idol identity. Idols, whose primary purpose is to sell products, appear on television on variety shows, in dramas, and on commercials, as well as in print media through magazine spreads, advertisements, and news coverage. Idols thus do not exist in one frame only, as a singer or actor or television personality; rather, an idol's identity is constructed simultaneously through appearances in all these media. Within these distinct platforms, idols may appear in both fictional and nonfictional contexts, confusing their existence as fictional characters or real people. They may appear on one show to promote another program or a product and often make references to a past known only by Japanese viewers, using nostalgia, a powerful emotion in modern Japan,[16] to captivate and connect with an audience. This complex intertextuality of the Japanese media system makes idols "not only identifiable but familiar. In the daily routine of life in contemporary Japan, one might have more contact with a particular idol or celebrity than with one's own family" (Galbraith and Karlin 2012, 9). This creates a particularly intimate relationship with Japanese audiences but alienates others, as idols do not easily translate cross-culturally (ibid., 12). In fact, according to Hiroshi Aoyagi, they should be "above average" but not so outstanding that they alienate their audience, who above all should feel intimately connected to the persona (2005, 66–73). In creating this sense of intimacy, idols should maintain "social ties" with their fans and not become aloof. They should be perceived as "companions," with many events designed to foster this perception.

The play between real and imagined persona by idols—between the public and the private—is fostered through the ideologies of *honne* and *tatemae*, a pervasive understanding in Japanese culture in which one assumes a public persona or front *(tatemae)* while maintaining a private version of oneself for family and close friends *(honne)*. Japanese, therefore, are quite accepting of the idol system, which is grounded in a constructed identity but is so often critiqued by outsiders. Idols as intertextual images—fictional characters completely separate from reality—do not even require a human body to exist, as in the case of the virtual idol Eguchi Aimi, who was fashioned from features of forty-seven human members of AKB48, the immensely popular Japanese idol group consisting of young girls in matching costumes prancing and preening across the stage. Eguchi Aimi appeared in a commercial in 2011 alongside her human colleagues (Black 2012, 222; Galbraith 2012, 193).

Hatsune Miku is an especially adept idol, but unlike the human idols of Japan who are unable to succeed in cross-cultural contexts, she is also immensely popular globally. As a virtual character born through transmedia creation, she *is* intertextual media and therefore is able to signify in ways that are meaningful to her consuming public without her personal baggage interfering. Human idols must hide their personal lives from fans to maintain the illusion of their fantasy persona (they must separate the *honne* from the *tatemae*), but Hatsune Miku cannot cause trouble and draw negative attention to herself (there is no *honne*).

Miku has no personality to interfere with fans' desires, and thus fans can generate whatever qualities they want, controlling her every move and creating a tremendous sense of intimacy with her image. And Miku's relationship with both her fellow Vocaloids, as depicted in many prosumer videos both in Japan and beyond, and her fans consistently creates this sense of accessibility. Daniel Black confirms, "the very fact that no part of her exists outside flows of commodities and digital texts enables relationships with fans that are far more intimate and all-encompassing than those available with a living star" (2012, 225).

Though Miku's ability to serve as an ideal idol extends far beyond Japan, Aoyagi describes specifically Japanese idols as "personified symbols" of social significance, capable of revealing shared values and shaping norms (2005, 9). Miku, as a virtual idol (Black 2012; Condry 2013) is especially adroit at functioning as a personified symbol, informing the socialization of her Japanese fans—particularly in the ways young women identify with and emulate idols and middle-age men project their desires on idols. Miku once again shows herself quite capable of meeting the diverse needs of her consumers, in turn revealing much about gender relations in contemporary Japan.

Female Idols

Female idols influence conceptions of gendered selves among young men and women in Japan. The quality of the femininity performed by them is extremely complicated, at times serving as a means of escaping traditional expectations of appropriate gendered behavior, while at the same time affirming stereotypes of a woman's proper role in society.[17] Aoyagi, for example, highlights two types of female idols popular through the 1990s: the "cute" and the more overtly sexual "post-idol." As will be seen, these performance types offer contradictory means for young women to rebel against the pervasive view of women as "good wives and wise mothers" *(ryōsai kenbo)* established in the Meiji period (1868–1912) through which a woman's place became firmly situated within the private sphere, and in turn man's in the public (Aoyagi 2005, 86–95).[18]

Cute-style idol performance, according to Aoyagi, "one of the most infamous forms of escapism for young Japanese girls in the 1980s" (98), involves singing in a high-pitched, childlike voice and maintaining a certain youthful innocence in dress and demeanor. By enacting this childlike style, girls can avoid growing up, where they have to act as "good wives and wise mothers." But this style lost some of its appeal as a form of rebellion in the 1990s when the popularity of idols momentarily waned. These cute idols came to be seen as a weak representation of femininity and catering to the desire of men, hence Aoyagi's labeling of them as infamous.

In the 1990s, as the innocence of the cute idol lost its appeal and ideas about female sexuality transformed, a new, more assertive style of idol came into fashion, exemplified by performers such as Namie Amuro, who embraced her sexuality and brought this essence to the stage. Her fans are in no rush to marry and are perceived as more independent. Today female idols often walk a fine line between being cutesy and being sexy. Indeed, within Japan, the cute is often conflated with the sexy in a somewhat disturbing way, as seen, for example, in the copious amounts of pornography featuring girls who appear to be prepubescent, sporting school uniforms. In the case of idols, these styles reflect "different visions of the appropriate image of Japanese adolescent femaleness, which are then manufactured by male idol producers" (Aoyagi 2005, 120–121) to appeal to both young females and actually many middle-aged males alike.

Miku, as a virtual idol, is especially adept at personifying this complexity of contemporary femininity embodied in female idol performance. Because she is not attached to any body, she is able to slip back and forth between codified idol performances and at once serve as the epitome of cute and the coquette; her visual character is innocent, with her schoolgirl uniform, pigtails, and youthful face—she will, after all, never age—but also sexy, with her long legs and short skirt towering above her predominantly male fans' heads live in concert (Itoh 2013a). Although it is impossible to view the thousands of versions of Miku generated by the collaborative hub of creation, she generally maintains these essential dualistic qualities—this is her essence—at once to be cute and innocent, requiring the work of others to educate and direct her, while as the coquette also teasing them without actually intending to engage in sexual relations.

In fact, men who desire to avoid the hassle of dating, marriage, and the responsibilities associated with both may turn to female characters in manga, anime, and of course Vocaloids for companionship. Men who find women who do not comply with the discourse of "good wife and wise mother" alienating, as these women may be too demanding and difficult, may also turn to such characters for solace. In Aoyagi's work, some male informants reveal a desire to celebrate and preserve traditional Japanese femininity in the face of changing real women in Japan, who are perceived as more liberated (2005, 204–231). Often these young men turn to idols because of their inability to socialize with women, and here again, Miku may serve as the ideal because of her ability to be manipulated.

As Miku is a manga character with a recognizable type of voice, fans around the globe feel comfortable with her, especially *otaku* (someone perceived as unhealthfully obsessed with manga or anime),[19] who prefer engaging with "2-D characters" rather than real human beings. Black adds, "the virtual idol very clearly ties together the otaku obsession with computer technology, animation technology, robotic or otherwise artificial bodies, and the kind of femininity represented by the live idol" (2012, 216). The male consumer of virtual idols is attracted to "youthful innocence, vulnerability, and meekness, and a lack of remoteness or self-sufficiency. The qualities are endearing in their lack of threat and suggestion that the idol is dependent upon the support, encouragement, and indulgence of her fans" (Black 2012, 219). *Otaku* may feel a strong attraction *(moe)*, even sexual, for a manga, anime, or video-game character and in turn a desire to take care of the character and tremendous devotion. *Otaku* are able to control production of female bodies through virtual idols; indeed, these "2-D women" are completely dependent on their creators. Miku thus can be "an otaku's own, 'personal' idol" (Black 2012, 224)—the ultimate fantasy constructed, in the case of these male fans at least, within an essentially heterosexist gaze (Black 2012; Condry 2013).

Miku's accessibility is further evidenced in the 2013 Domino's Pizza Japan advertising campaign—"Domino's Pizza feat. Hatsune Miku app for iPhone"—launched to cater to just these types of fans. Now people are able to place an order with their iPhone (without actually talking to anyone) and then aim the phone at the top of the pizza box to make Miku give a special private dance on the tiny little screen in the privacy of their home (Kendall 2013).

But this idealness does not always make Miku ideal for Japanese men and women, as her ability to become the dream girl of her male fans has potential negative ramifications for real-life women who may pale in comparison to the ever-accommodating, unrealistically proportioned Hatsune Miku (Condry 2011, 14), while *otaku* continue to suffer from poor social skills and further withdraw from society. Despite these serious concerns about Miku's potential adverse effects, she clearly has an intimate relationship with her prosumers, making her the ideal idol. Her lack of personality, beyond the basic characteristics outlined by Crypton, and the need to maintain certain essential traits make her available to be molded into whatever fans need. This malleability is of course most pronounced with her voice, which can be manipulated by any prosumer in the world.

The Diva with the Disembodied Voice

> Create Melody + Input Lyrics = I sing. Hatsune Miku V3 English is a futuristic voice synthesizer software that allows you to easily create vocal parts from scratch by just entering a melody and lyrics. (Crypton marketing materials)
>
> Add vibrato, dynamics and other effects to change the expression of Miku's singing voice. Compose songs using Miku as your main singer, demo vocalist, chorus singer or experiment with new vocal styles for remixing and other electronic music projects.[20]

Idols are often discussed as visual objects whose performances reflect, challenge, and even affirm societal values, at times simultaneously, but little is written in academic or popular literature about their vocal qualities and the music they perform, beyond a passing comment on a hit song's album cover and lyrics—a result no doubt of the general perception that idols are invented characters whose primary purpose is to market goods and be marketed themselves, rather than singers. In fact, as noted earlier, a successful idol typically cannot possess any great talent for singing as this may actually undermine one's ability to remain accessible to fans. Idols therefore cannot be too talented or too attractive, as this may distance them, while lacking certain attributes or skills in turn rallies fans behind a particular idol, encouraging him or her to succeed (Galbraith 2012, 192). However, these performers are singers, and therefore the sonic attributes and qualities of Miku should be considered in this analysis of her as an ideal idol. Her persona, after all, originates as music synthesizer software, as described earlier, through which users enter lyrics and create melodies. Even the design of her costume, in both the original "Japanese" version (see figure 15.1) and the more recent "Western" interpretation, is based on the original synthesizer, highlighting Yamaha's signature turquoise (see figure 15.2). In addition to the many songs and videos posted for Miku online, she has a successful recording career, releasing numerous professionally produced songs and albums. She is the featured star on the Karent label, which specializes in Vocaloid recordings,[21] and several of her recordings have even reached the top of the Oricon charts, the Japanese music industry standard for measuring popularity (Kenmochi 2012, 5387). Miku is clearly garnering much industry recognition as a singer, albeit one completely controlled by her predominantly Japanese male prosumers.

There are actually three main components necessary to "make Miku sing" in the Vocaloid system:[22] "(a) Score Editor, where users can input lyrics and notes additionally with some musical expressions [in Musical Editor, Lyric Editor, or Singer Editor], (b) Singer Database, which includes diaphone and sustained vowels of a human singer,[23] and (c) Synthesis Engine, which receives inputs from Editor (a) and selects necessary segments from Singer Database (b) and concatenates [links] them" (Kenmochi 2012, 5,385).

In the basic software package, prosumers manipulate the pitch, bend, vibrato, and other features, in all sixteen tracks, thus allowing for a rich texture. The malleability of Miku, as a virtual singer, extends to varied aspects of her vocal identity including gender. Within Score Editor, prosumers use Singer Editor to control breathiness, brightness, cleanness, and gender factor (see figure 15.2), which involves raising and lowering pitch and adjusting timbre.[24] Raising the gender factor results in a thicker, "calm," more masculine quality, while lowering it creates an increasingly feminine, "bright," even squeaky, chipmunk-like voice common among female performers in Japanese popular culture. Crypton also developed an expansion package to further adjust the quality of Miku's voice; the V3 version includes original, sweet, dark, soft, solid, and English.[25] The solid setting is also often understood by prosumers as sounding more masculine.

As a synthesized, disembodied voice, Miku enjoys a greater flexibility than a human singer, and thus numerous qualities of her vocal identity can be manipulated and controlled. As such, Vocaloid software reveals the voice "as an increasingly malleable instrument, . . . [challenging] notions of voice as revealing something essential about the body, resulting in works that subvert traditional expectations of bodies based on pitch and timbre" (Bell 2016, 223). Miku's prosumer is able to play with the vocal persona, which accompanies her clearly young female body. One could therefore create a video featuring Miku's pigtails flopping and skirt flying as she dances along to "her" middle-age, low-pitched, "male" voice with a dark timbre, in a bold gender-bending move. Indeed, Mikuo is a popular fan-made Vocaloid based on Miku, now

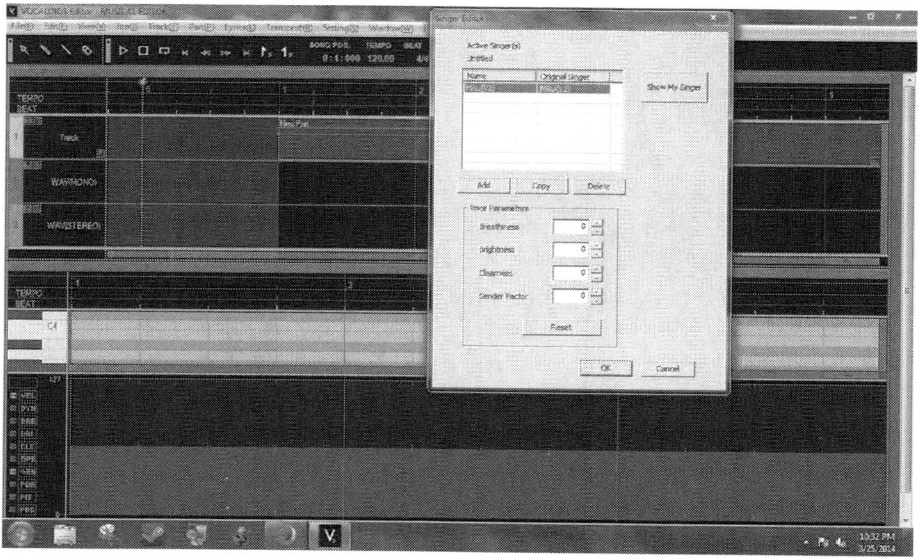

Figure 15.2. Screen shot of software featuring "Gender Factor."

rendered male with chin-grazing turquoise hair, slim black pants, and a necktie (see figure 15.3).

Miku's facial features are masculinized to varying degrees in different prosumers' visions, but Mikuo typically remains feminine by Western standards. It is important to note, however, that androgynous masculinity is widely accepted in Japanese popular culture (Darling-Wolf 2004; Nagaike 2012), perhaps offering another means of playing with and even escaping the strict gender roles in society outlined earlier and therefore paving the way for Mikuo's gender ambiguity. "His" voice results either from using the gender factor or simply through lowering pitch, with the latter more common. There are a number of genres of Japanese music in which we find similar play with gender. In classical puppet theater *(bunraku),* for example, male narrators *(gidayū)* provide the voices of all characters, while male actors in kabuki, another theatrical form, specialize in performing either male or female roles. In the popular all-female vaudeville theater known as Takarazuka, women must perform the male roles, with stylized masculine movements and low-pitched voices. Japanese may therefore be flexible about gender and the body, allowing for one person to sing multiple gendered identities or perform a different gender than his or her own. But "Vocaloid affords the manipulation of sounds within a singer library to a point at which pitch and timbre are not reflections of gender, but function outside biological 'male' and 'female'" (Bell 2016, 231). Japanese, as well as increasing numbers of global fans, may so easily accept Miku's cross-gender performance as gender

Figure 15.3. Mikuo (male rendering of Miku).

increasingly comes to be seen as a flexible and not fixed category, as evidenced, for example, by the recent acceptance of transgender celebrities. However, though the potential exists for other voices, Miku is most typically rendered as a young female voice to match the young female body. But the potential to play with her disembodied voice to this extreme speaks to Miku's versatility and thus only increases her potential as an ideal idol.

Miku theoretically can be adjusted to sing in an extremely wide range and numerous styles, making it possible for her to sing any song. Regardless of the settings, however, Miku remains distinct and easily recognizable by fans, many of whom are attracted to the digital nature of her voice. Tom Flint (2014) argues that "ultimately, Hatsune Miku is always going to sound a little bit electronic, no matter how much expression is applied, but that's not necessarily an issue." In fact, this may be one of her greatest strengths. Though digitally processed voices have been controversial for years in the popular music industry globally, today's young listeners, used to voices processed with tools such as Auto-Tune, may have different expectations of vocal quality and authenticity than in the past and therefore "don't find it wanting" when a Vocaloid sings (Black 2012, 211). And Miku's distinct, electronic voice is actually one of the main impetuses for her immense popularity.

Both Miku's active prosumers and more passive consumers throughout the world cut their teeth on manga, anime, and video games, hearing synthesized high-pitched voices from an early age. This perhaps accounts for why there is so little written about the quality of her voice.[26] In general, users are attracted to the unique quality of her digitized voice, with all its imperfections. Her fragmented vocal phrasing offers something new and different, something perceived as cool in popular music. Miku quite simply can do things that humans cannot. Itoh in fact believes that Miku's "charm lies in the imperfectness—sometimes sounding really machine-like adds to the 'personality' of the voice. It wouldn't be attractive if it could perfectly imitate the human voice" (Jarnes 2013). And composers may choose to work with Miku essentially because of the sound of synthesizers and "vocoders" for electronic speech production, the "robot sound," and the idea of working with singers without having to worry about breath and range—without having to work with actual singers.

To be sure, working with a virtual singer has a number of advantages. Hideki Kenmochi of Yamaha Corporation, for example, argues, "From the creator's point of view, the merit of using singing synthesis can be 'We can make musical tracks whenever you want, even in the midnight or early in the morning without any complaints'" (2012, 5,388). But more importantly, Kenmochi stresses the potential intimacy possible through Miku, who as a virtual idol has no emotions of her own to interfere with the direct communication between the composer and the listener. Without an actual human, nothing comes between the producer and the ultimate product. Rather, Miku is a personified symbol, to return to Aoyagi's terminology for idols, through which the emotion of the composer is transmitted directly to the listener (Aoyagi 2005; Kenmochi 2012, 5,388). He or she is able to express his or her own emotion more immediately to listeners, as opposed to the emotions of the human singer.

But not everyone celebrates this aspect of Miku, as her technicalness can inhibit one's ability to express emotions when one desires to do so. Because the phonemes are tied to note duration, subdividing rhythm is awkward. Composition is driven by trying to fit the text, rather than a desired rhythmic melody. Nonetheless, those fans who are less concerned with the details of Miku's musicality often associate her songs with the people who created them rather than the character, supporting Kenmochi's argument.

Despite some difficulties working the software, Miku once again is an ideal idol, able to work long hours with a composer, serving as a conduit for exactly what he or she wants to say with her disembodied voice, all without requiring union pay. Her ability to convey a composer's intent and capture her audience's collaborative spirit is best seen in her live performances, which are impressive in their range and technical sophistication.

Hatsune Miku "Live" in Concert

Originally inspired by SEGA's "Project Diva" game, through which prosumers create their own videos to share of Miku, complete with costumes and accessories,[27] Crypton premiered her "live" in concert as a 3-D hologram with actual musicians (guitar, bass, keyboard, and drums) at the Animelo Summer Live in Saitama in 2009 (Itoh 2013b). Since her debut, Miku has performed similar popular concerts around the world in Singapore (2009), Comic Con in New York City (2010), Anime Expo in Los Angeles (2011), Taiwan and Hong Kong (2012), and most recently on her "Hatsune Miku Expo 2016 America" tour through Canada, the United States, and Mexico (see figure 15.4), routinely pulling in from five to seven thousand fans (Itoh 2013a).

Miku sings—or, better put, "warbles coyly" (Kelts 2012)—songs created by prosumers and posted on her various video-share websites or marketed through karaoke that have gained global popularity, immediately creating the intimacy her fans so desperately desire. For the 2016 tour, Crypton organized an international songwriting contest. The grand prize winner—CircusP—received products from Sonicwire but more importantly two tickets to hear Miku perform the winning song "Ten Thousand Stars," featured at all the concerts on the seven-city tour (Miku Expo n.d.). When Miku performs pop music, her backup band follows her programmed singing and dancing, while audience members wave glow sticks in the air, bouncing along to the beat (see figure 15.4). "Unhappy Refrain," with music and lyrics by Wowaka and performed at the Hammerstein Ballroom in Manhattan on May 28, 2016 (Wowaka 2016), illustrates well a typical live performance, with a guitar-wielding Miku with her Japanese backing band straddling the projection screen. Programming such events, however, is no simple matter, involving multiple engineers who manipulate her every move and at great expense to all involved in the production (see figure 15.5).

In 2012, Miku also performed *Symphony Ihatov*, referring to a scenic location in Iwate Prefecture in the northeast of Japan (Tomita). In this work, she collaborated with "the Japan Philharmonic Orchestra and veteran electronic-music

Figure 15.4. Hatsune Miku "live" at Hammerstein Ballroom on May 28, 2016.

composer and pioneer, Isao Tomita," who was at least in part motivated by his desire "to see if Miku could sing along with the orchestra, sing properly by following the conductor" (Kelts 2012). Miku, the "prima donna" of the performance, both looms above the three-hundred-member orchestra on-screen and strides through the musicians as a ten-foot-tall vaporous and ethereal apparition. Though she is still the starring attraction, she must follow the conductor, with engineers once again controlling her movement and vocal production in real time (Itoh 2013b).

Miku's prima donna status continued to blossom when she starred in the opera *The End* by Keiichiro Shibuya and Toshiki Oakada (Shibuya and Oakada 2013), for which Marc Jacobs with Louis Vitton designed the costumes (Kelts 2012). The opera premiered in 2013 at the Yamaguchi Center for Arts and Media and was performed again at the Theatre du Chatelet Opera House in Paris. "'The End' promotes itself as a new style of opera, one comprising computer-created music and video, free of human appearances" (St. Michel 2013). With only Vocaloids, there is no traditional staging, with the expected props, but just a set of screens with a cube in the center in which Miku appears (St. Michel 2013). Patrick St. Michel (2013) describes the visuals as stunning, "using every

Figure 15.5. Hatsune Miku engineers at Hammerstein Ballroom on May 28, 2016.

inch of the projection screens to immerse the audience. The view can get trippy—lasers, giant eyeballs and waves of Miku's aqua-green hair flowing across all the screens." Miku's image transforms throughout the performance, and her "digi voice makes [the songs] more intriguing, adding a digital imperfection," so celebrated by her fans (St. Michel 2013). In *The End,* Miku makes a magnificent spectacle of herself, with her unreal voice floating through the disjointed digital images.

Miku is even featured on the infamous Japanese noise band Hijokaidan's album *Hatsune Kaidan* (2013), though when the band performs live, a human stands in for her (Hijokaidan). This perhaps is the most interesting collaboration, with the emphasis on play with digital technology in both Miku and noise music (Novak 2013) but with such drastically different results. Here we find a real mash-up of differing digital music-making.

The contradictory nature of Miku, as a performer who appears to be acting on her own but who is actually being programmed by someone else, is highlighted in her stage performances as she renders live songs written by her fans. Thus, though Miku appears to command the stage, she has no control over her musical selections and does not imbue her personality into the emotional quality of the songs. She is in fact an empty receptacle performing at the bidding of the audience, but she in turn empowers them. She resembles the dolls of *bunraku,* and "writing for Vocaloid Software is a bit like pulling strings of a puppet. Miku does what a composer wants, albeit a little jerkily" (Rao 2014). Miku thus once again lives up to the claim that she is the ideal idol in these examples. She can collaborate with amateur prosumers or highly accomplished professional artists and composers without complaint, revealing unheard-of versatility in a mere human singer, who likely would be more limited and potentially more demanding.

Hatsune Miku Goes Global

But like all idols, Miku must market goods not directly related to her work as a singer (Lieb 2013). And her malleability once again makes her extremely skilled at doing so. Miku has inspired the LOVE exhibit to commemorate the ten-year anniversary of the MORI art museum in Tokyo (Itoh 2013b). And she has become the muse of fashion designers such as Earth, Music and Ecology, a popular Japanese brand. Her influence is reaching well beyond even earth—with her image currently emblazoned on a metal plate on a Japanese spacecraft headed to Venus. It is no surprise that the Japanese minister of economy recognized Crypton for its work with Miku (Itoh 2013b).

Miku clearly is not just a model pitching goods; she has become a global icon. Itoh (2013a) describes how "at concerts everywhere around the world, the fans hum the phrases of the songs and sing along in Japanese": "Every time I see this happening before my very eyes, I realize that, in a way, we are promoting Japanese culture to people overseas." Miku's international success is no doubt fueled again by her malleability—she easily can be reinterpreted in local terms and shift ethnic and national identities to become whatever the consumer needs. For example, the marketing materials for Hatsune Miku V3 in English picture her as decidedly more Western, with much more angular features and mature face and hands (see figure 15.6). She is still manga but not nearly as cute, instead exuding a more overt sexuality. A human idol could not practice "ethno drag" so easily.

Hatsune Miku thus is without place, completely global, connecting a cyberworld with vanishing geographical, ethnic, and national boundaries, yet she somehow still feels entirely Japanese and not just because she is rendered with wide anime eyes. She was born in Japan but also connects to something beyond the borders of the country.

Miku has spread to the degree that she is now the most globally recognized Japanese idol of all time, punctuated by her appearance as the opening act of Lady Gaga's 2014 summer tour and, later that same year in October, when she

Figure 15.6. Hatsune Miku (English version).

entered mainstream America with her debut on David Letterman, amid a swirl of radiant blue flame. And of course she headlined her own international tour in spring 2016. She is an ambassador of Japan throughout the world on par with Hello Kitty, whose success is also grounded in her malleability (Kelts 2012; Yano 2013), and has released the most successful exports of Japanese popular music since "Sukiyaki and Chips" hit number one in the United States in 1963. As consumers become increasingly comfortable with constructed idols and computerized voices, Hatsune Miku's position as the ideal idol seems quite secure (Zhou 2013). She may even be the path to a future musical utopia, living up to her title as "the first sound of the future," always one step ahead.

Hatsune Miku and the Future of Making Music

On June 10, 2015, the Avex record label Dimension Point released "B Who I Want 2 B" by the famed human idol star introduced earlier, Namie Amuro, featuring none other than Hatsune Miku (Amuro). Produced by the British artist Sophie, the piece is billed as a "collaboration between popular Japanese singer Namie Amuro and Crypton Future Media's virtual Vocaloid singer Hatsune Miku" (Anime News Network 2015). Both stars are listed as equal participants. The lyrics, cowritten by Sophie and the Vocaloid producer Mitchie M, are a mix of Japanese and English, with Amuro's digitized human voice alternating with Miku's humanized digital voice, swapping lines. The voices, albeit distinguishable, are incredibly similar in their mechanical quality. Is Amuro trying to sound like Miku, or Miku like Amuro? It is becoming increasingly difficult to distinguish the real from the virtual. And Miku's performance—whether in amateur-produced songs posted on Piapro or in multimillion-dollar live 3-D productions—raises many questions about the potential effects of Vocaloid software on the future of making music globally.

When I first encountered Miku, I personally was not moved by her singing quality, was surprised at her massive popularity, and was deeply troubled by the potential adverse affects of such digitization on the careers of actual musicians. Some listeners, myself included, may have trouble connecting with the high-pitched, cloying, electronic sound and may further question her authenticity as a performer given that everything about her is created by someone else. Will such avatars eventually replace human performers and all that they bring to the stage? To my surprise, Miku even performed with top-level professional kabuki actors in spring 2016, revealing her infiltration into the classical theater of Japan as well, no doubt to attract young audiences to an increasingly esoteric art (Chō-kabuki 2016). And the more I listen and look, the more I understand why Miku, or at least some version of her, is here to stay as consumers become increasingly comfortable with these modes of creation and dissemination (Bell 2016).

Itoh of course believes Miku is here to stay as well, stating, "Now, with the release of the English version of Hatsune Miku, with improvements in the interface, it's going to be a standard tool for creators to make music, with more people using it. With that, there will be more types of music being created, with unpredictable, totally unique uses of Miku" (Jarnes 2013). Masataka Goto feels that the increased use of vocal synthesizers such as Miku is certain. He argues, "As music synthesizers generating various instrumental sounds are already widely used and have become indispensable to popular music production, it is historically inevitable that singing synthesizers will become more widely used and likewise indispensable to music production," particularly as the quality of sound improves (2012, 220–221). Others are even attempting to develop robot musicians who can perform not only with precision but with emotion and nuance (Lim, Ogata, and Okuna 2012; Lim et al. 2010). And, as noted earlier, AKB48 has already performed with a virtual member (Black 2012, 222).

Miku may be ahead of her time in terms of compositional techniques, as prosumers recreate each other's works. What sounds derivative to some listeners now may sound perfectly original to her current consumers and even more people in the future, as the idea of musical authenticity being connected to a "new" idea further diminishes. Goto suggests, "The reuse or customization of existing music might be a more natural approach for the future. For example, 'mash-ups' that ingeniously combine and mix different songs, and 'touch-ups' (customizations) that modify or customize elements of existing songs (changing the timbre, phrase, and volume balance of singing voices and musical instruments)" are becoming increasingly relevant in the creation of music (2012, 218–219). Listeners are developing the skills necessary to hear mash-ups as new, creative material, and "by referring to the musical memory already in the mind of the listener, these mash-ups are able to raise the level of complexity acceptable for enjoyment while retaining popularity" (Goto 2012, 221–222). Miku herself is "a user-generated loop" (Kelts 2012) built on the collective memory of her prosumers. Miku thus may expand possibilities for composition, demanding intriguing new ways of thinking about authenticity and originality.

Advocates of Vocaloid software further argue that the Miku phenomenon is transforming not only the way we make music in a compositional sense but also the way the music business runs. Itoh explains,

> Traditionally, content has been created by professional artists or creators, promoted by companies, advertised by the mass media, and finally distributed and sold by retailers. . . . The method of sharing products on the Internet, and having them spread throughout society, did not exist. But the starting point for the content and music of the VOCALOID differs completely from that of existing business models, and the way of producing things is totally different too: here, people make their own music for fun and share it on the Internet. The songs aren't originally composed with business in mind. (2013a)

In Itoh's model, the Internet allows people to create content in new ways, connecting with other artists and spreading their ideas without an intermediary, all without money as a motivation.

Prosumers may now have unparalleled access to modes of dissemination and indeed may feel they are creating the musical utopia that Itoh extols, but Crypton is of course still capitalizing on Miku's success and, as evidenced by the sales statistics mentioned earlier, creating new products. Miku at the least is a commodity fetish that keeps prodding consumers to buy more; at the extreme, she is an addiction: you get a little taste with the original software and then must have the latest updates. A true musical democracy generated by Miku would demand that everyone in the world have easy access to a computer and the $149 required to purchase her. And then one still needs to acquire the libraries and updates to fully manipulate Miku. Software also goes obsolete relatively quickly, so although Miku's character may not age, her software will, rendering one's investment null and void.

Nonetheless, we cannot ignore the immense impact Miku has had on equalizing the process of creating and disseminating music around the world. Condry argues that it does not make sense to set up a binary between producers and consumers of Miku (2009, 2011 and 2013). No one has "power"; rather, all work together for the common, for some shared value—for the characters (Condry 2009, 2011 and 2013). Miku thus "demonstrates new possibilities for an unusual model of musical production—the crowd-sourced idol" (Condry 2011, 12). Although now some prosumers do in fact register compositions with JASRAC, the primary licensing agency in Japan, thus securing royalties, no one really "owns" Miku, as her fans work collectively to bring her to life. No record label or management company controls access to her. No one has a monopoly on her creative content. And the software itself does not require formal training in music to begin composing. In this way, though originating as a commodity, Miku could potentially create the utopia that Itoh envisions, even as he uses this very rhetoric to sell more Miku.

Despite concerns with the underlying commercial conflict, Hatsune Miku is indeed able to connect people in creative labor throughout the world. She is at once Japanese but not limited by ethnic or geographical boundaries. Capable of fueling heterosexist expectations of passive female behavior, she simultaneously embodies challenging ideas of femininity as she fills stadiums and commands the stage, strides over an orchestra, supplies all the voices in an opera, tackles technology in noise, tours internationally, and releases a new single with one of Japan's premier and longest-lasting living idols. Incapable of determining her own personal identity, she can engage in relationships with unlimited numbers of diverse fans, meeting their individual emotional needs and creating a much-needed sense of intimacy. Her voice, though grating to some listeners, is capable of unprecedented versatility and presents great aesthetic beauty to others. And she cannot control her schedule so is able to collaborate at any time of day with anyone anywhere. She is indeed the ideal idol available and ready to sing for you.

Acknowledgments

Thank you to the students who first introduced me to Hatsune Miku and expanded my understanding of her significance, especially Qin Zhou, Alex Dubose, Shanna Saldana, Steven O'Branovich, Stanley Jiang, and Jessica Gilbert. This chapter is the result of the passionate dialogue possible with bright and engaged students such as these. Thank you also to Andrew Weintraub and Bart Barendregt for their work on the VAMP project and careful reading of this chapter—and for all the feedback I received delivering versions of this chapter at the University of Pittsburgh, MIT, Bowdoin College, Union College, and Bard College.

Notes

1. See Crypton Future Media, Inc. (Japanese) official Hatsune Miku page at http://www.crypton.co.jp/mp/pages/prod/vocaloid/cv01.jsp.

2. Miku was updated to coincide with the release of Vocaloid 4.

3. See the Piapro network at http://piapro.net/.

4. Generally speaking "J-pop" refers to popular music mass-produced in Japan, with more specific subgenres (e.g., J-rock or J-rap) now common.

5. According to the Vocaloid Wiki—a comprehensive and collaborative Internet forum devoted to all things Vocaloid—there is a distinction between Japanese as opposed to "overseas" fans, but no further details are given (Vocaloid Wiki Contributors n.d.-a. and n.d.-b.). Indeed, it is difficult to find specific statistics on the demographics of consumers, in large part because national, ethnic, and gender identity are not always apparent on the Internet sites on which Miku primarily exists. She is a global phenomenon, but fandom is generational, cultural and gender specific, and therefore unique to each context. There is a general assumption in the ways that Miku is discussed in anime and Vocaloid fan literature that the Japanese audience comprises many middle-age male fans, confirmed by quick scans of audiences at her "live" performances in Japan, while globally fans include more younger women; but more work is necessary in diverse locations to truly explore how different fans engage with Miku. In the context of Japan, for example, men and women may connect with her in both similar and differing ways; what she means may even vary individually, thus requiring far more fandom studies to fully comprehend the Miku phenomenon.

6. Details from this lecture are supported by a translated interview with Itoh published in *Wochi Kochi Magazine*.

7. "The company now has over 50 business partners in the U.S., Europe, and other countries around the world, and sells over a million sound contents based on the licenses in Japan" (Itoh 2013a).

8. All characters in manga and anime are provided basic biographical sketches from which fans may create new content.

9. The manga artist Kei Garō designed Miku's character.

10. See, for example, "Kaito," at http://www.crypton.co.jp/mp/do/prod?id=27720.

11. See Crypton Future Media, Inc. (English), at http://sonicwire.com/product/vocaloid/special/mikuv3e.

12. Crypton has redeveloped various supporting software packages to work with the new English version, and though past Vocaloids were offered only for PCs, Hatsune Miku V3 was made available for Macs as well (Itoh 2013b).

13. For additional information on the initial spread of Hatsune Miku on Niko Niko Douga (http://www.nicovideo.jp), see Okada 2007.

14. See Hatsune Miku's YouTube channel at http://youtube.com/HatsuneMiku and her virtual community at http://mikubook.com.

15. Jarnes (2013) credits Wakamura P as labeling Miku as an "ideal idol" but does not go into further detail.

16. For further consideration of the importance of nostalgia in shaping modern Japanese identity, see Milioto Matsue 2016.

17. See Choo 2008 for a discussion about how complex notions of femininity are manifest in manga and anime.

18. Aoyagi explains, "Officials in the Ministry of Education differentiated women from men in the 1890s and universalized the image of women as homebound agents of biological and social reproduction. Ever since, women have been simultaneously typified as 'protectorates' (so to speak) of the patriarchal rule—a characterization that continues to influence the public imagination of womanhood in Japan today" (2005, 91).

19. See Kinsella 1998 for additional information on the origins of the term *otaku* within the amateur manga community. A negative interpretation of the term refers to any type of antisocial "nerd" or "weirdo" obsessed with a particular hobby, while more recent arguments position the *otaku* as a positive form of resistance to mainstream pressures to conform (Galbraith 2016).

20. See Crypton Future Media, Inc. (English) at http://sonicwire.com/product/vocaloid/special/mikuv3e.

21. See Hatsune Miku's official music label at http://karent.jp/.

22. For additional discussion on how the software functions, see Bell 2016.

23. As of July 2015, Vocaloid could work with Japanese, Chinese, Korean, English, and Spanish, assisted by the "Singer library," which contains all possible combinations of phonemes (consonants and vowels) and sustained vowels for each language (Kenmochi 2012, 5,385). In the freeware Utaloid, consumers may record their own voices in any language and create similar works.

24. For additional discussion on how the software functions, see Bell 2016.

25. The qualities are written on Crypton's official website in English only, with suggestions for appropriate genres, tempo, and ranges in which they can be used in Japanese. Sweet, dark, English, and solid are demonstrated in this order at HatsuneMiku 2013.

26. Interviews were conducted with four students at Union College to supplement research on blogs (http://www.mikufan.com; http://www.vocaloidism.com/blog/) and published sources.

27. See SEGA Project Diva at http://www.gamestop.com/ps3/games/hatsune-miku-project-diva-f/109941.

References

Amuro, Namie. 2015. "B Who I Want 2 B featuring Hatsune Miku." YouTube, 9 June. https://www.youtube.com/watch?v=Y2V_Y26JTSw.

Anime News Network. 2015. "Namie Amuro & Hatsune Miku's New Song Previewed Online." http://www.animenewsnetwork.com/news/2015-06-10/namie-amuro-and-hatsune-miku-new-song-previewed-online/.89089.

Aoyagi, Hiroshi. 2005. *Island of Eight Million Smiles: Idol Performance and Symbolic Production in Contemporary Japan.* Cambridge, MA: Harvard University Asia Center.

Beauchamp, Zack. 2013. "Are Traditional Gender Roles Destroying Japan?" *Think Progress,* 21 October. http://thinkprogress.org/health/2013/10/21/2810191/japan-traditional-gender-roles/.

Bell, Sarah A. 2016. "The dB in the .db: Vocaloid Software as Posthuman Instrument." *Popular Music and Society* 39 (2): 222–240.

Black, Daniel. 2012. "The Virtual Idol: Producing and Consuming Digital Femininity." In *Idols and Celebrity in Japanese Media Culture,* edited by Patrick W. Galbraith and Jason G. Karlin, 209–228. New York: Palgrave Macmillan.

Chō-kabuki. 2016. "Chō-kabuki featuring Hatsune Miku." http://www.chokaigi.jp/2016/booth/cho-kabuki.html.

Choo, Kukhee. 2008. "Girls Return Home: Portrayal of Femininity in Popular Japanese Girls' Manga and Anime Texts during the 1990s in *Hana yori Dango* and *Fruits Basket.*" *Women: A Cultural Review* 19 (3): 275–296.

Condry, Ian. 2009. "Anime Creativity: Characters and Premises in the Quest for Cool Japan." *Theory, Culture & Society* 26 (2–3): 139–163.

———. 2011. "Post-3/11 Japan and the Radical Recontextualization of Value: Music, Social Media, and End-Around Strategies for Cultural Action." *International Journal of Japanese Sociology* 20:4–17.

———. 2013. *The Soul of Anime: Collaborative Creativity and Japan's Media Success Story.* Durham, NC: Duke University Press.

Darling-Wolf, Fabienne. 2004. "SMAP, Sex, and Masculinity: Constructing the Perfect Female Fantasy in Japanese Popular Music." *Popular Music and Society* 27 (3): 357–370.

Flint, Tom. 2014. "Crypton Hatsune Miku English." *Sound on Sound,* March. http://www.soundonsound.com/sos/mar14/articles/sample-shop-0314-04.htm.

Galbraith, Patrick W. 2012. "Idols: The Image of Desire in Japanese Consumer Capitalism." In *Idols and Celebrity in Japanese Media Culture,* edited by Patrick W. Galbraith and Jason G. Karlin, 185–208. New York: Palgrave Macmillan.

———. 2016. "Real(ity) Problem: 'Otaku' and the Politics of Imagination." Public lecture, Union College.

Galbraith, Patrick W., and Jason G. Karlin. 2012. "Introduction: The Mirror of Idols and Celebrity." In *Idols and Celebrity in Japanese Media Culture,* edited by Patrick W. Galbraith and Jason G. Karlin, 1–33. New York: Palgrave Macmillan.

Google. 2012. "'Tell Your World' (Google Chrome Commercial MV)." YouTube, 3 April. http://www.youtube.com/watch?v=VYLYk6PpRkw.

Goto, Masataka. 2012. "Grand Challenges in Music Information Research." *Multimodal Music Processing* 3:217–226.

Hamasaki, Masahiro, Hideaki Takeda, and Takuichi Nishimura. 2008. "Network Analysis of Massively Collaborative Creation of Multimedia Contents: Case Study of Hatsune Miku Videos on Nico Nico Douga." *Proceedings of the 1st International Conference on Designing Interactive User Experiences for TV and Video*, 165–168. ACM.

Hatsune Miku. 2013. "[Hatsune Miku V3] Six Greetings (Long ver.)." YouTube, 23 August. https://www.youtube.com/watch?v=3ejUVQGSKq0.

Hijokaidan. 2014. "Hatsune Kaidan @ Tusk Festival 2014." YouTube, 25 November. https://www.youtube.com/watch?v=ZtqqeamuLRw .

Itoh, Hiroyuki. 2013a. "Hatsune Miku, the New Social Phenomenon." *Wochi Kochi Magazine.* Japan Foundation Information Center. http://www.wochikochi.jp/english/special/2013/02/hatsune-miku.php.

———. 2013b. Public lecture at the Japan Foundation in New York City, 8 October.

Jarnes, Mark. 2013. "The Father of Hatsune Miku—On the Future of Music and Everything." MTV 81, 30 August. http://www.mtv81.com/features/interviews/the-father-of-hatsune-miku-on-the-future-of-music-and-everything/.

Kelts, Roland. 2012. "Hatsune Miku Goes Highbrow." *Japan Times*, 21 December. http://www.japantimes.co.jp/culture/2012/12/21/music/hatsune-miku-goes-highbrow-2/.

Kendall, Philip. 2013. "Domino's Pizza Japan Teams Up with Hatsune Miku, Releases Fantastic Cringeworthy Video." *Rocket News 24,* 8 March. http://en.rocketnews24.com/2013/03/08/dominos-pizza-japan-teams-up-with-hatsune-miku-releases-fantastic-cringeworthy-video/.

Kenmochi, Hideki. 2012. "Singing Synthesis as a New Musical Instrument." *2012 IEEE International Conference on Acoustics, Speech and Signal Processing (ICASSP),* 5,385–5,388.

Kinsella, Sharon. 1998. "Japanese Subculture in the 1990s: *Otaku* and the Amateur *Manga* Movement." *Journal of Japanese Studies* 24 (2): 289–316.

Kitamura, Yūko. 2008. "Gender Equality Dilemma in Japanese Society: How Traditional Ideas Affect both Women and Men." *Journal of the Faculty of International Studies Bunkyo University* 19 (1): 65–76.

Lieb, Kristin. 2013. *Gender, Branding, and the Modern Music Industry: The Social Construction of Female Popular Music Stars.* New York: Routledge.

Lim, Angelica, Tetsuya Ogata, and Hiroshi G. Okuno. 2012. "Towards Expressive Musical Robots: a Cross-modal Framework for Emotional Gesture, Voice and Music." *EURASIP Journal on Audio, Speech, and Music Processing* 2012 (1): 3.

Lim, Angelica, Takeshi Mizumoto, Louis-Kenzo Cahier, Takuma Otsuka, Toru Takahashi, Kazunori Komatani, Tetsuya Ogata, and Hiroshi G. Okuno. 2010. "Robot Musical Accompaniment: Integrating Audio and Visual Cues for Real-Time Synchronization with a Human Flutist." *IEEE/RSJ International Conference on Intelligent Robots and Systems (IROS),* 1,964–1,969.

Miku Expo. n.d. "Miku Expo 2016 Song Contest." Accessed 15 January 2016, http://mikuexpo.com/contest/?/.

Milioto Matsue, Jennifer. 2016. *Focus: Music in Contemporary Japan.* New York: Routledge.

Nagaike, Kazumi. 2012. "Johnny's Idols as Icons: Female Desires to Fantasize and Consume Male Idol Images." In *Idols and Celebrity in Japanese Media Culture,* edited by Patrick W. Galbraith and Jason G. Karlin, 97–112. New York: Palgrave Macmillan.

Novak, David. 2013. *Japanoise: Music at the Edge of Circulation.* Durham, NC: Duke University Press.

Okada, Yuka. 2007. "Unprecedented Demand for 'Hatsune Miku,' the Music Maker Spread on Niko Niko Douga" (in Japanese). IT Media, 12 May. http://www.itmedia.co.jp/news/articles/0709/12/news035.html.

Rao, Mallika. 2014. "Meet Hatsune Miku, the Sensational Japanese Pop Star who doesn't Really Exist." *Huffington Post*, 10 October. http://www.huffingtonpost.com/2014/10/08/hatsune-miku-letterman_n_5956420.html.

Shibuya, Keiichiro, and Toshiki Oakada. 2013. "The End." YouTube, 17 November. http://www.youtube.com/watch?v=gxeZLj6ZOQc.

St. Michel, Patrick. 2013. "Vocaloid Opera 'The End' Starring Miku Lives Up to the Hype in Stunning Fashion." MTV 81, 17 June. http://www.mtv81.com/features/live-reports/vocaloid-opera-the-end-starring-hatsune-miku-lives-up-to-the-hype-in-stunning-fashion/.

Takahashi Akiko. 2008. "I Want to Be a Creator Who Supports Creators: President of Future Crypton Media Itoh Hiroyuki (Part One)" (in Japanese). Internet Watch, 12 May. http://internet.watch.impress.co.jp/cda/president/2008/05/12/19477.html.

Tomita, Isao. 2013. "Miku Hatsune ＋ Orchestra 2012 11 23 ／written by Isao Tomita [Symphony Ihatov]." YouTube, 25 February. http://www.youtube.com/watch?v=MsFUNkgKtUI.

+Vocaloid Wiki Contributors. n.d.-a. "Kaito." Vocaloid Wiki. Accessed 15 July 2014, http://vocaloid.wikia.com/wiki/KAITO.

+———. n.d.-b. "Using the Parameters." Vocaloid Wiki. Accessed 15 July 2014, http://vocaloid.wikia.com/wiki/Using_the_Parameters.

Wikipedia. 2014. "Hatsune Miku." 15 March. https://en.wikipedia.org/wiki/Hatsune_Miku.

Wowaka. 2016. "Unhappy Refrain." YouTube, 31 May. https://www.youtube.com/watch?v=RftOv48yklo.

Yano, Christine. 2013. *Pink Globalization: Hello Kitty's Trek across the Pacific.* Durham, NC: Duke University Press.

Zhou, Qin. 2013. "Manufactured Idols and Vocaloids: A Mix of Technology and Japanese Anime Culture." Final paper for AMU 136: Popular Music in Modern Japan. Union College, New York.

CONTRIBUTORS

Bart Barendregt is an associate professor at the Leiden Institute of Cultural Anthropology. He has an interest in popular and digital culture, and has published on Southeast Asian performance, new and mobile media, and (Islamic) pop music. Barendregt is currently working on a book dealing with Islamist boy band music and the mixing of religion, youth culture, and politics among Malaysian and Indonesian student activists. He is the editor of *Sonic Modernities in the Malay World* (Brill, 2014), and coeditor of *Green Consumption: The Global Rise of Eco-Chic* (Bloomsbury, 2013), and the volume *Recollecting Resonance* (Brill, 2013).

Yifen Beus received her PhD in comparative literature from Indiana University and currently teaches film studies at Brigham Young University Hawai'i. Her teaching and research interests include modernity, reflexivity, intertextuality, minor (trans)nationalism, and de-Westernizing storytelling in cinema (Sinophone and Francophone). She is the author of *Towards a Paradoxical Theatre: Schlegelian Irony in German and French* (2003). Her work has appeared in the *Quarterly Review of Film and Video, Nineteenth-Century French Studies,* and the *Journal of African Cultural Studies,* and she has contributed, among other publications, to *Storytelling in World Cinemas* (2013), *De-Westernizing Film Studies* (2012), and *New Zealand, France and the Pacific* (2011).

Farzaneh Hemmasi is an assistant professor of ethnomusicology in the University of Toronto's faculty of music. Her research concerns Iranian popular music, migration, media, and politics. She graduated from Columbia University in 2010 and has held fellowships with the University of Pennsylvania's Penn Humanities Forum and Columbia University's Middle East Institute, as well as Columbia's Institute of Social and Economic Policy and Research. Her publications have appeared in *Ethnomusicology* (2013), the edited volume *Muslim Rap, Halal Soaps, and Revolutionary Theater* (2011), and *Mahoor Musical Quarterly* (2008), and she has presented at a number of North American and international conferences. Hemmasi has taught ethnomusicology at the University of Pennsylvania, Columbia University, and Hunter College in the City University of New York. She is currently writing a book that examines the intersection of popular music, affect, technological mediation, and politics in Iran and its diasporas from the 1960s to the present. In the fall of 2011, she began a new project documenting sound and musical practices associated with New York City's Occupy Wall Street movement.

Hee-sun Kim earned a BA and an MA from Seoul National University's Department of Korean Music and a PhD in ethnomusicology from the University of Pittsburgh. Formerly a research fellow at the Asia Research Institute of the National University of Singapore (Cultural Studies) and a research fellow at the Asian Music Institute of Seoul National University, she is currently an associate professor at Kookmin University, and the director of the music research division at the National *Gugak* Center in Seoul. Kim serves as vice-president of the Music of East Asia study group of the International Council for Traditional Music and member-at-large for the Association of Korean Music Research of the Society for Ethnomusicology. She is the author of *Contemporary Kayagŭm Music in Korea: Tradition, Modernity and Identity* (2008), as well as many articles in books and journals. As a *gayageum* practitioner, she has given lectures, seminars, concerts, and workshops on Korean music in major cities and universities of Asia, Europe, North America, and Oceania.

Soojin Kim received her PhD in ethnomusicology from the Ohio State University in 2011. Upon graduation, she taught at the University of Cincinnati (2012) and served as a Korea Foundation postdoctoral fellow at the Center for East Asian and Pacific Studies, University of Illinois, Urbana-Champaign (2012–2013). Since 2014, she has taught at Gyeongju University in South Korea as an assistant professor. Her academic interests include diaspora, transnationalism, and the globalization of East Asian / Korean music cultures.

Jennifer Milioto Matsue (BA, Wellesley College; MA and PhD, University of Chicago) is an ethnomusicologist specializing in modern Japanese music and culture. She has conducted research on a variety of music cultures in contemporary Japan, including the Tokyo hardcore rock scene, *nagauta* (a type of traditional chamber music featuring the three-string lute, *shamisen*), electronica and trance raves, and most recently, the increasingly popular world of *wadaiko* (Japanese ensemble drumming). She is interested in how performers find meaning through participating in such music worlds, with a particular focus on women's roles in music-making. She is the author of the monograph *Making Music in Japan's Underground: The Tokyo Hardcore Scene* (2008), as well as several articles on related topics. She is working on a new book on music in contemporary Japan, which explores *wadaiko* in Kyoto within the context of broader musical practices, as well as an article that problematizes the classification of *wadaiko* as a genre. She is director of Interdisciplinary Studies, Asian Studies, and the World Musics and Cultures Programs and serves as a professor in music, Asian studies, and anthropology at Union College in Schenectady, New York.

Joshua D. Pilzer, an associate professor of ethnomusicology at the University of Toronto, is a scholar of Korean and Japanese music. He is interested in the place of music in the texture of postcolonial Korean life, in music's everyday social utility and poetics, in music as alternative history, and in women's music. He is the author of *Hearts of Pine: Songs in the Lives of Three Korean Survivors of the Japanese "Comfort Women"* (2012) and is currently conducting fieldwork for his next book project, an ethnography of music and song among Korean victims of the atomic bombing of Japan and their children.

Russell P. Skelchy holds a PhD in ethnomusicology (2015) and an MA in Southeast Asian studies (2012) from the University of California, Riverside. His dissertation focused on *keroncong*, a genre of Indonesian popular music, and examined how this genre provided a narrative of modernization in postcolonial Indonesia. Skelchy is a recipient of the Fulbright IIE Fellowship (2011–2012) and the UC Pacific Rim Research Program Fellowship (2011–2012). In 2008, he founded Orkes Pantai Barat (the West Coast Orchestra), a *keroncong* ensemble comprising students and faculty that has performed at benefit events and Indonesian festivals in California.

Tan Sooi Beng is a professor of ethnomusicology at the School of the Arts, Universiti Sains Malaysia (USM). She is the author of *Bangsawan: A Social and Stylistic History of Popular Malay Opera* (1993) and coauthor of *The Music of Malaysia: The Classical, Folk and Syncretic Traditions* (2004). She has edited books and DVDs including *Representations in the Creative Arts of Southeast Asia: Negotiating Meanings and Identities* (2012) and *The Multicultural Performing Arts, Crafts, Festivals and Food of Penang* (2011). Her resent research on the Peranakan cultures and recordings of Malay music prior to independence demonstrates intercultural links in the Southeast Asian region. Tan is actively involved in engaged theater for young people and participatory research in Penang.

Ricardo D. Trimillos is a professor emeritus of ethnomusicology and past chair of the Asian Studies Program at the University of Hawai'i at Manoa. He specializes in issues of identity, gender, performance practice, and education related to multiculturalism. His research areas are the traditional and commercial musics of the Philippines, Japan, and Hawai'i. He studied at San José State University, the University of Hawai'i, the Ateneo de Manila, the University of Cologne, and UCLA, where he received a doctorate in ethnomusicology. He performs a number of Asian musics, including *rondalla* and *kulintangan* of the Philippines and *koto, gagaku,* and *kabuki* percussion of Japan. He has served as international consultant for arts public policy for the governments of Hong Kong, Malaysia, the Philippines, Poland, and the former Soviet Union, as well as for UNESCO.

Yiman Wang is an associate professor of film and digital media at the University of California, Santa Cruz. She is the author of *Remaking Chinese Cinema: Through the Prism of Shanghai, Hong Kong and Hollywood* (available from University of Hawai'i Press, 2013). She is currently working on two book projects, one on Anna May Wong as a transnational "minor" performer-worker, the other on animals and cinema. Her articles have appeared in numerous journals and edited volumes.

Amanda Weidman is a cultural anthropologist with interests in music, performance, technological mediation, and gender. She has conducted research in Tamil-speaking South India since the mid-1990s. She is currently working on a project on playback singing in relation to the cultural politics of gender in South India from post-Independence to the postliberalization period. Her publications include *Singing the Classical, Voicing the Modern: The Postcolonial Politics of Music in South India* (2006); several articles on performance, embodiment, and technological mediation in relation to South Indian classical music, film songs, and historic South Indian sound recordings; and a review article on voice for the *Annual Review of Anthropology.* She is also a Karnatic violinist.

Andrew N. Weintraub is a professor and past chair of music at the University of Pittsburgh, where he teaches graduate and undergraduate courses in ethnomusicology and popular music and directs the University Gamelan program. He is the author of *Power Plays* (2004) and *Dangdut Stories* (2010), editor of *Islam and Popular Culture in Indonesia and Malaysia* (2011), and coeditor of *Music and Cultural Rights* (2008).

Christine R. Yano, a professor and past chair of anthropology at the University of Hawai'i, has conducted research on Japan and Japanese Americans. Her publications include *Tears of Longing: Nostalgia and the Nation in Japanese Popular Song* (2002), *Crowning the Nice Girl; Gender, Ethnicity, and Culture in Hawaii's Cherry Blossom Festival* (available from University of Hawaiʻi Press, 2006), *Airborne Dreams: "Nisei" Stewardesses and Pan American World Airways* (2011), and *Pink Globalization: Hello Kitty and Its Trek across the Pacific* (2013).

INDEX